HETEROSEXUAL DICTATORSHIP

MALE HOMOSEXUALITY IN POSTWAR BRITAIN

PATRICK HIGGINS

HETEROSEXUAL DICTATORSHIP

MALE HOMOSEXUALITY IN POSTWAR BRITAIN

FOURTH ESTATE • *London*

For Robert

First published in Great Britain in 1996 by
Fourth Estate Limited
6 Salem Road
London W2 4BU

A catalogue record for this book is available from the British Library

ISBN 1-85702-355-2

Typeset by Rowland Phototypesetting Ltd,
Bury St Edmunds, Suffolk
Printed in Great Britain by
Clays Ltd, St Ives plc

The one duty we owe to history is to re-write it.

Oscar Wilde

We maintain we have the right to exist after the fashion which nature made us. And if we cannot alter your laws, we shall go on breaking them. You may condemn us to infamy, exile, prison – as you formerly burned witches. You may degrade our emotional instincts and drive us into vice and misery. But you will not eradicate inverted sexuality.

John Addington Symonds

Contents

Illustrations

(Illustrations are from the author's collection unless otherwise stated)

Acknowledgements

Mike Shaw, my agent, has been a continuing source of encouragement and support. I am grateful to him and his assistant, Sophia Janson, for all their hard work on my behalf. Sophia has helped with numerous queries with exemplary patience and enormous efficiency, I am much in her debt. Christopher Potter, my editor at Fourth Estate, has been a wise counsellor and a tower of strength. He has done much at Fourth Estate to ensure that gay literature and history reaches the widest possible audience. His intelligent reading of my first draft greatly improved the final text. Dr Rictor Norton, the copy editor, and Leo Hollis, the editorial assistant, both worked hard to polish my prose and produce a more readable book. Dr Norton provided many useful suggestions and saved me from many errors: it was a great pleasure to work with such a distinguished historian of homosexuality.

Noel Annan, Julian Jackson, Jon Parry and John Venning all read earlier drafts of this book and their comments helped me a great deal when it came to revising the manuscript. It was kind of them all to give up their time so generously. In their different ways all have done much to stimulate the interpretation developed in this book though they may not recognise, or even accept, the end product. Julian and John have had to endure long monologues while the work was in progress and their questions and comments did much to shape my approach. Julian Jackson asked really awkward questions and has repeatedly put the other side of the argument. John Venning placed his immense erudition, learning and precision at my disposal. I am grateful for his help with the proofs. Jon Parry continues to teach me history, a role he has performed for almost two decades, he has given me the confidence to generalise and encouraged me to make and follow connections. He was responsible also for an invitation to speak at an early stage in this work on the Wolfenden Commmittee to the Modern British History Seminar in Cambridge on 21 November 1994. The questions and comments made after my paper produced many useful insights, I am particularly grateful to Boyd Hilton and Alastair Reid for their observations on that occasion.

Books invade one's whole life and the research and writing for this book was at times peculiarly taxing. My friends provided all manner of support, they listened, they encouraged and most importantly of all they distracted me. Thanks to Carol Macready, James Laurenson, Duncan Garrow, Lucy Akrill, Tim Carter, Chris Clark, Sarah Heard, Chris Henshall, Jessica Kedward, Gabriel Kemlo, Nina Lubbren, Paul McHugh, John Morrill, Peter Salt, Akbar Shamji, Richard Shannon, Ben Stoll, Rachael Unsworth, Alun Vaughan, Emma Wilson. Jamie Laurenson deserves special praise; he has laboured alongside me long and hard in Bloomsbury, and he has comforted, consoled and amused me on a daily basis. He has also provided a constant stream of suggestions and advice. He's a real star.

The dedication of the book records the greatest debt of all. Robert Davies actually got me through the whole process. I can say without hesitation that without his support I would never have finished this book. He provided a framework and a philosophy, and in our conversations he taught me to understand. It has been an immensely stimulating experience, and the dedication is an inadequate payment for numerous acts of kindness that place me forever in his debt. As those who know him realise, he is more than an average guy.

Introduction

The telephone call from the Home Secretary's Private Secretary's Office on that summer morning in 1954 was entirely unexpected.
— *from* Turning Points *(1976), the memoirs of Lord Wolfenden*

The Englishman is by nature and upbringing a conformist. It is true that he likes to be able to criticise the group, whether it be nation, class or trade union, to which he belongs. But he likes to do this from the inside, from the security of the membership of the group. It is true that he likes to have within his range of vision and acquaintance a certain number of non-conformists, 'characters' or even rebels. But he normally regards them as amusing exceptions to his own safe and established majority pattern; their very existence as 'Outs' puts him 'In'. In general, he conforms, in speech, manners, and dress with the standards of the House of Lords, the Rotary Club, the suburban street, the youth club, the beatnik group or whatever sub-culture he accepts as his own . . . The ordinary conforming Englishman is a fairly easy-going person; he takes things and people as they come. Down the centuries he has come to accept whatever is there as part of the established pattern.
— *Sir John Wolfenden, writing in the* Jewish Chronicle, *28 September 1965*

It was an odd way to proceed. It was the way none the less that successive British governments have reacted when faced with difficult problems. They appoint a committee to explore the particular difficulty concerned, and after some time has elapsed, the committee produces a report. These committees are composed of people with as little connection with the problem under discussion as possible. Professional men with a sprinkling of upper-middle-class women, the committee generally contains a heavy concentration of academics. They are individuals with a reputation for detachment and discretion, willing to work for nothing more than titles, decorations, ribbons. They have played a major role in shaping official policy towards many aspects of human behaviour in modern Britain. In the decade after the Second World War governments established committees and commissions to examine many aspects of British society, most notably capital punishment, marriage and divorce, gambling, and in 1954 those odd bedfellows female prostitution and male homosexuality.

Sometimes the report might be ignored completely, future governments being unwilling to accept the committee's conclusions; the committee being merely a way of shelving a particular problem or of defusing a controversial issue. Other reports became the basis of new laws. Sometimes a decade might elapse before the recommendation of a committee reached the statute book. It was in this way that many new laws in post-war Britain were framed.

In 1967 the British Parliament passed a law which decriminalised all homosexual acts that took place between two consenting adult males, over the age of twenty-one, in private. This law can be traced directly back to the recommendations of the committee appointed by the British government in 1954, the Home Office Departmental Committee on Prostitution and Homosexuality, a committee which had reported in September 1957 and which provoked in the years after its publication numerous debates and discussions in both Houses of Parliament. The report generated a major debate on male homosexuality in British society during the late 1950s and 1960s, the first time that this issue had ever been the subject of prolonged public discussion in British history.

This curious process is a reflection of the quite extraordinary timidity shown by several British governments during the 1940s, 1950s and 1960s when they confronted social issues which excited strong moral objections. Ministers of both major parties feared that too close an association between their governments and the reforms proposed would damage them at the polls. Richard Crossman, a Labour cabinet minister who was leader of the House of Commons when the 1967 Act was passed, reflected in his diary at the time on the damage that the passage of that Act might do to the Labour Party:

> Frankly it's an unpleasant Bill and I myself don't like it. It may well be twenty years ahead of public opinion; certainly working-class people in the north jeer at their Members at the weekend and ask them why they're looking after the buggers at Westminster instead of looking after the unemployed at home. It has gone down very badly that the Labour Party should be associated with such a Bill.

This was despite the fact that the 1967 Act was not an official government measure but had been promoted by a backbencher. Support for the bill had divided the cabinet, with several of Crossman's ministerial colleagues opposing the measure, though few voted against it. Crossman, despite his grim prophecies of the electoral consequences, voted for the bill.

Governments found it expedient to use committees, commissions and backbenchers to promote social reform because they lacked the courage to address these questions themselves. It was a measure of the weakness of the British political élite that it was unable to tackle such problems directly during the post-war period.

Each generation contains a number of men and women whose main erotic preference is towards members of their own sex. A certain number of people are also attracted to both sexes. Western society for many centuries has condemned individuals who act upon such homosexual desires. Such condemnations have also become the basis of innumerable laws which have sought to inhibit such behaviour. Neither moral teaching nor law, however, have eliminated the practice. They have succeeded in stigmatising such behaviour but the records of every century disclose the presence of men and women who have expressed their homosexual desires.

In the nineteenth century some European states (notably France and Italy) began to adopt a slightly more tolerant attitude to homosexual behaviour by accepting that behaviour which took place between consenting adults in private was not the business of the state, a reform patterned on the legal code promoted by Napoleon. Laws remained in force prohibiting all public manifestations of homosexuality that might offend other citizens as well as laws designed to protect young people from homosexual assault. In 1861 the British Parliament passed a law which reformulated the 1533 Buggery Act in Victorian terms, criminalising all male homosexual activity, wherever it took place, and this remained in force until the passage of the 1967 Act. The only liberal element in the 1861 statute was that the act of sodomy which had carried the death penalty since the sixteenth century ceased to be a capital crime. Men convicted of sodomy after 1861 faced a sentence of life imprisonment instead. For well over a century British law remained out of step with much of the rest of Europe. Only Nazi Germany and the Soviet Union enacted laws similar to those in Britain in the 1930s, breaking with the tradition of European tolerance.

Incredibly, no one, in public at least, called for a reform of the laws in Britain until the autumn of 1953. In a six-month period beginning in October 1953 more space was devoted to homosexuality in the British press than at any period since the trials and conviction of Oscar Wilde during 1895. Most of the reports, letters and articles were hostile to reform. It is, however, a measure of the sensitivity of the British state to the opinions of élite newspapers and journals at that time that those articles suggesting that Britain adopt laws relating to homosexuality similar to those operating in France and Italy led the Home Office to take action.

In the summer of 1953 senior officials in the Home Office decided that it was time to 'clean the streets' of the capital of a growing army of prostitutes who stationed themselves across the city selling sex to passers-by. The numbers of prostitutes coming before the courts in the capital had increased from 2,966 in 1938 to 9,756 in 1952. There had been much adverse criticism of this development in the popular press and many overseas visitors expressed considerable disgust at the behaviour of these women. Two residents' associations, one in Paddington, the other in Mayfair, mounted well-organised campaigns after 1951 which increased the pressure on the Home Office to reform the laws regulating female prostitution.

Female prostitution was not itself illegal. Most prostitutes found themselves in court under a Victorian statute which allowed them to be prosecuted if the act of soliciting annoyed other citizens. Invariably the annoyance was reported by the police themselves. Magistrates' courts had the power to fine women for this offence if committed by a woman known to police as a common prostitute. The maximum fine was 40s. The women accepted this as a condition of employment and the police operated a rota system that brought different faces to the courts each morning. Like so much of the machinery for the regulation of sexual crime by the state, it was an elaborate charade.

The Home Office wanted to pass a new law that would tighten the penalties for women soliciting on the streets, increasing fines dramatically and including terms of imprisonment for repeat offenders. The Home Office anticipated that this would remove the women from the streets into flats where they could be approached via the telephone. In this way female prostitution would be hidden from view. Philip Allen, a senior Home Office official, was sent to the United States to study the policing of prostitution in major American cities. He was accompanied by a senior police officer from the Metropolitan Police force, Commander Ernest Cole. They also examined the operation of parking meters in those cities.

Allen's report supported the Home Office case for legislation: all the cities he visited regulated prostitution by heavy fines and imprisonment and as a result their streets were largely free of women selling their bodies. Call-girl operations flourished in all these places. The problem was that the civil servants perceived difficulties about selling this legislation to Parliament and the public. They feared that moral campaigners would try to introduce legislation to make the male clients liable to prosecution. This was never the intention of the Home Office officials, who accepted that female prostitution was a necessary evil; they wanted a law merely to regulate public decency. They decided that it would be necessary to establish a Royal Commission to investigate the problem and to propose a solution. The state might then act with the support of an impartial inquiry behind it.

To this end the Home Secretary, Sir David Maxwell Fyfe, proposed to the cabinet on 24 February 1954 that a Royal Commission be appointed. By this time the Home Office had decided that the commission should also study the operation of the laws relating to homosexuality as well as examine possible strategies for the treatment and the cure of homosexuality that the state might adopt. This was probably the first time a British cabinet had ever discussed the question of male homosexuality.

Maxwell Fyfe felt that there was

> a considerable body of opinion which regards the existing law as antiquated and out of harmony with modern knowledge and ideas, and in particular, represents that unnatural relations between consenting adults, which are not criminal except in Great Britain and the United States, should no longer be criminal in this country, and that the criminal law, in dealing with unnatural, and normal, sexual relations, should confine itself to the protection of the young and the preservation of public order and decency.

Maxwell Fyfe did not himself believe that there was a case for altering the law and he felt that the 'most profitable line of development is to improve, so far as finances permit, the facilities for the treatment of homosexuals sentenced by the courts', but

> there is a sufficient body of opinion in the country in favour of setting in train some inquiry into homosexual offences to warrant bringing the question before my colleagues ... a dispassionate survey by a competent and unprejudiced body might be of value in educating the public, which at present is ill-informed and apt to be misled by sensational articles in the press.

Other ministers were worried; they felt that the government would emerge with little credit, and by inference lose votes, if it attempted to amend the laws relating to homosexuality or indeed if it associated itself with the subject. The cabinet discussion shifted to the increasing amount of space devoted by the press at that time to trials for homosexual offences. A suggestion emerged that a backbencher would promote a private member's bill to test opinion in Parliament and in the country to see if there might be support for an Act restricting the reporting of such trials. This was a characteristically British response to a problem: censorship. It is clear from the discussion that ministers were alarmed by the increasing amount of space newspapers were devoting to the subject of homosexuality. They preferred a situation which had operated in the past whereby newspapers had simply ignored the subject.

In the course of the discussion opposition grew to the idea of a Royal Commission. Several ministers preferred that a departmental committee be appointed: such a committee was amenable to tighter control by the Home Office and its proceedings would be in private. Royal Commissions collected evidence in public and published all material presented to them. The discussion on 24 February eventually ran out of time and was deferred to a later meeting of the cabinet.

The Home Secretary brought the subject up again on 17 March 1954. He again tried to get fellow ministers to support the appointment of a Royal Commission. More ministers expressed their reservations; they preferred a departmental committee. Winston Churchill, the Prime Minister, ever cautious on domestic issues, opposed any form of inquiry. He preferred that the government do nothing, on either prostitution or homosexuality, except to encourage a backbencher to introduce a bill 'designed to prohibit the publication of detailed information of criminal prosecutions for homosexual offences'. Churchill felt that it was best to ride out the storm, gag the press and let the issue die.

Maxwell Fyfe refused to accept the Prime Minister's suggestion:

> he pointed out that such legislation, even if it had the effect of allaying public anxiety about homosexuality, would make no contribution whatever towards a solution of the problem of prostitution. This, in his view, was the more urgent and obvious problem. He had no doubt that the proper remedy was to increase the penalty for soliciting . . . but he was satisfied – and in this he had the support of the majority of his Cabinet colleagues – that there was no prospect of passing legislation to make these changes in the existing law without the support of an independent enquiry.

The matter was again deferred.

By the time the proposal had been reintroduced at a cabinet meeting on 15 April the Home Office had spiked Churchill's proposal for legislation to restrict reporting of homosexual trials in an authoritative and compelling memorandum:

> If such legislation were now introduced . . . and at the same time the Government announced that they did not propose to undertake an inquiry into the law relating to homosexual offences, it would be said that the Government had not merely declined to hold an inquiry, in spite of the great and unexplained increase in such offences and of

the fact that the existing law was regarded as unsatisfactory by many responsible people, but were endeavouring to suppress the publication of evidence which showed the need for an inquiry.

The Home Office was prepared to compromise: it would accept a departmental committee rather than a Royal Commission. The need for an inquiry was accepted by the cabinet and the decision to establish a committee was announced in the House of Commons a fortnight later. By 8 July, Jack Wolfenden, the forty-seven-year-old Vice-Chancellor of Reading University, had agreed to act as the committee's chairman. Six weeks later fourteen other professional men and women had agreed to serve on the committee and they met for the first time on the afternoon of 15 September in a room provided by the Home Office, Room 101. Wolfenden, who had taken his fellow committee members to lunch at his club, opened the first session with a short speech: 'The task which the Committee faces is difficult, and perhaps distasteful, and a heavy responsibility lies upon its members. It will be necessary to preserve a sense of proportion and a sense of courage.'

Jack Wolfenden agonised over accepting the Home Secretary's invitation to chair the committee. He was desperate for official employment and this invitation provided him with the widest possible platform to demonstrate his talents to the state. He sought the approval of the senior members of the university before he accepted; he did not want to do anything that might damage the reputation of Reading. They suggested that he accept the invitation but still he agonised, taking his doubts to the Chancellor of the university, Viscount Templewood. The Viscount is better known to historians as the Tory cabinet minister Samuel Hoare, friend and political ally of Neville Chamberlain. In his retirement Templewood became passionately interested in penal reform, having served as Home Secretary in the late 1930s, and he persuaded Wolfenden of the importance of the work that had been entrusted to him.

Wolfenden was a very ambitious man and he feared most of all that his employment in such an office might not advance his career, but rather damage it; these were subjects with which he did not want to be associated. 'I am', he told Templewood, 'rather grimly expecting that this will be about as unpleasant a job as I have ever tackled.' He would have to be careful.

Wolfenden came from a lower-middle-class background. He was 'a brilliant product of Chapel and grammar school, a walking vindication of the uses of literacy'. His parents were devout Methodists, but he joined the Church of England on reaching adulthood, a switch he frankly admitted that he made to help his career. He grew up in Yorkshire and won a classics scholarship to Queen's College, Oxford. After achieving a first in his finals he spent a year in America on a fellowship at Princeton before returning to a fellowship at Magdalen College, Oxford, where he taught philosophy.

A keen sportsman, Wolfenden played rugby and cricket as well as rowing for his college. Injuries on the sports field denied him the opportunity of playing rugby for his university or his country: 'a bit was chipped off my spine', he used to quip. 'It's been a fine excuse ever since for dodging gardening. I can't too highly recommend a broken back for that purpose.' Wolfenden was a master of understatement. He was able to play hockey for Oxford and won sixteen caps as a hockey international. He won golden notices for his performance guarding the English goal, 'a safe pair of hands' according to one critic. Both knees were injured at hockey and it is clear that he was something of a muscular Christian. Certainly his gritty character appealed to the governors of Uppingham School who in 1934 appointed him Headmaster at the age of twenty-eight. In 1940–1 he spent a sabbatical in Whitehall organising the establishment of the Air Training Corps.

In 1944 he exchanged the headship of Uppingham for Shrewsbury before returning in 1950 to university administration as Vice-Chancellor of Reading. He won his knighthood in 1956 for his chairmanship of the Home Office committee and in 1963 became chairman of the University Grants Commission. After six years dishing out Treasury grants to an expanding university sector he moved to Bloomsbury as the Director and Principal Librarian of the British Museum, which brought him a tied cottage in the West End. His tenure of this office was disastrous but he stayed until his retirement in 1974, having done much damage by his poor management to this important national institution. Later that year he was created a peer. Wolfenden had, it seems, satisfied his extraordinary lust for glittering prizes and collected innumerable honours in the course of an immensely successful public career (when measured in terms of prizes won rather than concrete achievements).

He had few close friendships (if any) and was so consumed by his career that he was never a very regular presence in his home. 'His wife believed he was more like an uncle than a father' to their four children. His biographer in the *Dictionary of National Biography* offers a fairly accurate assessment of his character: 'it is true to say that few got to know him well as a man, for he was essentially a very private person, sensitive and vulnerable to criticism, shielding himself from prying eyes behind a screen of courtesy, erudition, wit and civilized urbanity.' Pipe-smoking, balding and bespectacled, he struck many who met him as the quintessential Englishman. Philip Toynbee in a savage review of his opaque memoirs *Turning Point* tried to find a man behind the public mask:

> Here is a book which seems to have been written by a man wearing a mask and a false front . . . What is so desolating about this book is that for ordinary human beings the title of Lord Wolfenden's memoirs would suggest a whole set of real human events – bereavement; a first love; marriage; loss of faith; possibly a first job; a painful quarrel; a terrible personal humiliation . . . Lord Wolfenden's jovial success story *must* be hiding a real John Wolfenden – and one who would be far more interesting and endearing to readers than this almost grotesquely public man. My own reaction to the Great Cham whom he presents to us is one of friendly but exasperated irreverence. When I think of his braces my fingers itch for the scissors. When I think of the speaker – whom I once heard in full cry at a school speech day – I long to be invisibly at his side on the platform, whispering into his ear, 'How's the masturbation these days, Wolfenden?' or 'On your knees, Wolfenden' or 'Watch out, Wolfenden. Here comes Death!' . . . a man without a single close friend; with a wife and family who are scarcely allowed to intrude upon his smooth upward glide; a man who has never done wrong, or bitterly regretted it; who has never had an idea of his own; who has looked at all religious and anti-religious experience; who has never hated; has never had a disturbing row with a colleague (everyone in this book is a splendid chap: all the ships happy) . . .

One of the happiest ships, according to his memoirs, was the Home Office committee: 'Their devotion was complete, their patience unwearying and their industry unflagging.' He was pleased to report something as a former headmaster he most prized: they had developed 'a remarkable corporate spirit and throughout these years, in areas often distasteful and sometimes embarrassing, with precious little chance of light-hearted relief, nobody, so far as I can remember, lost heart or lost his temper.' For three years Jack Wolfenden, who regarded himself as an 'ordinary plain citizen', led these paragons in an investigation of the operation of British sex laws.

Wolfenden had helped select his colleagues in the summer of 1954 in consultation with the mandarins from the Home Office. They had drawn up lists in meetings sitting around the Home Secretary's private office trying to create a perfectly balanced membership. (A complete list of the committee is to be found in the Appendix.) There were representatives of the established churches of England and Scotland, there were three lawyers, three doctors, two Members of Parliament (one Labour, one Conservative), a peer, three academics and one Roman Catholic layman.

There were three women, four Scots and a Welshman, providing a proper representation of sexual and national 'minorities'. It was a cleverly constructed committee. Nobody on the committee, except of course for the lawyers and the doctors, had, as far as the Home Office knew, any connection with prostitutes or homosexuals, making them perfectly qualified for conducting an impartial inquiry into these two subjects.

The most important task of this committee was that it would support the amendments to the laws on prostitution suggested by the Home Office. As a consequence few strong moralists were chosen to serve as members. The committee was therefore more receptive to reform of the law than a slightly more conservative selection might have been.

British institutional life is constructed around a strict code of public secrecy. All British institutions feel that they have secrets to hide. The offices of state find it difficult as a consequence to release raw material to the historian. A thirty-year rule applies to most official records, but each year the guardians of the secrets of Whitehall regularly refuse to release records under this rule. Instead they impose longer periods of closure on their most sensitive records. Some involving the monarchy, the armed forces, the secret service and the police remain closed for at least one hundred years.

The documentation accumulated by the Wolfenden Committee was considered for release in 1988 but it was decided to restrict access to the material for a further twenty years, allowing citizens and scholars to examine them only at the beginning of January 2008. At this stage it seems that someone weeded out material considered too sensitive ever to be released, material either destroyed or removed into a category so secret that no date has been set for its release. This is material provided by the police forces of Britain on the way that they operated the laws on homosexuality. No scholar will probably be permitted to see this.

Researching a survey of attitudes to sex and sexuality in Britain since the Renaissance, the historian and biographer Richard Davenport-Hines secured the release of some of the committee's papers, the correspondence files maintained by the committee's secretary and the memoranda submitted by groups and individuals who gave evidence to the committee, material which he used in his book *Sex, Death and Punishment* (1990). The Home Office refused to provide him with access to the transcripts of the committee's proceedings, which would remain closed until the next century.

The first letter that I wrote to ask the keepers of the secrets in Whitehall to secure the release of the transcripts was ignored. My second was answered but the message was not encouraging. More letters were written;

John Wolfenden was Vice-Chancellor of Reading University when he was appointed chairman of the Home Office inquiry. A former public school headmaster, he was knighted in 1956 and created a life peer in 1976.

for every two letters written, one was received. After eighteen months the Records Officer of the Home Office agreed to open the transcripts but only after they had been thoroughly inspected 'for legal reasons' by one of their officers, a task which would take several years. More correspondence and eventually a new head of records produced a new decision, to release the transcripts without an inspection if I could prove that I was a bona fide scholar. I sent the most favourable review of my anthology *A Queer Reader*, a notice that had appeared in *The Times* written by Matthew Parris, which seemed to satisfy the archivist that I was a proper person to read the state papers. It was eighteen months from the dispatch of my first letter until I was allowed to read the transcripts; a guerrilla war in which I reckon I was unusually lucky.

According to the committee's secretary, W. Conwy Roberts, the 'meat' would be found in the transcripts and these documents make it possible to understand the dynamics of the Wolfenden Committee and to explain the way in which its members produced their report. So often in the past we have had to rely simply on the published report, a carefully constructed document, and the misleading memories of Jack Wolfenden. Commentary on the report has tended to be favourable to its contents, accepting a liberal spin, and it has tended to elevate the importance of Wolfenden so that by his death obituarists could describe him as the 'author of the homosexual report'. The other committee members have been entirely forgotten, supporting players in the star's big pageant. By the time of his death in 1985 Wolfenden had been elevated to the status of a liberal saint, the emancipator of the British homosexual, and the report remembered as one of the most important social documents of the post-war period. The documents, however, tell a somewhat different story.

PART ONE

VENTILATING PREJUDICE

1

The Wolfenden
Committee, 1954–7

It is always safer not to give reasons.
     – John Wolfenden to W. Conwy Roberts, 18 November 1954

The ordinary plain citizen like me.
     – John Wolfenden to W. Conwy Roberts, 22 November 1954

It is an extremely interesting enquiry, though in many respects a distasteful one.
     – John Wolfenden, 20 June 1955

...we are bedevilled throughout all these discussions by these confounded words and having to try to pin a label to various types of things when it is terribly hard to see where the boundaries come.
     – John Wolfenden, 31 October 1955

Collecting Evidence
The Wolfenden Committee met sixty times over a period of nearly three years. Generally, members gathered in a room provided by the Home Office in Whitehall for morning and afternoon sessions twice a month. During the first fifteen months of its existence the committee collected evidence. The committee listened, read and interrogated. It received over a hundred memoranda from interested parties, and cross-examined many of the individuals and groups on their submissions during thirty-two sessions devoted to the hearing of evidence.

A number of criticisms can be made about the management of the business by the chairman, Wolfenden, and the secretary, W. Conwy Roberts. Too much time was wasted on listening to evidence that was poorly presented, inadequately supported and extremely repetitive. Testimony rarely added much to the written submissions presented in advance. The only justification for spending so much time listening to evidence was that it made interested parties *feel* that they were being listened to. This was certainly how Wolfenden often perceived these proceedings, as a way of placating groups and individuals who believed that their opinions were being listened to in Whitehall. This, after all, was the real point of the committee.

Under a different regime the committee could quite easily have reported within a year. Far too much time was spent on testimony and even more time wasted on fussing over the final text. The committee spent nearly two years of its life drafting the report. Much of that time was spent by Wolfenden on what one committee member sarcastically described as 'textual criticism'.

Reading the evidence is neither a particularly enlightening nor edifying experience. Few groups and individuals did much more than put before the committee hastily prepared and rather scrappy memoranda. When surveys were made to provide some statistical support for these documents, they were generally based upon the smallest of samples and had very little academic or scientific rigour. The committee itself did hardly any independent research. The research that was done was undertaken personally by the secretary, a Home Office official, whose duties were temporarily extended to administering its business. Roberts was a middle-grade official with a limited imagination and an addiction to routine. His performance was criticised by members of the committee though he developed a close working relationship with Wolfenden who acted as his protector.

The entire enterprise cost just over £8,000, a sum which included the cost of printing the report. Most of this money went on the cost of bringing fifteen busy people, several of them located far from London, to the capital twice a month and providing them with their expenses. It was an extremely amateur affair, an inquiry conducted by fifteen men and women on a part-time basis.

Talking Dirty

People in the 1950s, especially professional people in positions of authority, were not accustomed to speaking to an official body on a sexual subject. It involved breaking a number of taboos. The ways that they usually conducted themselves in front of official bodies had to be modified as they reverted to modes of communication more suitable for private discourse. A particular problem felt by witnesses as well as by some on the committee was the fact that the membership of the committee was mixed – three ladies were usually present. This certainly inhibited Sir

John Nott-Bower, the Commissioner of the Metropolitan Police, who toned down his evidence because of the presence of the ladies. Wolfenden suggested to Roberts that the ladies sometimes excuse themselves when some particularly 'distasteful' (a favourite Wolfenden word to describe the business of his inquiry) item emerged. All the clerical work for the committee was done by females, and in order to save their blushes Wolfenden and Roberts employed euphemisms to cover the words 'homosexuality' and 'prostitution': Huntley's and Palmer's, the name of a famous firm of biscuit manufacturers. A rather typically English joke, a play on words, that would appeal to the academic and mandarin mind. Under this code homosexuals became Huntley's and prostitutes Palmer's.

Each session of testimony opened with an emollient greeting from the urbane chairman. These greetings were carefully calibrated on the basis of the importance of the delegation in the room. To put the representatives of the Metropolitan Police at their ease Wolfenden commented on this 'more distasteful part of our remit'; they had given evidence at a previous session on prostitution, a subject much less distasteful than homosexuality. Elaborate introductions were conducted according to almost oriental patterns of ritual, but, significantly, Wolfenden did not bother with even the minimum ceremony when Peter Wildeblood, a man convicted of homosexual offences, gave evidence; he was after all a criminal, a particularly distasteful experience for the law-abiding chairman.

Wolfenden clearly valued good manners and generally adopted a deferential tone that did much to weaken the impact of the interrogation of witnesses. Lines of critical questioning by Rees, Diplock, Adair, Curran or Whitby (the most critical members of the committee) were often diverted by Wolfenden as he came to the assistance of the embattled witness. In this way many of the contradictions contained in the testimony and the sloppiness of many submissions escaped scrutiny. It was, after all, quite a discovery to find that the secretary of the Public Morality Council did not know that homosexual activity between consenting male adults in private was a criminal offence. He had thought it was legal and wanted naturally enough to ban it. The lack of knowledge of this very poorly prepared witness did not prevent him giving 'evidence' to the committee and wasting its time.

The most important assurance that Wolfenden delivered at the beginning of each session was that nothing said during the sessions was to be placed on the record. The transcripts of evidence were simply *aides-mémoire* for members of the committee. Sir Lawrence Dunne, Chief Metropolitan Magistrate, asked Wolfenden about this:

Dunne: Everything said here is virtually off the record?
Wolfenden: Yes we speak with complete frankness . . .

'The record', as Wolfenden said on another occasion, 'is entirely off the record.' One of the delegation representing English barristers said, 'We can talk perfectly frankly without any punches pulled.'

Talking about sexual matters in this frank fashion by committee members and their witnesses was a considerable novelty. All business was conducted on the basis that nobody had ever met a homosexual other than in a court of law, a police station, a prison, a hospital or a clinic. Except for two sessions addressed directly by 'Huntley's' (the production of 'Palmer's' to present evidence proved beyond the organisational powers of the secretary), all witnesses kept their distance from the subjects of the inquiry. At the beginning, the committee started its discussion on the basis that no member had ever encountered homosexuality or prostitution in anything other than a professional capacity. Only one witness owned up to knowing homosexual men socially, Sir Theobald Mathew, the Director of Public Prosecutions.

There is no doubt that the creation of the Wolfenden Committee generated a tremendous amount of discussion about male homosexuality by groups and individuals across Britain. Professional bodies representing solicitors, barristers, doctors, psychiatrists, psychologists, probation officers, and local government officers worked out their positions on the problem. Lodged in archives across Britain is an enormous paper chain of these opinions collected for the production of the memoranda. Sadly, they simply expose the incredible level of prejudice against male homosexuality, the enormous ignorance of the subject and the amazing arrogance of British professionals at mid-century.

The men (and on a few occasions the women) who gave evidence possessed the most extraordinary amount of confidence in their pronouncements. In British culture at that time professionals rarely challenged one another, and those outside the professional group usually adopted a suitably deferential attitude to the pontifications of the 'experts'. An 'expert' delivered his judgement 'impartially'; he/she was invariably a 'responsible' person with a proper sense of discretion schooled over many years of indoctrination spent living and working in British institutional culture. This culture was probably one of the most extraordinary creations of modern times. The secretary of the committee tried to ensure that the committee heard evidence only from responsible bodies and individuals. Individuals or groups outside this magic circle were assumed to trade only in speculation and opinion. As we shall see, the frontier they imagined to exist was entirely illusionary.

The material collected presented an extremely negative description of homosexuality. No one except the 'Huntley' witnesses themselves said anything positive about homosexuality – indeed witnesses often seemed to compete with one another in their passion to vilify this activity. Much of the proceedings was a long litany, or catalogue, of insults that could be made against the homosexual.

Most witnesses bemoaned the absence of concrete data on which to shape policy, though this did not prevent them making up their minds on the limited data available to them. 'I think,' said Dr Eustace Chesser, one of the greatest experts on the subject, in a particularly Pythonesque session, 'the only thing we can do is to give a firm opinion. That is the only thing we can do; there is no real evidence.'

They hungered for *facts*. Writing in the *New Statesman* (4 July 1953), A. J. P. Taylor criticised 'the widespread modern belief that if we accumulate enough facts, we shall know the answer'. The professional men and women of the Wolfenden era had faith in the power of facts to illuminate problems. They comforted themselves with the notion that facts, particularly facts that could be rendered quantitatively, had a place in the hierarchy of knowledge far above that of any other source of information, especially anecdotal or impressionistic material. Repeatedly Wolfenden and his colleagues were frustrated at the failure of their many sessions to yield enough facts. They did not even know the numbers involved: 'our great difficulty is that we do not know how many there are'. They were reluctant to apply the Kinsey estimates, partly because they were American but also partly because the numbers were higher than many committee members and witnesses were willing to accept.

The problem of not knowing the number, or the extent of homosexuality, caused difficulties for the committee. Some witnesses minimised the numbers and others maximised them, using words that conveyed in general terms the size of the problem. Sometimes they both minimised and maximised the numbers in the same submission or testimony. This mainly occurred because all witnesses were keen never to compliment or praise the homosexual or homosexuality in any way. The only praise given, and then often only grudgingly, was to the celibate who sublimated his desires (preferably in work) and never owned up to what stirred his passions, what was usually called the 'controlled homosexual'.

Committee members and witnesses were often asked if homosexuality had increased in the past decade since the end of the Second World War. Most thought it had. This observation was usually based on the criminal statistics. Despite the fact that many committee members and witnesses realised that the increase in the numbers of cases coming before the courts was often a consequence of greater policing, they still used these figures to measure the extent of homosexuality. The committee also seemed to discount the information it gathered on the inadequacy of the official statistics and the lack of agreement about the figures that seemed to exist between different official bodies. Criminal statistics seemed to have a magical quality that made them immune from all sorts of potential reservations.

The committee and its witnesses operated on the assumption that homosexuality was a modern development, a particularly bizarre assumption in a committee chaired by a scholar of the ancient world. This was a deliberate attempt to deny any historical legitimacy for homosexual activity. It was as if it had all emerged suddenly in the late nineteenth century at the time of the Wilde trials, then largely gone underground again until the 1940s. This notion lulled committee members and witnesses into believing that this modern problem could in some way be solved, that something could be done to reduce if not eliminate the incidence of homosexuality. It was a confidence shared by many people, in many fields, who felt that they could shape the future and that the past offered few lessons for them in their task.

Essentially the committee addressed a succession of questions to itself and its witnesses. The responses to these questions shaped the final report:

1. Should male homosexuality between consenting male adults in private be decriminalised?

If the answer was 'yes' then a number of further questions followed:
    (a) Should decriminalisation include all homosexual acts?
    (b) What should the age of consent be?
    (c) What did 'private' mean?
    (d) Would decriminalisation lead to an increase in the incidence of homosexuality?

If the answer was 'no' then it was necessary to justify the complete criminalisation of all homosexual activity.

2. What measures should be taken to protect young males (a flexible category sometimes including men into their mid-twenties) from older homosexual men and from homosexual practice generally?

3. Was it possible to discover any course of treatment or even a cure that would reduce the extent of male homosexual practice?

4. How was homosexual activity policed? Were there any elements of

police practice or activity that justified criticism made in the wake of
the Montagu trials of 1953–4?

Witnesses generally perceived homosexuality as a danger and the proceedings of the Wolfenden Committee gave them an opportunity to articulate
their fears. While there were certainly individuals and groups who wanted
some reform of the law, this never extended beyond the proposal to
decriminalise homosexual activity between consenting male adults in private. There was a considerable measure of agreement between these
reformers and those individuals and groups who opposed any change to
the law: they all sought ways of marginalising and reducing the threat
from homosexuality to contemporary Britain. They hoped that it would
be contained in the future and that it would even decline, one of the great
fantasies of the heterosexual dictatorship.

Inverts and Perverts

Wolfenden and his committee decided that they would accept the Oxford
English Dictionary definitions of homosexual and homosexuality, and
accepted the distinction made by many witnesses that homosexual acts
did not necessarily mean that the individuals involved were 'homosexual'.
The committee encountered a bewildering number of schemes that sought
to classify the large number of homosexual types that seemed to exist.
These were often constructed by associations or societies which sought
to embrace the views of all their members, some inclined to blame nature,
others preferring nurture. This approach also allowed witnesses to cover
all bets. If they exclusively plumped for nature then there seemed to be
no necessity for any safety nets protecting young males from being converted to homosexuality. Few advocates of biological causation really had
the courage of their convictions, and they preferred to erect safeguards –
just in case. Witnesses exhibited a splendid display of intellectual timidity
disguised behind a smokescreen of scientific jargon.

Humanity, it seemed, was divided into two groups, heterosexuals and
homosexuals. Those naturally or environmentally created homosexuals
were usually referred to as inverts. They were freaks of nature or accidents
of some terrible environment, usually the product of strong and dominant
mothers and weak and absent fathers. The absence of so many men on
active service during the war created the comforting doctrine that the
increase in homosexuality was a generational aberration that would gradually be reduced as the impact of the returning warriors worked its beneficent magic on future generations.

The 'genuine' homosexual was a small minority of those men indulging in homosexual practices. Indeed it was often suggested that the real homosexual was under-sexed. They were easily distinguished from other men by their effeminate appearance, and the Victorian view that they were women trapped in a man's body still had some supporters (including Leo Abse, the Labour MP responsible for piloting the Sexual Offences Act of 1967 through the Commons). It was believed that inverts played the passive role in sex, and while they might talk more about sex, they indulged less often than their terrifying partner, the pervert.

It was the pervert who caused most problems associated with homosexuality. Most experts believed that the pervert was really a heterosexual who had lost his way: 'The pervert is not a homosexual, but a heterosexual who engages in homosexual practices.' 'So often', said one doctor, 'the homosexual is heterosexual', while another felt that they were 'simply dirty-minded heterosexuals'. Some of them sought this activity 'for an additional experience', others because they found it 'something more exciting to do, something which is forbidden'. Others had been 'corrupted in early youth'. Usually the pervert was presented as a heterosexual who refused to accept the 'rules' of heterosexuality as idealised in mid-century Britain – one woman in a lifetime of matrimonial bliss. Why perverts should prefer male partners to female ones was never satisfactorily explained. Sometimes he was, according to Dr Whitby, 'a person unable to achieve satisfactory heterosexual relationships'. Some experts believed that all humans were bisexuals who often went through a homosexual phase. Perverts were sometimes seen as men trapped in that phase. Genuine bisexuality, men who had sexual relations with both males and females, were seen as an even more dangerous species of the pervert. Bisexuality as described by the experts invariably ended in exclusive heterosexuality if nature took its proper course.

Perverts were more dangerous because they were less easy to detect through their manner, behaviour and demeanour. As the doctor who ran a VD clinic at a large London hospital explained in describing his patients who had indulged in homosexuality: 'Some of them far from appearing effeminate, are lusty he-men, e.g. physical culture experts, athletes, weight-lifters and champion cyclists.' In this way homosexuality could become a much broader challenge to British society and culture than that which was presented by a biological defect.

The pervert became addicted to homosexual sex, and Lord Hailsham, a minister wearing the mantle of Anglican moralist, compared it to heroin addiction. Perverts were sometimes described more generally as addicts. An Edinburgh-based expert thought that these men were 'compulsive characters'. Even reformers could subscribe to the addictive or compulsive nature of homosexuality. Gerald Gardiner, a man with strong liberal credentials, famous for his role as counsel to Penguin Books in the *Chatterley* trial, a leading agitator against capital punishment throughout the 1950s and Labour Lord Chancellor in the first two Wilson governments, could accept this idea. In a series of replies to Mischcon he could draw a distinction between men who 'interfered' with girls and men who 'interfered' with boys. 'I should have thought', said Gardiner, 'in relation to girls if you send [such a man] to prison he will stop. In relation to a man who feels like that with boys it is an obsession. It is a medical problem. It has a compulsive quality about it.'

This division of homosexuality into two broad categories was repeatedly used by commentators in writing and talking about homosexuality. The attributes could sometimes be confused. At a trial in 1954 Peter Wildeblood, who was accused of several homosexual offences, emphasised his respectability and his impotence; as a consequence he was described by the prosecutors as an invert while the two airmen on whose evidence much of the case rested were described, despite their effeminacy, as perverts. What seems to have mattered here was the fact that the airmen admitted to being promiscuous. It was the fact that homosexually-inclined men did not always pattern, or aspire to pattern, their relationships on the heterosexual ideal that seemed to offer the greatest challenge to the social ideal of 'normal' heterosexuality. The good homosexual was allowed to find one partner from the same class and same age band as himself and settle down to a chaste life faithful to that one partner. Sir Theobald Mathew, Director of Public Prosecutions, knew men like this and regarded them as offering no challenge to society as long as they lived discreetly. According to Dr Eustace Chesser, 'the normal homosexual – in other words, the homosexual who behaves with another homosexual in a normal manner, here you have a parallel with the heterosexual as well.' The bad homosexual, the pseudo-homosexual as he was sometimes called, challenged that ideal. That was his greatest crime.

There must of course have been heterosexual infidelity and promiscuity in Britain at that time. Yet the committee and the witnesses seem to have acted on the assumption that there was not much. In an amazing piece of double-think the committee could study prostitution without ever speculating about the clients who went to the prostitutes. What did the rising number of prostitutes on the streets of London suggest about the sex lives of thousands of ordinary British citizens, many married, sometimes living happily, more often unhappily, in the suburbs? The committee decided to punish and control the women while ignoring their clients, its main interest being to 'clean up' the streets of the capital.

Perversely perhaps, the man taking the active part in buggery was more often seen as the more heterosexual of the two men involved in the activity. According to one expert, 'the sodomist is closer to heterosexuality than any other form of perversion' which was, he claimed, an 'observed fact'. A member of the prison medical service suggested that 'buggery is an offence that the bisexual goes in for. That is to say if he is chiefly a heterosexual then he will desire to simulate the sexual act with women as far as possible and therefore goes in for buggery . . . You get a cruder type of personality. The more fastidious man will never commit buggery.'

Of course homosexual acts were committed that were not dangerous. Men sometimes indulged who were drunk, and alcohol really did seem to excuse this behaviour unless a pattern of activity could be discovered. The Procurator Fiscal of Glasgow, James Robertson, thought that 'generally speaking, one could say that these offences, indecency with males, are all half drunk men you are dealing with and not perverted types at all'. This also covered the behaviour of boys indulging in homosexual activity at public schools. Wolfenden, a former public school headmaster, offered his opinion: 'My own private view which is not to be considered binding by anyone else, is that sort of behaviour in [public] school has very little to do with the problem of homosexuality.'

Vampires

Except for the small number of inverts, who were perceived as biological mistakes, it was generally assumed that most men or boys 'caught' homosexuality in their youth or adolescence, infected by a virus passed on by adult men. Much of the business of the Wolfenden Committee revolved round what might be described as the 'vampire' theory of homosexuality, a theory effectively articulated by the representative of the Magistrates' Association Mr J.P. Eddy, JP: 'It [homosexuality] lives I believe in corrupting youth because I believe that in general, an adult homosexual is not particularly attracted by an adult homosexual. He wants youth, he wants boys; therefore I think this foul thing lives on corrupting youth.' Lord Hailsham told the committee that it was his belief that 'if you go far enough back in the life of a homosexual . . . you will find an active initiation'. This view was implicit in a question that James Adair asked the police: 'Where do young people or those accused first [learn] the practice?' This idea that there is a moment when the corruption takes root was widely held, and shaped the policy of many members of the legal establishment when dealing with homosexual offenders.

The psychoanalysts thought that homosexuality 'was laid down in infancy' but that the events of puberty, especially hero worship, 'might influence it in one way or other', a good example of bet-hedging. Goronwy Rees wondered facetiously if 'the British public's admiration for Mr Churchill' might not be 'a minor trait bordering on homosexuality'? Perhaps the cult of the wartime leader had led to the increasing incidence of homosexuality.

To assist them in their campaign of corruption, 'experienced homosexuals' possessed 'certain antennae' by which they could recognise 'the vulnerable subject', the view of Dr Dicks of the Tavistock Clinic. Sir Lawrence Dunne, Chief Metropolitan Magistrate, thought that 'homosexuals have a curious attraction for each other. There is something by which they seem to be able to distinguish each other, and they do tend to foregather together.' Another doctor from the Tavistock Clinic propounded a view which commanded much support, that 'the greater the disparity of the ages . . . the greater the damage'.

Perverts, it was thought, turned to youth on what was popularly described as the 'rake's progress': 'Appetites are progressive, and a homosexual sated with practices with adults, without hindrance, will be far more likely to tempt a jaded appetite with youth' (Sir Lawrence Dunne). Sir Leonard Costello, chairman of the Devon Quarter Sessions, another pillar of the magistracy, suggested that 'if two men do these things in private in course of time they get bored with another or tired of each other, and they go out seeking fresh fields of operation'. This activity was called 'proselytising', the drive to convert others to their vice: 'this particular class of conduct', according to Costello, 'is entirely contagious and there is a tendency amongst persons who indulge in it to proselytise and thereby to contaminate other people'. Dr Roper, Senior Medical Officer at Wakefield Prison, even discerned this trait in the importuner, whose behaviour clearly rather puzzled him: 'they have this funny kink that they do not want to go back to the same person twice; they must pick up a fresh person and take this frightful risk in order to pick up a new associate'. They really did seem to be vampires.

By focusing on the act of corruption, commentators could indulge in their obsession with employing medical terms for social developments. By concentrating on this important act it was possible to associate homosexuality with disease. Corruption could set off 'contagion' and so homosexuality could be 'spread'. Many people believed this had happened since the start of the war. American servicemen had been one source of contamination, as had British servicemen overseas. Lord Hailsham thought that many British troops had brought it back from the Middle East. A baronet had indeed offered as his defence to charges of a homosexual offence in the 1930s that he had served in Mesopotamia in the Great War and had been infected by the practice. The BMA extended the net even further, mentioning the service of Britons in the Orient where many had learnt these shameful practices. Across the centuries the foreigner has been blamed as the source of corruption. A statute of Edward III in the fourteenth century blamed homosexuality on Italian merchants who had been trading with England. According to the BMA, 'Homosexual practices tend to spread by contact and from time to time they insidiously invade certain groups of the community which would otherwise be predominantly heterosexual.' This is what was believed to have happened in Britain since the 1940s.

One man who peddled the contagion theory of homosexuality was a clergyman, Revd T. Holland, DD, who attended the committee as a member of the delegation sent by the Public Morality Council. Goronwy Rees challenged him to support his theory. Holland seems to have annoyed Rees. Perhaps it was his support for special prisons to be established for homosexual offenders where they would remain indefinitely until they were cured. He wanted the closure of a whole 'crop of private clubs devoted to this particular form of indoor sport':

Rees: Would it not be true to say, Dr Holland, that you believe that this thing is very catching . . . ?
Holland: Yes.
Rees: And [have] you reason to believe that?
Holland: I have, yes.
Rees: What kind of reason?
Holland: I have read about certain schools and I have met the masters who teach in them and I know how the thing has gone.
Rees: Is it based on the experience of schools?
Holland: That is an element of it.
Rees: I really would like to know what kind of evidence there is for it being rightly catching, what that kind of evidence is like, because it does seem to me that this really [is] the basis of your objection, given what you have said already, the basis of your objection to an alteration in the law?
Holland: My pause is not at all occasioned by facts, but discrimination of facts, schools, schoolmasters. Certain parts of the country I go round, I am a missioner and I go from church to church and give pep talks and that sort of thing. There are certain areas where clearly the thing has begun just from one pair and has flared out enormously, involving a neighbourhood of boys and young men from just a tiny beginning. I am thinking of special cases and I would ask not to be questioned more about it, if that suits the Committee.

Presumably he saw Rees ready to pounce with another question and sent up the white flag. A fellow delegate from the Council tried to come to his aid with more evidence that he had 'read on lavatory walls'. Rees closed his examination with a sarcastic comment on the testimony of the Council: 'We congratulate ourselves on being normal.' Said one of the delegates: 'We base the law on normality. We have some idea of that.'

These acts of corruption through which homosexuality spread were the source of many other fears. Homosexuality seemed to be no respecter of class and this, as the RAF suggested, had implications for national security:

> the removal of homosexuals is of vital importance in an armed force. The homosexual cannot exist in isolation; he must have an accomplice, usually several, and in seeking to extend his corrupting influence he is no respecter of rank or person. Homosexual practices bring together men of widely different ranks and position to the prejudice of discipline. There is also a security risk since the man compromised by homosexual conduct may yield to pressure for the disclosure of secret information.

A number of trials for homosexual offences in the 1950s reveal the alarm felt by courts when men sought partners across different classes, which seemed to challenge the established order. It could undermine British youth. Miss Davidson of the British Psychological Society was worried that if young men had a satisfying homosexual experience between the ages of sixteen and twenty-one then they would not 'move on to heterosexuality'. Of course the act of corruption was often perceived as a very complex process. Another representative of the British Psychological Society, Dr E. B. Strauss, thought that if

> a boy of 16 or 17 is seduced by an older man and seduced in a very subtle way, that is to say, by being given expensive presents, taken for expensive holidays, introduced to all the pleasant and delightful sides of life, and he himself found the emotional experience for the stage of development he has reached, there again I would claim, although it is not obvious, but undue persuasion had been used. The offering of the good things of life to a boy who could not get it in other ways, that in itself might be a traumatic experience ... that might impede the boy's subsequent development towards [the] adult [i.e. heterosexual] pattern of behaviour.

Those who opposed the decriminalisation of any homosexual act in whatever circumstances believed that a change in the law would send the wrong signal. More perverts would move on to the rake's progress and begin the systematic corruption of British youth. This would open what moralists described as the 'floodgates', with dangerous consequences for the state and society.

Against Society

According to Dr Sessions-Hodge, a specialist and an expert on homosexuality operating from a hospital in Taunton, men who indulged in homosexual acts were 'persons who have thrown off, in many respects, the yoke of society'. Such sentiments were echoed by other witnesses. The Law Society reminded the committee about the 'damage to the State if these tendencies get too strong a hold'.

The BMA regarded the homosexual man as 'an enemy of the State', 'attached to an alien ideology' opposed to 'a constructive [heterosexual] ideology which is really the basis and strength of democracy'. It was, according to the BMA, 'a basic and fundamental essence of a democracy and the way of life in which we take pride in this country, that individuals take responsibility; and if there is a weakening of that sense of public responsibility in an individual whoever he is, then the whole community may suffer'. Wherever Sir Leonard Costello the Devonshire magistrate went he found 'the same ugly story'. He did not 'know what is happening to this nation. The percentage of cases of this class which we have to try today is absolutely terrifying. If this evil is allowed to spread, it will corrupt the men of the nation.'

Dr Sessions-Hodge was a pioneer, experimenting in his hospitals with giving his patients massive doses of oestrogen which he believed made them better 'adjusted': 'The common report from the persons concerned has been that they are more effective in their daily lives than they were before – they are free of the incubus, they are free to act normally amongst their fellows, and one indeed has subsequently made so much money that he has been able to retire.' Sessions-Hodge and others promoted an image of the citizen as a social slave working productively for the benefit of the nation. This type of doctrine had been powerfully reinforced during the 1940s. According to Ray Gosling the 'idea of a consumer society was very foreign to my parents. The idea you could purchase at whim, because something looked nice or someone tells you so. The idea of credit was anathema. Life was productive, and that's how it should be. You provided for your needs, not your fancy. Work was necessary and of value, almost a virtue.' A nation at war tried hard to inspire its people to greater efforts to defeat Britain's enemies.

This doctrine did not cease being propagated in 1945; if anything, the Labour government of 1945–51 made this image a key element in its

There were few opportunities to celebrate male beauty in the popular press. These advertisements and features were unusual because they licensed, and possibly encouraged, some degree of male vanity.

message to the British people. The state provided benefits such as the National Health Service, better and easier access to housing, free education, and in return the citizen worked hard and lived a respectable life, as spouse, parent and worker – the essence of the heterosexual dictatorship. Labour leaders were unhappy about the sort of consumption ethic encouraged by the Conservatives after they returned to power in 1951.

There was a strong puritan element in Labour ideology which did the party much long-term electoral damage. The Conservative Party reaped an extraordinary electoral advantage from its promotion of consumerism. As a consequence many élite moralists found themselves in the strange situation of preferring the rhetoric of the Labour Party to that of the Conservatives, even though their temperament, their past history and associations inclined them to the Conservative Party. Geoffrey Fisher, Archbishop of Canterbury from 1945 to 1961, a fairly natural supporter of the Conservative Party, often found himself at odds with the party after 1951, and delivered a savage attack on Harold Macmillan when he boasted in 1959 that the British people had never had it so good.

One of the consequences of the doctrine which promoted the image of the citizen-producer was that it rested so firmly on the assumption that everyone aspired to be a model heterosexual. The producers were encouraged to work harder for the benefit of the next generation; the hard work and effort that they made would pay dividends for their children and even grandchildren. It provided much comfort to many people who found in the contemplation of the future well-being and prosperity of their offspring a justification for their present existence. The 'normal' heterosexual was a national hero doing his bit for his country. Inevitably, homosexuality was a major challenge to this system. Homosexual men would not make sacrifices for offspring they might never have, might spend disposable income on luxuries and pleasure and might indulge in promiscuous sex, causing further disturbance to the *status quo*.

It is difficult now to capture the mentality of the early 1950s when extremely patronising descriptions of 'the people' were uttered by figures in authority without the slightest public challenge or rebuke. It seems incredible that the Queen could deliver in her 1954 Christmas speech the following thoughts about the lives of her people:

> In the turbulence of this anxious and active world many people are leading uneventful lonely lives. To them dreariness, not disaster, is the enemy. They seldom realise that on their steadfastness, on their ability to withstand the fatigue of dull repetitive work and on their courage in meeting small adversities depend in great measure the happiness and prosperity of the community as a whole . . . the faithful

toil and devotion to duty of the great bulk of ordinary citizens. The upward course of a nation's history is due in the long run to the soundness of heart of its average men and women.

And so it is that this Christmas Day I want to send a special message of encouragement and good cheer to those of you whose lot is cast in dull and unenvied surroundings, to those whose names will never be household names, but whose work and loyalty we owe so much.

May you be proud to remember – as I am myself – how much depends on you and that even when your life seems most monotonous what you do is always of real value and importance to your fellow men.

Similarly Spartan sentiments were echoed by Geoffrey Fisher, Archbishop of Canterbury, in his Christmas message for 1954: 'We never really find life interesting or find our own capacities until we find ourselves engaged (at work and elsewhere) in a cause, a skill, a loyalty that takes us *outside* ourselves . . . [during the] War we found that good cause and lived by it.'

Mr J. P. Eddy, who had been for many years a stipendiary magistrate in the East End, delivered an incredible rant to the committee, in which he articulated the citizen-as-producer doctrine at its most explicit:

the national interest requires we shall do all we can to encourage ordinary, decent family [life] . . . unnatural practices [are] . . . against the national interest . . . I regard homosexuality as just a canker eating into the roots of ordinary, decent human relations, and I ask you this – you will no doubt consider it – What do we gain? What does this country gain? I care nothing about the practices on the Continent. We do not take our morals from the Continent. What does this country gain by giving licence to men . . . to indulge in filthy practices? Then can there be the slightest doubt that homosexuality will increase? Can that possibly be doubted?

Protestantism in Britain had traditionally set up Britain as a model nation, a chosen people, which seems to have been easy to believe if you and your congregation lived in Aberystwyth, Paisley or Lurgan. It was a Scot, a Scottish Sheriff, who put the objections to homosexuality in the crudest terms of all:

I believe the practice of homosexuality tends to discourage the practice of heterosexuality. In other words a man who is a homosexual will associate with men and will not associate with women, and as social practice that will eventually strike at the birth rate and will eventually lead to the deterioration of the race . . . [it is] so obviously against the order of nature . . . it destroys a man's capacity to enjoy the fulness of married life.

Dr Matheson, Senior Medical Officer at Brixton Prison, articulated these utilitarian sentiments even more explicitly:

the State has an interest in the proper use of the sex instinct, viz. to procreate children. Each child born is of potential value to the State, economically and socially; economically for the productive value to the State when the child becomes an adult; socially for the contribution which can be made to the general welfare of the State by each member of it.

The representatives of the Tavistock Clinic wanted the committee to educate the British people about the danger they faced: 'The homosexual should be thought of and proclaimed in the public mind as an immature, sick and potentially "infectious" person and the whole subject divested of the glamour of wickedness as well as aesthetic superiority.'

Moral Education

When official and semi-official committees and commissions had collected material on sexual and moral offences before the Second World War their proceedings had been dominated by moral educators. Such individuals and groups optimistically believed that better moral education was all that was required to reduce sexual offences or, some naïvely hoped, to eliminate them altogether. This argument was less often developed by those coming before the Wolfenden Committee.

It is possible that the Second World War had changed perceptions about the nature of the problem, that all sorts of evidence (higher levels of venereal disease, illegitimacy, homosexuality and divorce) may have undermined the old arguments because they all seemed to point in the same direction of a moral collapse. One member of the committee speculated that they had been appointed to stop things going further downhill. The extent of the trouble was so great that it needed more drastic solutions than simply education.

There may be a link between the decline of the rescue missions to save female prostitutes during the 1940s and 1950s and the declining appeal of this argument. Prostitution rescue work before the Second World War usually rested on the argument that women went on the game because they were driven there by economic necessity or by unscrupulous men (the infamous white slavers). From the 1940s this view of prostitutes was successfully challenged, especially with the establishment of the Welfare State. Prostitutes were increasingly perceived as females addicted to sex and glamour. The representatives of the probation officers thought these girls were in 'revolt against domesticity'; prostitutes were 'associated with glamour, high-lights and colour' and had 'a longing for exhibitionism' not satisfied by family life.

The men, but mainly women, involved in rescue work were a disappearing breed. The representatives of groups like the Association for Moral and Social Hygiene and the National Council of Women were decidedly antique. They often peddled the same solutions to the problems of sex crimes as they had done in the 1920s. Mrs Ashby, LLD, of the Association of Moral and Social Hygiene, tried to persuade Wolfenden and his colleagues to lead a great campaign of re-education: 'An appeal from you, for instance, for greater respect – self-respect and respect between the sexes – to the press and to the great organs of advertising that they should refrain from this very blatant incitement to sex, would be beneficial.' Such an appeal was unlikely to cut any ice with the popular press. Mrs Ashby drew Wolfenden's attention to the incitements to vice sanctioned by London Underground: 'one travels on the Underground. There may be rows of pictures of almost naked women in suggestive attitudes – drink, cabaret – all that incitement to debauchery.' Mrs Ashby remembered past triumphs, most notably and memorably the work of Josephine Butler which acted as an inspiration to generations of middle- and upper-class ladies who sought to curb, tame and eliminate male lust. 'For Heaven's sake', Mrs Bligh of the National Council of Women told the committee, 'start teaching the men and the boys something about the sanctity of sex . . . We have to make our young people character-proof against temptation.'

Throughout the testimony it is possible to discern a very strong bias towards a Protestant morality. Many of those giving evidence were lapsed Christians but they retained a strongly moral framework that owed much to the Evangelical revival of the nineteenth century which so strongly reinforced the connection between puritanism and the British and which has done much to shape attitudes to sex and morality in twentieth-century Britain. Even liberals like Gerald Gardiner, QC, could think that 'the whole trouble really . . . is the decrease in moral standards; moral education is what is wanted'. Frank Powell, a metropolitan magistrate, suggested that 'there is such a thing in life as self-control, and I do not see why that should not be exercised . . . most crime is caused, in my view, by uncontrolled natural instincts, unmastered common human feelings, an immoral and irreligious attitude to life, and things of that sort.' References to self-control recur throughout the testimony of many figures of authority, especially those involved in the law.

Victorian clergymen and their fellow-travellers had successfully persuaded their contemporaries and their descendants that there was a connection between religious behaviour and belief and improving moral behaviour. As religion declined so, it was suggested, immorality became more prevalent. It made a nonsense of the Christian message and western history but it was gratefully embraced by men in authority eager to find something to ward off evil thoughts and actions amongst their charges.

It might seem odd, in 1955, that the group which invested most heavily in moral education and the protective powers of Protestant Christianity was the nation's doctors. The British Medical Association, representing the 'family' doctors of Britain, was proud to place itself in the forefront of the battle against homosexuality. 'Everything', they proclaimed, 'which helps to encourage health, social responsibility and stable family life is the concern of the medical profession for on these factors are founded the virility and soundness of the national life.' The proper use of sex was 'creative', which was related 'to the individual's responsibility to himself and the nation, and the [BMA] . . . believe that the weakening of personal responsibility with regard to social and national welfare in a significant proportion of the population may be one of the causes of the apparent increase of homosexual practices and prostitution.'

The BMA was still bitter about its defeat over the establishment of the National Health Service and eager to detect every sign of the weakening of individual responsibility as fresh evidence of a moral decline accelerated by the welfare policies of the Labour government. Given its members' extraordinary greed and selfishness in their negotiations with Aneurin Bevan, it is amusing to read their lectures on the promotion of 'unselfish living': 'What is needed is responsible citizenship where concern for the nation's welfare and the needs of other's takes priority over selfish interests and self-indulgence.'

They had a long list of things to which they objected: 'the behaviour and appearance of homosexuals congregating blatantly in public houses, streets and restaurants, are an outrage to public decency. Effeminate men wearing make-up and using scent are objectionable to everyone.' The solution lay in a 'healthy social environment' which sprang from 'secure and happy homes'. The BMA described the recipe for creating the ideal home that would keep the homosexual menace at bay:

> homes which give a sound background of character training and where sex is kept in its rightful place, would be the greatest prophylactic. Boys and girls from homes where high moral standards are aimed

at, where there is parental harmony, sensible, but not over-strict discipline, a general recognition of personal responsibility and sincere
religious faith will not fall easy prey to the seducer's invitation to
homosexual or heterosexual misconduct.

The great panacea offered by the BMA was religion: 'There should ... be
a recognition of the fact that homosexuals can acquire a new direction
in their lives through religious conversion, and opportunities should be
available to them to discover for themselves a basis of life that proves a
reality to many people.' An Appendix to the BMA memorandum gave
detailed case histories of men who had been cured of homosexuality
through their commitment to Jesus.

There could no doubt about the Christian commitment of Quintin
Hogg, second Viscount Hailsham, a fact which Hailsham was extremely
keen to advertise. It is still difficult to understand why Hailsham should
have volunteered to give evidence to the Wolfenden Committee, the only
politician to do so. It seemed an opportunity to express his disgust. Hailsham has often tried to use the moral issue to boost his support within
the party. Wolfenden was delighted by the presence of the peer and
crawled shamelessly. He told Hailsham at the end of his testimony that it
was 'a most refreshing testimony'. Amongst the many profound comments
uttered by Hailsham, pride of place should be given to the way that he
sanctioned his prejudice. 'The instinct of mankind', he told the committee,
'to describe homosexual acts as "unnatural" is not based on mere prejudice'; 'the element of corruption is rarely absent in homosexuality' because
it was 'a proselytising religion'. A lawyer, Hailsham was sceptical about
the things that homosexuals said about themselves, as they 'all tend to
deceive themselves' that they are exclusively homosexual. He had 'a great
deal of reserve about believing anything I am told by these people about
their own past history'.

It was a stellar performance from one of the nation's leading moralists;
appropriately enough he would end his political career three decades later
as a Lord Chancellor in the Thatcher government.

The Church of England has often been credited with an important role
in shaping the Wolfenden Report. The evidence, however, does not support such a suggestion, which seems to be a piece of pure propaganda.
Religious bodies and religious consideration did not play major roles in
the life of the committee. Neither of the two clergymen on the committee
put forward a particularly religious or moral agenda. Canon Demant was
mainly interested in re-drafting the report into more elegant prose than
in pushing any particular proposals and Revd R. T. Scott of the Church

of Scotland resigned from the committee in March 1956 on his appointment as Moderator of the Church of Scotland, which required him to spend most of his time north of the border. One of the most remarkable features of the proceedings of the committee was the indifference of the churches generally, which showed little interest in its activity. The Church of England was the only church that sent either memoranda or delegations to the committee. It is important to appreciate that these representatives did not speak officially for the church, and many churchmen certainly would not have given their blessing to their report.

The Church of England Moral Welfare Council had grown out of various Anglican bodies established to rescue prostitutes. It had been at work on a report on homosexuality since 1952. The reports that it submitted to the committee reflected the work done by one of the council's officers, the Revd Sherwin Bailey. The most significant proposal in the report was the support it gave to the campaign for decriminalisation by endorsing the formula of supporting consenting male adults in private. This was hedged about by a large number of reservations and historians have sometimes been too eager to read the headlines without examining the small print.

Bailey had a bee in his bonnet about misinterpretations of the biblical story of Sodom and Gomorrah. Bailey believed that this story had not been about sodomy at all, but about hospitality. The citizens of the cities on the plain had been torched by God because they were inhospitable. Bailey really believed this reinterpretation and supported it with a mass of learning. It was all the fault of the Jews who had deliberately misinterpreted the story, to advance their own demographic agenda, and so found its way into the myths of western civilisation. The exercise is a wonderful example of the sort of arrogance that can overcome biblical scholars as they set about testing the good book against critical scholarship.

Bailey had an interesting cocktail of beliefs, that need to be taken into account by those keen to find a place for him in the pantheon of homosexual law reformers. Bailey believed that homosexuality was a sin, not a crime, and for this reason he supported law reform. Like many other witnesses, Bailey thought that the future was heterosexual, because he thought that modern people would create better marriages, which in turn would make better homes, producing children who would naturally follow the right sexual path. The document he presented to the committee celebrated 'the vital experience of normal, heterosexual life'. One kind proposal he made to alleviate the 'suffering' and 'loneliness' of these sad men was for well-adjusted heterosexuals to invite homosexuals into their homes to share some of their joy with them. They might even be encouraged to establish homosexual partnerships patterned on these idealised heterosexual unions, but without of course the blessings of a church service or children.

Bailey's fieldwork led him to see the invert as a kind of noble savage:

The inverts are sensitive, sometimes biased, often dogmatic about their situation, and give the impression that they believe attack to be the best form of defence; they suffer, they resent, they are afraid – and yet not a few have a dignity of their own . . . yet for all that he *is* unfortunate, and we have learnt to deal kindly with other unfortunates in our midst.

Society, he felt, had to take the blame for the invert (though not of course for the pervert):

'Society gets the homosexuals it deserves' declares one invert – and his charge is well-founded. By unhappy marriages and homes, by inept handling of youthful problems, by prolonged segregation of the sexes, and by war and its consequences (to mention only a few factors), society itself creates just those situations which cause inversion, or lead to adoption of a homosexual attitude to life.

Society therefore had a responsibility to take pity on the invert, that it had created, while hoping that normal service would be resumed after the tempestuous decades of the early twentieth century, and that homosexuality would inevitably decline. Bailey was alive to a further danger, which did not attract his sympathy, lesbianism. This was 'socially more undesirable than male homosexuality', a tremendous source of marital breakdown in British society, he believed.

The Bishop of Rochester, Christopher Chavasse, the leading evangelical amongst the episcopate, could not stomach the report of the Moral Welfare Council. He wrote to his friend the chairman to tell him so, disassociating himself and others from the report which

recommends that homosexuality can be legally practised between male persons in private if they are above the age of seventeen years. I am quite certain that this is not the view of the Church of England as a whole, and only represents the Moral Welfare Council. Some of us had experience of homosexual clubs. The Police know about them and we should not be happy that such should be allowed to operate with lawful sanctions.

A week later he explored his thoughts further:

I find myself personally feeling more sympathy with a curate or scoutmaster who has offended with a boy (horrible though this is: I have had to deal with such cases) than with two grown men misbehaving together. There is something healthy (with a deterrent force that is powerful) in the strong public disapprobation of homosexual *practice* that demands punishment. But my big point was, and is, that Sodomy Societies and Sodomy Weekend House Parties must not be made legal. I believe, too, that homosexual practice can be, and is, indulged in by those by nature abnormally heterosexual; that homosexual practice is alarmingly catching.

Chavasse, like Bailey, denounced the pervert as a malevolent social agent. He was the only bishop to offer his opinions to the committee and he did so informally, not as an official witness.

St Alfred

Wolfenden and most of his colleagues did not really approve of Alfred Kinsey and his research. Generally they, and most witnesses, rejected the applicability of his findings on American homosexuality to Britain on the grounds that the Americans were different. Dr Sessions-Hodge thought that there was more homosexuality in America because there were more broken homes in the United States. Kinsey was not called as a witness, but a small delegation from the committee did interview him informally when he was on a visit to London. Dr Curran, Dr Whitby, Mrs Lovibond, the Revd Scott and the committee secretary Roberts met him on 29 October 1955.

Kinsey challenged much of what the Wolfenden delegation thought. He was very sensible and extremely funny. 'We have seen everything', he announced authoritatively of his work and of his Institute. He spoke easily about sex, about outlets and urges:

> We propose to the teen-age boy who is at the peak of his sexual capacity that he should develop a heterosexual pattern, but simultaneously we interpose laws against intercourse; and many a parent hopes that the boy will not even start dating girls until he gets much older, and so the restraint which custom imposes, even if the law does not impose it, the ban on heterosexual conduct, is in our opinion one of the prime factors which makes individuals so often move up the scale of homosexual rating . . . Think of the many situations in which our society allows males to congregate and females to congregate, and the much more limited number of instances where males and females are allowed similarly to congregate. Sixteen-year-old John comes home with a boyfriend from school and asks if he may stay over the weekend and his parents are delighted. Sixteen-year-old John comes home with Susan and asks if Susan can sleep with them

over the weekend and the parents raise tremendous objections.

Kinsey upset and shocked Mrs Lovibond with one of his case histories. He told the delegation of a prison clinic where the authorities encouraged a paedophile to develop homosexual affections with men of his own age who were also in the institution. Mrs Lovibond thought it dreadful that the authorities would sanction such behaviour, even though it was eminently sensible. Kinsey did not convince the delegation that his report would help them in making their report. As one witness suggested, Wolfenden and his colleagues were 'fortunate' that they did not have to 'solve American problems'.

Straight Talking

Soon after the first meeting of the Wolfenden Committee in the autumn of 1954, Wolfenden wrote to Roberts about the possibility of hearing some evidence from the 'Huntleys' and 'Palmers':

> What about our Huntley's and our Palmer's? What are their complaints about the police? What are their grudges against society? They are not likely to come as official witnesses and if they did they would hardly be at their best when cross-examined by a committee. But I hope that some groups can find ways of meeting some of those who are in daily touch with the realities of our enquiry and get them to talk off the record about what really happens under the surface of the law and its administration.

Roberts tried to think of ways of bringing this about, but seemed to be confronted with a number of problems. What was the legal position of men confessing to criminal activity before a government inquiry? Prostitutes were in a happier position because prostitution was not illegal, only the act of soliciting if it annoyed a member of the public. Some homosexual men wrote to the committee but Wolfenden read their letters with distaste – they were 'exhibitionists'. A man called R. Devereux Shirley offered to give evidence 'to represent the beliefs and needs of the big majority of the 500,000 homosexuals in Britain'.

The idea was floated that an advertisement in a newspaper or weekly magazine might attract potential witnesses. Over Christmas 1954 Wolfenden got cold feet about this idea, weighing up, in his characteristically cautious way, the damage that might be done by this action: 'The more I think about it, the more frightened I am about a public advertisement. But if it is thought to be necessary as cover for the Committee I suppose we must go through with it.' The matter was discussed at a meeting of the committee a few days later, and the idea was dropped: 'Some members felt, however, that a public invitation would be a mistake and likely to attract in the main exhibitionists. The secretary explained that the announcement of the Committee's appointment was of itself an invitation to give evidence and had evidently been so regarded by some individuals' – a grand total of three in fact. With this skilful piece of footwork the secretary was able to put Wolfenden's fears at rest.

In the event, the three men who came before the committee and were willing to identify themselves all came through Goronwy Rees. He was approached by friends of friends and made the necessary arrangements. It proved to be a task beyond the ingenious secretary of the committee.

Peter Wildeblood liked to believe that his conviction for homosexual offences had led to the establishment of the Wolfenden Committee. In a way it contributed, but much less directly than he imagined. He had high hopes that the committee would act and clear up the many injustices revealed by the prosecutions of himself, Lord Montagu and Michael Pitt-Rivers in early 1954. He was eager to address the committee, and through intermediaries arranged to appear as a witness.

Wolfenden was reluctant to allow him to testify because he was a convicted offender, but eventually agreed. He was apprehensive about the session in advance. 'I confess', he wrote to Roberts, 'I am not looking forward to our interview with Mr Wildeblood.' Wolfenden's annotations on Wildeblood's memorandum to the committee suggests a very strong and deep hostility to Wildeblood. Alongside the following paragraph by Wildeblood: 'The imprisonment of men like myself is logically indefensible and morally wicked: it weakens the whole concept of Justice in our country' – Wildeblood at his most self-important and righteous – Wolfenden wrote: 'No, you broke the law.'

Unusually for Wolfenden, he did not introduce Wildeblood to the committee nor did he apologise for the low attendance of eight, partly caused by the proximity of the meeting to the General Election but possibly because others were as hostile to Wildeblood as Wolfenden and boycotted the meeting.

Wildeblood essentially trailed his hook. He attacked queens inside and outside prison and wore the mantle of the responsible and respectable homosexual: 'They just happen to have a male body. They think like women, and go to incredible lengths to get cosmetics and things smuggled in. I do not know why it is they are allowed to get away with these things.' It was Peter Wildeblood at his most strident. He was prickly, bitter and defensive. His testimony was poorly thought out and he went down several blind alleys. It is his desire to defend his conduct and his type that comes across most strongly:

> people of that sort are very often born like that ... What they are responsible for is their nuisance value. I think they are only a very, very small proportion altogether, but they do attract a tremendous amount of attention – I do not mean just in prison but outside as well – and I think they cause a lot of public feeling against homosexuals.

He contributed to the portrait of the self-hating homosexual by his comment that 'I cannot really imagine anybody choosing it [homosexuality], unless they were obliged to.' He also distanced himself from men who had sex with boys, adolescents or teenagers; he himself supported twenty-one as an age of consent: 'I probably take a stricter view about that than is usual.' He was *very* responsible. It is difficult, reading through his testimony, to see what he was trying to do, other than portray himself as a victim, the sort of 'good' homosexual who ought not to be punished. 'Good Homosexuals' wanted 'to lead their lives with discretion and decency, neither corrupting others nor publicly flaunting their condition'.

The most curious idea that Wildeblood attempted to develop was that 'The law ... has come to offend the public conscience'. He believed that public opinion favoured a change in the law. Canon Demant was sceptical of the anecdote Wildeblood used to support this notion. Wildeblood had suggested that he had been delighted and surprised by the reaction of his neighbours in the 'working-class district of Islington' where he lived on his return from prison: 'I found nothing but charity from everybody.'

Wildeblood criticised the treatment offered in prison as a sham, as if he wanted to be cured – which was not consistent with the line developed elsewhere in his testimony that he was a man trapped. He had taken the wrong turning. 'I tried very hard to go back', but he couldn't. It was a tortured performance, and a mistake.

It was known in certain homosexual circles in London that Peter Wildeblood had volunteered to give evidence to the Wolfenden Committee, and this knowledge spurred a number of individuals into action. They wanted to counter the potential damage that might be done by Wildeblood's testimony, as many people who had known him did not believe he would make the best representative for the cause, however eager he was to adopt that mantle. The proceedings of the committee were followed with interest in certain metropolitan circles of well-connected homosexuals, and it would seem that Goronwy Rees acted on occasions as a source of information. He was the member of the committee who organised the appearance of two men who sought to represent homosexuals to the committee. Initially three men were to have come before the committee but one of them, the novelist Angus Wilson, was unable to attend on the day appointed. This left the distinguished eye consultant Patrick Trevor-Roper and Carl Winter, a Fellow of Trinity College, Cambridge, and the Director of the Fitzwilliam Museum, to speak for the homosexual.

These were men who were bound to have an impact. They belonged to the same class as most members of the committee and they were well-respected members of the community. Trevor-Roper was a consultant to the sovereign and Wilson had recently left the staff of the British Museum to become a full-time man of letters. They offered some of the most impressive evidence submitted to the committee, and were willing to speak extremely personally about their own experiences, in contrast to Wildeblood who was largely grinding his own personal axes. They were also much more catholic in their willingness to accept and tolerate a wider variety of homosexual types and were not afraid to challenge the preconceptions of the committee. Their evidence was delivered with a great deal of authority. Rees welcomed them to the committee by commending their courage, though their identity was disguised: Trevor-Roper became the 'Doctor' and Carl Winter 'Mr White'.

Carl Winter died in 1966. Patrick Trevor-Roper is still alive and lives in London, aged 80. He continues to take a lively and active interest in a whole range of activities, and it was one of the great pleasures of preparing this book that I was finally able to meet this legendary figure who deserves an important place in the pantheon of British homosexuals. Trevor-Roper gave me many useful insights into the subject of this book. I had no intention of identifying him other than by his Wolfenden alias but Margaret Drabble in her biography of Angus Wilson (published in 1995) names him. She is incorrect in thinking that Wilson testified before the committee.

Patrick Trevor-Roper bears a very famous name; his brother is the historian Hugh, rewarded with a peerage in 1980, successively Regius Professor of Modern History at Oxford and Master of Peterhouse. The Trevor-Ropers were descended from border gentry and Patrick's father was a doctor in Northumberland. Educated at Charterhouse and Clare College, Cambridge, Trevor-Roper became one of the most distinguished medical men of his generation, building up a large practice from his rooms in Harley Street.

He was extremely well connected amongst the metropolitan intelligentsia. Angus Wilson dedicated *Anglo-Saxon Attitudes* to Patrick Trevor-Roper and his friend Christopher Arnold. Trevor-Roper also did his duty for the International Homintern, taking Yukio Mishima around the 'gay night life of London' when he visited Britain in 1960. Since 1965 he has been a part owner of Long Crichel, a Queen Anne country house in Dorset (not far from the home of Pitt-Rivers), a house which plays an important part in the history of British culture and British homosexuality. It had been bought in 1945 by Edward Sackville-West, Desmond Shawe-Taylor, Eardley Knollys and Raymond Mortimer.

What shines through the testimony of Trevor-Roper and Winter is their happiness and contentment at their sexual orientation. They both tried to give the committee an accurate picture of the homosexual lifestyle:

> Winter: . . . my point of view is that homosexual persons are a considerable proportion of the population and so many that I do not know what a normal person is. I do not wish to meet a strictly normal person . . . I live and have lived for a number of years in a society of which many members are aware that I am a homosexual. I have many friends who are known to be so. A large number of the extremely critical people among whom I live [Cambridge dons] have a very unfavourable view of this and do not wish to know me on that account, and I think it is fair to say without acrimony that I do not particularly wish to know them in return. I am content to know the sort of people I do know, which covers a very wide field, and we are all completely at ease in one another's company and the world in which we live, which is a much more extensive world, I think, than many people would suppose. We visit each other's houses, go abroad, travel, look at the sort of things that interest us, art, exhibitions, ballet, and have a satisfactory life within that sphere. Somebody from outside is every now and then caught up in it, somebody presents himself at one's door and if he is in character a sympathetic person he is admitted, if not, he is excluded.

Winter tolerantly admitted that the problem seemed to be the propensity of human beings 'including myself . . . to be righteous'. He suggested that homosexual experiences after puberty had no impact on a person's long-term sexual identity. He had an affair with another boy when he was twelve and he reminded the committee that the younger partner in a relationship might sometimes be the seducer. He had seduced his family's gardener 'against his will and against his better judgement'. 'It is,' he continued, 'very often the child who is the determining factor in the case. I think it must be very difficult for certain people: if their interests are at all susceptible in that way, to be attacked by a persistent small boy.' This was not the sort of testimony usually presented to the Wolfenden Committee.

Both men had wide circles of homosexual friends: Trevor-Roper calculated that he knew about 150 other homosexuals. Both men spoke with considerable frankness about their sexual development. Trevor-Roper suggested that as a medical student in London he had been 'unaware except for an occasional comment in the *News of the World* of the existence of homosexuality'. It was rather refreshing to encounter a pair of witnesses who accepted the genuineness of homosexual love and affection. Trevor-Roper thought that 'it is true of both sexes that people are physically most attractive between the age of 18 and 25', though he added, 'one is constantly surprised by the strange things people like and do'.

The committee was interested in how homosexuals met – were they 'recruited'? Trevor-Roper suggested that there was really no mystery:

one is introduced to them . . . my private life tends to be virtually restricted to almost the purely homosexual world and has become increasingly so . . . one meets by ordinary introduction . . . Two of my current students both approached me. Why did they approach me? They were frightened and felt out of society. They felt one would be sympathetic. They knew I was unmarried and, because I had dealings with them in the ordinary way they were in a position to lead up to it. I do not ask students, but over the last ten years one or two others have done the same.

Carl Winter suggested that his acquaintances were made 'spontaneously by a kind of telepathy that you see a person or persons and you realise that they are sympathetic or likeable, and a few words of conversation will establish the fact that they are also homosexual'. Sometimes such connections were sexual, more often they were not.

Both men powerfully argued for a change in the law, Trevor-Roper suggesting an age of consent at sixteen. Trevor-Roper collected evidence of the extent of homosexual blackmail and also suggested that the present intolerance led to a large number of young men taking their own lives. He made the point that the statistics 'are indications of the extent of police activity . . . not of the number of men with homosexual instincts'. He was puzzled at the existing laws given the potential over-population of the world. Winter said that the police ought to be investigated because they were employing 'disagreeable stratagems'. Rees deliberately presented the arguments for the existing law as a deterrent so that Winter and Trevor-Roper could emphatically reject them. Wolfenden referred to a homosexual 'community' and 'your community', suggesting a willingness to accept them as representatives of British homosexuality.

Three openly acknowledged homosexuals was an extremely small sample to consult, but it was a big step for Wolfenden and his colleagues, who presumably congratulated themselves on their open-mindedness in casting their net so wide.

The Boys in Blue

Almost certainly the best-prepared and best-briefed delegation to appear before Wolfenden were the representatives of the Metropolitan Police. Scotland Yard produced a memorandum which set out the situation in the capital, accompanied by detailed statistical material, maps and graphs. The Commissioner was flanked by senior policemen responsible for policing the West End, and by the head of the legal department at the Yard, an experienced solicitor. This delegation appeared twice, dealing at its first session with prostitution and later coming back to discuss the policing of homosexuality. The Commissioner also agreed to send along members of the force who were involved in the day-to-day policing of prostitution and homosexuality. Two policewomen talked about policing prostitutes and on another occasion two policemen talked about the policing of London's public lavatories.

The Metropolitan Police dealt with homosexual offences very differently from other police forces in England and Wales, and we shall examine this difference later. The main contact point for the Met was in policing the huge number of public toilets across the metropolis. Many men used these places to solicit other men for sex, and some had sex in the toilets themselves. The Met reported that it usually employed about half-a-dozen men each week in the most notorious public lavatories.

These men were almost always dressed in plain clothes when they went around the lavatories. A large number of cases suggested that for many years the Met had been using policemen to trap homosexual men in lavatories and that it was common for the constables in the course of the trial to lie about what had happened. This use of *agents provocateurs* was probably one of the most persistent abuses of police power in policing homosexuality since at least the 1930s, possibly earlier. The Metropolitan Police denied that such a practice occurred, despite evidence to the contrary. It seemed possible that the Wolfenden Report would criticise this practice, perhaps even condemn it quite strongly.

Scotland Yard took action to try to stop this happening. It produced two young policemen to give a worm's-eye view of the problems involved in policing London's lavatories. PC Darlington from 'B' Division and PC Butcher from 'C' Division gave evidence to the committee on 7 December 1954. This pair of 'pretty policemen' charmed the committee. One presumes that they were hand-picked, the very model of the young policeman.

The policing of lavatories was potentially one of the most difficult features of police work to defend, and by entrusting the task to two young constables Scotland Yard tapped the extraordinary goodwill that policemen excited among members of the British middle and upper classes. It was the sort of feeling that drew audiences to idiolise PC George Dixon in the film *The Blue Lamp* (1950) and in the television series *Dixon of Dock Green*. It certainly helped the police and saved them from too much criticism in the final Wolfenden Report.

Butcher patrolled the Mayfair and Soho districts of the West End, districts which continually caught the imagination of the readers of the popular newspapers, the one as the epitome of luxury and glamour and the other as the national den of iniquity. Butcher understood the seriousness of the accusation he could make: 'to accuse a man of importuning male persons is very nearly as serious as accusing him of murder, and it is the most awful thing that could happen to a man.'

Constable Butcher distinguished two different constituencies on his beat. In Mayfair the lavatories were busiest at lunchtime as men who worked in the area made assignations for the evening: 'I am not exaggerating when I say that 90 per cent of the people I have arrested in the Mayfair area are actually in their lunch hour.' These men included businessmen and clerks, individuals who worked in the huge number of offices to be found in Mayfair. In the 1940s and 1950s many of the great houses of the district were sold off and turned into offices, a trend that had important consequences for the sexual geography of Mayfair. Butcher identified three popular lavatories in the district, all clustered around Grosvenor Square: at Providence Court, at Three Kings Yard and George Yard. According to the constable these places were world-famous; a Russian (a friend of Guy Burgess?) had been arrested and had been found to have a map of the district on which the cottages were marked. The men who frequented the Mayfair cottages, according to PC Butcher, 'if I may put it this way, do it for the love of the thing, to satisfy their emotions, and that generally consists of the run round in the lunchtime ... get[ting] a great deal of satisfaction from the chase.' Butcher's testimony gives an interesting insight into the metropolitan lunch hour in the 1950s, and one is left with the picture of suited men planning their campaigns in the morning, contemplating the hunt in the afternoon and in some lucky cases planning the evening ahead.

The pattern of activity and the types of men found in the public lavatories of Soho were entirely different according to Butcher. Here Butcher met the queens with 'the mincing gait, the plucked eyebrows, they wave their hair and dye their hair, paint their finger nails and use cosmetics.' He regarded these men as prostitutes and informed the committee that they charged their clients £2 a time. They mainly frequented the Fitzroy public house off Tottenham Court Road. PC Butcher told the Wolfenden Committee that the Fitzroy was 'known throughout the world', and remarked on the large number of servicemen to be found there. It was all in the 'look': 'There is a certain look among these people, and if they look and the look is returned that is quite enough and they will enter into conversation.'

The constable had learned a lot from his hours working undercover in the West End wearing his 'Harris tweed sports clothes', size 11 shoes, reeking 'of being a policeman', all six foot three inches of him. Reminding us perhaps more of a London taxi driver than a London bobby, Butcher told the committee about all the men he had 'had', in other words those that he had arrested:

> I have had serving soldiers, members of the clergy, particularly from any occupation or profession that has an air of artificiality about it, like the acting profession, the creative professions like hairdressers, dress designers. These people, that sort of live in a world of their own, they adopt that manner in their business and they finish up like that. The majority of our people do come from those walks of life. It is very rarely that one arrests a coalman or a dustman or anything like that. The manual labourer never seems to come into that sort of thing. What more often happens is that a manual labourer will go into one of these urinals, get accosted by a person of the homosexual type and he will just hit him.

Butcher met many foreigners in his work, whom he did not like. They were more brazen: 'they are arrested more easily, much more easily than the English pervert, because they do it more openly.' Perhaps, speculated Butcher, they thought they were back in their own countries where the 'view in European countries is not the same as in Great Britain'. Americans were another hazard and in particular the American servicemen hanging out along Coventry Street, from the Prince of Wales Theatre to Piccadilly Circus, in what the Met called the 'Standard Front'. He thought American servicemen were addicted to this type of vice, specialising in giving and receiving blow-jobs which seemed 'to go more with them'. Dr Curran recalled that on a trip to the United States he had found that 'the mouth was very popular'. Americans, the constable said, sometimes performed sexual acts in doorways late at night. The policeman also identified the area around Piccadilly Circus underground station as one of the most popular cruising spots in the West End. Butcher was as much of an expert on homosexuality as any of the doctors.

PC Darlington's evidence from Chelsea, by contrast, was much less detailed except to record the fact that the amount of activity had increased over the previous four or five years. The busiest time of the year was the week of the Royal Tournament at Earl's Court, which created much more activity in the West London cottages due to the large influx of servicemen to the capital to participate in the Tournament.

Wolfenden thanked the policemen for 'talking so fully and so frankly on an extremely unpleasant subject'. The Wolfenden Committee *knew* that these policemen were lying about their use of *agent provocateur* methods, but Wolfenden refused to grasp the nettle, seduced by the boys in blue:

> It is terribly difficult, I think, to assess the extent to which the police do employ *agent provocateur* measures in this. We have of course, seen representatives of the police and I find it personally very difficult to decide the rights and wrongs of this question. I have not the least doubt that it occurs, but my own personal impression is that the men who are actually on the job – so far as we have been able to come across them – dislike the job, that side of the work very much. They seem to me – at any rate the ones we saw – very decent chaps, and it is awfully hard to see how much there is of it from the one, two, three, five, six or seven cases that one hears about. That there is any should be any I grant is a very dangerous thing.

It was a classic defence of the police in terms of the very difficult job that they do. The young constables had left a favourable impression on Wolfenden and presumably other members of the committee as well. For men like Wolfenden, who might agonise, the implication that British police officers might tell lies in court was too incredible to imagine. It was always wise at such moments to take comfort in the police force's favourite piece of propaganda, the few bad apples.

Plod

The Association of Chief Constables chose to represent them at the Wolfenden Committee, C. C. Martin, Chief Constable of Liverpool and K. H. Watkin, Chief Constable of Glamorgan, neither of them a very impressive witness. They showed limited knowledge of the submissions presented by the Chief Constables, expressing their disagreement with substantial parts of them. Neither was well-briefed and they chose to attend the sessions without any support staffs. The most alarming feature of their testimony was their limited knowledge of the law.

Martin gave a particularly comic turn. He expected a 'tremendous increase' if homosexuality was decriminalised for consenting adults in private. The law maintained higher moral standards in Britain, as opposed to other countries:

> the punishment . . . does keep it down, does control it very largely, and from my experience in other countries, in Scandinavia, France, Italy and America, I think that we are number one country in the world so far as moral standards are concerned. I think that is only because, really, our law is in such a state that it prevents this sort of thing from growing; . . . I do not think the moral standards in other countries are anything like they are in this country, except probably Canada and Fiji . . . I have consulted and spoken to policemen in other countries about it and I feel you never hear of any country with higher morals than this country . . . it is a form of wretched corruption which leads to all sorts of other things and I think generally undermines the moral standard of the country. If you go right back to the Bible, you will find it has been responsible for undermining the national structure of many countries and many civilisations.

His rambling commentary gives one an insight into the mentality of the man responsible for policing one of the largest cities in Britain.

The Wolfenden Committee had access to some police records, in the form of case histories. These files have been removed from the Wolfenden archive, and presumably will become available to historians fifty or sixty years in the future. Some of these files supplied material for case histories in the report and Roberts, the secretary, was led to think worse of 'the buggers' as a result of his exposure to this material.

Whistle Blower

Richard Elwes, QC, the Recorder of Nottingham, brought to the attention of the committee two cases in which he had participated while presiding over Derbyshire Quarter Sessions.

In the first case three Derbyshire men were charged with having committed acts of gross indecency with each other: Lewis Cluskey, Ralph Dennis and Stanley Hill. Three years before the prosecution the three men had committed sexual acts together in a hut beside a children's paddling pool in a park, acts which according to Elwes were 'comparatively trivial'. A man arrested for another offence had told the police about the incident. Cluskey and Dennis, both miners, had been seventeen. When confronted with the accusation Hill, who was thirty-four, had confessed, and he later attempted to commit suicide. His confession provided evidence against the other two: 'After some conversation about sex these men exposed their persons, and after feeling at each other some masturbation took place, and in Hill's case this resulted in ejaculation. Hill says it was either Dennis or Cluskey who masturbated him, but both the latter say it was the other man.' The police established that Hill had placed his penis in someone else's mouth – Dennis's or Cluskey's? According to the evidence Cluskey was inclined to be effeminate and his younger brother John, a minor, had been placed under 'care and protection' for indulging 'in homosexual practices with a number of men in this area'. The magistrates had been appalled that the police had brought such a stale and trivial case, and Elwes felt that it reflected an over-zealous policing of homosexual offenders. The accused had pleaded guilty and were fined, rather than imprisoned, by the Derbyshire magistrates.

Elwes's second case involved two men, Wilfred Pearce and Daniel O'Connell. Pearce, a miner for twenty years, was fifty and had left coal mining in January 1954 to work as a labourer with the local council's cleansing department after he had been incapacitated by a hernia. O'Connell, a native of Manchester, was twenty-eight and had drifted from one job to another, none of which he had kept long because of a poor record as a bad time-keeper. Pearce had looked after his aged parents for years, and when they died he had taken in O'Connell as a lodger. The two men slept in the same room and had sex together on at least seven occasions. One day O'Connell, a restless soul, left, taking some of Pearce's property. Pearce reported the theft to the police. While they were investigating the crime they toured Pearce's house and discovered that the two men had shared the same bed. They questioned Pearce and he confessed to their sexual activities together. The two men were charged with gross indecency and the case came before Elwes. He regarded the police action as improper and strongly criticised their activity in a series of documents that he submitted to the committee.

What Elwes did was unique. Most of his fellow judges would never have even contemplated shopping the police in this fashion. Unfortunately the implications of these cases and what they suggested about the policing of homosexuality were largely forgotten by the time that the report came to be written. Elwes offered an important and useful insight into provincial policing, but his material was largely ignored. Wolfenden and the majority of his colleagues preferred to believe the best of the police in spite of the accumulating evidence that suggested that there were serious defects in their practice and procedure. 'Can this explain why Derbyshire is among the counties with the highest number of homosexual offences "known to the police"?' Roberts asked Wolfenden.

Treatment

The most enthusiastic supporters of decriminalising homosexual acts in private between consenting adults were often the strongest supporters of a medical model of homosexuality. The idea that homosexuality was an illness or a disease was fairly common and contributed to the notion that it might be possible to find a cure, or at least offer these men some form of treatment. This differed somewhat from the notion of homosexuality as a form of contagious disease or moral sickness favoured by many who opposed decriminalisation. The cure was simple – greater self-control. Many reformers saw homosexuality more as a mental disorder that needed specialist medical help or treatment. 'It is', said one London magistrate, 'a case for the hospital . . . The poor fellow needs treatment . . . They are all ill, every one of them. They are ill: their doctors say so.'

The supporters of homosexual law reform suggested that a change in the law would allow more men to seek treatment and produce less homosexual activity. The Tavistock Clinic regarded 'homosexuality as an illness' and thought that the law should 'take this into consideration, so that it can become and be perceived as a public health problem in the same way, perhaps as tuberculosis [is perceived] as a public health problem'.

The purpose of most cures was to bring the individual as close to the model heterosexual as possible. The BMA boasted that through religious faith it was possible for people completely to reject homosexuality. All sorts of doctors peddled a huge variety of cures. Three of them, Eustace Chesser, Clifford Allen and R. Sessions-Hodge came together before the committee on 31 October 1955 peddling their own solutions to the problem.

Allen offered the simplest solution of all. Homosexuality was essentially a fear of women; homosexuals had been improperly socialised and had failed to develop a 'normal' relationship with a woman. Often the failure could be related to another woman, the man's mother. Allen's treatment was to banish this fear:

> My aim, first of all, is to show the man that women are desirable objects and that he must look at them as sexual objects. I am not using the term in a derogatory way, but he has to realise that women are a source of sex. To enjoy a social life and to mix freely with women and go to dances would help him a great deal. Some of these patients actually have to be told how to make love to a girl. That they do may seem surprising, but they are frightened of women. When they are able to be pushed in the right direction, at the same time one has to undermine the reason why they have not been

interested in girls – mother fixation or over-protection by the mother or an undesirable father – if you can break that down, then they do swing around and go straight ahead . . . Obviously you have to make the man realise – and he has to do it by experience – that normal intercourse with women is more desirable than with men.

Allen believed that he had achieved success when the man married or kept a mistress and had regular intercourse with her. Allen was supported by the Institute for the Study and Treatment of Delinquency. It was 'essential', they thought, 'in the environmental manipulation in treating a homosexual . . . to put him with women, as much as you can, in order to facilitate things.'

Allen believed that better results could be achieved if the state funded a network of special clinics across the country to treat homosexuals, an idea he had been promoting in print for several years, most notoriously in the *Sunday Pictorial* during their path-breaking feature on male homosexuality in the summer of 1952. He supported his proposal with some interesting evidence: 'I regard homosexuality as an illness. I think imprisonment increases the illness. It has been shown in America, by segregating rats, that you produce homosexuality in normal rats, and the more you segregate them the more homosexual they become. So why should it not be the same with men? It seems absolutely obvious.'

In 1960 Allen wrote that for parents 'The best insurance policy against one's child becoming a homosexual is to give it a happy home. It should have a chance of knowing, loving and respecting its parents, particularly that parent of the same sex. If he or she dies, or is lost by divorce, or by some other cause, every effort should be made to replace him or her by remarriage or a kindly relative' (*New Statesman*, 16 July 1960). An Eltham man wrote a letter in response to Allen's article: 'are we to think that all Greeks had unhappy home backgrounds?' (*New Statesman*, 30 July 1960).

Sessions-Hodge placed his faith in massive doses of oestrogen pumped into homosexual patients. This treatment gave a 'satisfactory response' in most patients with only limited side-effects. The drug could kill all desire for periods of up to four or five weeks, at which point it had to be readministered. The doctor did concede that it could sometimes lead to the enlargement of breasts, though he cited the case of one patient, a miner, who had grown hair on his chest during the period of treatment.

Chesser also hoped to persuade the state to support a network of clinics across Britain. These would supplement, not replace, the incarceration of offenders in prison. Without the deterrent of prisons Chesser thought that 'homosexuals would be parading quite openly' in the streets. The law, he felt, did act as a deterrent, and the threat of prison would concentrate the minds of offenders lucky enough to be sent to Dr Chesser's clinics, giving them more of an incentive to achieve a cure.

Many groups and individuals promoted the idea of special treatment clinics, 'some kind of medical institution where they can be both incarcerated for punishment as well as being treated'. The General Council of the Bar wanted a separate institution for convicts who had been twice convicted of sexual offences with males under twenty-one. The BMA favoured a network of observation and treatment centres with specially trained personnel to deal with the problem, with support groups modelled on Alcoholics Anonymous when the 'patient' returned to the community. The BMA clinics would be run by a team of professionals, a prison officer, prison doctor, psychiatrist, religious worker and social worker who would offer a fully integrated remedy on a number of different fronts simultaneously:

> The prison officer would exercise general supervision. The prison doctor would look after the prisoner's general health. The psychiatrist would advise the team on the causes of the homosexual's condition, and would undertake any necessary psychiatric treatment. The religious officer, who might be the prison padre, a Salvation Army officer or Church Army officer, would help the prisoner to obtain spiritual experience and strengthen and fortify him in his character formation. The social worker would enquire into the prisoner's history and background. After discharge the case would be followed up in order to ensure that all necessary aftercare was provided.

The homosexual, it seemed, was to receive care virtually from the cradle to the grave. Specially incorrigible homosexuals were to be sent to a special colony for psychopathic inmates.

Another popular reform, supported by the Labour Lawyers, the Howard League, the BMA and the Royal Medico-Psychological Society, was the idea of introducing compulsory psychiatric examinations of men convicted of homosexual offences. The test was to be administered after the verdict and before the sentence as a way of guiding the judge in dealing with the offender. Many problems were presented by this proposal. Several witnesses believed that there were not enough trained psychiatrists to cope with the extra work. The greatest problem was the fact that the test might discover many more offences and prejudice the judge against the offender. Gerald Gardiner for the Labour Lawyers believed that this did not really matter because this was 'an inherently medical question'. In that case he was prepared to accept the infringement of the offender's civil rights; these were of secondary importance compared to the primary purpose of curing the individual of his homosexuality. Gardiner overrode all objections based upon the defence of the individual because 'the main thing for the Court

[was] to know the truth'. This amazing remark came from a senior barrister with over twenty years of experience at the English bar. Dr J. A. Hobson of the Royal Medico-Psychological Society also brushed aside objections based upon the rights of the offender:

> it is for the psychiatrist to help the court as far as he can. If he is going to give new facts to the court and the Judge, as a result of those facts, feels it right to give a heavier sentence, why not? Why should the psychiatrist keep in the background to avoid a heavier sentence if that is the right thing to do? ... If it is right for people like this to be sentenced, why should we be concerned in getting a lesser sentence than is justified.

Desmond Curran on the committee thought that these examinations so seriously undermined the rights of the offender and in particular his relationship with his doctor that they should not be introduced. He very forcefully raised objections to this particular proposal. How could a doctor contribute to giving a man a heavier prison sentence? It was something that Curran believed should not happen and it is to his credit that he also persuaded his colleagues on the committee to reject the idea, even though it had a number of influential and persuasive supporters. One of the senior medical officers in the prison service who had sometimes reported on offenders before sentencing also rejected the proposal. 'In general', Dr Matheson said, 'I am against reporting to a Court where the Court do not ask for a report, unless I can report something which will be of use to the man.' He claimed that prison doctors always passed their reports to the defence if their examination revealed mitigating circumstances which could be used to persuade the judge to impose a more lenient sentence.

For many witnesses the greatest advantage of clinics and of a pre-sentence medical report was that it would increase knowledge amongst medical practitioners of homosexuality. Most witnesses pinned a lot of faith on the possibility that modern medicine, in the atomic age, would come up with a medical solution to the problem of homosexuality. The material collected in the clinics and in the courts might make all the difference in the hunt for a cure. Treatment would mean more facts and eventually better treatment – and fewer homosexuals. Gerald Gardiner, tireless campaigner in many liberal causes, warned the committee not to propose anything that curbed prostitution because that would increase the incidence of homosexual activity. It is difficult to predict what the consequences of these proposals would have been, but it is unlikely they would have improved the position of men unlucky enough to find themselves before the courts.

Many reformers felt it necessary in their submissions and testimony to the committee to balance their support for decriminalisation with a host of safeguards that revealed their commitment to containing and reducing the incidence of homosexual activity. It is not accurate to portray the arguments made before the Wolfenden Committee as a clash between reformers and reactionaries, as has sometimes been done, because the degree of hostility to homosexuality from almost all parties united them more than the few issues that divided them. All supported the same end, the reduction, and hopefully one day the elimination, of male homosexuality.

The problem that all the doctors faced was that they could point to so few cures. Even superficial examination of the material presented suggested relatively few cures. Dr Pearce of the Royal Medico-Psychological Society, one of the bodies pressing most strongly for compulsory court reports, believed that treatment 'is sometimes a euphemism . . . we have not been impressed by the efficacy of treatment, indeed in very few cases [does] it seem to have been very successful'. Dr Jeffries of the VD unit at St Mary's Hospital in London told the committee that many of his patients, 'having been referred to psychiatrists by the courts, [realise that] it is to their advantage to pretend that treatment has been a success or they might be sent to gaol. In fact, they say, it has no effect at all and carry on with their homosexuality as before only with more discretion.'

Sir Hugh Linstead, the Conservative MP on the committee, brought the committee right down to earth on this question by pointing out that no government of whatever party would ever find the massive amount of money needed to fund the elaborate system of clinics and court reporting proposed by all these bodies.

The Prisons

The most sceptical group of witnesses concerning the efficacy of treatment were the representatives of the prison medical service, who warned the committee about the difficulty of trying to find an easy solution to the problem. All of the prison doctors opposed any changes to the existing law because they feared that the floodgates would really open and society would be swamped by the numbers of emerging homosexuals. They thought it best to maintain the *status quo* and were worried that even a limited reform of the law would give the wrong signal to the British people and British youth. Dr Landers, Senior Medical Officer at Wormwood Scrubs, was worried about the social impact of any change in the law:

> One of the most important methods whereby young people's characters are formed is by example. To see young male prostitutes, or lovers, above an age of consent living in luxury would have a bad

effect on the decent-living industrious youth of the nation. There would also be a demoralising effect on young servicemen from being aware that older comrades and perhaps men of superior rank were indulging in homosexual practices with impunity. Homosexuality propagates itself unless checked by improving moral standards.

There were 1,069 men in prisons in England and Wales for homosexual offences at the end of 1954. They were mostly in their thirties. Three-quarters of the men were under forty-five, and the oldest prisoner was in his late seventies. The mean age was thirty-seven. Over a third (36 per cent) were serving sentences of one year or less, while just under a third were serving sentences of a year to three years. All but a few of the remainder were serving sentences of more than three years, 13.7 per cent serving five years or more. Most had been convicted of buggery (42 per cent) or indecent assault (32.6 per cent). Forty-three prisoners had been imprisoned for importuning (4.2 per cent). Three-quarters of the offenders were single, a fifth were married, the rest had been widowed or divorced. The married men were on average seven years older than the single men. Seventeen per cent of the offenders were fathers as well as husbands. They were overwhelmingly working-class; 92.3 per cent had received only an elementary education. Nearly 60 per cent (59 per cent) had been employed in unskilled or semi-skilled work. A fifth (21.3 per cent) were classified as skilled workers. Men who had worked in offices as clerks comprised 11.4 per cent of the total while only 2 per cent had never been employed. There were sixty-three professional men (6 per cent), over half of whom were employed in jobs where they had charge of boys or young men. Newspaper reports were highly selective and gave the impression that most offenders were middle-class men associated in some way with youth work. This was not so. The number of recidivists was also lower than newspapers might suggest: exactly two-thirds of the entire group had no previous convictions, while one in twenty had ten or more.

Each offender was interviewed by the prison doctor at the beginning of his sentence. The doctor asked him if he wanted treatment. Eight hundred and sixty-four of those in prison at the time of the prison service survey rejected treatment, over 80 per cent of the whole group. The doctor then tried to assess the remainder for their suitability for treatment, and by the end of this exercise just over a tenth of all offenders were found to be suitable, over a hundred or so men. Most of these men finished up at either Wormwood Scrubs in London or Wakefield Prison in Yorkshire, where the prison service centred most of their psychiatric resources. It was reckoned that about half of those treated in these units 'benefited' in some way. The prison medical service did not boast about cures, and the benefits chiefly involved teaching self-restraint and discretion.

The prison doctor on the basis of the initial interview classified the prisoners according to type: 37 per cent were 'genuine homosexuals' (i.e. inverts), 25.1 per cent were 'bisexuals' and a further 32.5 per cent were classified as 'pseudo-homosexuals'; together these two latter groups were what others generally described as perverts. Only 6 per cent were classified as prostitutes. A small number were assigned other labels: 'adolescent experimenters' (there were two), 'exhibitionists' (one) and the 'drunks' (five). On the basis of their answers to the doctor's questions, 71.9 per cent were classified as the active partners in sodomy while only 19.1 per cent owned up to being the passive partner and 6 per cent switched from one role to the other. Most men claimed to be chiefly interested in sodomy. None of these figures match any other data published since.

Many prison doctors were extremely sceptical about treatment. The Director of the Prison Medical Service, Dr H. K. Snell, was very doubtful: 'The most likely that can be hoped for in a majority of cases accepted for treatment is a better understanding of their condition and a better adjustment to society.'

The most bullish member of the medical service was Dr Roper who ran the special unit at Wakefield. He imposed his own scheme of classification on the inmates at Wakefield, dividing the offenders into 'Obligate, Facultative, Pederasts, Adult-seekers, Actives and Passives, Cultists and Non-Cultists, Promiscuous and non-promiscuous [sic], profit-seeking and non-profitseeking, Religious and Anti-Religious, Feminised and Virile, Sodomists and Masturbators'. He particularly detested Pansies, whom he placed in an entirely separate category: 'They live for notice and appreciation.'

Treatment at Wormwood Scrubs was more advanced. Convicts used psycho-drama, re-enacting past history with other prisoners. Plays were scripted by the patient, who coached his fellow prisoners to play out his sexual experiences with him. These scenarios were then discussed by the group. It was imagined that this activity might exorcise the sexual demons who tortured the offender.

Doctors in the prison feared that if homosexuality were treated as an illness it could have dire consequences for society. Dr Brisby from Liverpool Prison believed that 'Any connotation of irresponsibility is fatal to treatment, and that is the reason I deplore the impression sometimes given that every homosexual is a doctor's case. This may be very dangerous. It presupposes disease, something the offender cannot help. The issue of personal responsibility must ever be brought before the man, with Society rendering what help it possibly can.'

The prison service opposed the segregation of homosexual offenders: 'One would view with some apprehension totally homosexual institutions.'

The only difference in the treatment between homosexual offenders and other criminals was that the homosexual offender was assigned a cell to himself. Overcrowding, however, made this impossible to achieve in many prisons. There were accusations from other prisoners that homosexual offenders got the best jobs in prisons. According to the Prison Commissioners 'many types of homosexuals are prone to a facile religiosity' which often won them a privileged position as a consequence of their association with the chapel. In a rather remarkable passage the prison service suggested that 'In general, in the better type of prison the homosexuals are a stabilising and beneficent influence, and greatly assist the smooth running of the prison.'

The main trouble was with 'the temperamentally female type (not necessarily of effeminate appearance though often so) who is so often the canker . . . such types create an unfortunate emotional atmosphere'. Such sentiments would have been endorsed by the champion of the 'responsible homosexual', Peter Wildeblood. Many of these queens wore cosmetics, an extraordinary admission from the authorities running the prisons. One naïve female member of the committee wondered how make-up got into the prison.

The Scottish prison service classified its inmates somewhat differently from its counterparts across the border. Every prisoner entering a Scottish prison, not just those convicted of a homosexual offence, was asked if he were homosexual or not. On this basis there were 157 homosexuals in Scottish prisons at the end of 1954. A similar profile of the prisoners to that of England and Wales emerges from the data supplied to the Wolfenden Committee by the Scottish Office. The mean age was thirty-five and most prisoners were manual workers; the proportion of professionals and better-educated men was even smaller than in England and Wales. The sentences served were generally much shorter, with nearly three-quarters of the homosexual offenders serving sentences of a year or less. The proportion seeking treatment was slightly higher, a quarter of the total, but the facilities for treatment were even more limited than in England; only one Scottish prison had a full-time medical officer.

As the men who ran prisons across Britain told Wolfenden and his colleagues, the prison service did not have the resources for a massive programme of treatment. Their testimony did much to undermine the notion that a programme of treatment might be the answer to the problem of homosexuality. It was the prison doctors who pointed out that when the judge would announce that the convicted prisoner would receive treatment when he got to prison, this was done, according to one doctor, merely 'to salve other people's consciences'.

PART TWO

SHADOW BOXING:
THE WOLFENDEN REPORT

2

Men in Uniform

... one of the most susceptible ages is between 19 and 22 or 23 ...
the young guardsmen, Army cases ... we regard as the more serious
cases.
       – *Sir Theobald Mathew, Director of Public Prosecutions, in his testimony*
       to the Wolfenden Committee, 7 December 1954

... my view about it is this, that it is all due to the war, and to
conscription. It is men living together in large numbers in remote
places ... young men were corrupted when they went away during
the war and when they were living together or serving together ...
things they learned and got into when they were serving together
during the war, and even after the war, when they went on national
service.
       – *K. Martin, Chief Constable of Liverpool, in his testimony*
       to the Wolfenden Committee, 31 March 1955

It is quite easy to learn the art of killing and being killed. It is not easy
to get over these psychological tendencies.
       – *Claude Mullins, a retired metropolitan magistrate, in his testimony*
       to the Wolfenden Committee, 14 December 1955

Between 1939 and 1960 the British state operated a system of conscription
into the armed forces. Introduced soon after Hitler's destruction of
Czechoslovakia in the spring of 1939, it produced a wartime army, navy
and air force which at their peak numbered almost five and a half million.
The process of demobilisation was slow and there were still one and a
half million men under arms at the start of 1947. The Attlee government
decided to do something in that year that no British government had ever
done, introduce peacetime conscription. All males between the ages of
eighteen and twenty-one were eligible for what was packaged by Labour
as 'National Service'. There were a number of exemptions from the draft
but it was still the case that the majority of young male Britons coming

to manhood in the next thirteen years had to put on a uniform to defend their homeland. At first they were required to serve for one year but this was soon increased to two years. This radical measure, the militarisation of a state which had long prided itself on its repudiation of conscription, had a major impact on post-war society.

The decision to maintain conscription was a mistake. The military command never worked out a useful role for the conscripts, except as human fodder in the armed conflicts that punctuated the last years of empire. Principally the force was maintained to reassure Britain's allies of its willingness to fight the enemies of the West. It was generally believed that the failure to mobilise the nation before 1939 had contributed to Britain's military weakness at the beginning of the war.

Some elements of the Labour leadership also liked to depict the measure as the creation of a citizen's army for the New Jerusalem they were building through their social legislation. Ernest Bevin, wartime Minister of Labour and Foreign Secretary, 1945–51, was a strong supporter of the measure.

The poor reputation of National Service amongst Britons was largely due to the miserly attitude of the state, which consistently under-invested in the project. Servicemen were poorly paid and the authorities did little to provide the sort of leisure and recreation that might have made the experience attractive to young men – in stark contrast to the experience of their American allies. There was little for the men to do, and once training had been completed few real tasks to perform. The professionals in the Army were never enthusiastic about the conscripts, they simply saw them as a drain on hard-pressed resources. Even moralists attacked the scheme. Many would later depict the experiment as a means of disciplining youth, but at the time they presented National Service as a seminary of idleness in which older men taught their juniors bad habits, in particular ways to evade hard work. Several Conservatives saw a connection between Britain's poor performance as an industrial producer after 1945 and the experience of National Service.

The sexual consequences of the measure were considerable. As in the United States the mass mobilisation of males in their late teens and early twenties, at a moment when many were most curious about sex, provided plenty of opportunities for sexual experimentation away from the prying eyes of family, neighbours and peers. It did much to foster homosexual identities, networks and relationships between servicemen. It was possible during leaves to explore the nightlife of the capital and occasionally to visit even more exotic locations overseas. Post-war trials also provide evidence that suggests the importance of military service in building a more powerful homosexual subculture in Britain.

The low pay often provided an excuse for experimentation. Conscription greatly stimulated the market for male prostitution. This operated across Britain, though chiefly in London and the seaports. Quentin Crisp suggested that 'a visit to Portsmouth [today] would not be worth the train fare' but in the 1930s and 1940s it was 'the Mecca of the homosexual world'. Navy week in Portsmouth between the wars, an annual event, occupied an important place in the homosexual calendar, the inter-war equivalent of the Sydney Mardi Gras, 'the whole town like a vast carnival'. After 1939, as the spirit of egalitarianism took root, the pleasures of the carnival were more evenly spread across the whole island.

The authorities knew of this development, but it was something they could never admit in public. Between 1939 and 1945 it would have provided a propaganda coup for the Axis and after 1945 even more ammunition for the Yanks. They talked about it privately of course, and it was mentioned a lot in the privacy of the Wolfenden Committee. The issue touched many raw nerves, most notably the poor performance of Britons as soldiers in the field. After 1942 Singapore was rarely mentioned but it was a defeat that haunted the élite, probably the most humiliating reverse ever suffered by the British Army.

The existence of National Service during the 1950s shaped a major recommendation of the Wolfenden Committee, the decision to set the age of consent at twenty-one. The committee papers reveal that it was the protection of National Servicemen which led Wolfenden to press for twenty-one rather than eighteen as the homosexual age of consent.

The Age of Consent

All members of the Wolfenden Committee, soon after they began their work, seem (with one exception) to have accepted that they would recommend the decriminalisation of homosexual activity between males in private. A few members of the committee, including Wolfenden, would have excluded buggery from this recommendation. Buggery wherever it took place would remain illegal. This was the view of the Lord Chief Justice of England, Sir Rayner Goddard, whose testimony did much to shape the final report.

The most significant element in Goddard's testimony was his acceptance of the principle of decriminalising homosexual acts (excluding buggery) between consenting adults in private. Sir Theobald Mathew, Director of Public Prosecutions, while opposing a change in the law because it would send the wrong messages to society, accepted that the present law did not act as a deterrent. These views from such senior

There'll always be a Royal Navy

Never was there such an opportunity for a young man as there is to-day in Britain's New Navy. So immense are the developments in nuclear science that, within ten years, the Royal Navy will be completely revolutionised. You've plenty to look forward to in this young man's Navy — a really worthwhile career, higher pay than ever, and all the excitement of visiting new countries where the British sailor is always welcomed. Unquestionably, you'll be better off *and* happier in Britain's New Navy.

If you are over 15 you are needed in

BRITAIN'S NEW NAVY

You're better off in the Navy

Full details about life in the Navy are given in a new illustrated booklet "The Royal Navy as a Career".

As from April basic pay, allowances, and living-o*... allowances will be incre*... The Royal Navy offers *... responsibility, a continu*... career and high pay.*

AND YOU RECKON YOU'RE COLD!

These Fleet Air Arm gunners are training at their Lee-on-Solent barracks for the Royal Tournament. They start off with early morning P.T., followed by a ten-mile run; this is rounded off with a swim in the sea. By then they can hardly tell the difference between a carpet of snow and a Persian rug !

The military publicity machine tried to reassure young men that service in the armed forces could be fun.

figures in the legal establishment sanctioned the instincts of most members of the committee.

The more important question was, at what age should the law consider a man an adult? When thirteen members of the committee were polled on the age of consent after a year's service on the committee, Wolfenden was appalled to discover that seven of his colleagues supported eighteen as the age (Rees, Whitby, Curran, Diplock, Demant, Lothian, Lovibond). Sir Hugh Linstead, the Conservative MP, supported an age of consent of seventeen. Wolfenden found himself in the minority of four who thought twenty-one safer (Wolfenden, Wells, Cohen, Stopford). Two of the three women had gone for twenty-one, Mrs Cohen suggesting that the heterosexual age of consent should also be raised from sixteen to twenty-one at the same time. James Adair, though present at the poll, refused to express an opinion; he was implacably opposed to any decriminalisation of homosexual activity.

Wolfenden made it clear that he would never sign any report that recommended an age of consent as low as eighteen. In the months that followed he justified his opposition by enlisting the support of his old friend 'public opinion'. The committee ought not to go too far in advance of 'public opinion'. If it supported eighteen all its other recommendations would be disregarded and members would find themselves condemned as dangerously radical. In the end he won the battle, and twenty-one was set as the age of consent for homosexual sex. The recommendation was translated into law in 1967, with terrible consequences for many young men in the years that followed. Eighteen became accepted as the legal age of consent only in 1994, almost forty years after a majority of the Wolfenden Committee had supported that age. Wolfenden's action was partly motivated by his fears of the damage that a radical report might do to his reputation. He was also responding to the signals he was receiving from the Home Office, which wanted a cautious report.

A minority on the committee, most strongly Wolfenden, wanted to act in a way that would protect young and innocent sailors, soldiers and airmen from the predatory advances of older homosexuals. This consideration was behind much of the evidence given to the committee, and was in turn coloured by three contemporary trials.

The Croft-Cooke Case

One of these cases involved Rupert Croft-Cooke, an amazingly prolific writer, mostly of fiction but also of about a dozen volumes of reminiscences and memoirs, a biography of Lord Alfred Douglas and several cookbooks. Croft-Cooke travelled widely and wrote many books describing his excursions abroad. He had a special interest in circuses and gypsies.

His industry seems to have been reasonably well rewarded and while he never seemed to live at the Somerset Maugham-level he had what popular journalists in the 1950s would describe as a fairly luxurious lifestyle. He also had a splendid war record as an intelligence officer in the British Army.

By 1953, in his fiftieth year, Croft-Cooke was a well-connected author living in an attractive house in the Sussex village of Ticehurst with his secretary and companion Joseph Alexander, an Indian christian from Goa. Croft-Cooke entertained liberally and many guests from London came down to his house for the weekend. He believed that local residents resented his extravagance: they were 'for the most part [members] of the impoverished middle-classes, pathetically clinging to the bourgeois traditions of an earlier age'.

Croft-Cooke had long since rejected the bourgeois values of his parents, embracing a more bohemian lifestyle when he ran off at eighteen to work as a journalist in Buenos Aires. He had also written a book celebrating his Sussex house and his lifestyle, *The Life for Me*, 'a book which caused a good deal of resentment in the district'.

In the late summer of 1953 Joseph Alexander met two naval cooks, Harold Altoft and Ronald Charles Dennis, in the Fitzroy Tavern, a pub off Tottenham Court Road. He introduced them to his employer who issued them with an invitation to come down for the weekend to the country. The sailors accepted. A lively weekend was enjoyed, during which much good food, fine wine and spirits were consumed. The sailors would later claim that Croft-Cooke and Alexander had sex with them. As they left the house before returning to their ship, the two men were each given a pound note by Croft-Cooke.

On their return journey the sailors became drunk and assaulted a road-mender and a policeman. While being questioned on these charges the police were curious about their presence in rural Sussex and were told about the weekend at Croft-Cooke's house. They also made their allegations against Croft-Cooke and his secretary and the police offered them immunity from prosecution if they would give evidence against them. They agreed.

Croft-Cooke always maintained his innocence and suggested that he had been framed because of his nonconformist behaviour. The police force that arrested him sent ten men and made a thorough search of his premises without a search warrant. They took away bamboo canes used for training plants to suggest that Croft-Cooke's home was the site of all manner of debauched practices. His case came up before the East Sussex Quarter Sessions on 4 October 1953.

The case was presided over by an extremely vicious homophobe, R. E.

Seaton, who as a barrister usually working for the DPP's office prosecuted more homosexual cases than any other lawyer, about two hundred and fifty between 1951 and 1956, and many more before and after those dates. Seaton gave evidence to the Wolfenden Committee as a representative of the Council of the Bar, and enunciated the eleventh commandment: 'If you are found out then of course that is where the trouble starts.' He was quite amused about the effect he seemed to have on homosexuals, and regaled the committee with an anecdote: 'I know a man who is, to use a colloquialism, a flaming pansy. He is a waiter at my club and the best I know. I am sure he is a homosexual. I think he dodges me. I do not dislike him. I do not watch him. It is all right until you get caught.' Supposedly therefore it was perfectly legitimate to vilify the homosexual as Seaton did in his service as a crown prosecutor. In Croft-Cooke's case he was sitting as a magistrate and his assistance to the prosecution was so outrageous that Croft-Cooke's lawyers felt that there was a strong argument for appeal. Croft-Cooke decided to serve his sentence and leave England, putting the whole dreadful business behind him. He did not want to return to court.

Sir Compton Mackenzie, Lord Kinross and a gypsy, Ted Mathews, all gave evidence for Croft-Cooke, praising him as an honourable man and a distinguished author with an interest in the exotic. His counsel suggested that he had invited the sailors to his home to collect information for a book. The court rejected Croft-Cooke's version of events and preferred to believe the sailors. Croft-Cooke was represented by one of the leading advocates of the age, G. D. 'Khaki' Roberts. Roberts successfully depicted the two sailors as a couple of young thugs who had changed their stories repeatedly.

The jury retired for twenty minutes and found Croft-Cooke guilty. Seaton sentenced him to nine months in prison: 'From what we have heard, The Long House, Ticehurst has been a pit of iniquity.' Croft-Cooke was 'a menace to young men'.

After he left prison, Croft-Cooke went to live in Tangier with Alexander and continued to produce his books. He provided an account of his ordeal in *The Verdict of You All*. Unduly neglected, it deserves a much wider readership, especially his account of prison life. It has less of the bitterness towards effeminate men that does so much to mar Wildeblood's book. Croft-Cooke was willing to accept that different folks really did have different strokes and he seemed to revel in the diversity he found in homosexual society.

Philip Allen and the Croft-Cooke Case

The Croft-Cooke case had been reported in the press, and was reasonably well known at the time. The significance of the case for the Wolfenden

Committee lay in the way that a senior official tried to use the material from the case to influence the committee's deliberation on setting the age of consent. The official, Philip Allen, was a well-established figure in the Home Office who would eventually become head of the department. Ironically his period as Permanent Under-Secretary coincided with Roy Jenkins's tenure of the Home Office (1965–7), when the recommendations of the Wolfenden Report on male homosexuality eventually passed Parliament and became law.

Allen had been sent by the Home Secretary to the United States during 1953 to study the ways in which American police forces dealt with prostitution (he also examined the operation of parking meters). It was Allen's report which led to the decision to establish a committee to inquire into the operation of the laws on prostitution. He was responsible for presenting the department's evidence to the Wolfenden Committee and was accompanied by a junior civil servant, Michael Graham-Harrison. The Home Office presented the committee with a long briefing paper and their role was ostensibly to act simply as advisers. Allen was at pains to explain that he was merely a civil servant and there was much coy talk about those things he and his masters knew and those things he and his masters could not know. Asked about prosecution policies of the police, he gave a wonderfully mandarin answer: 'We [i.e. the Home Office] do not know. The Home Secretary has no responsibility for prosecution; he ought not to know the answer to that question and he in fact does not.' It is easy see how Allen rose to the top of the civil service.

Wolfenden purred approval for the draft that the Home Office had prepared: it had been drafted with 'admirable skill'. Allen was pleased but offered an apology.

> Allen: 'We apologise for using the word "alternative" in relation to more than two things.'
> Wolfenden: 'I hoped you would!'

Wolfenden, himself a man of few words, with a love for the language, admired the precision and exactness which Allen employed: all the better to hide your feelings and policies with.

As he gave his testimony, Allen became less reticent. Wolfenden raised the possibility of decriminalising homosexual acts between consenting males in private: 'may we speculate for a minute on what would likely to be the effect of any alteration in the law?' In answer to this question Allen took the committee in an intriguing direction: 'I wonder if the Committee might be interested in a recent case which came to our notice. The man involved might possibly be known by name to some members of the

Committee and I will keep him anonymous.' This was how men like Allen preferred to proceed, anonymously.

The case of course was Croft-Cooke's, which Allen proceeded to describe. 'He is a wealthy man with a large house in the country.' The house was actually modest, a glorified cottage, and it was Croft-Cooke's only residence.

> The police picked up a couple of sailors who were adults, I mean they were over 21, for some other offence and they told a gruesome story about how the individual and his servant [his description of Croft-Cooke's secretary-companion] had picked them up in a public house in London and taken them to the country mansion [the house was growing in stature], given them comfortable bedrooms and then at night their host and his servant both tried to interfere with them. The sailors resisted them, but they continued to stay at the house, and they continued to stay there another night. Then they left for their barracks next morning and got drunk on the way back to the barracks and got involved in some other irrelevant offence [assault] for which the police picked them up. If you washed out the present law that conduct would be quite legal, and I think the committee would wish to consider whether it is desirable that people of this kind, wealthy gentlemen, should be able to go out and pick up adults to gratify their desires. Some people may think that it is better to take the risk, but it is that sort of case that you have got to take into account. It is not only the case of the two consenting adults of the same sort of social status.

This extremely misleading account of the case is tinged with a good deal of lower-middle-class moralising. Allen's grammar school origins were showing. Another former grammar school boy, Rees, wondered if 'there is any reason why we should disapprove of that sort of conduct than similar conduct in relation to females under similar circumstances'. Allen's reply was artful: 'It is not for me to say, but on our information this sort of thing happens with men, and I do not know that it happens with women' – the old coy pose of knowledge and ignorance. It is difficult to believe that Allen had lived and worked in central London for twenty years, twenty years as a civil servant at the Home Office, without having acquired some knowledge of heterosexual corruption.

The purpose of Allen's story was to muddy the waters about decriminalising homosexual offences. We might be tempted to see Allen's excursion into anecdote as Home Office policy if we did not also possess the response of Graham-Harrison, the other Home Office civil servant present, who did much to undermine Allen's interpretation of the case. In the discussion James Adair had expressed some scepticism about the innocence of the sailors; he did not believe their stories of resistance. It was at this point that Graham-Harrison, an old Etonian, interjected: 'it began with two sailors being picked up in a place frequented by homosexuals. I do not think anybody could believe for a moment that they did not know what they were going for.' If there was a Home Office line then Graham-Harrison had not been told about it. Allen seems to have been planting his own prejudice. The Croft-Cooke case did not easily support an interpretation of wealthy and socially prominent men corrupting innocent servicemen. But the myth of the innocent serviceman would not disappear.

The Curzon Street Case

The most frequently cited case during the proceedings of the Wolfenden Committee, to which there are many references, took its name from a street in Mayfair. The case seemed to encapsulate the worst fears of those individuals terrified of the consequences of decriminalisation: luxury, a wealthy man and large numbers of servicemen – soldiers from the élite Guards regiments – and all-male parties, depicted as orgies, at which the wealthy man introduced the soldiers to his friends.

Arthur Robert Birley was forty-three, a man of independent means who had worked for the BBC and who owned an apartment in Curzon Street. In 1948 he struck up a connection with a young Life Guard, Corporal K. J. F. Stiles, who must have been about twenty at the time. Stiles arranged for other Guardsmen to visit Birley, and acted as his agent or procurer at the barracks. Groups of Guardsmen regularly visited the flat to attend cocktail parties at which 'BBC officials' were present. Birley was extremely generous and gave the soldiers many presents. Competition to join the circle intensified, creating tensions in the barracks and giving Stiles considerable power over his peers. It was, however, a tip-off from a neighbour that led the Military Police to Curzon Street. They ran an operation, with the consent of the Metropolitan Police, to catch Birley in the act. Unfortunately he did not close his curtains, and policemen were able to station themselves on ladders and in surrounding buildings to watch him make love to Trooper George Baldwin, twenty-three, a Life Guard stationed at Hyde Park. The newspaper reports were extremely reticent, the *News of the World* providing the fullest account: 'Police and military authorities saw through a window what took place at the flat. Birley was partly undressed. Baldwin was in his uniform. [The prosecutor] did not propose to go into detail.' The prosecutor was R. E. Seaton, notching up another triumph in a homosexual case.

Birley and Baldwin were put on trial at the Old Bailey in April 1951. The Recorder of London, Sir Gerald Dobson, thought that it was 'the worst story it had been his misfortune to hear for [many] a long day . . .

Young soldiers are very easily corrupted.' In fact, neither at this trial nor at the court martial of five Guardsmen held later that month did any of the soldiers suggest that they had been coerced. They agreed that they had all consented to whatever had taken place. During Birley's trial the Recorder asked his attorney if Birley had paid these men. 'There is no doubt at all that he has given all these soldiers sums of money', he replied, 'but they were not forced to go there.'

Birley was presented by his counsel as a sick man, wrecked by his 'terrible' appetites, for this was a case 'of how appetite grew as appetites' were satisfied: '[he] is a man as sick as a man can be. Had it not been for his mental affliction it may be that when these desires came on him that he would have repulsed them. His powers of resistance and control were far less than that of the ordinary man.' The counsel's eloquence struck a chord with the judge, who accepted his interpretation of Birley's actions. Judges were often reluctant to accept medical evidence in homosexual cases but Dobson did believe that Birley needed treatment:

> Up to the present time the Legislature has been unable to provide any machinery of a hospital character to deal adequately with cases like yours. It required some degree of self-control or self-discipline to avert the dire misfortune which has now overtaken you. It is clear that you should be removed from the community. You will if necessary, receive psychiatric treatment. You are not without hope. You are a man who can rescue yourself.

Dobson sentenced Birley to eighteen months' imprisonment. Baldwin he bound over for two years: 'You have been led into this, but take warning. If you cleanse yourself by hard work, there is no reason why you should not return to the ranks of decent, honest soldiers.'

The Army was not so keen to welcome the soldiers back into the ranks. Five Guardsmen at a court martial were sentenced to terms between eighteen months and two years in military prison and discharged from the army. Many other Guardsmen escaped with a warning.

It was the Commissioner of the Metropolitan Police force, Sir John Nott-Bower, who first introduced this case to the Wolfenden Committee:

> I do know about the case of the Horse Guards, if you want to know about that one. There was a gentleman, whose name I will not mention, and in the flat above there happened to be a major of the Guards, and he was surprised to find a number of Horse Guards troopers and NCO's going frequently to that flat. In the end there were 31 found . . . The mainspring was a man who had guardsmen up to his flat and who spent a lot of money on them. One of his odd ideas

was that they should all be dressed by Moss Bros. in beautiful riding kit – that cost him about £300. We did have the advantage there of having a fire escape from which we could see what was going on.

The operation had become part of the Metropolitan Police folklore. PC Butcher, who gave evidence to the committee, had been a member of the party that had observed the premises: 'they had the guardsmen riding around in a harness and they were chasing them with whips. These guardsmen were being paid quite large sums, they were in the nude and they had a harness on and these perverts were chasing them around with whips to get the satisfaction . . .'

The Drummer Boys at Windsor
Mr Justice Hilbery knew Wolfenden socially and he invited him to attend a trial for men charged with homosexual offences so that he could see the law in practice. On 14 January 1954 Wolfenden wrote to Roberts: 'Hilbery asked me to sit with him yesterday to hear this awful Windsor case. I could not do that, but I am lunching with him today and he is going to let me see all the papers. When I was talking to him last night he told me that it was a typical sample of the really bad case.' Five days later he reported again: '[Hilbery] let me read the depositions. It seems to be a fairly typical sample of its kind, and I suspect it will get a good deal of publicity.'

In fact most newspapers did not cover the case. Some were reacting to pressure for greater reticence from readers. The Women's Institute had launched a national campaign in 1954 that was reducing the number of reports of homosexual trials in some districts. The Windsor papers covered the trial patchily and the *News of the World* used that material to produce only a brief report.

The depositions that shocked Wolfenden concerned a group of men in Windsor who had sex with a number of drummer boys attached to the Coldstream Guards. The boys were all teenagers, sixteen, seventeen and eighteen, who as boy-soldiers were receiving particularly low wages. The men gave them presents and often also paid for their services.

The Conversion of Wolfenden

These three cases had an impact upon Wolfenden's thinking about the age of consent. Mrs Cohen seemed to have been persuaded by them as well. At a session of the committee on 30 March 1955 Wolfenden explained why he believed that there should be such a wide difference between the ages of consent for heterosexual and homosexual activities:

we have a good deal of evidence that young men doing their period of National Service are at present very much tempted – if that is the right word – by others, and there is a good deal of evidence, that inducements of one kind or another, often straightforward financial ones, are brought to bear on them and with the point . . . made here of the segregation of large numbers of them into one-sex communities for a long time, I suppose there is more likely to be – if one may just put it that way – more likely to be opportunity for them to indulge with them and on them during those ages than perhaps any other time, and it was simply on that prudential ground – I mean really to protect them – that it has been put to us that the age for men might be higher than the age for girls.

Rees immediately challenged him, what did he mean by 'evidence': 'we have had no evidence that the age of military service has an effect upon offences of that kind.' Wolfenden's reply was very lame: 'There is no evidence in the strict sense of being able to say that this would not have happened to them otherwise but I think no doubt a fair amount of evidence that it goes on substantially.'

The testimony of Lord Chief Justice Goddard seems to have had a major impact on Wolfenden, more so than upon any other member of the committee. He had said that:

> The age of consent presents a problem on which there is likely to be wide divergences of opinions. After much thought I incline to 21. My reason is that I believe National Service is to some extent responsible for the undoubted increase. Then from conversations with officers attached to the London Command I believe that elderly male perverts do tempt young soldiers to lend themselves to these practices for money . . . I feel it would be advisable not to put the age of consent too low.

Wolfenden was good at taking cues from figures in authority, a skill which certainly helps to explain his astonishingly successful career. Such obedience and deference endeared him to the gerontocracy that ran many of Britain's élite institutions.

Wolfenden would not move from twenty-one as the suggested age of consent, despite all the problems that his colleagues foresaw at setting such a high age. Diplock set out the problems for the courts in dealing with individuals who were in every other way adults and yet who would in this instance be treated the same as children. All sorts of hypothetical cases were suggested but Wolfenden would not budge.

The Evidence of the Armed Forces

The three armed services gave their evidence to the Wolfenden Committee on 25 May 1955. One immediate difference emerged between them in their attitude to 'homosexual crime'. The Army and the Royal Navy tended to play it down, assumed that their service personnel were usually the innocent party when they had been involved in homosexual activity and clearly tried to protect the members of their service. The Royal Air Force, with its reputation as a more democratic and meritocratic service, adopted a much less paternalistic attitude. Air Commodore Pride, Provost-Marshal, ran special investigations to search out homosexual personnel and felt that they represented a serious threat to the RAF, one that he was determined to eliminate. It was Pride who was responsible for the kit-searches that led to the discovery of the incriminating letters of Montagu, Pitt-Rivers and Wildeblood in December 1953, resulting in their conviction for homosexual offences in 1954. Neither the Army nor the Royal Navy invested in such tactics. T. Royle in his history of National Service, *The Best Years of Their Lives* (1986), suggests that 'in many units tacit approval was given by senior officers to long-standing homosexual "marriages"'.

Pride seems to have made a special study of the problem. He found that there was a higher incidence of such activity in units that served overseas. This he explained in terms of the limited recreation facilities available in overseas bases and the shortage of women, but he also thought it possible that in hotter countries airmen in common with others wore less and the exposure of flesh excited their comrades towards lustful thoughts and actions. The incidence was higher amongst the less educated. He discerned a relationship between more education and resistance to homosexual activity. He suggested that there existed networks of homosexuals within the RAF and it is clear that he was using some of the methods and practices employed by some English police forces in prosecuting these networks. 'Most of our cases', he told the committee, 'arise from searches of kit for one purpose or another, revealing letters or compromising material that sets the investigation on foot. One of the more recent developments is the tendency to confess freely. Once they are put on the spot they tend to tell the whole story, and one case turns into half a dozen.'

As a justification of his activities, Pride predictably enough cited the testimony of a Russian defector who said that the entrapment of homosexuals was an important element in Soviet subversion of the West. Homosexuals, because they were weak characters, tended to be security risks. It was an idea rejected by the head of the Naval Law Board; the Royal Navy could find no evidence to support the security risk theory.

Both the Army and Royal Navy seem to have turned a blind eye. Some of the activity was simply 'schoolboy' stuff and not serious, the sort of approach that would have infuriated the Director of Public Prosecutions who would have warned them of the addictive nature of all homosexual activity, however minor. The representatives of the Royal Navy believed that it never took place on board its ships. The Army representative questioned by Wolfenden on the Windsor case suggested that the 'incitement' to an offence 'always was by the civilian rather than the soldier'. This comforting doctrine was combined with the notion that alcohol consumption diminished all personal responsibility for acts committed under the 'influence'. G. A. Macdonald, a solicitor from Portsmouth and a member of the Law Society delegation, told the committee of his experience of the naval port: 'A man might be drunk by accident. In my experience young sailors frequently commit acts of gross indecency very nearly by accident. The habitual practitioner is seeking the young sailor very often.'

Neither the Army nor the Royal Navy wanted scandals. Officers seemed to have a paternalistic attitude to their charges, the sort of attitude found in the Church of England and in the public school system that minimised and hid homosexual activity. This attitude was challenged by men like Pride and Sir Theobald Mathew, the Director of Public Prosecutions. The Army and the Royal Navy adopted what might be perceived as a traditional approach as opposed to the modern attitudes of the RAF. In contrast to the RAF, the Royal Navy did not encourage confessions: 'Those who confess to homosexual practices are often very willing to implicate others, and their confessions if taken at face value might give the impression that homosexuality is rife. However the self-confessed homosexual is apt to be an unreliable witness, and no action is taken against those whom he implicates unless there is independent evidence to support the allegation.' Voluntary confessions led to an ordinary discharge with no disciplinary action for the confessing sailor.

The courts martial that took place in this period might give a different picture. But the services are intensely protective of such records, and a majority of courts martial even for the First World War are still not open. An Act of Parliament in 1950 gave servicemen punished by a court martial the right to appeal to a panel of civilian judges. The records of these proceedings are open for inspection under the thirty-year rule but the sample is so small that it is difficult to discern much about the policy of the different services. All the records for the early and mid-1950s have in any case been lost, disappearing down some bureaucratic black hole.

Towards the end of the session an interesting speculation developed concerning the preponderance of homosexuals in some of the ancillary branches of the armed forces:

> G. B. Dodds (representing the Royal Navy): . . . there is some indication that the kind of people who go in for this tend to be people like mental nurses, and people who do what might be called women's work.

> E. W. Handley (RAF): I do not know whether we should be able to say whether homosexuals are naturally attracted to medical work, or whether medical work makes them homosexual.

Kind Hearts and Brutes

Within homosexual circles much information circulated about the availability of servicemen. There were clearly many convenient points for making contact. Pubs in the West End were a favourite place for rendezvous. Some like the Fitzroy Tavern drew a mixed crowd, while others attracted a more specialised clientele. The Golden Lion in Soho always had the reputation of a place where soldiers selling their bodies could be found – it was completely trade. Railway termini connecting the capital with garrisons, airfields and the ports were also much favoured. One man remembered those evenings:

> When trains arrived from the port with sailors on leave the stations of the main London terminuses (Paddington, Victoria and Liverpool Street) offered some possibilities.
>
> On arrival of the train there would be scores of young sailors tumbling out of the train, all it seemed in violent need of a good piss. They ran helter-skelter into the large lavatory on the platform, and pulling down the flap of their trousers, pissed for all they were worth . . . If they happened to note some eager looker, they would exclaim: 'He's a beauty isn't he? Like him up your bum, chum?' This sally would be followed by gales of laughter from the other pissing fellows. If the pubs were still open, one at once said: 'Come along for another one, Jack, before the boozers shut.' And, once safely behind a pint at the bar, as often as not one succeeded in dragging him back to one's room.

Homosexual folklore traditionally presented the sailor as an altogether more accommodating source of pleasure than the Guardsman, who was often the archetypal rough trade. These stereotypes are supported by the evidence from the trials of the period.

It was a distinction made by Quentin Crisp, in his splendid autobiography *The Naked Civil Servant* (1968):

> I and most of the homosexuals whom I knew best wanted 'something in a uniform'. When any of my friends mentioned that he had met a 'divine' sailor he never meant an officer . . .
>
> When I was young the word 'soldier' meant one of the red-coated guardsmen who strutted up and down Knightsbridge in the evenings. These men were willing to go for 'a walk in the park' for as little as half-a-crown . . .
>
> Sailors never asked for money but, on the contrary, had large sums of money to spend in short spasms of shore leave. They also never turned nasty. Perhaps the act of running away to sea was an abandonment of accepted convention and, after a sojourn in strange ports, they returned with their outlook and possibly their anus broadened.
>
> The fabulous generosity in their natures was an irresistible lure – especially when combined with the tightness of their uniforms, whose crowning aphrodisiac feature was the fly-flap of their trousers. More than one of my friends has swayed about in ecstasy describing the pleasures of undoing this quaint sartorial device.

Joe Ackerley, literary editor of *The Listener*, was something of an authority on Guardsmen and he was certainly not oblivious to their faults. In his search for the 'Ideal Friend' (looking for what Francis Bacon, the painter, called 'the Nietzsche of the football team'), he encountered many soldiers. Ackerley had written in 1930, 'It would be the blackest ingratitude to disparage the guards – these brave soldiers are of incalculable use to a great many lonely bachelors in London – but it must be said that the usual disadvantage attaches to them that attaches to all prostitutes, they are mercenary.' According to Ackerley's biographer Peter Parker, nothing was more admired amongst Ackerley's friends than 'the scarlet jackets and gold epaulettes of His Majesty's Brigade of Guards . . . The guardsmen . . . in a time-honoured tradition combined ceremonial duties and casual prostitution . . . it appears that young recruits were frequently "broken in" by their elders when they joined the colours'.

Gangs of off-duty Guardsmen often prowled around Hyde Park robbing punters, often beating them up as well. These violent robberies were a regular feature of the business at the magistrates' courts in the West End. The park was a major cruising ground, a space shared each evening by several hundred prostitutes according to police estimates. In the manner of such places these different groups (the clients looking for sex with men or women and the men and women offering their bodies) might mix at the all-night coffee stalls near Marble Arch but they occupied different parts of the park and guarded any encroachments upon their territory with the same ferocity that the nation state might exhibit. The stalls were one of the chief casualties of the Street Offences Act, 1959, the statute that embodied the recommendations of the Wolfenden Report on prostitution, moving the prostitutes off the streets, thus killing a nocturnal street culture that had survived many generations of moralists.

James Pope-Hennessy who often cruised the area has left a number of vivid descriptions of the district in the diary he kept during the early 1950s. The biographer of the royal matriarch Queen Mary (a book with a homosexual subtext; one chapter is entitled 'Country Cottages') met his partner and lover Len Adams, a paratrooper, in a lift at Holland Park underground station in 1948. Many homosexual couples in London began as liaisons in which the younger serviceman decided to settle down with the older man he had met cruising. Adams has been described by Pope-Hennessey's biographer as

a beloved friend and chief supporter, filling a multiplicity of roles – confidant, travelling companion, aide-de-camp, bodyguard, household-help and general nanny, even in times of crisis, a trusted privy purse. Len's sole defect, from James's point of view, was his somewhat pugnacious disposition, which, again and again, in Martinique or Siena or Oslo or Hyères, precipitated some resounding conflict that involved them with the local police.

It was possible to take the soldier out of the uniform but not always possible to tame the fighting man. Adams was not hidden when guests came to call at their home in Ladbroke Grove. On one occasion the Duke and Duchess of Windsor came to call: 'They were received by James and Len.' The other guests were Diana Baring, Pope-Hennessy's literary agent, 'James's close friend Lady Victor Paget (to whom the Duke had long ago paid court)', the writer Patrick [Lord] Kinross (who had gone into the witness box to testify as a character witness for Rupert Croft-Cooke) and 'a trooper from Knightsbridge Barracks, at the moment James's reigning favourite'.

Some Guardsmen sought out rich patrons to buy them out of the Army and make them their companions. These relationships might last a long time. Others ended too quickly and the ex-Guardsman, losing his looks and possibly out of shape, found himself with a taste for a better life but without the means to provide for a luxurious existence. Some turned to crime, in particular to blackmail. One soldier in the 1930s took his own life. Reginald Jacobs, twenty-one, an ex-Grenadier Guardsman, was found dead in July 1936 in the London flat of Colonel Munro Cuthbertson, a member of the Consular Service at Cairo. His father explained to a journalist what had happened:

> My son was expelled from the Army for his association with Col. Munro Cuthbertson . . . He came home to me [from Egypt] on January 10, 1936. I was not at all satisfied with the cause of the discharge being an old Sergeant-Major myself. I wrote to the C.O. at Cairo with the result that I had an appointment at Chelsea Barracks. I came home and told my boy he would have to leave [the family home]. He went but returned next day, April 12, when I again requested him to leave. Ultimately I forced him out of the house . . . He was not fit to associate with his brothers and sisters.

A post-mortem examination revealed that he 'had habitually indulged in a certain malpractice'.

Simon Raven in a classic study of male prostitution in London, 'Boys Will Be Boys', *Encounter* (1960), introduced the reader to a Guardsman, Tom:

> I enquired, did not these expeditions do violence to his proper sexual nature? Apparently not. Tom regarded 'what happened' as a form of masturbation: he would close his eyes and think about 'girls and things' while his partner provided the necessary mechanical stimulus – a service which Tom performed unthinkingly, with an almost automatic movement of the hand, in return. Thus Tom was able to persuade himself that he was not at all 'queer' by nature, and that what occurred was of no sexual significance. However, it is evident that a person who is not at least slightly homosexual in taste could never begin to tolerate such a situation; and I strongly suspect that Tom, along with most soldiers who behave like him, has a definite if narrow homosexual streak. He is, in fact, bisexual – a judgement which, in its general implications, is confirmed by some remarks made to me by a young Lance-Serjeant (also of the Brigade). 'Some of us get quite fond of the blokes we see regularly . . . You go to their flats and have some drinks and talk a bit – they're nice fellows, some of them, and interesting to listen to. And as for the sex bit, well, some of the younger ones aren't bad looking and I've had some real thrills off them in my time.'

It was one of the wonderful paradoxes of British life that the soldiers guarding the sovereign, whose parades provided so much of the daily pageantry of the capital and who were always present at the most important ceremonies of the state, should have been composed of so many men who in their spare time hustled their bodies for sex with other men.

Newspaper cuttings collected for the 1960s suggest that there were more homosexual cases involving Guardsmen during that decade than the preceding three. In 1968 another scandal erupted involving Guardsmen in a Curzon Street flat, a circle including dozens of soldiers. Seven years later serving Guardsmen were discharged after it was discovered that they had regularly posed for photographs in a gay pornographic magazine. The story was exposed by Cudlipp's *Daily Mirror*, which also revealed that a corporal in the Life Guards was running a call-boy service, supplying his friends from the barracks to men who called him. The tradition continued.

Most people did not connect. Members of the Wolfenden Committee heard so much about the innocent serviceman that they forgot about Guardsmen. Goronwy Rees, however, was on hand to remind them:

> *Sir Hugh* [Linstead] thought that the public regarded male prostitutes with contempt rather than disgust. *Dr. Curran* said that homosexuals regarded them as 'pansies' lowering the status and reputations of themselves (i.e. the homosexual) [they] simply would not associate with male prostitutes. *Mr. Rees* however pointed out that Guardsmen seemed not infrequently to be male prostitutes and they were scarcely figures of disgust or contempt. (Minutes of a meeting, 21 February 1956)

A characteristic Rees intervention: he kept his colleagues on their toes, always ready to challenge their more ludicrous pontifications. But it was destined to be the last meeting of the committee that Rees attended.

3

Thin Ice

Goronwy Rees attended a meeting of the Wolfenden Committee on the afternoon of 21 February 1956. That morning he had seen his literary agent, directing her to sell a manuscript that he had written about his friend the spy Guy Burgess. Within a few days she entered into negotiations with the *People*. They agreed to serialise the manuscript over five weeks and paid Rees about £1,000. The first article appeared on 11 March, the last on 8 April. Before the end of the series Rees had been identified as the author by the *Daily Telegraph*. The revelation destroyed Rees's academic career. A number of his colleagues at Aberystwyth called for his resignation because of his association with Burgess, whom he described in the articles as his 'closest friend'. An official inquiry by the college authorities recommended that he should be dismissed, and after many months of wrangling he resigned his post.

Guy

Rees had been born in Aberystwyth but had spent most of his adult life in England. A grammar school boy like Wolfenden, he won a scholarship to Oxford but he outshone Jack, academically and socially. He won a prize fellowship at All Souls after distinguishing himself in the Honours School of Politics, Philosophy and Economics. John Sparrow, a fellow of All Souls, had been attracted to the dark and handsome Welshman when he met him as an undergraduate and launched him into a glittering social circle that extended from Oxford and Cambridge to bohemian London and brought Rees into contact with a considerable number of artists, aristocrats and intellectuals. He met Guy Burgess at a dinner party in 1934 and they became close friends. The Soviet spy confessed his treachery to Rees in 1937 and it is probable that between then and the outbreak of the war Rees passed information to Burgess. The war made Rees a patriot and in the years after 1945 he became strongly pro-American and anti-communist. An active cold warrior, he must have bitterly regretted his employment, however briefly, as a Soviet agent.

His association with Burgess continued up until the defection of Burgess and Maclean in May 1951. Rees was one of the last people Burgess tried to phone before he left for the Soviet Union. Rees was not home and his wife took a message from Burgess who told her that he was 'about to do something which would surprise and shock many people but he was sure it was the right thing to do'. Burgess had been a regular visitor to Rees's home and he was godfather to one of his children. By 1950 Rees had also known the identity of two other members of the spy ring, Anthony Blunt and Donald Maclean. He would later explain that he had not revealed this information to the authorities because he had no intention of being the British Whittaker Chambers, a reference to the American who had exposed the spy Alger Hiss in the United States, but he did go to see MI6 soon after Burgess and Maclean had defected.

The men who saw him did not believe him. Indeed, on one occasion Blunt was brought along by the deputy head of MI5 to hear Rees's story over lunch. Nobody listened to Rees, suspecting that he too had been a traitor. Blunt managed to discredit Rees's reputation with the senior members of British intelligence and Rees grew increasingly bitter over his treatment.

Rees's career flourished in the early 1950s. He moved in 1953 from All Souls (where he had been Bursar) to run Aberystwyth. In 1954 he had been appointed to the Wolfenden Committee which gave him the opportunity for regular outings to the capital. He was, as we have seen, an extremely active and important member of the committee, probably the most powerful voice promoting law reform amongst its members. By the time the Wolfenden Report appeared in September 1957 he was no longer a member of the committee. A footnote to the report explained that he had resigned in April 1956. The Home Office had never publicly announced his resignation because it was terrified that some enterprising journalist might make the connection between Burgess, Rees and the Home Office inquiry into the laws on homosexuality. The popular press would have had a field day.

This was the sort of nightmare that had terrified Wolfenden from the moment of his acceptance of the chairmanship, a scandal that would overshadow the work of the committee and more importantly damage his own career. He was on holiday with his wife and daughter on the Gower peninsula when the *Daily Telegraph* identified Rees as the author of the *People* articles. He wrote immediately to the Home Office:

Holidaying for the weekend in the depths of South Wales I have just seen . . . the *Daily Telegraph* 'Peterborough' references to Goronwy Rees. He is a member of the Departmental Committee . . . If Peterborough is right in identifying him and of Rees['s description of] . . . himself as Burgess's 'closest friend', I think this makes considerable awkwardness for the Committee. Further if it turns out – as it will – that the Committee recommends some 'liberalisation' of the law about male homosexuals in private we really shall be in rather a mess, such a recommendation will be a good deal discredited if it is signed by 'Burgess's closest friend', would obviously be criticised in many quarters and [the report] would be discredited from the start . . . It is pretty damaging in any case that one of the members of the Committee should now be revealed as having this particular connection with a notorious homosexual.   •

Wolfenden got into a flap. Sir Frank Newsam, Permanent Under-Secretary at the Home Office, wrote back to assure Wolfenden that everything was under control. By 18 April Newsam had secured Rees's removal from the committee. They both agreed that it would not be announced, the 'awkward and embarrassing little problem' had almost been solved. On 5 May a journalist from the *Sunday Pictorial* phoned the Home Office and asked for a list of the present committee. He was given the runaround. Nothing more was heard of the request. Roberts was preparing for the worst: 'if they come through here we shall have to give them a list, from which they can draw their conclusions. I wonder what they know?' The journalist did not telephone again, the connection was never made.

Rees found employment as a journalist and writer but on a much reduced income, and he never held another academic office. The articles overshadowed his whole life and it was only in his last weeks, dying of cancer, that he got his revenge by unmasking Anthony Blunt as a spy in the autumn of 1979. There has been much speculation about why he chose to sell the manuscript to the *People*. Burgess thought he had done it for the money – he was always short of cash, and he supported a fairly extravagant lifestyle. But there were possibly stronger motives that had been triggered by the appearance of Burgess and Maclean at a press conference in Moscow on 11 February 1956, the first time they had surfaced since their defection. It was a news item that made headlines across the world. It unnerved Rees. Possibly he felt that Burgess was about to name him as a collaborator in the 1930s. He decided to get in first. He had written the manuscript some time before and he took it with him to London when he went up for his monthly session of the Wolfenden Committee.

The irony is that behind closed doors in Whitehall he was doing much to promote tolerance towards homosexuality and puncturing the prejudices of the many reactionary moralists who had given evidence to the committee, but through his articles he did much to support the transformation of Burgess into the greatest homosexual demon of the decade. What is more, he called for a witch-hunt, and he identified the members of Burgess's social circle, many of them prominent members of the élite. It is difficult to believe that the sceptical voice in Whitehall was the same man who could produce the vilification of the spy that appeared in the tabloid:

> He was a human monster and a Jekyll and Hyde who used his depravity to gain possession of vital information about the espionage activities of the Foreign Office . . . For 20 years one incredibly vicious man used blackmail and corruption on a colossal scale to worm out Britain's most precious secrets for the rulers of Russia . . . [he] wrought more damage to Britain than any traitor in our history . . . men like Burgess are only able to escape detection because THEY HAVE FRIENDS IN HIGH PLACES WHO PRACTICE THE SAME TERRIBLE VICE.

In the same article he boasted about his friendship with this 'monster': 'We were constantly in each other's homes. We shared anxieties and joys. We went to parties together. We had the same friends . . . He wrote to me frequently when we were separated. He has even sent me messages of friendship from Moscow . . . I was exceedingly fond of this strange and in many ways terrible man . . . Guy had a complete charm that made all of us forgive his excesses.'

Such prose seemed to suggest they had been lovers rather than friends. Rees always maintained that they had never been lovers but he lied about so much else that it is not always easy to believe him. At one point in the series he revealed that he was not going to express 'any opinion about the legal and moral guilt of homosexuals', yet he would present Burgess's homosexuality in the following fashion:

> The most painful part of the entire Guy Burgess affair is the story of his incredibly depraved private life.
>
> For this man who was the greatest traitor Britain has ever known – and who was for a long time my closest friend – indulged in practices that repel all normal people.
>
> Yet I must place the facts before you because they disclose a state of affairs in high places that remains to this day a terrible danger to Britain's security.
>
> Guy Burgess was not only guilty of practising unnatural vices. He also had among his numerous friends many who shared his abnormal tastes.

The spy Guy Burgess, whose treachery cast a long shadow across the British élite, provided many opportunities for critics to attack the decadence of the 'establishment'.

And he was in a position to blackmail some of them – including men in influential positions – to get information for his Russian masters.

Rees used the series to warn the nation, and to call for a witch-hunt:

the public must be worried about the dangers still to be faced from men like these.

For it is certain that Maclean and Burgess were not the only Britons in positions of trust who were recruited into the Soviet spy ring.

I believe that Burgess and Maclean staged their reappearance in Moscow as a warning to those remaining traitors – a warning that they can be exposed if they do not continue in the service of Russia.

The articles led neither to an official inquiry nor to any sort of witch-hunt. Instead, they brought about the ostracism of Rees; many of his friends broke with him for his behaviour, and it made him even more of an outsider. Nöel Annan later explained the reaction of his circle: 'Rees lost his head and his obsession destroyed him . . . [he produced] an indictment not only of Burgess but of his friends and in particular all those friends who were in high places or had been in the security service during the war . . . His friends took the line that to start a witch-hunt five years after the birds had flown was inexcusable.'

Jeremy

Two years before Wolfenden had been approached to become chairman of the Home Office committee, his eighteen-year-old son Jeremy had laid 'all my cards on the table', by telling his father that he was gay. At the time he was doing his National Service with the Royal Navy between school and university. Aboard HMS *Shipstone* he wrote to a friend, 'Afloat! Afloat! I know I have queer tastes but I'm rather enjoying this.'

On a cryptography course in Devonport he met another homosexual but he was 'sadly "camp"'. Apparently Jeremy Wolfenden 'preferred to seduce womanisers. He and his new friend had an excursion one evening to "a pub renowned as one of the 'queer' centres of Plymouth" where they were bought drinks by a drunken Petty Officer with whom they managed to avoid going to bed. Wolfenden found the evening memorable chiefly for the fact that he was able to get drunk on an outlay of less than ninepence.' Some time before, this self-confident teenager had described his predicament to a friend:

Where do we go from here? . . . I am not going to end up as Anthony Blanche arty-tarting around the art galleries . . . I am queer; so much is physically evident. But I have a lot more important things to do than waste my time hunting young men. It is a charming hobby, and for the sake of physical and emotional well-being a certain amount of it is of course necessary. But it is not an essential part of my life, and the more 'self-fulfilment' I achieve in my work and my thought and my writing, probably the less I shall need it. I may end up with an undemanding and unsensational menage with a single boy-friend; I may end up unsatisfied except for an occasional Sloane Street tart . . . I may, I suppose, turn to heterosexuality; but if by a pretty mature (physically) eighteen I am not attracted by girls either physically or emotionally or aesthetically it seems unlikely. One can but wait and see, and not get too involved, or waste valuable time. Waste of time is the one mortal sin.

This letter throws into relief some of the more extraordinary comments made by a procession of experts to his father's committee a couple of years later.

Jeremy Wolfenden wanted it all and it seemed that he was destined to get it. After a top scholarship at Eton, he won another scholarship to Oxford and went up to the university to read Politics, Philosophy and Economics in the same autumn that the Home Office committee began its work. According to Jeremy's biographer Sebastian Faulks, Jack Wolfenden wrote his son a letter at the time making two requests: '1] That we stay out of each other's way for the time being; 2] That you wear rather less make-up.' Stories have percolated down the years, probably apocryphal, about blazing rows between father and son during this period, with the younger Wolfenden championing the cause against the cautious attitudes of his father. One tale even suggests that Jeremy cultivated Peter Wildeblood, whom he admired, a connection which greatly irritated his father.

Jeremy won election to All Souls after achieving a first in finals. As a fellow he may have run into Goronwy Rees, who maintained some association with his old college. Jeremy decided to become a journalist and he explored London's homosexual subculture: 'the shallow emotions and the casual treacherous, cynical sort of love I now associate with the homosexual underworld in London ... an atmosphere in which sordid homosexuality is the only practicable form of self-expression ... the catty cynicism of the queer bars and camp little flats in Earl's Court Road.'

During his early twenties he fell in love with a young man who later became a distinguished historian, and for a time he was happy. Sadly, Jeremy Wolfenden became an alcoholic and his addiction to liquor probably killed him, a few months after his thirty-first birthday. By then he had served as a foreign correspondent in Paris, Moscow and Washington and had become entangled with the world of espionage. In Moscow he got to know Guy Burgess: 'The two would put on their Old Etonian ties and get drunk together.' They spent their time gossiping about Eton, Oxford and Bohemia. When Burgess died in the autumn of 1963 Jeremy Wolfenden was a pallbearer at his funeral, and Guy left him the pick of his library.

According to Sebastian Faulks, the 'two pivots of his character were his intellectual brilliance and his homosexuality'. Had he been arrested at any point in the mid-1950s, the event would certainly have made the papers; it would probably have damaged the progress of the Wolfenden

Committee, and possibly brought his father the sort of notoriety that Jack knew could spike his own progress up the greasy pole. They all skated on very thin ice. Our knowledge of Jeremy Wolfenden's proclivity makes his father's performance as chairman of the Home Office committee even more remarkable.

4

Dark Corners

... the homosexual community, and I fear it is a community.
    *– Sir Lawrence Dunne, Chief Metropolitan Magistrate, in his testimony
to the Wolfenden Committee, 4 October 1955*

I can envisage men walking down the street, arm in arm, possibly
holding hands, and at dances perhaps wishing to dance together and
even caressing in public places ... it is a shocking example to young
people.
    – Dr A.D.D. Broughton in his Commons speech, December 1958

The Wolfenden inquiry was badly flawed. Without doubt its chief weakness was its failure to understand or appreciate (except in the most negative terms) the importance of the homosexual subculture. The committee had a number of glimpses into this world but, as with so much associated with the 'distasteful problem' of homosexuality, it preferred to keep its distance.

All sorts of evidence, anecdotal as well as documentary, suggest that there existed across Britain networks of homosexually-inclined men and that a number of social venues (cafés, pubs, steam baths and even clubs, and in London the YMCA) which catered for these groups. There was a concentration of such facilities in the capital but contemporary trials (some of which are surveyed in Part Three) suggest that they had their counterparts in the provinces as well.

Queens

British accounts of homosexuality tended to be written from either a legal or medical point of view, focusing on the homosexual as either a criminal or a patient. These surveys tended to ignore the sociological and historical perspectives. It was not that many people did not know about the homosexual subculture, simply that they did not understand its positive role in the creation and maintenance of homosexual identities. Reactionaries increasingly used the existence of a subculture as a way of further vilifying homosexual culture. Richard Hauser, a Viennese sociologist, examined that subculture in a book which appeared in 1962:

> Although few generalisations can be made about individuals, cliques of homosexuals possess very definite characteristics. This is partly because individuals of a particular type are specially attracted to such cliques, and partly because homosexuals, like any other unwanted minority, react by forming their own special outlook and conventions in defiance of the hostile majority. One of the consequences of the presence in our midst of large numbers of men living under the threat of ostracism and persecution is the existence, unknown to most normal persons, of a vast underworld of sexual deviants. In the normal company the homosexual preserves a front ... but among the secret community of his fellows he can throw off the mask. In this strange underworld they have their own little social coteries, their own conventions and slang, their own favourite bars, restaurants and meeting places ... Entry into this camaraderie is a matter of visiting the right places in the right clothes and knowing the right conversational gambits and *double entendres* ... Among these circles the initiated make themselves understood by the use of a slang that is almost a Masonic code ... These comments apply only to homosexual society as it manifests in large centres of population where unorthodox groups can find a footing ... For the minority who find attraction in homosexual cliques, the 'gay life', as they call it, has a certain fascination. The sense of self-importance derived from belonging to an 'underworld' group, and the enjoyment of laughing behind society's back, compensates them for inferiority in other directions. They can feel a little superior to normal men living dull, routine lives. By mixing in these circles and cultivating promiscuous habits some ordinary young men find they can make contacts beyond the scope of their usual humdrum environment. Having no wives or children to tie them, they can travel easily, and wherever they go they can be sure of making 'interesting' contacts.

It must be remembered that for much of the 1940s and 1950s (and possibly even for the 1960s as well) social and recreational facilities were particularly underdeveloped in Britain. Campaigns launched in the nineteenth and early twentieth centuries to make urban life respectable and to police public spaces and gatherings in cities and towns so as to inhibit social interaction did much to weaken associational culture in Britain. It was the high price British society paid for the evangelical revival; successive waves of social puritanism made Britain an increasingly dull place in which to live. The coming of television in the 1950s did much to aid this trend, temporarily at least. Music halls, repertory theatres, cinemas and spectator sports all saw their audiences slump dramatically in the 1950s. This was not all due to television; the post-war baby boom also tied many young families to the home, and women who made up the bulk of the cinema audience in the 1940s increasingly found themselves trapped in their domestic tasks.

London escaped much of this puritanism, and continued to support a lively and diverse social life throughout this period, giving it the appearance increasingly of the nation's pleasure ground. This widened the difference between London and the provinces, increasing the capital's attractiveness for those restless spirits who found provincial life grim. Contemporaries, particularly moralists and foreign journalists, depicted London as the modern Babylon.

The American authorities responsible for the entertainment of their troops in the 1940s found the situation incredible. Manchester, reported one consul, 'has the appearance of a very grim town. It is particularly lonely on Sundays when the soldiers come in.' Another American consular official described the situation in Birmingham: 'Outside of two very expensive and relatively small restaurants operated by the leading local hotels there is in cold fact not a good eating place in the town. Moreover, aside from cinemas and a limited number of cheap but rigidly regulated dance halls, there is virtually nothing to interest the average soldier.'

Provincial Britain at mid-century was a miserable place. To establish any sort of social base in these places was a considerable achievement. Most local police forces and municipalities discouraged the development of any new social amenities and tied in a mass of red tape those who tried to open new places. That a subculture should have existed at all in such a wasteland was nothing short of miraculous. That it did survive was largely due to the determination, tenacity and defiance of that most vilified segment of homosexual society, the queens – the men who chose through their camp manner, their effeminacy, their use of cosmetics and flamboyant dress to advertise their revolt against the heterosexual dictatorship.

Too little is known of how these men negotiated their lives, though court records offer some revealing insights. It was the queens who formed the nucleus of the subculture. Their patronage and their visibility attracted camp followers to the places where they established their court. The men who came to pay court often ridiculed and despised the queens, indeed it was almost a matter of course that they should do so, part of the normal ritual expected by the queens. The men who clustered around them wore all sorts of labels but all were interested enough in homosexual sex to seek out this world. There were others who either confined their activities to the cottages or resisted all temptation and stayed away, too terrified in many cases to make any sort of contact with a wider homosexual community. There is even some indication that there were emerging in Britain at this time homosexual men who rejected the old camp stereotypes and chose instead an exaggerated masculinity through body-building and the gym, but such a movement was thwarted by the failure of tight-fisted local authorities to support adequate sporting facilities. It was the queens who provided the social space which was the lifeline for many homosexually inclined men in post-war Britain.

Many of those who gave evidence to the Wolfenden Committee knew of the existence of such places. They habitually described them in the most lurid ways, turning them into 'sodomy clubs', 'schools of vice' or even 'dens of iniquity'. All were agreed that such places were evil. The Wolfenden Committee was as keen as everyone else that these places should disappear. They excited all sorts of fears, most notably as venues for the infamous 'homosexual orgies' that haunted the imagination of committee members and witnesses alike. It was fear of such orgies that determined the committee's definition of what might constitute a private situation. A situation was private only if two adult men were quite alone; the presence of any other person (male or female) rendered any acts performed illegal, even if the other person was not a participant. This definition developed in discussions of the committee, but in the final report the committee agreed to leave the definition of privacy up to the courts.

The authorities wanted to destroy the limited social space occupied by male homosexual culture. As was suggested earlier, the Wolfenden proposals to 'clean up the streets' by removing prostitutes from them had a very damaging impact on the homosexual subculture. Many social venues attracted female prostitutes as well as male homosexuals. In Cambridge, for example, the Baron of Beef where the city's prostitutes drank was also the local gay bar. American servicemen were much in evidence in the bar, attracted chiefly by the girls, but a few also took the chance for a walk on the wild side. The committee had never thought about this connection but most of its members would have been pleased by the consequences of their proposals.

The complementary connection between prostitutes and homosexuality is vividly captured by the testimony of John Alcock, a Birmingham boy evacuated to Herefordshire during the war. When he was teenager he

used to meet a lot of soldiers and American airforce men in the street and I'd stand outside the USO canteen and ask American soldiers for chewing gum. I was a very pretty boy and I was always being taken for cups of tea and things like that. I used to stand outside public toilets, not knowing what I was there for but I knew there was action of some sort there. And I remember a lovely lady by the name of Nellie, who was a prostitute. She warned me about the police and said if anyone was to ask for a woman to come and fetch her, and if anyone asked her for a boy then she would fetch me! I can't remember her ever bringing me any customers and I'm sure I didn't take her any either, but I would always get a constant supply of cigarettes from Nellie.

Venues such as the Baron of Beef were an essential feature of homosexual life. A police campaign directed at these places would have been more damaging to the practice of homosexuality in Britain than any witch-hunt. It was in these places that homosexually inclined men could meet not only lovers, but could establish their own circle of friends. The café, the pub, the club or the steam bath played a significant role in the transmission of homosexual identities. They provided the participants in these activities access to an accumulation of homosexual folklore, a rich cultural tradition passed down from generation to generation. It was a way of countering the dominant heterosexual ideology promoted by much of the rest of British society and culture.

In a characteristic lapse of imagination the Wolfenden Committee never considered how the responsible and respectable homosexuals it so cherished were to meet their partners so that they could establish their pseudo-heterosexual 'marriages'. Neither did it contemplate how someone in his teenage years or early twenties would make contact with like-minded souls with whom to share and explore his guilty secret. The emphasis instead was on 'exhibition', 'proselytisers', 'corrupters of youth' and the ubiquitous orgies. This really was an intellectual evasion, a simple refusal to think out its position. Committee members could accept that adult homosexuals existed, but imagined that they would simply refrain from expressing their sexuality until they reached adulthood.

The experts on homosexuality agreed that men who identified themselves as homosexual tended to be unhappier than their peers. Dr Gibbens of the Institute of Psychiatry thought they were 'an unhappy group, who know they are on the edge of a lot of trouble socially and from the mental health point of view'. Canon Demant went further: 'There are certain predisposing constitutional causes which make them both unhappy and homosexual.' A comforting doctrine for the heterosexual dictatorship to peddle.

Connected to this generalisation was a complaint about the sense of superiority exhibited by the more openly homosexual men (predominantly queens) which clearly rattled those in authority. Policemen, lawyers and judges were much irritated by their show of defiance. There is no doubt that men who adopted a defiant attitude and did not show proper penitence in the dock were rewarded with tougher (and usually custodial) sentences. The sense of superiority that they described was often a result of exposure to the subculture, generating a pride in their membership of a wider homosexual community and as heirs to a particular cultural and historical tradition. A recurring feature of such philosophies was the strong appeal to the past combined with a powerful optimism about freedom in the future.

Laura Hobson in her novel *Consenting Adult* (1975) conveys the sense of power that comes from such meditations on the past. Jeff, the young homosexual hero, remembers that there 'were people who were homosexual that you could be proud of, Leonardo and Michelangelo and Plato and Tchaikovsky and also plenty of living people, famous playwrights and composers and conductors and authors. The string of names came quickly because he had so often gone over them. Telling my beads, he had once thought . . .' Such lists of famous men, living as well as dead, who were identified as homosexual provided another way of countering the prevalent assumption propagated by scholars as well as journalists and other writers that the past had been almost exclusively heterosexual.

The belief in a better future was usually focused on a repeal of the laws against homosexuality. Repeal of the laws would certainly bring benefits to homosexually inclined men, but fewer than they liked to think. They simplistically assumed that a change in the law would produce a transformation in the position of the homosexual in society. What they tended to underestimate was the power of homophobia, an ugly word for a peculiarly unpleasant sentiment, which has deep roots in our society and many well-placed advocates to perpetuate it. This naïvety embraced the Wildeblood interpretation of the 1950s, and in particular disposed homosexuals to a peculiarly benevolent attitude to Wolfenden who came to be seen as their emancipator – a role which he himself found rather difficult to embrace. In the 1940s and 1950s it was easy to believe in the paramount importance of Parliament and the law. Such institutions went virtually unchallenged at the time, and citizens were lulled into the illusion that the legislative activities of the Mother of Parliaments really could make a difference to their lives.

In the last four decades a considerable improvement has taken place in the position of gay men in British society. Principally this has been achieved by the massive expansion of the subculture, the thing least desired by the Wolfenden Committee or those liberals promoting homosexual law reform. In achieving that progress pride of place must go to the men and women radicalised by Gay Liberation in the early 1970s, some of whom established a gay press in Britain which greatly strengthened the subculture. The courage, the talent, the ingenuity and persistence of the men and women who created *Gay News* in the summer of 1972 deserve wider recognition because it stimulated the greatest leap forward in the history of homosexuality in Britain, a truly heroic moment.

However, facilities today are still concentrated in London and the largest cities, and for those living in small towns or villages the situation is often as bleak as it was in the 1950s. It is still difficult for teenagers to explore their homosexuality since most families remain hostile to the homosexuality of their offspring, even those liberals who preach tolerance for others. At the other end of the spectrum, many older men feel alienated by the commercialisation of the homosexual scene and a culture that appeals primarily to the young. It is possible that the networks of the 1940s and 1950s adopted a more tolerant attitude to the older men, who came to have some of the privileges accorded the parish elder. Nevertheless, however one draws up the balance sheet the credit side undoubtedly far outweighs the debit side and, in the major cities at least, there appears to be some acceptance of homosexual equality – a concept alien to the vast majority of Britons forty years ago.

Victims

Social hostility in a culture so aggressively heterosexual and intolerant of difference often exposed homosexually inclined men to blackmail and sometimes led them to take their own lives. There is a good deal of anecdotal evidence to suggest the prevalence of both blackmail and suicide, and such testimony has helped to shape our perception of the post-war era. Trevor-Roper in his memorandum to the Wolfenden Committee makes a powerful case against the existing law by documenting blackmail cases and suicides in his circle and the circles of his friends. The exposure of men to blackmail was the most powerful weapon in the reformer's armoury; it dominated the rhetoric of the reformers up until they achieved victory in 1967. It is of course difficult for the historian to test, something about which he must remain largely sceptical. Examinations of the criminal cases involving blackmail and the coroners' reports on suicides expose many facts which make us qualify the prevailing myths but cannot be assumed to be anything more than a rather arbitrary selection of cases, the tip possibly of an iceberg that will always remain hidden from the historian however ingeniously he tries to expose it.

In 1961 the film director Basil Dearden and producer Michael Relph, the team that produced *The Blue Lamp*, brought out another documentary thriller, *Victim*, starring the villain from their earlier film, Dirk Bogarde. Bogarde had a good 1950s: the Rank Organisation turned him into a matinée idol, a wholesome native pin-up whose cheerful manner endeared him to the home audience. Between *The Blue Lamp* and *Victim* Bogarde made many films, most of them pap, but sometimes the mask slipped and exposed his darker and more sensual side (much in evidence in his portrayal of the police killer Riley in *The Blue Lamp*). There was also, but this was rarer still, the camper Bogarde, a sensibility he articulated in 'a gay Mexican western about a bad bandit and a good priest', *The Singer Not the Song*. *The Times* film critic, John Russell Taylor, observed that he looked 'like a latterday Queen Kelly'; his black shiny leather pants, so tight they looked as if they were sprayed on, were much admired.

Accepting the role of Melvin Farr, the homosexual hero of *Victim*, was an extremely brave act by Bogarde. Other leading men had turned the role down because of the damage that it might do to their careers. In Bogarde's case it allowed him to turn his back on his career as a matinée idol and become a leading actor in European cinema during the 1960s, when he would be directed by Losey, Visconti and Fassbinder. Accepting the part 'was the wisest decision I ever made in my cinematic life'. The film was a 'tremendous success, pleasing us and confounding our detractors. The countless letters of gratitude which flooded in were proof enough of that, and I had achieved what I had longed to do for so long, to be in a film which disturbed, educated, and illuminated as well as merely giving entertainment.'

The film looks incredibly dated today, and it is not easy to understand its impact, but it was the first time in the British cinema that one man had said to another that he loved him. Bogarde wrote that scene and insisted that it should be included: 'I said "There's no point in half-measures. We either make a film about queers or we don't." I believe the pictures make a lot of difference to a lot of people's lives.'

The film told the story of Farr, an upper-middle-class barrister living in an elegant house in West London with his wife (played by Sylvia Sims). They are childless, a state to which there are many allusions. Farr has had a homosexual relationship with a young working-class wages clerk, Jack Barrett, who lives in a bed-sit. A blackmail gang secures a photograph of Farr and Barrett together and blackmails Barrett. Desperate, he tries to contact Farr, who refuses to see him, thinking that he is trying to blackmail him. Barrett starts to steal from his employers and is caught and arrested by the police. While in custody he commits suicide. Evidence links him to Farr who is seen by the police. Farr decides to seek out the gang even if it means that he must sacrifice his own marriage and career. He admits his homosexuality to his wife and they part. After many obstacles are thrown in his path, Farr finds and breaks the gang, in scenes similar to those in *The Blue Lamp* when the police search for Riley. One of the blackmailers has a picture of Michelangelo's *David* on his wall.

There were no queens in *Victim*; the homosexuals portrayed were of a type that Peter Wildeblood would have approved. Dennis Price and Anthony Nicholls played toffs, upper-class poofs, and nobody was displayed who might frighten the general public. One scene was set in the Salisbury in St Martin's Lane, which was then and for many years afterwards one of London's leading gay pubs.

The messages that the film reinforced may have helped the passage of homosexual law reform, but they fostered illusions about the homosexual community that also did much harm. The film-makers' desire to sanitise the homosexual subculture by excluding queens denied the importance of what was a key element in the culture and eliminated the homosexual who most annoyed a straight public by his visibility and difference. Bogarde and his friends, upon whom, as one character says, 'nature had played a dirty trick', were not much different from everyone else, with a healthy desire to conform. In a film that was marketed as a realistic slice of life this was a serious omission. More problematic was the propagation of the idea that homosexuals were victims who needed the pity of straight people in order to have a tolerable life. This may have increased public support for the Wolfenden proposals, as is sometimes suggested, but it was at a high cost. When more aggressive homosexuals became visible in the early 1970s the shock was considerable and it inevitably fuelled a backlash against repeal that claimed that homosexuals had abused the freedom they had been granted. The subculture was certainly vulnerable to unscrupulous characters but it was also stronger and more menacing than liberals liked to think. Even in the 1950s there were homosexual men who did not want the sort of assimilation into the mainstream offered to them by the reformers. The film's most dangerous message was its sympathetic portrayal of the police, several of whom emerge as decent, compassionate and efficient fellows, not too different from the chaps encountered all those years ago in Dock Green. But the good policeman was as much a myth as the homosexual victim, and it is amusing that it should have been the same team that produced both films.

The American authorities refused to give *Victim* a general release in the United States. *Time* magazine explained that 'what seems at first an attack on extortion seems at last a coyly sensational exploitation of homosexuality as a theme – and what's more offensive, an implicit approval of homosexuality as a practice . . . Nowhere does the film suggest that homosexuality is a serious (but often curable) neurosis that attacks the biological basis of life itself.'

Playing Down

At the first meeting of the Wolfenden Committee the chairman asked Philip Allen from the Home Office about blackmail: 'It is commonly believed, is it not, that one of the difficulties about the present law is that it does encourage blackmail?'

Almost all articles and many letters advocating homosexual law reform suggested that the present law encouraged blackmail. Usually they cited in support two distinguished authorities, Sir Travers Humphreys, a former high court judge, and Lord Jowitt, another eminent lawyer who was Attorney-General in the second MacDonald government (1929–31) and Lord Chancellor in the Attlee government (1945–51). Humphreys, who had been a junior counsel at the Wilde trial, repeatedly described the Labouchère amendment as the 'blackmailer's charter'. He is chiefly responsible for the exaggeration of the importance of that amendment which has been a feature of much modern writing on male homosexuality. Bizarrely he completely ignored the 1861 Act under which men were as liable to be blackmailed as they were under the 1885 Act. Humphreys believed strongly in homosexual law reform and supported repeal of the Labouchère amendment which he believed had caused much mischief. Jowitt observed in a speech delivered in the House of Lords in May 1954 that when he had been Attorney-General 95 per cent of the blackmail cases had involved homosexuality.

One barrister estimated that three-quarters of all suicides were blackmailed homosexuals. Sir Compton Mackenzie, a writer with many homosexual friends, overheard the remark which began him thinking of the story that he would publish as *Thin Ice*, about a homosexual politician who is blackmailed. The main character was mainly based on his friend Lord Lloyd (who had died in 1941) but had elements of Tom Driberg and Chips Channon as well.

It was essential for the Home Office that the Wolfenden Committee did not endorse or support this connection, or at least that it would not be given too much prominence in the final report. Wolfenden accordingly resisted pressure to include homosexual blackmail in the final report on the grounds that the issue was too 'emotive' and that the committee had not been satisfied on the basis of the evidence that they had received that such a connection existed. This conclusion was a personal triumph for James Adair, the Scottish attorney, who repeatedly challenged reformers to demonstrate the connection. Adair promoted the argument that blackmail would occur with or without the decriminalisation of homosexuality, in that victims were more afraid of social exposure than criminal prosecution. As a practising lawyer with considerable experience of criminal law he possessed a much better understanding of blackmail cases than any other member of the committee or, it would seem, of any of the reformers who came before them as witnesses.

Philip Allen set the ball rolling on 15 October 1954, replying to Wolfenden's question with his usual precision:

Allen: Yes [it is commonly believed that there is a connection] but I do not think anyone has produced any facts to support it.

Rees: Would the Home Office on the whole agree with that?

Allen: I think we should be extremely cautious and say there is no evidence on which to form any opinion.

Rees: You would say there is no available evidence?

Allen: Yes.

Curran: I remember hearing Lord Jowitt in an address referring to section 11 of the Criminal Law Amendment Act, 1885 [the Labouchère amendment] as the 'blackmailer's charter'. It is very important to refute such a generalised view [?]

Allen: I can hardly speak disrespectfully of a former Lord Chancellor, but I do not know on what he was basing the remarks.

Wolfenden: I think it is fair to say, as they [the Home Office] said in their paper and as we considered it yesterday, that it is probable that the blackmailer relies on his fear of social exposure rather than his fear of criminal proceedings. That presumably would hold whether the law stays as it is or not . . .

Adair: One must link it up in some way, because after all, it is because of the skeleton in the cupboard that the possibility of blackmail arises, but it is the desire not to have that skeleton produced that produces the money.

Wolfenden: Yes, but there is a distinction whether the production of the skeleton is feared because of legal consequences or whether it is feared because of social disrepute. I do not know whether there is any connection between those two or not.

Rees: In the mind of the person blackmailed, very close. The man being blackmailed is not in a position to draw these very fine distinctions.

Wolfenden: Mr. Wells produced yesterday a piece of historical evidence that blackmail was operative in this sort of field before 1886.

Wolfenden's response to a critical comment from Rees is the characteristic introduction of a *non sequitur*. Wells had raised the case of Lord Castlereagh, British Foreign Secretary 1812–22 who committed suicide in 1822. It was rumoured that Castlereagh had taken his life because he was being blackmailed by someone who had discovered that he was having a homosexual affair. Wells, an MP, probably heard the story from his parliamentary colleague, the ubiquitous Harford Montgomery Hyde. It was one of Hyde's party pieces. He had worked for Castlereagh's descendants, the Londonderrys, during the 1930s and was well-versed in the family's scandal. The family were extremely sensitive about the story and invested much energy, as late as the 1930s, to spike the tale, even supporting sympathetic historians willing to produce other explanations for the suicide. Hyde eventually turned his story into a rather thin and disappointing book. By then he was convinced that the blackmail story was true and that Castlereagh had had a homosexual affair. The book, however, does not convince and the only verdict that can be returned even after considering Hyde's special pleading is an open verdict.

What did the possible blackmailing of a famous British statesman have to do with the possible connection between blackmail and the laws criminalising male homosexuality? The fact that blackmail existed before 1886? Wolfenden was clearly no historian – this really was clutching at some very flimsy straws for a man usually cautious about according any piece of evidence or information the accolade of 'fact'. Rees returned to the matter in hand:

Rees: But the fact that there were cases where people were blackmailed for social exposure does not mean merely the social exposure and no criminal prosecution . . .

Allen: . . . there is a very strong public impression that there was a close connection between the present law and blackmail in this matter – distinct altogether from, or distinguishable from the social disrepute involved. I am sure a lot of people think that – and apparently a former Lord Chancellor thought so . . .

Diplock: The two must inevitably be connected. So long as there is criminal sanction the victim, if he is being blackmailed, knows there will be full publicity. If there is no criminal sanction perhaps only his wife and friends know and not the newspapers, and the penalty for paying is much less.

Wells: I would not like extreme decisions to be drawn from my example, because obviously a Foreign Secretary is different from other people!

The problem of course, as Allen was quick to point out, was evidence. How can one establish that a connection existed? The court cases offer one way of examining the issue, but it is possible that the vast majority of cases never came before the courts and we are thrown back on speculation.

Eighty to one hundred and ten blackmail cases came before the British courts during the 1940s and 1950s each year. Most were metropolitan and most involved the threat to expose some sexual action, activity or connection. The vast majority of these cases involved heterosexual sex, activity that was not criminal. The victims were principally rich men, middle-aged and older, many of them professionals but with a large number of businessmen and independently wealthy men amongst their number. Many had been drawn into paying for sex in some way. Homosexual blackmail often developed out of an association with a male prostitute. Most men threatening to expose another's homosexuality were usually homosexual themselves, and blackmailers usually operated within the metropolitan homosexual subculture. Scrutiny of the cases from 1929 to 1959 does not support Jowitt's memory – at no point were 95 per cent of blackmail cases associated with homosexuality.

A study of blackmail in mid-century Britain shows how keen respectable men were to protect their reputations from any accusation of sexual impropriety. Many of their neighbours were only too ready to suggest that there was no smoke without fire. The evidence confirms how tightly conformist much of British society was. Any sexual activity outside marriage was damaging. As a consequence many middle-class men took risks when they travelled away from home, especially to London, to indulge their sexual tastes and inevitably many were trapped by unscrupulous men and women who bled them of their wealth. Homosexual men faced a double risk in so far as they might face criminal prosecution as well. It is possible that this inhibited them from approaching the police and denouncing their blackmailer. The situation was, as Trevor-Roper pointed out, further complicated by the existence of blackmailers working from within the protection of the police station.

The record of the police on blackmail generally seems to be good. The anonymity of the victim was achieved and the only case that can be discovered where a victim was unmasked was done on the orders of Mr Justice Devlin, who believed in a 1950 case that the homosexual crimes of the victim far outweighed the activities of his blackmailer and refused to continue the case unless the man revealed his identity. The man refused, but it was academic; encouraged by the judge's action, the newspapers named him. The police were angry. They managed to charge the black-mailer with blackmailing another man and suceessfully prosecuted him.

The Wolfenden Committee did as the Home Office bid it. On 12 March 1956, it came to the following conclusion: 'Blackmailing was mentioned and it was agreed that the subject should be brought up, and played down in the report: the "blackmailer's charter" dictum must be modified. The change in the law would not in any event remove the risk of blackmail, which often used a threat of social rather than criminal exposure.' It was a victory for Allen and Adair.

These sentiments made their way into the final report. Despite what many thought, and often suggested in speeches after the publication of the Wolfenden Report in 1957, the committee provided much less support for the connection between blackmail and the operation of the existing law in the final report:

> These figures [for blackmail cases] represent an average of eight cases a year, and even allowing for the reluctance of the victim to approach the police, they suggest that the amount of blackmail which takes place has been considerably exaggerated in the popular mind.
>
> We will certainly not go so far as some of our witnesses have done and suggest that the opportunities for blackmail inherent in the present law would be sufficient ground for changing it. We have found it hard to decide whether the blackmailer's primary weapon is the threat of disclosure to the police, with the attendant legal consequences or the threat of disclosure to the victim's relatives, employer or friends, with the attendant social consequences. It may well be that the latter is the more effective weapon; but it may be true that it would lose much of its edge if the social consequences were not associated with (or indeed dependent upon) the present legal position.

The Soho Blackmail Gang of the 1930s

A succession of cases between the war revealed the existence of a highly organised blackmailing racket based in the West End of London. This racket trapped wealthy men, often visitors to the capital, by setting them up with pretty younger men who would lead them to their lodgings, where the pair would be disturbed as they began to make love. An older man would then arrive who claimed to be the brother of the young man and who would demand that the wealthy man should compensate the family for the injury that he had done them by corrupting the young man. More money might later be extracted to pay for the younger brother's passage overseas to remove him from the temptations of the capital. The man who ran the racket and played the part of the older brother was usually Harry Raymond.

Raymond had been convicted of blackmail in 1933 and sentenced to five years. He was released in October 1936 but convicted again at the end of 1937 to a sentence of seven years, after which point he disappears from view. Raymond, who was as old as the century, owned a café in Rupert Street, Soho, described by police 'as the resort of male perverts and women of ill-repute'. He also owned other property in Soho and he let rooms to prostitutes. A former actor, he was described by the *News of the World* as 'long-haired and glassy eyed'. He had resorted to blackmailing as his acting career collapsed in the early 1930s. He was caught mainly because he boasted so much of his activities, which it was claimed brought him £60,000 a year. He gambled heavily; his lounge suits cost £20 each, and he had thirty in his wardrobe. His stage name was Robert Clive Gould. He appeared in West End shows: *The Rising Generation* with Ivor Novello at Wyndham's; *The Fire Brand* and *Seven Days Leave* at the Lyceum. He had been a member of the cast of the first production of Barrie's *Peter Pan*. He ran forty agents who sought out their victims in cinemas, theatres, hotels and restaurants; almost all, like Raymond, were members of the homosexual fraternity. This blackmailing gang functioned as did many blackmailers from within the subculture. The cases of the 1950s, however, do not reveal such an organised group, as blackmail then appears to have taken place on a much smaller scale.

The Warhurst Case

A particularly disturbing blackmail case came to trial in March 1955. Two police constables from the Metropolitan Police, Thomas Collister, twenty-two (of Herne Hill) and John Warhurst, twenty-four (from Tulse Hill), both stationed at Brixton police station, were found guilty of blackmailing Kenneth Lindsay Jefferies. Jefferies was a commercial traveller staying at a hotel in the West End when he was stopped by Collister in Leicester Square. Collister asked him for a light. He told Jefferies that he was on leave from the Merchant Navy but that he had no money and no place to stay. Jefferies offered to pay for his accommodation at his hotel. After he had made the offer Collister produced his police warrant card: 'I am going to take you to the police station on a charge of importuning for an immoral purpose.' At this point Warhurst arrived and was introduced by Collister to Jefferies as 'my sergeant'. After some discussion they agreed to take some money from Jefferies and agreed to collect more from him the following evening.

Jefferies went immediately to the police who supervised his meeting the following evening with the two off-duty constables. After Jefferies handed a £5 note to Warhurst, police arrested him and his colleague. They both pleaded not guilty, claiming rather lamely that they were giving Jefferies some counselling 'regarding his tendencies'. The jury found them guilty and sentenced them each to two years' imprisonment. The prosecution also brought to the attention of the court the savings of Collister, which in the months before the Jefferies incident amounted to a great deal more than he could have earned as a policeman.

A report of the case appeared in the *Manchester Guardian* on 30 March 1955, at a time when all the London newspapers were on strike. A man sent the cutting to Wolfenden. Wolfenden did not acknowledge the letter. The cutting was put away in a file and not circulated to the committee.

Suicide

Roger Walker was a nineteen-year-old undergraduate reading History at Pembroke College, Cambridge. In the summer of 1955 he sat Part One of the Historical Tripos and was three days away from the announcement of the examination results when he took his own life. It is the custom in Cambridge for suicide inquests on undergraduates not to probe very deeply. Colleges wish to minimise the embarrassment caused by such events and coroners are usually willing to resolve the business to their satisfaction. At the Walker inquest the coroner was about to commence his summing-up when the boy's parents asked that some further evidence be heard.

Peter Gray, another historian who lived in a neighbouring hostel, was a friend of the deceased. He told the court that Walker was optimistic about the examination results; he predicted that he would get a first (in fact he got a 2.1). He had, however, 'psychological worries'. Asked by the coroner if he could explain Walker's action, he replied that he had 'had a mounting fear of persecution – fear of being regarded as a sexual invert or as a social outcast'. Walker had apparently said certain things that Gray had not taken seriously.

Brian Wedmore, another friend, a second-year lawyer from Jesus, was the next person to come into the witness box. He told the coroner that Walker had been a homosexual:

Coroner: That is to your knowledge?
Wedmore: Yes. That is to my knowledge, and he did suffer from the unfortunate ignorance of this subject and the number of people who are involved in it. And I think he would have wished his death would do something to alleviate . . .

The coroner interrupted him:

> Well, I do not think we can have that. All you know was he was
> homosexual and was suffering persecution? I do not think he was
> really being persecuted, but suffering from that barrier that seems to
> exist between people who are homosexual and people who could
> help if only the sufferer would seek help.

Wedmore added that Walker had moved out of college the previous term
because of certain incidents and had taken a room in one of the college
hostels in Lensfield Road.

Walker's father, a hotelier from Barrow-in-Furness, was then at his own
request recalled to the witness box. He told the court that he had been
surprised and shocked at what he had heard and wished them mentioned
so that they could benefit others:

> Coroner: You mean mention of this case might be a deterrent to
> other men?
> Mr Walker: Not so much a deterrent as to lead them to seek advice.
> Coroner: I am sorry that you should have learned what you say since
> you have been here.

Mrs Walker then came forward and told of the persecution her son had
suffered at his grammar school. He was apparently troubled, sensitive at
being different from others and there had been jealousy of his ability. She
told the court of her son's experiences and of her desire that the persecution of homosexuals should end. The coroner interrupted her:

> . . . this is a court to find the cause of death. There is no evidence before
> me of persecution – in the sense that the word implies. You cannot go
> beyond saying this will act as a deterrent to other young men who might
> feel similarly disposed. I think that is as far as you can go.

The final witness was Walker's closest friend John Russell Taylor, another
second-year student from Jesus. Taylor was reading English and was a
few days away from notching up the first of his two firsts.

> He told me more than he told others. Most of the events of which
> he spoke took place this term and some last term, the effect of which
> were to depress him and make him feel friends and people who knew
> him could not understand his problem and that people were against
> him. He was subjected in his own college and in the street to insults.
> He dressed unusually and that was generally the first cause of insult.
> People saw his clothes and ridiculed him.

The coroner asked Taylor if Walker had dressed 'in the Edwardian manner'.

'Well,' replied Taylor, 'he dressed artistically. His clothes were unusual.' Taylor said that Walker had been depressed when people shouted things at him. Walker, being very sensitive, was deeply upset and would be dejected for two or three days by the most minor slight. The coroner was puzzled: 'Is this not the reason why he should not have mended his ways?' 'The position', Taylor said, 'was more complicated than that; it was not a mater of choice. He had said he wished to discuss matters with a psychiatrist, but had very little hope of becoming completely normal.' After these interruptions the coroner returned to his summing up:

> One looked [he said] to ascertain as far as possible why such a promising young man should have taken this course and as much as one would have liked to have kept some of the circumstances in the background, that was not now possible; the circumstances were put forward as the possible reason for the act. The Coroner advanced the view that a correct course would have been to have sought advice.
>
> While Mr. Wallis [the Coroner] was putting this view, the deceased's mother called out 'Oh, no!' leading the Coroner to ask her not to interrupt.
>
> Continuing, he said deceased had not co-operated with [the] psychiatrist and was in a frame of mind indicating fear of being persecuted. He (the Coroner) had yet to learn why persecution was good and sufficient reason for a young man to take his own life.
>
> With that uppermost in his mind, it had been shown, he regarded himself as an outcast and could no more look other people in the face. In that frame of mind he decided to end his own life and [he] did so by carbon monoxide poisoning.

Many national newspapers carried reports of the inquest.

On the morning of the inquest Walker's friends had met his parents and they talked about him. They told them that he had been homosexual, and while neither was completely surprised, it was something that helped them better understand why their son had taken his life. Both his mother and his father were, as the court record shows, unusually tolerant of homosexuality. With the other undergraduates they became determined to use Roger's death as a way of advertising the plight of young homosexuals. The parents probably believed this more than the undergraduates. The students did see the advantages of ascribing Walker's death to this cause for the sake of the wider movement, so that he would not have died entirely in vain.

John Russell Taylor, who progressed through many posts in arts journalism since serving as *The Times* film critic in the 1960s, is now art editor of that newspaper and vividly remembers the death of his close friend. Looking back he is less certain that Walker took his life for the reasons he suggested in court, and now thinks that it had more to do with his results. Walker desperately wanted a first to achieve an academic career and had been disappointed by his performance that summer. Since then Taylor has discovered that the Walker family had a history of mental instability; his father some years later committed suicide in front of the entire family.

Far from being an outcast, Walker had been at the centre of a homosexual network with connections across the university. It was composed almost entirely of grammar school boys like Walker; for much of the post-war period a sort of social apartheid operated in most Cambridge colleges, dividing the products of the public schools from their contemporaries who have come from the grammar schools. There was a suspicion amongst the grammar school boys that they had much less homosexual sex than their public school peers. These grammar school undergraduates erected their own subculture within the university largely based on an addiction to the 1890s and the 1920s, with a particular devotion to Beardsley and Firbank, while according a special place of reverence to Wilde. They were camp and dressed, as Taylor told the coroner, 'artistically'; fluffy angora sweaters were much in evidence.

Walker was determined to get to know every queer undergraduate at Cambridge and was a great collector of gossip. He collected names for a census and could count at least one hundred and twenty committed homosexuals among the undergraduate population. (Representatives of the Cambridge LesBiGay Society told me in February 1996, when I was giving a paper on 'Queer History' at Fitzwilliam, that four hundred undergraduates were on their mailing list but only a quarter of that number came to social events. The university has expanded hugely since the 1950s and Walker's census suggests that fairly visible gays made up a larger proportion of the university at that time than they do today.) Walker and his friends held giant parties to which they invited queers from across the university, along with a few pretty straight guys for decoration. They went to two city pubs, the Baron of Beef and the Sugar Loaf, which had strong gay associations; the bar staff at the Sugar Loaf, unusually, were themselves gay. Walker and others believed in making their homosexuality obvious. Taylor believes that relations with the rest of the undergraduate population were good, and that the insults Walker received came from townies. Taylor even remembers gays who played on the rugby team.

Many members of the group had already done their National Service, which probably made them more independently-minded and knowledgeable than most undergraduate generations. Walker's was the year which had come up to Cambridge in the autumn of 1953 and experienced at first-hand the reaction to the Gielgud conviction and the Montagu cases, and the accompanying media coverage of the problem of homosexuality. Walker also belonged to a group which met the poet Thom Gunn when he returned to Cambridge after a visit to the USA and saw the uniform of the future, the leather jacket and levis that Gunn now wore.

Taylor remembers his friend as the possessor of a 'clever, insightful mind . . . quick and mercurial' but easily bored and with an 'underlying melancholy'. He loved the movies and, like many gay men before and since, idolised the screen goddesses – he had a special attachment to Joan Crawford and Greta Garbo. Cambridge undergraduates were lucky in possessing possibly the best cinema in Britain, the Rex, run by Leslie Halliwell. It was the only cinema in Britain that showed Marlon Brando's *The Wild Ones* when it was released in 1954. Walker was better situated than most other teenage homosexuals in 1955, and yet he took his own life.

The Walker suicide exposes the problem of trying to explain why somebody kills himself. My trawl of the coroners' reports produced no pattern that would point to a higher suicide rate amongst homosexually inclined men than other social groups. The only pattern that emerged exposed another casualty of the heterosexual dictatorship, the high number of lonely spinsters who decided that they were better off dead. Even contemporaries realised that London's bed-sitterdom produced a large number of middle-aged female suicides, women who felt out of place in a society that prized marriage above everything else. These middle-aged women were much worse off than their male homosexual contemporaries. They earned substantially less and did not have access (unless they belonged to a church) to a social network that would allow them to meet others who shared their predicament.

Patrick Trevor-Roper brought the Walker case before the Wolfenden Committee, but the records of the committee suggest that it was never discussed.

5

Report and Response

The actual writing of the Wolfenden Report was the work largely of three men, Wolfenden, Demant and Roberts. From an early stage of the work Wolfenden identified Demant as a sympathetic ally. They shared many interests, most notably a commitment to Anglicanism, and considerable experience of academic administration. They were both the type of dons who found themselves sitting on committees and delivering judgements, whether weighing the relative merits of individuals for posts and places or resolving the sorts of conflicts that developed within institutions. They were both very skilful operators with a wide experience of British institutions that gave them a natural sympathy for authority, an ability to turn a blind eye at the appropriate moment and to avoid confrontations.

Foxy Dons

Wolfenden, as we have seen, was extremely skilled at taking cues from authorities that mattered. He treated the senior civil servants and the legal establishment much as he might have courted the governors when he was a public school headmaster. He knew how to ingratiate himself with men senior to himself, and figures in authority found his manner and his mode of address particularly pleasing. He was extremely discreet and reticent and could as a consequence be trusted with confidential material. The Home Office never needed to tell Wolfenden precisely what to do, for he did it instinctively anyway, which made him a perfect chairman of the committee.

During the committee proceedings Demant often came to Wolfenden's assistance when one of the more difficult members of the committee challenged him. Over the three years, Wolfenden constructed a working majority who came to trust his judgement and would as a result support him against the awkward squad. There was only one major issue where he failed to carry the committee with him. Wolfenden wanted to recommend that buggery remain a criminal offence even if performed in private between consenting male adults. This was what Goddard had recommended in his testimony and it is clear that Wolfenden desperately wanted to shape the committee's recommendations according to the prejudices of the Lord Chief Justice of England, a man he much admired, as did many other Britons at that time. But the committee overwhelmingly rejected the proposal – Wolfenden's only major defeat. Wolfenden nevertheless was able to ensure that the following paragraph be inserted in the final report: 'We believe that there is some case for retaining buggery as a separate offence; and there may even be a case for retaining the present maximum penalty of life imprisonment for really serious cases.'

Wolfenden also enjoyed the support of the secretary, W. Conwy Roberts. Wolfenden was a busy man with fingers in many pies and he appreciated the assistance that he received from Roberts. Unfortunately Roberts's ineffectiveness as an administrator and a draftsman were exposed during the process of writing the report. Wolfenden foolishly delegated this task to Roberts and the result was an extremely clumsy and ill-prepared draft. The early drafts were so poor that they ought to have been ripped up, but instead the committee spent months amending and adjusting them, with Wolfenden and Demant indulging their passion for linguistic fastidiousness and ambiguity. The two dons spent much time and energy fussing over the text. Both men believed that their report, whatever its conclusion, was dynamite and they devoted their energies to minimising the explosion: 'The report would have to contain a very positive introduction and stress that the legal change would not mean that every act between consenting adults in private were unobjectionable morally and socially.'

Wolfenden and Demant tried hard to anticipate the reaction to their findings and as a consequence attempted to produce a document that could satisfy reformers as well as moralists. At a meeting on 12 March 1956 Demant insisted that 'the Committee's wording must be of the essence of tact and respectfulness'. Wolfenden and Demant were for ever trying to second guess the reaction of the Home Office, Parliament and the press and throughout they amended the Roberts text to this end.

In a justly famous passage the committee announced that homosexuality was not a disease – a fairly radical suggestion in the mid-1950s. But Wolfenden and Demant ensured that a qualifying coda was added that gave a slightly different spin to the comment, converting a liberal concession into a more respectable proposal that might win over the more conservative reader: 'the claim that homosexuality is an illness carries the further implication that the sufferer cannot help it and therefore carries a diminished responsibility for his actions. Even if it were accepted that homosexuality could properly be described as a "disease" we should not accept this corollary.' It becomes a point about personal responsibility;

the sting is taken out of the concession. It rejects the disease model on conservative grounds. The report then goes on to underline its conservative credentials by suggesting that 'The existence of varying degrees of self-control is a matter of daily experience', a sentiment which all moralists could applaud. The sentence ends with an example which is almost a joke: 'the extent to which coughing can be controlled is an example.' This wonderfully off-beam remark raises as many questions as it settles. 'In what way is abstaining from sexual activity like disguising a cough?' is the sort of question that would give much pleasure to the schoolmen and is typical of the sort of convolutions to which Wolfenden and his friends were often driven.

Wolfenden's intention was to produce a document that would satisfy both reformers and moralists, but readings of the report have ignored the way in which he balanced the document to achieve this end. He failed in his intention, for readings of his report have been unanimously liberal. This was due to three developments that Wolfenden did not anticipate: the impact of the Adair minority report; the radicalism of the two doctors Curran and Whitby whose proposals attracted most readers' attention; and the immediate adoption of the report by the reform lobby, which frightened off the conservatives who had in the Adair report an immediate counterblast to the majority report. Wolfenden found himself increasingly the prisoner of the reform lobby, the process by which he would find himself canonised as a liberal saint.

Adair

Undoubtedly the cleverest tactician on the committee was James Adair. His complete refusal to contemplate any change in the law relating to homosexuality, reflecting the overwhelming opinion of the legal establishment, was evident from the outset. Adair was a particularly skilful interrogator and used his questions to undermine the liberal report that he saw emerging. He continually sought to show that blackmailing thrived not because of the law but as a consequence of social fears, and while others spoke speculatively of the long-term mental damage that might be done by homosexual activity between men and boys and adolescents he collected information about the physical damage that might be done through the act of buggery.

Wolfenden obviously found him completely exasperating but seems to have believed until quite late in the proceedings that he could manage to keep him on side; 'the more we take him with us', he wrote to Roberts in March 1956, 'the better'. He often found his intransigence useful and appealed to more liberal elements on the committee to compromise in the hope of getting Adair to sign the majority report. It took some time for him to understand that no form of words, no linguistic formula, no fudge, no piece of horse trading was going to placate Adair. English mandarins have never really understood 'No surrender', and stubbornly believe that they really can find some ingenious device to present a united front to the rest of the world.

Adair embarked on his own campaign to sell his minority report after the publication of the majority report and became a hero to the moralists. His principal converts were the Church of Scotland, of which he was an elder, and the *Daily Telegraph*. He warned readers of the *Evening Standard* on the day that the report was published about the possible consequences of accepting Wolfenden's report: 'I do not know what will happen if these recommendations become the law, but I would have the darkest fears for the future . . . I had a closer acquaintanceship with this social problem than some members of the committee.'

The most widely cited passage from Adair's report exposed possibly the greatest fear of the heterosexual dictatorship: 'The presence in a district of, for example, adult male lovers, openly and notoriously under the approval of the law is bound to have regrettable and pernicious effect on the young people of the community.' The existence of an alternative was impossible to contemplate. Privately, Adair had pleaded for the committee to remember another group in society that would be affected by reform: '[Adair] apprehended that the proposed change in the law would have a very fearful effect on many people, especially on the attitude of mothers.'

The Doctors

Equally exasperating for Wolfenden were the two doctors on the committee, Curran and Whitby, in whose hands the report would have been an exceptionally radical document. They regarded themselves as the experts and were able to win many arguments by appealing to the mysteries of science. They were consistently sceptical about the claims of witnesses (a characteristic they shared with Diplock, Rees and Adair). They were certainly the most hard-working members of the committee, doing most of the homework. It was this pair who rejected the division of homosexual types into inverts and perverts (they tended to prefer the Kinsey model of a six-point scale) which ran counter to most of the evidence they heard. They also established a distinction which had even more profound consequences. They suggested that there was a difference between homosexual men who sought adult partners and those who sought partners amongst boys who had not reached puberty. This ought to have persuaded the committee to suggest an age of consent at puberty but this was too radical even for the doctors. This created one of the major contradictions in the report: a fixed sexual identity by puberty and an age of consent set several years later. This placed the teenagers in exactly the same position as young boys. The committee was desperately keen to show its hostility to any corruption of youth, even though many other conclusions rejected this widely-accepted notion, and recommended that punishments for men over twenty-one who had sex with youths aged sixteen to twenty-one should be increased from a maximum of two years to five years, a recommendation which found its way into the 1967 Act.

It was Curran and Whitby who spiked the idea that homosexuality was contagious. They rejected the idea that a change in the law would open the floodgates and they dismissed the notion of the rake's progress as a fantasy. They were also keener than Wolfenden to emphasise the possibilities of blackmail. They educated their colleagues and did much to shape the final report. It was Wolfenden and Demant who qualified their conclusions and erected the safeguards to assure the moralists, much of whose testimony had been rejected by the doctors.

Curran and Whitby wanted much greater openness about the workings of the committee, in particular more direct quotation from the memoranda and the testimony, 'in some detail if necessary'. Wolfenden dismissed this as merely 'counting heads'; he saw no 'useful purpose in it', and he refused to countenance it. They also wanted the report to be written in a more direct style with fewer qualifications. They were impatient at the time that the draft was taking. Curran, who could be wonderfully waspish, felt that too much time was being 'consumed' in 'textual criticism'. He proposed that it would be more 'profitable . . . to concentrate on general issues that called for decisions leaving the exact wording until later'. The doctors suggested that a series of sub-committees be established to work on different sections of the report, but Wolfenden rejected this because it was 'impracticable'.

The biggest clash between the doctors and Wolfenden arose over the policing of homosexuality. Curran and Whitby seem to have been genuinely shocked by what they heard and they wanted to include an exposure of such activities in the report. They wanted to make a severe criticism of the police, particularly on the use of *agents provocateurs*. Wolfenden defended the police, drafting a passage that exonerated their conduct in entrapping men on sexual charges in public lavatories in the following terms: 'We feel bound to record that we were on the whole favourably impressed by the account they gave us of the way in which they carried out their unpleasant task. It must, in our view, be accepted that in the detection of some offences – and this is one of them – a police officer legitimately resorts to a degree of subterfuge in the course of his duty.' Legitimately? The police were being sanctioned to lie in court. At the time, such police practice was generally confined to the big cities, but within a few years it had taken root across the whole of England and Wales. The committee's failure to condemn these practices had very serious consequences for many individuals. When we assess the Wolfenden Report we should bear these men in mind. A tougher condemnation of this practice on the lines preferred by Curran and Whitby might have inhibited the spread of this police tactic in the decades that followed. Even sadder was the fact that after the mid-1950s local newspapers regularly recorded the names and addresses of men caught in lavatories, a custom which encouraged some forces to adopt this form of policing to advertise to their community their virtue, campaigning fearlessly for public decency and acting as moral guardians of the people. To suggest that police officers could 'legitimately' resort to such activity effectively licensed it.

Roberts had written to Wolfenden about the problem of how to present the police in the final report, suggesting that 'Possible corruption of the police ought perhaps to be put in and knocked down.' This suggestion followed an important discussion the previous month during which Curran had urged the inclusion in the report of a passage strongly condemning and exposing the use of *agents provocateurs*. Adair and Demant said that there was no evidence to support such accusations. Mischcon, the solicitor, tried to find a compromise between the two positions but feared that if homosexual importuning became rife then it would be necessary for the police to take tough action and he did not want to weaken police power should that happen. Sir Hugh Linstead, the Conservative MP, came to the aid of Curran. He thought that the police took 'advantage of the psychological condition of men, often of poor education, to extort confessions', and he criticised the way that the police pried into 'private lives on some very thin pretexts such as the presence of one bed in a room where two men slept'.

At this point in the discussion Demant intervened to try to defuse the disagreement by suggesting that they should not 'criticise a situation they sought to remove' – an amazing comment. If these practices were attacked the police would be much less likely to drop them, according to Demant. Far better, he suggested, just to have a quiet word with those responsible, no need to wash too much dirty linen in public. Wolfenden found himself heartily in agreement with these sentiments. In September 1956 Curran again tried to persuade Wolfenden to adopt a more honest approach to this question: '[We] must publish evidence from the police because of its damaging character in showing public opinion how bad they are.' Whitby and Curran were allowed to insert a point about the injustices produced by the unevenness of police activity across the country and the difference in sentences between individual judges and magistrates.

Effectively Rees and Diplock often found themselves working with Curran and Whitby, but both men tended to hunt alone. All four men (along with Adair) showed much less deference to Wolfenden than the rest of the committee and were less willing to accept his agenda. Rees's departure in April 1956 removed a strong advocate for a more radical report, and Diplock's promotion to the High Court as a judge in 1956 considerably reduced his commitment to the committee. These two developments certainly helped to make the report less radical, depriving the doctors of useful supporters in the drafting battle.

The Recommendations

The committee made the following recommendations to the Home Office in its report:

1. That homosexual activity between consenting adults over the age of twenty-one in private be no longer a criminal offence.
2. That no proceedings be taken in respect of any homosexual act (other than an indecent assault) committed in private by a person under twenty-one without the sanction of the Director of Public Prosecutions or the Attorney-General. Persons under twenty-one found guilty of a homosexual offence were to receive a compulsory examination by a psychiatrist before sentencing.
3. That, except for some 'grave reason', proceedings were not to be instituted in respect of homosexual offences incidentally revealed in the course of investigating a blackmail allegation.
4. That the prosecution of any homosexual offence which had taken place more than a year before was to be banned by law – except in cases of indecent assault, for which there was to be no time limit.
5. That new offences be created to make male prostitution illegal, as were the crimes of living off the immoral earnings of a male prostitute or operating a male brothel.
6. That the maximum penalty for a man over twenty-one found guilty of a sexual act with a sixteen to twenty-one-year-old male be five years' imprisonment.
7. That men charged with importuning be entitled to a jury trial.
8. That a prisoner found guilty of a homosexual offence could if he wished receive oestrogen treatment while in prison.

9. That more research be supported by the Home Office 'into the aetiology of homosexuality and the effects of various forms of treatment'.

Meet the Press

On 4 September 1957 the Wolfenden Report was published. It was an immediate best-seller. It appeared on a Wednesday morning and dominated the front pages of newspapers that evening and the following morning. The weekly journals gave it prominence that Friday and in the weeks that followed. There was also extensive coverage in the Sunday papers. Homosexuality had never received so much press and media attention. Wolfenden presented the report to the press and gave a succession of interviews on radio and television. He became a media personality. His benign presence and his lack of affectation made him a reassuring figure and the exposure greatly benefited his career. A journalist interviewing him for the *Daily Mail* in 1958 thought that he was 'the living image of a fading concept – the correct Englishman, polite, fair, modest and (his favourite words) "objective and dispassionate"'. He was repeatedly congratulated for his bravery and his courage in leading the distasteful inquiry. He had produced 'the most important social document of the decade', 'a most sane, sober and scientific treatment of the whole subject', 'clear, conscientious and courageous'.

The reaction to the report was determined by informal Home Office briefings for the media which took place on the morning of publication. The journalists were told that the government would act on Wolfenden's recommendations on prostitution but would not do so on those concerning homosexuality. Reporters and leader writers knew when they wrote their articles that legislation on homosexuality was a distant prospect, and this often helped some waverers adopt a more generous attitude to the report. The Home Office subtly distanced itself from Wolfenden. The department had achieved its objective: support for legislation to 'clean the streets' of the capital.

London-based newspapers were generally supportive of Wolfenden's chief recommendation on homosexuality, the decriminalisation of homosexual offences between consenting male adults in private. The major exceptions to this support were the newspapers of Lord Beaverbrook (the *Daily Express*, the *Sunday Express* and the *Evening Standard*) which immediately adopted a hostile attitude to the report, as did the *Daily Telegraph* and the *Daily Mail*. John Gordon in the *Sunday Express* described the Wolfenden Report as the 'The Pansies Charter'. A *Daily Express* editorial asked:

Why did the Government sponsor this cumbersome nonsense? Anyone would think prostitution and perversion were a widespread problem. In fact the majority of British homes never come into contact with either.

It is up to the Home Secretary to see that family life remains protected from these evils. If the law needs stiffening he should get on with stiffening it.

Calling in an outside Brains Trust and making a public song and dance about it is a foolish way of tackling the matter. For all the help he will find the Wolfenden Report he might as well tear it up.

The *News of the World* was extremely hostile the following Sunday – it had a tradition to maintain. It entitled its editorial 'The Wages of Sin':

The moment the State officially condones such behaviour, an entirely new outlook would result. No longer would homosexuality be something to fear or be frowned upon, it would become rather respectable and a 'thing to do'.

Not only would a boy gain the key of the door at 21 – he would gain a key that would lead to the most dreadful corruption and pollution. There is no knowing where it would end from a national standpoint . . . let's leave ill alone.

The provincial press came out virtually unanimously against the report while Scottish newspapers were particularly repelled by any suggestion of changing the *status quo*; James Adair was much celebrated by them. The weeklies – the *New Statesman*, the *Spectator* and the *Economist* – all supported Wolfenden's main proposals.

The attitude of the *Daily Mirror* and its weekly sister the *Sunday Pictorial* is more difficult to gauge. Their editor Hugh Cudlipp concentrated on prostitution and supported the proposals with sensationalising headlines because he argued that it was better to keep vice hidden from public view. The daily paper ran a poll that collected over 10,000 votes. The readers overwhelmingly accepted Wolfenden's recommendations on prostitution but rejected those on homosexuality: 4,880 supporting them with 5,393 voting against.

The *Daily Mirror* found in its poll that a larger majority of women were against the homosexual recommendations than was the situation amongst the men. Mrs Jean Mann, a Scottish Labour MP, warned television viewers that 'we may even have husbands enticed away from wives' as a result of the report. Jeanne Heal, a journalist and television personality, believed that women were more aware of the dangers than men. In her column in the *Empire News* she took on the mantle of the super-heterosexual and spoke as a mother. She opened modestly enough:

I believe I speak for the majority of mothers when I say I was profoundly shocked by the Report of the Wolfenden Committee . . . To mothers – more perhaps than to fathers – this is not just an academic discussion of a social question. It vitally concerns the future happiness – and perhaps the health – of our own children, and it is because I believe our first duty is towards our children that I find this report shocking.

I was shocked by the excessively cynical, worldly attitude the committee has adopted towards perhaps the most deeply profound problem surrounding our personal lives . . .

I read the Wolfenden Report as a mother – full of personal hopes and worries for the future of my own son and daughter . . . as I read the report I read it as a mother, with the future of my own children in mind. I realised I should be far more worried if my son were attacked by a man than if my daughter were.

A sexual attack by a man on a girl seems to me to be a violent and horrible excess of something which is basically a normal thing. But an attack by a man on a boy is to me, by contrast entirely abnormal – and far more likely to have permanent frightening results . . .

I have grave misgivings . . . that homosexual practices between consenting adults in private (yes, even in private) should be no longer a criminal offence. Surely if the practice of homosexuality is to be reduced – and that must be our aim – this is entirely the wrong way to go about it . . .

Personally, if I had no son, I might shrug my shoulders. But I do have a son. And I would fight to the death to prevent such an attitude by the law.

The worst heterosexual nightmare, a faggot for a son.

The best critique, and the most accurate reading of the report, appeared in *The Times* editorial. Its author was more knowledgeable than most of those who pontificated on the subject of homosexuality on the evening of the 4th and the morning of the 5th:

The report finds no great fault with police methods dealing with prostitutes, and less fault than one might have been expected with their methods of catching male importuners. It trenchantly reviews the varying police procedures for cautioning street walkers and, notably, for obtaining evidence (particularly confessions) of homosexual offences. Yet its conclusion that the Judges' Rules must be strictly

Daily Mirror
TUES SEPT 10 1957
2ᵈ FORWARD WITH THE PEOPLE
No. 16,716

Mirror Public Poll backs Wolfenden Verdict that—

HIDDEN VICE IS LESS HARMFUL

BUT—

HERE are the first results of the Mirror Public Poll on the Wolfenden Vice Report. Of nearly 7,000 votes so far analysed OVERWHELMINGLY the voters wish to clear prostitutes off the streets.

So do the Wolfenden Committee.

OVERWHELMINGLY the voters believe that "hidden" prostitution is less harmful than the temptation—especially to the young—of open vice.

This view agrees with that of the Wolfenden Committee.

On the next two issues, there are sharp clashes between PUBLIC OPINION (as reflected

so far in the Mirror Poll) and SIR JOHN WOLFENDEN'S COMMITTEE ON VICE.

More than a third of the men and women who have already voted in the Mirror Public Poll are in favour of licensed brothels — which the Wolfenden Committee opposed.

BUT THE WIDEST CLASH OF OPINION IS ON THE PROBLEM OF HOMOSEXUALITY.

More than half of the voters disagree with the Wolfenden Report recommendation that it should no longer be a criminal offence for homosexual behaviour to take place in private between consenting adults aged twenty-one or over.

than the public parading of the prostitute's wares before ordinary citizens—especially young people. Do you agree or disagree?

5,876 voters AGREE.
943 voters DISAGREE.

③ The Wolfenden Report says that— Licensed brothels would imply that the State recognised prostitution as a social necessity; would encourage some women to enter the trade, and could lead to trafficking in women.

The Report therefore declares that licensed brothels should NOT be adopted. Do you agree or disagree?

4,158 voters AGREE.
2,654 voters DISAGREE.

④ The Wolfenden Report recommends that—

While the law already still protest

● More than a third of the men and women who voted SUPPORT—

Licensed brothels

[The Wolfenden Report said NO.]

DAILY MIRROR, Wednesday September 11, 1957 PAGE 7

That VICE Report

WHAT POLL SAYS

● In the South 7 to 1 for 'hidden' vice

● But in the North it is 5 to 1

Hero Simba is dead

WANTED BY THE POLICE—A YOUNG ALSATIAN OR LABRADOR DOG TO TAKE THE PLACE OF A DEAD POLICE DOG HERO.

This appeal was issued by Scotland Yard yesterday after Simba IV, who worked with Police-Constable Alan

Wilkinson, 30, was put to sleep following an accident with a car at Wimbledon Common.

Simba had been a police dog for less than six months but he had helped in six arrests.

Until a new dog is found, Constable Wilkinson will go back to normal police duties.

BY late last night the Mirror Public Poll on the Wolfenden Vice Report had swollen to:

10,336 VOTES.

Analysis of the voting shows that it varies considerably in different parts of the country.

In the SOUTH OF ENGLAND and SOUTH WALES there is a 7 to 1 vote FOR the Wolfenden Committee view that "hidden" prostitution is less harmful than the temptation of open vice.

In the NORTH OF ENGLAND, however, the vote drops to 5 to 1 in favour of this Wolfenden Committee view.

In SCOTLAND the vote in agreement with the Wolfenden Committee view is still substantial. But it is only 4 to 1 compared with the national average of about 6 to 1.

There is a similar difference in voting on the

Latest Figures in

THE MIRROR

issue of licensed brothels—which the Wolfenden Committee opposed.

So do Mirror voters. But voters living in the SOUTH (including SOUTH WALES) are less opposed to brothels than voters living in the NORTH or SCOTLAND.

● In the SOUTH: 60 voters in every 100 oppose licensed brothels.

● In the NORTH: 66 voters in every 100 oppose licensed brothels.

● In SCOTLAND: 75 voters in every 100 oppose licensed brothels.

In the total vote on licensed brothels there is a clash of opinion between Mirror voters and the Wolfenden Committee.

At least one voter in three disagrees with the Wolfenden Committee's opposition to licensed brothels.

But the sharpest clash of opinion is provoked by the problem of homosexuality.

Fewer Than Half

The Wolfenden Report recommends that it should no longer be a criminal offence for homosexual behaviour to take place in private between consenting adults aged twenty-one or over.

FEWER THAN HALF THE MIRROR VOTERS AGREE WITH THIS PROPOSAL.

And the further north voters live the less they appear to agree with the proposal.

● In the SOUTH OF ENGLAND and SOUTH WALES voting is almost equally divided for report recommenda-

---

The *Daily Mirror* conducted a poll of its readers on the findings of the Wolfenden Committee. The majority of readers wanted all evidence of 'vice' to be kept out of sight.

observed in such cases reads a little lamely after its plain indication that Scottish procedure shows a greater care for individual rights . . .

In some other respects the report is less thorough and consistent, and divisions appear among its authors. Disturbed by the court sentences for homosexual offences, the committee conclude only that psychiatric reports should be obtained before young offenders are sentenced. They did not note the Cambridge survey's finding of a rather higher rate of imprisonment of first offenders (for importuning the proportion was nearly half) nor the Home Office Advisory Council's recent recommendation that no adult first offender should go to gaol unless there is no appropriate alternative. Though their own arguing points to eighteen as the 'age of consent' to homosexual relations, by majority the committee recommended twenty-one.

Of the huge coverage given to the report this was the only one to spot the inconsistency that the report's recommendations were designed for an age of consent at eighteen, not twenty-one. *The Times* leader writer was the only journalist to comment on the curious disparity that the recommendations proposed by the report would create between the way the law treated males and females:

> Existing maximum penalties for what will remain homosexual offences are retained. The maximum penalty for seducing a youth over 16 is raised to five years' imprisonment (seduction of a girl of the same age is not punishable). All penalties are much more severe for equivalent offences against females. Two years' imprisonment for male soliciting contrasts with the present 40s. and proposed three months for female soliciting; ten years for indecent assault if the victim is masculine with two years if feminine . . . [these proposals] reflect the committee's necessary and proper determination to make it clear beyond doubt that the proposed exemption of adult inverts from legal penalty is in no sense a sign of tolerance of paederasts or corrupters of youth.

In a parliamentary debate in May 1965, Lord Lothian, who had been a member of the Wolfenden Committee, explained its approach to the subject of homosexuality, an account supported by the unpublished material and one reinforcing *The Times*'s interpretation:

> Looking back to when the Report was published, one gets the impression that many people, possibly the majority, thought that the Wolfenden Committee were condoning homosexual crime, or at any rate appearing to 'play it down'. Of course, this, it is clear, sprang from our recommendations concerning homosexual acts between

Many newspapers presented the Wolfenden report as a way of brushing the problems of female prostitution and male homosexuality under the carpet: this cartoon by Illingworth appeared in the *Daily Mail*.

consenting adults in private ... I believe that this impression was based on a mis-reading of the Report and, to a certain extent, on a misinterpretation of what the Wolfenden Committee were trying to achieve ... we took the view that homosexual acts are wrong and harmful – some very gravely so – and therefore to be deplored. I think we also agreed that, in general, homosexuals are more often than not unhappy people, maladjusted and sometimes degraded. This, I suggest, is in line, not only with ordinary decent, Christian opinion, but also with a good deal of medical evidence as well. From this, two things follow: first, that the young and the weak must be protected; and secondly, that homosexuals must, so far as is practically and medically possible, be assisted towards cure. I think that this constructive, curative approach forms the basis of the recommendations in the Wolfenden Report ... I do not wish it to be thought the Committee were condoning homosexual acts. That was very far from the case.

The *Daily Mirror* said that the report had fallen like a 'bombshell' on the West End, many of the girls thinking that it was now the law: 'Observers said only a quarter of the normal number of prostitutes were on the streets.' Peter Vane, a reporter on the *News Chronicle*, tested opinion on those streets, asking 'ordinary people' their reaction to Wolfenden:

'Among the 60 people I spoke to one point raised particular ire – the recommendation to legalise adult homosexuality. The majority passed cynical comment, ruthless in its bandying of household names whose owners, the man in the streets believe, will benefit if the recommendations become law. Said Bill Hamilton, a gas worker of Battersea: "At least this will please —," naming a well known personality.' The idea that homosexuality was the prerogative of the élite was well entrenched, as Vane's survey suggested.

Looking back, Wolfenden professed himself pleased with the reaction. By the end of September the battle-lines were clear: a group of liberals pressing for a reform resisted by a conservative group defending the *status quo*. There was only a limited and rather tenuous connection between the liberals and homosexually inclined men in British society. They did not *represent* them, they did not listen to their complaints or aspirations and they pursued an agenda which ultimately did little to address the principal problems facing such individuals. Nevertheless the cause of homosexual law reform had been strengthened by the Wolfenden Report. It helped those politicians, intellectuals and journalists who wanted to 'civilise' Britain, and to do this through the medium of a series of laws that would, they imagined, make Britain a more tolerant state.

A year after the report Wolfenden told the *Daily Mail*: 'You see I've tried not to *campaign* about the report. We tried to take an objective and dispassionate look at two distasteful and embarrassing subjects. Once we had reported, we'd done our jobs . . . I've always tried not to *argue* a case. My task has been explanatory rather than expostulatory . . . We had to be dispassionate. We had to be objective.'

The cabinet discussed the Wolfenden Report on 28 November 1957. It endorsed the Home Office's recommendations to act on the prostitution element and shelve the recommendations on homosexuality. The government needed to take account of 'public opinion' before it acted.

The Chief Constables had been absolutely incensed by the Wolfenden Report. They discussed it at their meeting on 27 February 1958. Captain Peel of Essex placed it on the record 'that the Chief Constables did not accept the views of the Wolfenden Committee as to the lack of uniformity in the administration of the law relating to homosexual offences'. Sir Theobald Mathew, Director of Public Prosecutions, who was present, agreed. He believed that the Wolfenden report had been wrong. Sir Frank Newsam, Permanent Under-Secretary at the Home Office, also assured the sensitive policemen, 'the Home Office had no intention of interfering in any way with the discretion of Chief Constables in the investigation and prosecution of offences'.

6

Implementing the Report, 1957–67

False Starts, 1957–60

The Macmillan government accepted the Wolfenden Committee's recommendations on prostitution, which were embodied in the Street Offences Act of 1959. It had, however, no intention to implement the recommendations on homosexual law reform. It was not until fourteen months after the publication of the report that the Commons would be provided with an opportunity to discuss its contents. The Lords had debated it in December 1957 on a motion from Lord Pakenham. Neither debate led to a vote, so opinion was not tested on the issue, though many peers who spoke seemed to support the recommendations.

Debating honours were more evenly matched in the Commons. Plenty of excited homophobes predicted the end of civilisation if homosexual acts were decriminalised between consenting adult males in private. A Labour MP, Fred Bellenger, described homosexuality as 'a malignant canker in the community, and if it were allowed to grow, it would eventually kill off what is known as normal life . . . humanity would eventually revert to an animal existence if this cult was so allowed to spread that, as in ancient Greece, it overwhelmed the community at large.' There was indeed much discussion that day about ancient Greece and Rome. The great fear was that a change in the law might lead to some public manifestations of homosexuality. Dr Boughton, a Labour Member representing Batley in Yorkshire, spoke as a psychiatrist:

It is better, I think, if we have a festering sore, to keep it covered and out of sight rather than have it exposed, a revolting sight to decent people and a possible cause of infection among the young . . . I feel very sorry for these people. They do not know what they are missing . . . I have a fear, based on what I know of homosexuals, that some, certainly not all, homosexuals will repress their feelings less. They may go to the extent even of showing some signs of affection that they have for one another in public. I can envisage men walking along the street arm in arm, possibly holding hands, and at dances perhaps wishing to dance together and even caressing in public places ... If we see a man and woman walking along arm in arm, we approve of it ... if we see two men showing affection for one another in public it gives most people a deep sense of disapproval. It is unnatural, it is biologically wrong and worst of all, because it is biologically wrong, it is a shocking example to young people ... We have, most unfortunately, both prostitution and homosexuality with us. I wish that they could both be cured, but, until they can, I think it best we should keep them out of sight of the general public.

Reformers, who were not at this point an organised grouping, tried to counter such speeches by arguing that reform of the law would make homosexuals more responsible: they would come to pattern their lives on these of the ideal heterosexual. Sir Hugh Linstead, Conservative MP for Putney, who had served on the committee, suggested that reform could promote assimilation:

From the point of view of those forming what I may call the homosexual community itself, the change in the law can put a new social and moral responsibility upon them. If we no longer impose a legal code of sexual behaviour which we do not extract from anyone else, we can surely expect homosexuals to accept the same responsibility as the rest of us ... [by] behaving themselves in public.

Many speakers against the Wolfenden recommendations smelled a conspiracy trying to promote reform. Jean Mann, a Scottish Labour MP, had 'never known a Report which was so well boosted ... [it was being promoted] by a very powerful and influential body ... The evil thread runs through the theatre, through the music hall, through the Press, and through the BBC. It has international ramifications.'

All MPs had received a copy of Peter Wildeblood's book *Against the Law* and a pamphlet also written by Wildeblood, *The Homosexual and the Law*. Several MPs were outraged that they should have been sent such material. It lent support to their fantasy of a homosexual lobby.

The pamphlet produced by Wildeblood had come from a newly created organisation, the Homosexual Law Reform Society (hereafter abbreviated to HLRS). The society had been created in the early months of 1958 as the result of a correspondence in the *Spectator*. Dr R. D. Reid, from Wells, wrote to the magazine to tell readers about the prosecution of a group of adult homosexuals in Somerset, all charged with consensual sex acts and all of them over twenty-one, who were all sent to prison. He described this as a 'provincial pogrom'. He suggested that a society ought to be established to help the victims and their families. Many people had expected the police to moderate their enforcement of the laws after the Wolfenden Report, but in fact in many areas it had the opposite effect.

A few weeks after Reid's letter another letter, this time in *The Times*, announced the establishment of HLRS. In the early months of its existence the main organiser of the society was Tony Dyson, an English Literature don teaching at Bangor in North Wales. His first aim was to collect the support of the great and the good. This campaign was constructed around the notion that they needed to secure the blessings of 'top people' to show that reform had the support of enlightened opinion. It was to be a fundamental characteristic of HLRS that it should court famous names. It proved to be a mixed blessing because many of the names were so cautious that they ensured that the society should adopt a timid campaign. In particular, they preferred to promote the idea of the responsible and respectable homosexual while condemning the homosexual subculture. Neither were they willing to support a campaign which exposed the police, so the society always soft-pedalled this issue, in public at least. The tone adopted was patronising and paternalistic. Effectively it was a front organisation for the liberal establishment.

The signatories of *The Times* letter inaugurating the society included many liberal dons: Noel Annan, Freddie Ayer, Isaiah Berlin, Lord David Cecil, Julian Huxley and A. J. P. Taylor, to name only the most famous. A clutch of clergymen, two bishops, the anti-apartheid campaigner and later co-founder of the Festival of Light, Father Trevor Huddlestone, the leader of CND, Canon John Collins and that promoter of all radical causes, the President of the Methodist Conference, Donald Soper. The only politician to sign was Bob Boothby. Intellectuals included J. B. Priestley and his wife Jacquetta Hawkes, Bertrand Russell, Stephen Spender and C. Day Lewis. The left-wing publisher Victor Gollancz, one of the leaders of the campaign to abolish capital punishment, agreed with Collins, Hawkes and Spender to serve on the committee of HLRS. There was considerable overlap between the much larger campaigns to destroy Britain's nuclear weapons and the campaign to abolish hanging – for many of those involved felt that a measure of homosexual law reform was a necessary element in civilising British society.

The campaign was enthusiastically supported by three pillars of the liberal establishment: the *New Statesman*, the *Spectator* and the *Observer*. All provided access to a wider liberal audience and many articles were published in these journals promoting the cause. David Astor provided financial help to HLRS from his private fortune (E. M. Forster was another benefactor) and Kingsley Martin, editor of the *New Statesman,* served for a time on the committee of HLRS.

HLRS eventually worked from an office in Shaftesbury Avenue with a small staff. The secretary from 1958 until 1960 was an Anglican clergyman, safely married with children. The society was so terrified of frightening potential backers that it hesitated when offered the services of A. E. G. Wright as secretary, a lawyer who had worked for several years as a parliamentary lobbyist for the iron and steel industry and an executive in a public relations company. Wright was gay and lived with another man. A more cautious individual it would have been difficult to find, but still the committee hesitated. In the end they agreed to appoint him for a probationary period. He was to stay with the group for much of the rest of his career. Wright always used the pseudonym Antony Grey for his homosexual work, and during the 1960s he busied himself promoting the cause of homosexual law reform.

Time has not been kind to Grey. Without doubt he did much good work, particularly in promoting the counselling arm of HLRS, the Albany Trust. Characteristically the Trust took its name from the chambers, in the Albany building on Piccadilly, belonging to J. B. Priestley and Jacquetta Hawkes where it held its first meeting. HLRS found it impossible not to advertise and celebrate its connection with the élite. Wright devoted enormous energy during the 1960s (and later) to lobbying Members of Parliament, participating in debates and discussions across the country and writing many articles and letters to further the cause. He had a powerful sense of the injustices faced by homosexually inclined men and titled his autobiography *Quest for Justice: Towards Homosexual Emancipation.* Unfortunately he is condemned to be depicted as an Uncle Tom, a collaborator, whose efforts were shaped by the agenda of the liberal establishment whose policies were ultimately almost as hostile to homosexual society as those advanced by conservative moralists.

The greatest weakness of HLRS from the point of view of homosexual men was that they could not become members. The society collected famous names but it did not encourage ordinary people to join. It had no roots in the provinces and its homosexual element was predominantly metropolitan, middle-class and professional. Peter Wildeblood was an early activist. The pamphlet that he drafted to be distributed to parliamentarians in 1958 for HLRS endorsed much of what he had advocated in *Against the Law.*

HLRS encouraged homosexual men to earn the respect of their peers through their responsible attitude and their respectability. The society did not encourage the subculture and it tried to present an image of the homosexual that excluded the wide variety of men who wore that label.

There was no place for effeminate men or queens in HLRS. The counselling arm of the organisation, while doing much good work, encouraged the notion that homosexuals needed to adapt to the dominant culture and discouraged the establishment of alternative networks of support within the subculture. The society never built on the success of a public meeting that it held on 12 May 1960 at Caxton Hall in London, attended by over a thousand people. For many of the homosexual men who did attend that meeting it was a liberating occasion, yet there were no further meetings and no place for them in the cause. They were not encouraged to become too closely involved. HLRS did not want to embarrass its sponsors who were terrified of being seen as propagandists for homosexuality.

As a lobby HLRS was weak. It played an extremely marginal role in the passage of the Act and would have brought more benefits to homosexuals had it disassociated itself from the Act and advertised its weaknesses, instead of which it was driven along by the strength of the current to endorse something which brought only marginal benefits to homosexual men. The campaign after 1960 was dominated by a group of sympathetic peers and MPs who believed that HLRS should keep out of sight. They over-reacted to the angry comments of reactionary MPs in 1958 and did not want to suggest that a homosexual lobby was pushing for reform. As a result Grey and his colleagues worked in the shadows and killed the chance of creating a body that might have built on the success of Caxton Hall. By the mid-1960s there were almost one hundred and thirty homosexual groups and societies in the United States pressing for change – in Britain there were only two.

The 1960 Debate

The first major parliamentary test of the Wolfenden Report occurred at the end of June 1960, soon after the Caxton Hall meeting. Kenneth Robinson, a Labour frontbencher with a reputation as a progressive, put down a motion calling on the government to act on the recommendations of the Wolfenden Committee regarding homosexuality. For the first time MPs were called upon to express their opinion of the Wolfenden Report. Three hundred and twelve MPs did so, just under half of the House of Commons.

R. A. Butler, the Home Secretary, tried to persuade the Commons that the government wanted time, time to do further research on this intractable problem and time to allow public opinion to digest Wolfenden. They must not, he suggested, move in advance of public opinion; that would be extremely dangerous. He added a twist of his own that would be echoed in some speeches from opponents of reform in succeeding debates on the subject. We were living, he told them, in a peculiarly disturbed time which was not a suitable period for experiment and change. Religion was in decline, the old moral certainties were under attack, and there were people who needed the guidance of the law to form their moral values: 'There are, unfortunately, people today to whom criminal law and moral law are co-terminous in the sense that they have no other point of reference. They consequently consider that if conduct is not prohibited by criminal law, there is no reason why they should not indulge in it. The restraints which the criminal law imposes, therefore still remain important.' In this way he justified the maintenance of the *status quo*. Research projects costing a few thousand pounds helped a couple of academics make limited studies of the 'problem', none of which contributed much to the literature on the subject. Butler's promotion of the research projects bought him time and got him out of a tight corner.

The debate provided an opportunity for the homophobes to explore their fears with the nation. Godfrey Lagden, fifty-four, Conservative MP for Hornchurch, who had exchanged a job as a sales rep for a career at Westminster, conjured up a succession of fantasies that would, he imagined, become reality if Wolfenden's recommendations became law:

> In my opinion, all right-thinking people would at best – and put it at best – think of these homosexuals as people with warped minds who have little self-control . . . in the general run the homosexual is a dirty-minded danger to the virile manhood of this country . . . it is important for any country to have a virile manhood and to see that it is not corrupted by such men as these . . . we may well be in the position, of doing what we are asked to do, of seeing notices outside anyone's house saying 'Homosexual experiences can be had within'.

Lagden was trying to keep the world safe for sales reps.

To William Shepherd, MP for Cheadle, homosexuals were 'revolting creatures of odious femininity who want to flaunt themselves before the public and who are nauseating members of society'. Shepherd set himself up as the defender of the heterosexual dictatorship as he contemplated the fate of the homosexual: 'A life without children and without normal family existence, a life in which one goes into public lavatories looking for one's associations, is not something to which any individual ought to be committed.' Ever hopeful, Shepherd wanted the United Nations to organise a global research project into the causes of homosexuality and to search for a cure.

There were two professional psychiatrists in the House, one a member of the Conservative Party the other a member of the Labour Party. Both opposed the recommendations of the Wolfenden Committee, sanctioning the prejudices of their colleagues with their professional expertise. Dr Boughton, who had spoken in the 1958 debate, believed that the pressure for this measure was coming from homosexuals, a powerful pressure group he claimed. He articulated a recurrent fear of opponents of decriminalisation – the possibility that it would encourage the greater visibility of homosexuality in society. '[Homosexuals are] severely damaged personalities', pronounced the doctor. Many of them

> were obviously effeminate, flauntingly exhibitionist and deeply resentful anti-social types. Given a change in the law, I believe that [they] would snap their fingers in the face of public opinion. I think there would be a display of homosexual feeling and a development of a homosexual cult, all of which would be objectionable to the majority of people.
>
> We are aware that already some homosexuals gather together in groups and instances occur of the seduction of others. Drinking parties are organised as a preliminary to the practice of homosexual offences, and the culprits lack all sense of sin in this respect. Their type of sexual behaviour gives them great enjoyment and that is all they care about. With the state condoning homosexuality, I fear that that practice would grow. There might even be cases of men who are by their make up, shall we say, 60 per cent heterosexual and 40 per cent homosexual, living normal respectable lives, being led astray . . . we might expect to find a display in public of homosexual feelings, particularly by the exhibitionist types. I fear that bullies and seducers in positions of authority might make homosexual demands on their subordinates . . . I look upon homosexuality as biologically wrong, and I think, therefore, that any encouragement of it would damage society.

It was an argument listened to often by the Wolfenden Committee and it would be repeated in both Houses of Parliament until the passage of the Act in 1967. Society would be destroyed, its heterosexual foundations undermined, if Wolfenden's recommendations became law.

Robinson and his allies made an appeal to reason and to compassion. The reform campaign was constructed largely around the attempt of the reformers to arouse the pity of their audience for the plight of the homosexual. Robinson repeated the main findings of the Wolfenden Report, in particular the fact that only 'a very small minority' of homosexuals were 'effeminate, depraved and exhibitionist'. The vast majority were 'useful citizens who go about quite unrecognised and unsuspected by most of us'. The existing law made them anti-social, whereas reform would allow them to integrate better into society. He did not believe it would increase the amount of homosexual activity or the number of homosexuals; in common with most reformers he believed that the number of homosexuals was biologically fixed. He painted a picture of the sad and wretched lives lived by homosexuals in Britain: 'these unfortunate people deserve our compassion rather than our contempt.'

Robinson would depart from the Wolfenden Report only on the subject of blackmail. None of his opponents exploited the ambiguity of the passages in the Wolfenden Report on blackmail. Indeed, throughout the Commons debate opponents of reform paid insufficient attention to the text of the Wolfenden Report. There were many nuances that they might have turned to their rhetorical advantage, chiefly because reformers claimed so often that they were constructing a case based on the Wolfenden Report. A bit more homework would have paid dividends in the debate. Robinson cited the figure that Lord Jowitt had produced in a Lords debate in 1954 that 90 to 95 per cent of all blackmail cases that he had come across when he was Attorney-General between 1929 and 1931 involved homosexual men. This inaccurate statistic would find its way into most speeches during the struggle for law reform. Blackmail was the key used by reformers to enlist the sympathy of their colleagues.

By 1960 many groups had come out in support of the Wolfenden Report. This allowed Robinson and other reformers in the debate to suggest that they had the support of 'informed', 'educated' and 'enlightened' opinion on their side. He made a great deal of the endorsement given to the Wolfenden recommendations by the main British churches. By 1960 the Church of England, the Roman Catholic Church and the Methodists had officially accepted the need for a reform of the law along the lines recommended by the Wolfenden Committee. This was a card that particularly annoyed the opposition, and the reformers played it repeatedly. Despite the fact that only a small number of Britons still went to church regularly they still overwhelmingly considered themselves a religious people. The support of the churches mattered and the opposition knew it.

Roy Jenkins, whose progressive credentials had been boosted in 1959 with the passage of the Obscene Publications Act, which made the censorship of serious literature by the state more difficult, in one of the speeches winding up the debate for the reformers said that he wanted Britain's laws to be in line with other civilised nations. Throughout the debate reformers had compared Britain unfavourably with other European democracies. Why, the reformers wondered, had Sweden been able to pass a similar measure to that proposed by Wolfenden in 1942 without any of the apocalyptic consequences imagined by the opponents of reform? Why were the British going to react differently – were they really so much more depraved than their European neighbours?

The main arguments for reform were developed in a series of powerful speeches by five Labour MPs: Robinson; Jenkins; Douglas Jay, the economist who sat for Battersea North, and who like Jenkins was closely identified with Hugh Gaitskell on the right of the party; Anthony Greenwood, who occupied a position more on the left and who made the first of many interventions on the subject; and their colleague Eirene White, who tried to treat the subject as 'scientifically' and as 'objectively' as possible. The five speeches were well-organised and clearly co-ordinated. Reformers throughout generally sang from the same choir sheet, while opposition speeches were generally delivered off the cuff and had a tendency to degenerate into rants.

Boughton and others tried hard to depict the reformers as operating in the interests of the homosexual lobby, sadly a creation of their overheated imaginations. All the reformers distanced themselves from this accusation. Robinson accepted that this was a subject 'distasteful and even repulsive to many people'.

Ninety-nine MPs supported Robinson in the division lobbies. Seventy-three Labour MPs, twenty-two Tories and four Liberals. Drawn from across the House, this was obviously a diverse group but some common characteristics can be identified. Most of those voting for reform were university educated, with a strong ideological commitment. It is notable that on this issue two of the most consistent supporters of reform, Margaret Thatcher and Enoch Powell, should come from the right in what has traditionally been seen as a left-wing issue. Many future Thatcherites supported reform including John Biffen, Keith Joseph and Nick Ridley. Amongst Labour supporters there was a similar profile. Ideologues like Anthony Crosland, Roy Jenkins, Barbara Castle, Dick Crossman and Tony Benn were amongst the most consistent and active supporters of the measure. It is possible also to identify strong support for reform amongst the Jewish MPs in the Commons. It was Leo Abse, MP for Pontypool, who introduced bills on three occasions to implement reform.

Opposition came mainly from the Tory backbenches with a small group of supporters from amongst Labour trade unionists, many of them working-class MPs with little formal education. At its peak this group numbered almost fifty but over the following seven years the numbers dwindled. The Tory opponents were usually drawn from the backbenches, most of them coming from the ranks of small business. The typical Tory opponent was a self-made man, the sort of character who had done well out of the 1950s economic boom.

Towards the Act

The First Bill

On 9 March 1962 Leo Abse proposed that some of the recommendations of the Wolfenden Report should become law. His was a modest bill which suggested that the police could not prosecute offences revealed in the course of blackmail investigation and that all decisions to prosecute in cases involving consenting adult males in private should be made by the Director of Public Prosecutions. Introduced under the ten-minute rule, the measure was talked out by Sir Cyril Osborne, Conservative MP for Louth, a businessman whose father had been a miner. Osborne was a prominent figure in the opposition to homosexual law reform. Unaccustomed to speaking in the Commons even though he had first been elected a member in 1945, Osborne was much ridiculed on the Labour benches and his speeches were continually interrupted by laughter.

Arran's Bill

Arthur Gore, 8th Earl of Arran, an eccentric journalist who wrote a column in the *London Evening News,* proposed a motion in the Lords on 12 May 1965 to discuss homosexual law reform. The debate was so encouraging that a day later he proposed a one-clause bill that would implement the main recommendation of the Wolfenden Committee, the decriminalisation of homosexual acts in private between consenting male adults. This bill passed its second reading on 24 May 1965 by a large majority, ninety-four votes to forty-nine. A group of peers led by the former Conservative Lord Chancellor, Viscount Dilhorne, tried to wreck the bill during its committee stage; they failed. In a series of mammoth debates Dilhorne tried to exhaust the reformers. The committee stage on 21 June lasted for eight-and-a-half hours. In all, the House of Lords spent twenty hours discussing the bill that summer and autumn of 1965.

The Home Office provided Arran with draftsmen to produce a proper bill that would bring into law all the rest of Wolfenden's recommendations. This was essentially the measure which became law in July 1967. The bill achieved its third reading on 25 October 1965 with a huge majority of seventy, one hundred and sixteen peers supporting the measure.

Arran was to be involved with the measure throughout its parliamentary passage. He never revealed to the House his motive in pursuing the bill so vigorously, but it was probably his way of atoning for the way that his aristocratic family had treated his elder brother Lord Sudley, a writer and translator. Sudley regularly brought Guardsmen back to his home in Chelsea, one, a Scot, becoming his companion. The family felt that Sudley was being exploited by the former soldier, who had moved his wife and children into the house, and the family managed to send Sudley away to a home where he remained until his death. It is clear that Arran was drawn to the measure because of the tragedy of his brother.

The bill enjoyed the support of the Archbishop of Canterbury, Michael Ramsey. A handful of bishops also offered their votes, though most of the episcopate stayed away from the debates. Ramsay certainly helped to rally support for the bill but his involvement in the debates did much damage to his reputation. He revealed on one occasion that he knew the difference between anal and oral sex. Another peer claimed that he had turned Hansard into a piece of pornography as a result of this admission. Throughout the debates in both Lords and Commons it was often repeated that the recommendations of the Wolfenden Report were supported by the Church of England, the Roman Catholic Church, the Methodists and the Quakers.

The opposition directed most of their attacks on Ramsey. Dilhorne was peculiarly offensive, delivering a succession of sarcastic speeches intended to embarrass the Archbishop. Dilhorne had a reputation as a bully and he tried hard to bully Ramsay. Dilhorne became obsessed with stopping the measure. It is not easy to understand why he should have put so much energy into opposing a bill which repeatedly secured large majorities amongst the peers. He tried hard to rally opinion against the measure but he could never persuade enough peers to support him. Lord Devlin, a contemporary, thought that he was 'an uninspiring advocate; a poor forensic tactician; a man of limited and no flexibility'. But he was dogged, and an amazingly hard worker. Several people believe that he provided the model for the character of Widmerpool in Anthony Powell's sequence of novels *A Dance to the Music of Time*. Devlin wrote:

> What was almost unique about him and makes his career so fascinating is that what the ordinary careerist achieves by making himself agreeable, falsely or otherwise, Reggie achieved by making himself disagreeable ... His disagreeableness was so pervasive, his persistence so interminable, the obstructions he manned so far flung, his objectives apparently so insignificant, that sooner or later you would be tempted to ask yourself whether the game was worth the candle ... He was neither a saint nor a villain. But since most of his convictions were wrong-headed, he was ineluctably a do-badder, by which I mean a person whose activities bear the same relation to villainy as those of a do-gooder do to sanctity.

His greatest triumph was that he secured one amendment which defined privacy in such a way that if a third person were present, intentionally or accidentally, this would render the homosexual act public and therefore

illegal. It was an amendment designed to prevent the legalisation of homosexual orgies.

Dilhorne's support came chiefly from a small group of Conservative
peers who found themselves at odds with the leadership of their party
and the Church of England. Most, like Dilhorne, were lifelong Anglicans.
Dilhorne was regularly supported by his predecessor as Lord Chancellor,
the Earl of Kilmuir who, while Home Secretary, had been responsible for
establishing the Wolfenden Committee. Kilmuir had moved to the right
during the early 1960s and he remained bitter at his dismissal from the
cabinet in July 1962.

Dilhorne could also count on the support of England's most reactionary
judge, the former Lord Chief Justice, Lord Goddard. The former Chief
Scout was also a determined opponent of the bill. The war hero Field
Marshal Viscount Montgomery of El Alamein was much stirred up by
the bill:

> To condone unnatural offences in male persons over 21, or indeed,
> in male persons of any age, seems to me utterly wrong. One may
> just as well condone the Devil and all his works . . . a weakening of
> the law will strike a blow at all those devoted people who are working
> to improve the moral fibre of this country. And heaven knows! It
> wants improving . . . Do not let us forget that it is the present young
> generation who will have to handle the problems that lie ahead in
> this distracted world of politics, war and mixed-up values. They will
> need all the help and guidance that we older ones can give them . . .
> Far from helping these unnatural practices along, surely our task is
> to build a bulwark which will defy evil influences which are seeking
> to undermine the very foundations of our national character – defy
> them; do not help them. I have heard some say . . . that such practices
> are allowed in France and in other NATO countries. We are not
> French, and we are not other nationals. We are British, thank God!

He facetiously proposed a wrecking amendment that would have raised
the age of consent to eighty:

> . . . after the age of 80 it does not matter what we do. I myself am
> rising 78, and the great thing is that at the age of 80 at least one has
> the old-age pension to pay for any blackmail which may come along.
> I regard the act of homosexuality in any form as the most abominable
> bestiality that any human being can take part in and which reduces
> him almost to the status of an animal . . . [this bill is] 'A Charter for
> Buggery'.

Arran, in contrast, made much use of the analogy of homosexuals as disabled individuals who needed help: 'They are the odd men out: the one's [*sic*] with the limp.' They were more likely to seek help if homosexual acts were decriminalised. There was much celebration in his speeches, and those of others, of the pleasures of heterosexuality: 'Will any man or woman . . . tell us seriously that a man, out of perverseness, and not perversion – purposely renounces the joys of love with the opposite sex, the joys of having a wife, the joys of having children? Is there a man in the world who would be, not so wicked, but so silly?'

Lord Francis-Williams, a Labour peer with many years' service as a journalist, believed that decriminalisation would remove some of the glamour that he suggested often attached itself to homosexual society:

> What we are now doing is to turn homosexuality into a secret society, with all the attraction that a secret society offers to the unbalanced young. And we appreciate that only those who are in some measure unbalanced, are likely to be attracted to homosexuality since the normal life, with its immense rewards in love and affection and achievement which are not offered to the homosexual, has so much more to offer than the homosexual life. But to those who are unbalanced, to those who are perhaps on the edge of a homosexual nature, the appeal of what can be presented as a secret society is immense. Any who have moved at all in homosexual circles, some of which also try the spurious appeal of a kind of intellectual Bohemianism, will know how strong that appeal of a secret society can be.

Kilmuir believed that the bill would encourage the subculture and that the cult would flourish. The recurring nightmare was the display of homosexual affection in public.

One of the most ridiculous participants in the Lords debates was Bob Boothby. Ennobled in 1958 by his mistress's husband, Harold Macmillan, he used the debates as an opportunity to boast that he had been responsible for the establishment of the Wolfenden Committee, a piece of fancy that some historians have believed. He only wanted to see a repeal of the Labouchère amendment of 1885, which would simply have removed the crime of gross indecency from the statute books. Always the man of the world, the man in the know, Boothby even suggested that this was what Wolfenden really wanted: 'Sir John Wolfenden has said to me on more than one occasion: "The guts of my Report was the repeal of the Labouchère Amendment. If I can get that, that is what I really want. That is what matters." And I quote Sir John Wolfenden as having said that again and again, and it is what I have always said.'

Boothby's own homosexual activities were widely known, and certainly known to many of his fellow peers. He was a regular visitor to the public lavatories at Victoria Station. In June 1964 he had been identified in the *Sunday Mirror* as a friend of Ronnie Kray, the East End gangster. A story claimed that he had attended homosexual parties run by Kray. The newspaper withdrew the accusation and he received substantial damages but many believed the stories, including several members of his own party. Boothby, possibly as a consequence, was more sensitive than others about this particular problem, and he might have been better advised not to have spoken at all. One speech he made suggesting that blackmail would be reduced if the bill was passed angered his party colleague, Lord Conesford:

> What astonishes me in this whole controversy is the quite extraordinary view that, if we pass this Bill or something like it, the blackmailing of homosexuals will cease. Why on earth should it? The noble Lord, Lord Boothby, said quite rightly, that to a public man the reputation of being a homosexual could be very harmful. Therefore the revelation that he is a homosexual –

He did not finish the sentence; Boothby rose: 'I really must protest against that. I never said that I was a homosexual – "The revelation that I was a homosexual".' Conesford denied that he had done any such thing: 'I said nothing of the kind. The noble Lord is not always the person concerned if he is concerned at all . . .' Again Boothby rose and stopped the peer mid-sentence: 'Be careful.' Conesford continued: 'I will be careful. It is damaging to a public man to be known to be a homosexual, whether it is a criminal offence or not.' Boothby, who was often drunk in the chamber, returned to the acrimonious exchange in a later speech: 'The noble Lord has been beastly to me, and I do not see why he should because I have been a great friend of his for over thirty years.'

Commons Defeat

Attempting to capitalise on Arran's success in the Lords, Leo Abse introduced a similar bill into the Commons on 26 May 1965. The debate lasted for twenty-two minutes with Osborne once again braving the jeers of other members in a long rant against the evils of homosexuality. The bill failed to pass its first reading, 178 MPs voting against it. The reformers came perilously close to success: they secured 159 votes in favour, and had many of their supporters not expected the bill to pass and simply failed to turn up then a majority would have been achieved. The General Election of 1964 had brought a large number of MPs favourably disposed to homosexual law reform into the House. The 1966 General Election would bring even more to Westminster. An examination of the Commons in the summer of 1965 shows that there were many more MPs committed to reform than those opposed. The pattern of the 1960 vote was broadly replicated, most of the reformers were drawn from Labour, who provided 124 MPs in favour, and those opposing reform were drawn mainly from the Tories, 127 MPs coming from that party. More Labour MPs voted against than in 1960, fifty as opposed to forty. They had a similar profile to the group that had opposed Wolfenden in 1960, a heavy concentration of Scots, northerners, former miners, railworkers and Catholics. Thirty-nine Tories supported Abse.

The failure of the bill to pass the Commons meant that Arran's bill was lost at the end of the parliamentary session of 1964/5. The Labour Government had a small majority and was expected to go to the country in the spring. There seemed little point in starting the bill again in the new parliamentary session that started in the autumn of 1965, as it was bound to run out of time.

Berkeley's Bill

Despite this problem, Humphry Berkeley, an upper-middle-class Conservative MP who represented Lancaster and who worked in public relations, brought a bill before the Commons during the session of 1965/6. Berkeley was himself homosexual, a fact known to many at Westminster and in Fleet Street, but kept hidden from the public. This bill drew much more Conservative support than later or earlier bills simply because of the party allegiance of its sponsor. Even on non-party measures MPs continue to maintain party loyalties. Berkeley's bill had its Second Reading on 11 February 1966. It secured 164 votes against 107, and became the first bill on this subject to win a vote in the Commons. Forty-nine of those supporting Berkeley were members of his own party.

Few Labour MPs bothered to vote against this bill, realising that it had no chance of getting through. Frank Tomney, a trade unionist and MP for Hammersmith (he numbered Joe Ackerley amongst his constituents), was upset by the tone adopted by the sponsors:

> I object to this intellectual superiority and sophistication on the part of the people who think they know better and who look down with snide remarks upon people who have the other point of view. The Bill is signed by people who in the main cannot be described as the horny-handed sons of toil. [It] is supported by those who, in my opinion, have never had to lead the life of the ordinary people outside, the mums and dads carrying the responsibilities of society and of rearing this country's citizens ... I am not concerned with what happens on the Continent. I know what happens on the Continent. But once we start, by legislation, to debase our minimum standards

in a period of a lush rich civilisation of material greed and advancement, we are really heading for trouble . . . I only know, coming from the class of society that I do, that our experience of sexual life was gained in a way which is still applicable to about 99 per cent of the population – at the local cinema, the ballroom, taking an occasional girl home. That is the way most of us learned. It is the natural way, and most of us enjoyed it. Those who do not find it enjoyable and are genuinely afflicted have my sympathy. Let not Parliament judge this issue. It hits at the very roots of our society.

The Labour MP cannot have been happy at the sarcastic reaction he provoked from Norman St John-Stevas, one of the chief promoters of the bill: 'I am sure we all congratulate the honourable member for Hammersmith on his notable contribution to the debate. I only hope that he will not look down on those of us who have not had his advantages in life.' The reformers certainly used to their advantage the fact that they could present the bill as an enlightened and modern measure and could present their opponents as reactionary backwoodsmen. They used to the full the advantage of possessing so many of the best speakers in the Commons. Most of the opposition to the bill sat silently, not willing to rise to their feet because of the mockery they knew they could expect. This certainly inhibited many Labour opponents to the bill from speaking, but it often encouraged members of the hard right of the Conservative Party who courted the disapproval of more liberal members.

Some of the most determined individuals promoting reform included that group which had voted for Wolfenden in 1960. By 1966 Barbara Castle, one of the most active supporters of homosexual law reform, was a cabinet minister. The 11th of February found her, as Minister of Transport, locked in negotiations with the rail unions over pay. Her colleague George Brown, the deputy Prime Minister, led the government's negotiating team. Castle was not going to miss the vote:

we had retired to the room of George Brown, leaving the N[ational] U[nion of] R[ailwaymen] to chew it over. For four hours the minutes ticked by while we waited. George and the rest started to drink, while I worked on some office papers. George's manner began to change rapidly; he got noisy and aggressive, abusing his officials in what he no doubt considered a jocular way and shouting at everyone. At 3pm I said mildly that I hoped I shouldn't be prevented from voting at 4pm on the Second Reading of the Sexual Offences Bill. This set George off on a remarkable diatribe against homosexuality. As an Anglo-Catholic and a Socialist, he thought society ought to have higher standards . . . the officials argued with him good-naturedly, he got passionate: 'This is how Rome came down. And I care deeply about it – in opposition to most of my Church. Don't think teenagers are able to evaluate your liberal ideas. You will have a totally disorganised, indecent and unpleasant society. You must have rules! We've gone too far on sex already. I don't regard sex as pleasant. It's pretty undignified and I've always thought so.'

Brown's homily was interrupted by a message that the NUR had rejected the government's offer, and it would be beer and sandwiches at 10 Downing Street as the Prime Minister, Harold Wilson, took over the negotiations. Castle voted, gratified that they had a comfortable majority. Brown, like a number of other senior members of the Labour leadership including Harold Wilson and James Callaghan, abstained, as they had done on every vote on this subject.

Arran's Second Attempt

Two weeks after Berkeley's triumph in the Commons Parliament was dissolved, and Labour was returned to power with a majority of ninety-seven, a victory which greatly increased the numbers supporting homosexual law reform. Probably two-thirds of the Commons now supported the cause. The problem was getting enough parliamentary time. Private members have only limited time to pass legislation because the government tends to monopolise time for its legislation. A bill would pass only if it were given time by the government.

Arran decided to start the ball rolling by re-introducing the bill that he had successfully piloted through the Lords the previous year. The bill received its First Reading on 26 April and a Second Reading on 10 May after a division that the reformers won seventy to twenty-nine. Dilhorne continued to oppose the bill and he insisted on putting forward the same old amendments to the bill, pushing most of them to votes, every one of which he lost. The speeches were shorter as the peers covered familiar ground and the debates lasted less time. Dilhorne managed to rally many more peers for the Third Reading on 16 June, hoping to catch the reformers out. Certainly many reformers stayed away but the bill still passed seventy-eight to sixty. The Lords had again registered their support for law reform. Dilhorne's speech in that debate was almost wholly directed against Ramsey and the bishops, whom he castigated for their dereliction of duty. It was, according to Boothby, 'a vicious attack', and certainly 'the most disgraceful speech I have ever heard in Parliament'. Dilhorne had come to believe that the bill would not have passed had it not enjoyed the support of the Church of England.

Opponents increasingly set the bill in the context of what was coming to be called the permissive society. The 1966/7 session saw the passage of David Steel's Abortion Act, which provided more support for the notion of declining moral standards. Kilmuir, in one of his last speeches in the Lords before his death, explained that 'it is becoming more evident to more people every day, rolling quickly down the slope of the permissive society'.

Abse's Bill

On 5 July 1966 Leo Abse introduced a bill on this subject in the Commons for the third time, this time as in 1965 a measure based on Arran's bill, which had been drafted by the Home Office. It received its First Reading by 244 votes against 100. The majority was composed of 187 Labour MPs, 46 Tories and 11 Liberals. The Liberal Party had supported this reform consistently since 1960. The length of time that it took to implement Wolfenden was certainly increased by the fact that although the Liberals invariably collected a large number of votes the parliamentary system ensured that they were massively under-represented in the Commons. In the seven years of divisions on the subject only one Liberal, a Scot, voted against reform. In 1966 no Liberal went into the division lobby against this measure with the 70 Conservative and 30 Labour MPs who voted against Abse's bill.

That vote allowed the group of cabinet ministers supporting reform to argue that the measure ought to be given parliamentary time. On 27 October 1966 Roy Jenkins, the Home Secretary, raised the matter in cabinet. He had the support of Dick Crossman, who as Leader of the House managed the government's business in the Commons. According to Crossman, 'Roy was able to make a persuasive case. I didn't make any comment and listened to Callaghan [the Chancellor of the Exchequer], the Prime Minister, George Brown and others asking why time should be given at all to such a Bill.' Jenkins prevailed, winning over the others by suggesting that it was better to get the bill out of the way well before the next election. This victory in cabinet ensured the passage of the bill.

On the Second Reading on 19 December 1966, Crossman and the government Chief Whip, John Silkin, mobilised support for the bill, effectively using the whip to secure support. As a consequence, the bill's supporters came increasingly from Labour and fewer Conservatives came into the division lobbies. A small group of Conservatives continued to register their support, a group which had helped the bill throughout its passage: Sir Edward Boyle, Paul Channon, Sir Charles Fletcher-Cooke, Hugh Fraser, Ian Gilmour, Martin Maddan, Enoch Powell, Nick Ridley, Margaret Thatcher and Richard Wood. The bill won a division before the Second Reading by 194 votes to 84. Only twenty-two Tories supported the bill on that division. Another consequence of making this a Labour measure was to reduce Labour opposition to the bill; only twenty-two Labour MPs voted against in December 1966, and by the summer of 1967 only three opposed the bill in the lobby.

Abse's speeches supporting the bill put plenty of distance between himself and homosexuality. He believed that the bill would reduce homosexual activity and bring about the better integration into society of those homosexuals who could not be treated. He believed that social education could help:

> among fatherless boys there is a disturbingly high rate of homosexuals. A lad without a father, lacking a male figure with whom to identify, is sometimes left with a curse, for such it must be, of a male body encasing a feminine soul.
>
> All in this House, on both sides and all sections of opinion, I know wish to see a diminution in the incidence of homosexuality. But I believe that education in mothercraft, and what is perhaps even more important, education in fathercraft, the mobilising of our social resources to lend more aid to the fatherless, the provision of more male child care officers and more male teachers are far more likely to succeed in this respect [depending on] our penal system.

By late 1966 members were simply repeating the same speeches and the debates aroused a decreasing amount of passion. A small group of Labour MPs from Merseyside, most of them working-class Catholics, tried to wreck the bill by tabling a motion about the protection of the Merchant Navy but this tactic failed. As the bill passed its report stage opposition increasingly fell to a small group of Tories led by Ray Mawby, a Conservative trade unionist. Most of those supporting him were self-made businessmen, few of them university educated and with no prospect of sitting on the front bench.

The bill finally passed the Commons after a long all-night sitting on 3/4 July 1967. It passed its final division by ninety-nine votes to fourteen at 5.44 a.m. The bill was sent to the Lords where it cleared all its stages in a few days. Arran and Abse were much congratulated by their colleagues. This was not, however, Arran suggested, a moment of triumph:

> This is no occasion for jubilation; certainly not for celebration. Any form of ostentatious behaviour; now or in the future, any form of public flaunting, would be utterly distasteful and would, I believe, make the sponsors of the Bill regret that they have done what they have done. Homosexuals must continue to remember that while there

may be nothing bad in being homosexual, there is certainly nothing good ... no amount of legislation will prevent homosexuals from being the subject of dislike and derision, or at best of pity.

The bill became an Act when it received the royal assent on 27 July 1967.

Good Behaviour

The Homosexual Law Reform Society had played its part in promoting the Act, but behind the scenes. The parliamentarians insisted that they should stay out of sight. For nearly seven years the HLRS was content to play the role of a lobbying organisation that rarely popped its head above the parapet. In those seven years after the Caxton Hall meeting in 1960 it never attempted to mobilise opinion outside Parliament or build any sort of grassroots organisation for homosexuals across Britain. It was a foolish strategy that placed HLRS entirely at the mercy of the parliamentary promoters of homosexual law reform. Antony Grey, secretary of HLRS, felt physically sick as he listened to Arran's speech in July 1967.

Grey, a sensitive man, has defended his role in his memoirs. He offers a strong defence of his actions while recognising the strength of the criticisms that have been made against them. His view in 1992 was 'that a better piece of legislation could have been achieved in the 1960s as easily as the Arran/Abse Act, because the vehemence and value of opposition to any reform at all remained constant, regardless of the detail of what was being proposed'. This is a significant admission. The sponsors of the reform were so obsessed, like Wolfenden, at winning over the opposition, that they continually delivered concessions that never attracted any extra support but only succeeded in further emasculating the eventual Act. It was a case, as Grey says, of 'placating the implacable'. Ultimately, though, Grey thinks that 'Paris *was* worth a mass: and that to dress, behave and speak in ways calculated to win the sympathetic attention of those you wish to influence is simply common sense.'

Antony Grey read history at Cambridge, at Magdalene, in the late 1940s. Whether consciously or unconsciously, he seems to have bought into a series of myths often propagated by academic historians about the peculiarity of British history, what Herbert Butterfield sneeringly described as the 'Whig Interpretation of History'. It was a set of myths that presented the recent history of Britain as a succession of liberalising measures produced by an ever-enlightening public opinion in co-operation with a sensible élite that through the medium of Parliament and a free press effected the necessary change. It was possible to present the extension of the suffrage in this way. Gradually more and more men, and then women, got the vote until Britain became a fully fledged democracy: 1832, 1867, 1885, 1918, 1928, each act increasing the numbers eligible to vote. The prototype of all these campaigns was Wilberforce's promotion of the abolition of slavery, which employed tactics used later by the campaigns for the Factory Acts, the repeal of the Corn Laws and Josephine Butler's campaign to raise the age of consent for females and abolish controlled brothels.

To some extent Grey and others patterned the cause of homosexual law reform on these movements, but without building the sort of extra-parliamentary campaign that was a feature of most nineteenth-century agitations. It is odd that Grey, a qualified barrister, did not think of the benefits that might derive from helping men charged with homosexual offences negotiate the legal system. Many men accused of these crimes had good cases against the police but were forced to use lawyers hostile to their interests; once arrested, they were at the mercy of a legal system increasingly designed to secure their conviction. It is even more odd that resources were not used to publicise the cases that came before the court, to analyse them relentlessly and expose the fact that homosexual men were denied their civil rights once a policeman arrested them.

One man who did try to promote an alternative model to Grey's was Alan Horsfall, a young Labour activist from Lancashire. Horsfall worked for the National Coal Board as an administrator. He served briefly as a Labour councillor in Nelson, from 1958 until 1960. When he was elected he was thirty years old. He had a powerful sense of the pressures faced by homosexually inclined men in villages and small towns, though he himself belonged to the privileged homosexual coteries of the metropolis: 'the pressures for social and legal conformity [in villages and small towns] bore down most heavily on homosexuals. Whereas in the cities it might be possible . . . for homosexuals to be themselves, the small towns offered no such possibility.' In the northern towns he knew where there were some sort of meeting places, they reinforced existing stereotypes of the homosexual: '[homosexuals] tended to congregate in the bar of the better hotels because it was there that people felt least prone to the prying curiosity of others, but it was an arrangement that served to reinforce the pervading misconception that homosexuality was something alien to the working-class.'

Horsfall tried to work for homosexual rights through the Labour movement but he encountered little sympathy and much hostility: 'They saw the condition as a product of the public schools from where it was carried into the decadence of those upper-echelons of society to which they were implacably opposed.'

Horsfall decided to establish a branch of HLRS in the north-west. After prolonged negotiation the society refused to let him affiliate, so the North Western Law Reform Society (NWLRS) was from its first meeting in Manchester during June 1964 an independent group. Horsfall suggests that the executive committee of HLRS took the view 'that sympathetic MPs [and peers] would withdraw their support if it became apparent that some of the demand for it was coming from homosexuals themselves!' There was a strong Anglican presence in the north-western society and a bishop sat on its committee (the Gay Liberation Front later boasted that it was the first pro-gay society not to have a bishop in its ranks). The chief difference from HLRS was that there was a larger membership which included many gay men, and the society had much more grassroots support. After 1967 it turned itself into the Campaign for Homosexual Equality, of which Horsfall was secretary until 1970.

The most novel feature of the Manchester-based group was that it wanted to extend the social space accessible to homosexually inclined men. Some club owners were amongst its supporters. According to Grey, the Manchester group was 'within a few weeks of the Arran/Abse Act reaching the Statute Book ... deep in plans to set up a chain of gay social clubs across the North of England and the Midlands and were approaching breweries for backing. I endeavoured to slow down this premature initiative, knowing only too well that it was likely to provoke loud disapproval from Lord Arran and Leo Abse.' HLRS had fallen into the pocket of their parliamentarian heroes.

The Act

According to the Wolfenden Committee one hundred men aged over twenty-one were each year convicted of homosexual offences with other men aged over twenty-one, and forty of them were sent to prison. The hundred represented about 10 per cent of all men convicted of homosexual offences. Obviously this was only a tiny fraction of the numbers of homosexual acts committed in private between consenting adults. Of those convicted only two or three each year came from London, the city with the highest concentration of homosexual men. These men would no longer be regarded as criminals after 1967. They were the principal beneficiaries of the 1967 Act. Clearly the law would make many men feel better and it would assist those who did not fear any social stigma from being blackmailed by their partners or others. This is the principal benefit that the 1967 Act brought to homosexual men. As a first instalment it was a step in the right direction.

The parliamentary debate that developed following the publication of the Wolfenden Report had exaggerated the importance of reform; it was the inevitable result of the polarising process of debate. Reformers tried to show that the measure would bring many benefits while opponents inevitably focused on the huge damage that would be done by the passage of the bill. Few parliamentarians actually spelt out the limited nature of the measure. Ramsey, trying to sell the measure to churchmen, told the Lords in May 1965 that 'the alteration of the law . . . would still leave by far the greater number of homosexual crimes and convictions unaltered, and it would be a gross misrepresentation of this particular change to say, in sweeping words, that such a change would legalise homosexual behaviour'.

As the bill passed the Commons, Quintin Hogg, who had been the only politician to give evidence to the Wolfenden Committee, consoled opponents with a rather sober assessment of the Abse bill:

I have been connected with the legal profession for 35 years, and, although at one time or another I have had to deal with a number of homosexual cases, never have I handled a case in the criminal courts that would have been affected by the Bill.

In every case with which I have had anything to do, either the act was done in public or it was done to a person under 21 years of age. Therefore, the idea that a very large number of people should utter loud cheers because we have removed from the field of criminality something which is virtually never prosecuted excites my surprise rather than my enthusiasm.

It is a small measure which will have little effect on our social life.

The 1967 Act may have great symbolic importance but it cannot be judged a great achievement, however much the liberals such as Jenkins and his friends like to suggest. Unfortunately the Act was treated as a once-and-for-all measure of homosexual emancipation. The issue ceased to occupy the attention of legislators and journalists, and homosexual reform groups found it virtually impossible to enlist their interest. It removed only one grievance, but there were many more that needed to be addressed. The police, who generally disliked the passage of the Act, grew even more homophobic and found it easier to make prosecutions under the new law. In particular, they ensured that the definition of privacy was kept as rigorous as possible and they prosecuted whenever they discovered any possible infringement. They used the new measures of the Act which increased the penalties for men who had sex with males between sixteen and twenty-one to increase their harassment of homosexually inclined men. A twenty-one-year-old man who committed a consensual sexual act with a twenty-year-old, for example, usually found himself liable to a much heavier prison sentence than a man found guilty of raping a female. The police exacted their revenge. There were many more prosecutions for homosexual offences in the 1970s than there had been in the 1950s: the numbers finding themselves before the courts tripled. In the two years Roy Jenkins was at the Home Office from 1974 he witnessed many more prosecutions than had occurred during Maxwell Fyfe's three years in the same post.

Police prosecutors did not need to seek approval for prosecutions for importuning. There are no figures for these offences, but newspaper reports and court records suggest that the practice of using *agents provocateurs* spread like wildfire across the nation. In the 1950s it had largely been confined to the larger cities but by the 1970s every force, however small, invested in elaborate equipment to trap men in public lavatories. Court cases reveal all sorts of devices and secret observation posts established by the police in this task. By the 1970s local newspapers were willing to publish the names and addresses of men convicted.

The 1967 Act did not include Scotland or Northern Ireland, and it excluded the Merchant Navy and the armed forces. An amendment to a Criminal Justice (Scotland) Act tabled by Robin Cook in June 1980 secured the extension of the 1967 Act to Scotland. Cook set his amendment in a wider international context: 'The House is given to developing a strong line in criticising the neglect of human rights in the Soviet Union. Those criticisms are well-deserved. However in this instance the state of our law is no better than that in the Soviet Union. It would be more constructive to put our own house in order first.' The amendment passed by 203 votes to 80. The *Sun* headlined it as the 'McGay's Charter'. It had a stormy passage in the Lords but eventually reached the statute book in the summer of 1980.

It took two more years to extend the Act to Northern Ireland. A very brave young man, Jeff Dudgeon, fought and won a case for discrimination against the government at the European Court of Human Rights and this led to legislative action at Westminster during 1982.

The prohibitions on the merchant marine and the military remain to this day, leaving Britain one of the few western countries to deny its homosexual servicemen (and servicewomen) the right to acknowledge their sexuality publicly. That battle continues. The age of consent, linked by Wolfenden to the armed forces in the 1950s, was not modified until 1994 when it was lowered to eighteen, the age which a majority of the Wolfenden Committee had supported in 1955.

★   ★   ★

There is one institution and one set of actors that usually hide well out of sight, the Home Office. It was the mandarins in that department who shaped the development of the issue from 1953 until 1967 and who deserve more credit for their role. Ironically the retiring Sir Philip Allen, sent by Maxwell Fyfe to study prostitution and parking meters in America in 1953, and who through his poisonous evidence to the Wolfenden Committee tried to muddy the waters on the issue of homosexuality, was by 1967 Roy Jenkins's right-hand man, the bureaucratic architect of the permissive society. Sir Philip had become Permanent Under-Secretary at the Home Office in 1966 after a palace coup. During his six years in that post he earned more rewards for his management and creation of the British security state in Northern Ireland. James Callaghan sent him to the Lords in 1976.

It was the mandarins who early in 1954 sold Maxwell Fyfe the idea of defusing the problem of homosexuality by combining it with prostitution as the subject of a Royal Commission. This was a reaction to the media interest in male homosexuality that had erupted in the autumn of 1953. Maxwell Fyfe accepted their arguments and brought the proposals to the cabinet who demoted the inquiry to a departmental committee. By a wise selection of chairman and committee members the Home Office secured a report on the two subjects that suited their needs. The police, of whom the Home Office is extremely protective, were not heavily criticised and the recommendations were accepted as coming from independent elements in society. The recommendations on prostitution quickly became law, the object of the bureaucratic manoeuvre of 1953–4.

On homosexuality everything depended on the attitude of the Home Secretary. If he wanted to block reform the Home Office had plenty of arguments ready, chiefly the unsuitability of the moment and the need for more research and time. In this way they stonewalled during the Home Secretaryships of Butler and Brooke. When a reformer arrived in 1965 they were ready for a limited measure which did little to change the *status quo* but gave the appearance of significant advance – a measure which they found difficult to sell to the police and judiciary but which protected, even strengthened, the position of the legal establishment. The Act had the further benefit of seeming to be independent of the Home Office, sponsored by backbenchers as a private member's bill, when in fact the basis of the Act was the Wolfenden Report (to which the Home Office input had been considerable) and the bill had been drafted by Home Office draftsmen.

It is the job of government departments to protect themselves and the special interests they represent. In the Home Office that means the legal establishment, and over the fourteen years from 1953 they succeeded in doing so with considerable skill. They also achieved their secondary aim of ensuring that ministers were protected from what often threatened to be a controversial issue. The situation was contained.

PART THREE

HOMOSEXUALITY ON TRIAL

7

Introduction

On 19 December 1966 Leo Abse's Sexual Offences Bill passed its Second Reading in the House of Commons. A day later Joe Orton, a young playwright who lived a few miles to the north of Westminster in the borough of Islington, started a diary. The last entry he made in that diary was on 1 August 1967, five days after Abse's bill received the royal assent, having passed through both Houses of Parliament. Eight days later, on 9 August, Orton was killed during the night in a frenzied attack by his long-time companion Kenneth Halliwell.

In the eight months that he kept the diary Orton, an active homosexual, makes only one mention of the Abse bill: 'Saw Peggy [Ramsay, his agent]. She's quite extraordinary. Being v. sophisticated about my taste "for little boys" . . . "Well you're legal now," she said, showing her ignorance. (The homosexual law becomes law today). "It's only legal over twenty-one," I said, "I like boys of fifteen." She looked rather bright. Great attempts at modernity' (4 July 1967).

The bill did not excite Orton, there was no great hymn of praise on its passage or relief that 'the prison doors were now open' (to borrow a phrase from Arran). On Sunday 23 July he discussed the bill with his friend, the actor and comedian Kenneth Williams, when Williams came to see him and Halliwell. Williams was depressed and feared that he would never satisfy his sexual desires. Orton gave him a pep talk, and Williams recorded their kindness in his diary: 'Went up to see Joe Orton and Kenneth. They were v. kind. We chatted about homosexuality and the effect the new clause [i.e. the Abse bill] would have. We agreed it would accomplish little. Joe walked with me to Kings X.' On that walk Orton outlined his own sexual philosophy:

> I walked [Kenneth Williams] to Kings Cross where he caught a bus home. On the way we talked about sex. 'You must do whatever you like,' I said 'as long as you enjoy it and don't hurt anyone else, that's all that matters.' 'I'm basically guilty about being a homosexual you see,' he said. 'Then you shouldn't be,' I said. 'Get yourself fucked if you want to. Get yourself anything you like. Reject all the values of

society. And enjoy sex. When you're dead you'll regret not having fun with your genital organs . . . Fucking Judaeo-Christian civilisation!' I said, in a furious voice, startling a passing pedestrian. (23 July 1967)

The fact that all homosexual practices were illegal did not stop Orton living openly in north London with his partner nor did it stop him seeking other sexual partners. The diary describes a succession of casual sexual encounters beginning on 23 December when he met 'an ugly Scotsman who liked to be fucked' (a desire that Orton satisfied) and ending with 'a dwarfish creature' who sucked him off in a public lavatory in Brighton. In all, he records ten encounters that took place in England, supplemented by five Moroccan lads he met on an eight-week stay in Tangier. His activities would have disgusted the honourable lords, ladies and gentlemen debating homosexual law reform inside the Palace of Westminster.

Orton was thirty-four, and except for a brief flirtation with the opposite sex in his late teens his exclusive erotic interest for all of his adult life had been directed towards his own sex. Orton's experience reminds us of the existence of individuals uninterested in law reform who negotiated a homosexual lifestyle for themselves in the unpromising terrain of post-war Britain. Orton had spent six months in prison, but not for a sexual offence: the local magistrates had imprisoned Orton and Halliwell for the heinous crime of defacing library books. Orton believed, however, that the magistrate Harold Sturge had sent them to prison because 'we were queers'. Sturge had written a memorandum for the Wolfenden Committee expressing his strong distaste for homosexual activity, so Orton was probably correct in detecting his prejudice in sentencing the lovers.

It is an accident that we know about Orton's private life and thoughts. His agent preserved his diary for posterity and passed it on to his biographer John Lahr. Lahr made good use of it in his life of the playwright and eventually published the complete document, an extremely valuable record for the historian of homosexuality in this period. The amount of documentary material that has survived about homosexual experience in the post-war period seems to be negligible. We are usually able to see homosexual men only through a heterosexual filter, forced to accept a picture that satisfied heterosexual fantasies. Orton's diary allows us to challenge these. Orton was neither afraid nor ashamed. He was defiant and used his writing as a way of articulating his hostility to the aggressively heterosexual society in which he lived:

we walked in the direction of Brighton – along the front . . . Here and there were numbers of nearly-naked young boys. This made me unhappy. After passing a fifteen-year-old youth lying face-downward, wearing red bathing-drawers, I said, in a rage, 'England is intolerable.

I'd be able to fuck that in an Arab country. I could take him home and stick my cock up him!' 'This is verbal exhibitionism!' Kenneth said, glancing at a number of evil-faced old women in a shelter. 'Look at them – crouching like Norns or the spirit of fucking British civilisation,' I said. 'I hate this tight-arsed civilisation.' (28 July 1967)

He wrote this entry less than fortnight before his death, and one day after Abse's bill became an Act. It encapsulates much of Orton's social outlook, an outlook which owed much to his experience as a gay man. In the mid-1960s Orton was lionised for his savage satires on contemporary society. In his plays he at last had the opportunity of publicly attacking the sort of conventional society held so dear by the legislators at West-minster. Sex was his chosen instrument for exposing its follies:

Kenneth who read *The Observer*, tells me of the latest way-out group in America – complete sexual licence. 'It's the only way to smash the wretched civilisation,' I said making a mental note to hot up *What the Butler Saw* [the play he was writing at the time] when I came to re-write. 'It's like the Albigensian heresy in the eleventh century,' Kenneth said. Looked up the article in the *Encyclopedia Britannica*. Most interesting. Yes. Sex is the only way to infuriate them. Much more fucking and they'll be screaming hysterics in next to no time. 'Innocent III', Kenneth said, 'did for them.' 'It isn't going to be so easy to mount a crusade this time,' I said. (26 March 1967)

Nobody could claim that Orton was typical. Yet none of his sexual partners went on to win fame or fortune: they were 'ordinary people'. Orton had sex with eight men between December 1966 and July 1967 (which hardly justifies his reputation as a voraciously promiscuous homo-sexual), and they displayed similarly positive attitudes to homosexuality. Most were working-class, most it would seem, like Orton, migrants to London. They knew where to meet other men for casual sex and like Orton they had plenty of fun with their genital organs:

. . . went down to [the public lavatory on] Holloway Road in search of a bit of sex. It was a grey day . . . I passed through the place, looking to see if any were worth having and suddenly noticed that one – a youngish man – wasn't bad. He followed me out and we walked under the bridge. He was Irish. He had a pale face, hollow cheeks, but pleasant. I said, 'Have you anywhere to go?' 'I share a room with a mate,' he said. I thought this meant that he had nowhere to go. So I said, 'I don't know anywhere round here.' 'Do you like threesomes?' the young man said. I shrugged. 'It depends who the other fellow is,' I said, thinking at the time that this was a very sensible remark because his mate might be hideous. 'You can come back with me,' he said, 'if you like.' 'Won't your mate mind?' I said. 'I wouldn't be taking you back if he did, would I?' he said, which was another sensible remark to put with mine.

His name was Allan Tills. He was a security guard. I thought he meant police at first, but this wasn't the case. His mate worked in a bar. They had a flat in Highbury . . . his mate was introduced to me as Dave. I realised at once that luck was with me: he was well-worth the effort. He had pale blue eyes and had a day's growth of beard. He wore jeans and a check shirt, under the shirt a white vest. He was about twenty-five years old and came from Burnley in Lancashire. He had a softness about his body which wasn't the softness of a woman . . . 'Where d'you come from?' he said, a bit later. 'Leicester,' I said. 'I've got a mate who plays for Leicester City,' he said. 'I slept with him on the night before his wedding.' 'You must've ruined his wedding night,' I said, more for want of something to say, since the remark hardly made sense. 'Yer,' Dave said.

After they had their tea, the three of them made love. They invited Orton to call again – he never did. 'I thought they were both nice fellows', he remarked.

Such encounters were occurring every day across Britain. Most are lost to history, unlike the piles of paper recording the disgust and prejudice of the men and women who talked to Wolfenden and the reams of Hansard that contain the agonised debates of the politicians contemplating a modicum of sexual freedom. Were the two men, Allan and Dave, lovers or just friends? How many accommodating couples were there like them across the country, working at ordinary jobs and just living their own lives on their own terms?

The path from Wolfenden through the parliamentary debates of the 1960s is a false trail, ending in a symbol, a piece of legislation which did nothing to promote tolerance or equality for homosexual men. Neither did it address the sorts of legal harassment faced by many homosexuals in Britain at this time. The material collected in this section of the book comes mainly from law courts and newspaper reports and allows us to get some idea of the sort of world in which Orton and men like him operated.

8

The Operation of the Law

Homosexual Offences

Until the passage of the 1967 Act through Parliament all homosexual activity between men was illegal. Under English law there were eight homosexual offences with which men could be charged, crimes created by three different statutes:

(a) Sodomy or buggery: an offence created under a statute of Henry VIII in the sixteenth century which carried the death penalty. The court had to be satisfied that a man had inserted his penis into the anus of another person or animal. In 1861 this crime ceased to carry the death penalty. The maximum penalty under the 1861 Act was life imprisonment.

(b) Attempted sodomy or buggery: statutory offence created in 1861. It has been unduly neglected by commentators. It carried a penalty of ten years' imprisonment and covered every homosexual act apart from sodomy, comprehending everything from fellatio to a kiss. This offence also covered invitations to a sexual act, so that if one man wrote to another suggesting that they made love he was guilty of attempted buggery. It was not even necessary for the participants to touch at any point during the commission of an act for them to be deemed guilty of this offence.

(c) Assault with intent to commit sodomy: another offence carrying a penalty of five years created under the 1861 Act, rarely used. It has not been possible from a survey of indictments to find a single individual charged with this offence.

(d) Indecent assault on a male person by a male person: an offence created by the 1861 Act that carried a penalty of ten years. This covered the performance of any sexual act by a male over sixteen on a male below that age.

(e) Acts of gross indecency between male persons: an offence created by section 11 of the Criminal Law Amendment Act, 1885 (what has come to be called the Labouchère amendment). This crime carried a penalty of two years. It was similar to the crime of attempted buggery in covering every homosexual act except buggery. 'Gross' was employed as a pejorative as in 'a gross act': it merely expressed the condemnation of the legislators, it did not mean that there were lesser offences labelled 'petty indecency'.

(f) Procuring acts of gross indecency between male persons: an offence which sharpened the elements of attempted buggery that concerned invitations to sex. This part of the statute covered an individual who might for himself or for someone else procure a sexual partner. It carried a penalty of two years.

(g) Attempting to procure an act of gross indecency: exactly the same as (f) except that no actual act actually took place. It carried the same penalty as all the other offences created under the 1886 statute.

(h) Persistent soliciting or importuning of males by males for immoral purposes: an offence known as importuning or cottaging, created under section 1 of the 1898 Vagrancy Act. This carried provision for fines and a maximum penalty of six months. Most men charged with importuning after 1898 were still charged under local bye-laws which regulated public spaces. Unlike the other crimes, this charge was usually tried only in a magistrates' court without a jury.

Almost all homosexual offences had been created by two Victorian statutes. The 1861 Act was a consolidating measure drafted by the state, bringing together all the crimes that could be described as offences against the person. As a consequence the Act covered bigamy, abortion and rape, as well as homosexuality. All these activities were crimes under old statutes and what the 1861 Act did was bring them together in one statute and attach new penalties for these offences. As a consequence sodomy ceased to be a capital crime. The newly-defined offence of attempted buggery was designed to fill the resulting gap in the new law. Courts had been reluctant to convict a man of the capital offence of sodomy and prosecutors in any case found it difficult to secure convictions because it was extremely difficult to prove evidence of penetration. It was hoped that by reducing the tariff from life to ten years juries might become less stringent. Attempted buggery provided prosecutors with a second charge that might be made on an indictment if the charge of buggery failed to stick. The 1861 Act therefore marks a major change in the way offences relating to homosexuality were prosecuted.

The 1885 Act, as is well-known, has its origins in a clause inserted by a Radical MP during a late-night sitting of the House of Commons. The Act was primarily concerned with raising the female age of consent from thirteen to sixteen, on to which Henry Labouchère tacked the following amendment:

Any male person who, in public or private, commits, or is party to the commission of, or procures or attempts to procure the commission by any male person of, any act of gross indecency with another male person, shall be guilty of a misdemeanour, and being convicted thereof shall be liable, at the discretion of the court, to be imprisoned for any term not exceeding two years.

This clause has often been misleadingly interpreted. It did not extend the laws against homosexual practice; it could not have extended them because the crime of attempted buggery already covered everything except sodomy. Repeatedly in discussions of the evolution of the law relating to homosexuality this myth has gone unchallenged. In a Lords debate on 12 May 1965 the Earl of Dundee articulated the interpretation which has generally been accepted: 'Until then [1885] sodomy had been the only kind of homosexual act which came within the range of the criminal law. This new Labouchère clause brought every other kind of homosexual act within the range of the criminal law.' This was not true. Further, a study of a random sample of cases at assizes from 1861 until 1886 suggests that neither the prosecutor nor the court drew any distinction between public and private; men were often convicted for committing homosexual acts in what Wolfenden and his committee would describe as private. The offence proved popular with prosecutors because sceptical jurors were more inclined to find a man guilty of an offence carrying two years than one carrying ten years. The offence gained considerable notoriety because it was under the 1885 Act that Oscar Wilde was charged and convicted in 1895.

An amusing feature of much writing on homosexuality has been the attention that is paid to analysing the official statistics for these crimes. It is often assumed that the prosecutors graded offences so that the most serious offence would be covered by the crime of buggery and the less serious offences by the crime of gross indecency. This sometimes may have been true but fails to take into account the process under which men were charged. Two delegations coming before the Wolfenden Committee suggested that there were men convicted of buggery who had not in fact committed the act, but performed another homosexual act. Police charged men opportunistically. There was also a problem of language for some men, in that they sometimes had no words to describe what they had done. A policeman might be able to persuade them to accept the label 'buggery' for what they had done and proceed to charge them with that offence.

The police also took the precaution of charging a man with two or three charges for the same act. This gave them scope for bargaining at a number of points during the case. In a contested case the prosecutor might be able to persuade a man charged with, say, attempted buggery to plead guilty to the lesser charge of gross indecency. This was a common practice.

There is a further complication in the way that the statistics were compiled in that the guidelines, before the 1950s at least, were extremely flexible, leaving much to the discretion of local police authorities to provide material from which the Home Office produced the national figures. Some forces were more efficient than others at the task and there seem to have been few attempts to resolve the potential ambiguities produced by dozens of different authorities classifying similar offences and categorising them according to local tradition rather than central dictat. Lord Trenchard discovered when he took over the Metropolitan Police as Commissioner in 1931 that the force recorded many crimes in a lost property book so that their overall detection rates did not cover crimes they found difficult to solve, so as a consequence these crimes did not show up on the official record.

The biggest change in the statistics in the post-war period occurred in 1949. Before that point offences were counted on the basis of all those charges on which an individual had been convicted. Because of bargaining at every stage of the process this meant only a fraction of charges were included in the figures. After 1949 the figures were constructed from the charges made when a man was arrested. As a consequence there seemed to be a much bigger jump in the amount of crime between 1949 and 1950 than actually occurred. This was less significant for crimes such as murder or manslaughter, where an accused man might be accused of a small number of charges, but produced a great inflation in crimes such as homosexual offences, where the accused was charged with a large number of offences but convicted on only a small number of them. As a result it seemed in the early 1950s as if there had been a big leap in the amount of homosexual crime. Though the trend was certainly upwards, it was much less than the much-cited figures suggested. In London the new mode of calculation made it seem as if homosexual crime had increased by 30 per cent between 1949 and 1950, and in some provincial areas by as much as 60 per cent.

This study has largely eschewed quantifying homosexual offences, except in the most general terms, because a close examination of the figures reduces any faith one might have in them. Figures do exercise an extraordinary impact on the human imagination: it always seems that quantification makes something clearer. Certainly individuals in the 1940s and 1950s reacted very strongly to the crime figures. During the war, criminal statistics were not published, so the first run of crime figures for 1946 which appeared in 1947 were eagerly scrutinised and showed, as moralists had already felt, a massive increase on those for 1938, the year that was thereafter taken as the base for what many regarded as the norm. The publication of those figures created a public perception of a breakdown of law and order that fuelled the post-war panic over the dissolution of British society, of which the homosexual press panic of 1953–4 was only one manifestation. It is my intention to try to re-work the figures for homosexual crime between 1861 and 1967 using court records. This is a task that will take many years, but the impressions so far gained, combined with the material presented by the police to the Wolfenden Committee, provide the basis for the following survey, which is a highly speculative and tentative first instalment.

Patterns of Prosecution

A number of observations on the basis of this survey can be made, observations with considerable implications for the history of homosexuality in Britain.

During each decade since 1861 the number of men charged with homosexual offences has increased, accelerating particularly after both the First World War and the Second World War.

In the period before 1914 most men charged with a homosexual offence faced one, possibly two, charges relating to one incident. In nine cases out of ten the defendant challenged the prosecution and placed the case before a jury. Conviction rates were low, sometimes less than 10 per cent, so this was not always a rewarding field of police activity. Even in cases where an individual pleaded guilty or was found guilty he might try to use the defence that this had been an isolated act, probably the consequence of excessive consumption of alcohol. This might encourage a magistrate or a judge to be more lenient.

By the 1950s relatively few men were ever charged with a single homosexual act: most were charged with several. Evidence was constructed to show that the accused's actions were part of a wider pattern indicating that he was a homosexual. This made it more difficult for an individual to plead that his action had been an isolated action. Most indictments listed a succession of homosexual acts performed by the individual. Police also increasingly used supporting material, including letters and diaries, to portray consistent homosexual behaviour. Confessions were particularly important in this process. Several judges and magistrates suggested in the late 1930s and early 1940s that these were becoming franker and more depraved. Increasingly policemen encouraged the accused to make their statements as frank as possible.

Another reason for establishing a pattern of homosexual behaviour was to convince judges, particularly in the high court, that these were more than trivial offences. Some judges in the 1920s dismissed cases of gross indecency that came before them and criticised the police for taking these cases. By setting the individual's behaviour in a wider pattern they could convince the judge or magistrate of the seriousness of the crime. This in turn alarmed judges and magistrates who read this increasingly as evidence of growing depravity. Judicial homilies as a consequence became more common on this subject. This also brought benefits for the police because the homily was usually the only part of a sex case that the press would print; in this way the police could advertise their virtues to their local constituency.

A key element in the changing pattern of cases was the fact that whereas before 1914, and still probably before 1939, a majority of homosexual offenders pleaded not guilty and were as a consequence able to have their cases tried before a jury, by 1954 only 6 per cent of men facing a trial pleaded not guilty; all the rest were convicted before a judge or magistrate in a brief case that might only last a few minutes and they would be convicted on the basis of their own confession.

By the 1950s police rarely prosecuted men who did not confess. They took cases they could win. As a consequence, and in marked contrast to the periods earlier in the century, conviction rates on this offence were extremely high.

Increasingly lawyers found themselves defending men who had pleaded guilty to homosexual offences. The old defence of an isolated episode was no longer possible, so defence attorneys increasingly invested in medical explanations of the accused man's behaviour. The wealthier the accused, the more medical testimony could be collected. Judges and magistrates were often sceptical of such evidence, but it had a reasonable chance of success with a middle-class professional. His lawyer would show that he was a respectable character with an unblemished record except for this one aberration. Family members would be persuaded to testify and many judges and magistrates were prepared in such circumstances to be lenient, fining the man or placing him on probation, with a recommendation that he seek medical treatment. The 1948 Criminal Justice Act made it easier for courts to send a man to a mental hospital for a specified period instead of prison. The sentence usually lasted a year. The medical defence was thus chiefly a way for middle-class men to avoid prison, and their families might not lose so much face if their relative was regarded as suffering from a sickness rather than labelled a criminal. This device was one of the main ways in which the notion of homosexuality as a sickness was disseminated. After a time some judges and magistrates themselves came to articulate the idea that it was a sickness, a consequence of repeated exposure to the argument.

A key element in court cases was the class of the individual accused. Working-class men rarely had access to proper legal advice, and as a consequence their defence was limited. They were unlikely to be able to call character witnesses and as a consequence the case revolved around the approach of the prosecution. As a result working-class men were more likely to be sent to prison and for longer periods.

At the turn of the century about 10 per cent of cases concerned an adult man and a boy under sixteen. By the 1950s three-quarters of cases involved this combination.

These developments can be explained in a number of ways. It is significant that after both world wars the number of prosecutions increased. Both conflicts produced major social dislocation in Britain. Young men were taken away from home and frequently separated from their families and from females for long periods of time. The amount of homosexual behaviour and homosexual prostitution increased considerably. This greatly strengthened and expanded the homosexual subcultures. The wars also produced much greater sexual liberation generally and this produced a moral reaction that is evident during the early 1920s and the late 1940s and early 1950s.

In the period after the First World War the recruitment by British police forces of women officers was of critical importance for policing sex crimes. The women who joined the police were very different from their male colleagues. Policemen were generally drawn from the working classes but the spinsters who made the police their career were drawn from the middle and upper classes. Most of those women joining in the 1920s were suffragettes, a movement which had greatly sharpened their belief in achieving social change. The movement for women's suffrage had created a strong *esprit de corps* and a powerful sense of personal empowerment. Some of these women developed a taste for policing during the war when they had worked as auxiliaries or in the squads of moral vigilantes that patrolled the large cities to expose sex criminals.

Police forces used women to deal with other women and children. Many of the women belonged to that British moral tradition deeply rooted in nineteenth-century British Protestantism that believed that the reduction, even the elimination, of male lust was the only way to remove the chief evils of modern civilisation. They campaigned for laws against the consumption of alcohol, for laws on incest and for more policing of female prostitution. The existence of a small number of women police officers provided moral campaigners with well-placed allies in their war against male lust. The greatest battle of course was against organised prostitution, what was called 'white slavery'. Between the wars the League of Nations devoted many resources to a major investigation into this international problem and many moralists hoped that the international organisation would be able to stop the global traffic in women and children for prostitution.

Homosexuality was never a major priority of such groups, but the greater care taken by courts to listen to children as witnesses increased dramatically the numbers of men charged with sex crimes against boys and youths. Women police officers tended to believe the children and possessed the social confidence to press for the conviction of the men they accused. In the years before the First World War defence attorneys were quite brutal with children who accused adults of sex crimes. By the 1930s such tactics had become counter-productive. Many parents were reluctant to allow their children to give evidence and this often made it difficult to prepare a case – but once again women police officers tried hard to persuade them.

Other developments in British policing between the wars led the police to take more cases in which men were charged with homosexual offences. Conviction rates were constantly under scrutiny and to achieve better results forces devoted more of their resources to specialised groups of detectives who could produce better-prepared cases that would be less easy for lawyers to challenge in court. Forces also faced a demand of almost continual retrenchment from the local authorities that supported them, so it often helped their local image to advertise their concern for public morals to the local communities they served.

It is clear that many forces felt it prudent to advertise their role as the guardians of public morality between the wars. This often offset other aspects of policing which brought them into conflict with the local community. Typically such a pattern seems to have grown up in rural forces first, where general crime levels were low and where the policing of sexuality and morality offered a way to justify the continued existence of the force. As a consequence by 1939 there were criminal assize calendars in the English provinces where one half of all the cases coming before the court were concerned with public morality. Between the wars homosexual offences were not the only moral crimes that produced more convictions: bigamy, carnal knowledge of girls under sixteen, rape and abortion all occupied an increasing portion of the courts' time. Invariably the police took only those cases they could win so the confession became crucial and conviction rates soared.

The Metropolitan Pattern

For homosexual cases two regional patterns emerged between the wars. In the larger cities, principally in London, the police rarely prosecuted or indeed investigated homosexual crime that took place in private. Police were possibly simply too busy. High levels of crime plus the increasing amount of police time devoted to the management of traffic meant that in the larger conurbations sexual and moral crimes largely went undetected. The police in these cities did, however, make concessions to the need to advertise their virtue. This was achieved by policing the public lavatories and public spaces.

The Metropolitan Police force established in 1930 a special force of officers to police the capital's lavatories. In the year 1930/1, 127 cases of soliciting by males were taken; only one was lost by the police. There was, however, one major problem: the arrest of a number of Guardsmen, which alarmed the military. A special Home Office conference was called to discuss the problem in May 1931 and the police agreed to co-operate closely with their military counterparts. The impact of the Met campaign had been dramatic: fifty men had been dismissed from the Brigade of Guards during 1930/1 for homosexual prostitution.

By the 1950s the policing of lavatories using plain-clothes policemen was a well-established feature of policing in the capital. In 1946 the Met usually had four policemen each week employed on this task. Groups of policemen rotated each month and always worked in pairs. By the early 1950s eight policemen were assigned to this task. The wastage of manpower was immense. In 1946, for example, 188 arrests were made for importuning; in 1953 it was 374, just over one man a day. The magistrate in the case involving Sir John Gielgud suggested that 600 such cases came before his court each year; this was absurd, but the figure passed into general circulation. This figure was taken up by the press and has been much cited since. If one magistrate's court had 600 cases per annum then the total number for the whole capital would have gone into thousands. The fact was that it was fewer than 400 cases per year for the whole of the Metropolitan Police district.

A police memorandum identified eighteen 'cottages' across London where they concentrated their attention:

Victoria Station (the most popular venue with cottagers)

South Kensington underground station

Dudmaston Mews, on Fulham Road

Clareville Street, off Brompton Road

Dove Mews, off Brompton Road

Piccadilly Circus underground station

Leicester Square

Babmaes Street, off Jermyn Street

Providence Court, close to Oxford Street

Dansey Place, off Shaftesbury Avenue

Falconberg Mews, between Soho Square and Charing Cross Road

Three Kings Yard, near Grosvenor Square

Grosvenor Hill, off Grosvenor Square

Brydges Place, off the Strand near Charing Cross Station (closed on police advice from February 1954)

Rose Street, between Long Acre and St Martin's Lane

York Place, off Villiers Street near Charing Cross Station

Dryden Street, near Covent Garden

Galen Place, off Bloomsbury Way near the British Museum

From police reports it is possible to discern cruising patterns in London at this time. It will be seen that popular cottages are clustered close together so that a cottager could move conveniently from one to another. In west London, for example, one might start at South Kensington underground station, walk up Fulham Road to check out Dudmaston Mews (where Gielgud was arrested), move back north to Brompton Road with visits to Dove Mews and Clareville Street before returning to South Ken. Similar circuits operated in the vicinity of Victoria, Grosvenor Square, Leicester Square and Charing Cross Station. These were the circuits that the policemen took.

Examination of importuning cases suggests that two groups were particularly vulnerable to arrest, out-of-towners and clergymen. Policemen found that the arrest of a clergyman brought publicity and praise for their activity. Magistrates often reserved their most savage comments for the clergymen who came before them and even reticent newspapers might be attracted by such remarks.

While Nott-Bower's information suggested that importuners came from 'all walks of society', they did detect a predominance of men employed 'in quasi-domestic occupations e.g. waiters, kitchen porters, barmen and chef'. The importance of noble households, hotels and gentlemen's clubs in supporting the metropolitan homosexual subculture has long been underestimated. The decline of domestic service may have had an impact upon homosexual practice in the capital, though anecdotal evidence suggests that the influx of building labourers in the 1950s and 1960s (a number of Orton's partners in 1966–7 were drawn from the building industry) provided a group that replaced the butlers, valets, chauffeurs and footmen who were having to find new livelihoods.

Police activity may have deterred some men but most cottagers believed that the chances of being arrested were slim; for some it added to the excitement. Even better were the cottages outside the central district, such as Joe Orton's *pissoir* on Holloway Road, which were targeted only occasionally. The regular patrols largely kept to central London.

Another public space that produced arrests was Hyde Park. In 1953 seventy-six men were arrested for acts of gross indecency in this area, most of them during the act of sex. The amount of activity in the park, especially during the summer months, was incredible. Cinemas were another site of activity where a few arrests were made, particularly the Biograph Cinema in Wilton Street near Victoria Station.

Policing in the capital was directed towards identifiable public places. The chances of being caught were small. Men found guilty of importuning on a first offence were usually fined; only second offenders were imprisoned. Sometimes a magistrate launched a crackdown, as Harold McKenna, stipendiary magistrate at Bow Street did in 1943–4. Such campaigns soon ran out of steam or became counter-productive, because so many first offenders seemed to be able to overturn a prison sentence at an appeal.

The Met did not collect evidence to prosecute homosexual networks or to prosecute homosexuality between consenting male adults in private. It was Peter Wildeblood who brought this to the attention of the Wolfenden Committee, pointing out that Sir Harold Scott, Police Commissioner from 1946 to 1953, had operated the Code Napoléon in the capital. In 1953 only two cases were prosecuted that would have fitted the 1967 Act.

The Met tolerated the homosexual subculture in the West End, partly due to prudence, because prosecutions would have brought in well-connected individuals and the police did not seek to antagonise the élite. There was also a strong element of corruption. For decades the Met had accepted bribes from publicans, club owners, bookmakers, pornographers and pimps to turn a blind eye to their activities.

Provincial Patterns

Outside the big cities homosexually inclined men faced a more ferocious pattern of policing which amounted to a series of locally sponsored campaigns to harass them. This pattern grew up in the 1920s and 1930s, starting in a swathe of counties in southern and western England. From court reports it is obvious that the area covered by the western circuit (Hampshire, Dorset, Wiltshire, Somerset, Devon and Cornwall) pioneered these practices. In these counties police used every method possible to launch provincial pogroms. They searched premises without legal authority, they collected names of all partners, and used diaries, letters and any other documentation to present the most graphically homosexual picture of the accused. In the late 1930s there were network trials in which several men were put on trial together. The earliest of these took place in Wallasey in 1937, followed closely by another group trial of men from Callington, Cornwall, during 1938. By the mid-1950s such trials were a regular feature of the Assize calendar as will be evident from Chapter 10. In the 1940s other provincial forces started to imitate these activities and by the late 1950s it was a national practice. It was during this period also that provincial forces began to launch campaigns against importuners.

Hampshire seems to have long had the most savage police force in dealing with homosexual offences. The presence of the port of Southampton, the naval port of Portsmouth and the largest military garrison in England at Aldershot made this a fairly obvious place for homosexual activity. The police in this county had more experience of homosexual activity than almost any other provincial force. It therefore does not seem to have been quite so accidental that it should have been the site of the most highly publicised case of the 1950s involving Lord Montagu.

Many of the provincial forces were vicious in their prosecution of homosexuality. They rarely showed any respect for status or class, so that networks including middle-class men as well as working-class men were prosecuted. Londoners accustomed to an altogether different system of policing were often vulnerable when they came to stay in the country if they behaved as they would back home.

The press coverage of 1953–4 highlighted a situation that had been developing for at least three decades. The problem for contemporaries was one of perception. Newspapers rarely reported homosexual trials, simply omitting them in their otherwise extensive coverage of the assize or quarter sessions. There was no way of knowing what was being covered up. As a consequence the much more extensive coverage after 1953 produced support for the notion of a witch-hunt. If one still wants to use that word then it might be applied to the locally-inspired campaigns against homosexuals that took root in provincial England between 1920 and 1960. They were directed not from the centre but from the locality, and London was not included.

Persuasion

Sir Robert Mark, Chief Constable of Leicester, was appointed to the Met in 1966, becoming Commissioner in 1972. He was appointed to root out the corruption in the Met. He was not entirely successful, as operations after he left office in 1976 showed. His memoirs, however, offer an important antidote to the prevalent George Dixon image of the British policeman which won the force so much popular support in post-war Britain. He shows policing in Britain during the 1940s to have been a very 'rough and tumble' business. His experience of the force led him to believe that policemen regularly used violence or threats of violence while interviewing suspects. Mark remembered a colleague,

> a very successful, fairly senior detective in Manchester, who, when dealing with hardened criminals, had his own version of the Judges Rules. It consisted of greeting the prisoner with the blunt enquiry, 'Will you talk or be tanned?' If the reply was in the negative, sometimes colourfully so, the prisoner was removed smartly to the lavatory where he was upended and his head jammed down the bowl. It usually took two to hold him whilst a third repeatedly pulled the chain until a waggling of the feet indicated a more compliant attitude. He signed a form headed by the usual caution against self-incrimination.

The inter-war improvement in police performance depended on their increasing success in extracting confessions. A man was arrested, whether in a public lavatory or as the result of a complaint, and a process of negotiation and persuasion started. The police were both the prosecutors and the detecting agency. They used all manner of threats and inducements to secure a confession. A particularly talkative suspect might be offered the possibility of turning King's evidence by giving evidence against his partners, but this was not always necessary. Evidence collected from houses and flats, letters, papers and diaries often persuaded men to talk. The accused would be led to believe that his sentence depended on how the police presented his case. Recalcitrant men were often taught a lesson by the police, who presented such a depraved picture of their activities that the court gave them a much longer sentence. Demeanour was always a critical element in determining a sentence. Police often reported the accused's reaction to his crime before the judge or magistrate passed sentence, thus colouring the judge's perception of the man about to be sentenced.

The way in which police collected evidence constituted a major infringement of the civil rights of the individuals arrested. Newspapers and politicians never took up such miscarriages of justice. They were entirely swept under the carpet, nobody listened to their complaints and they had no redress. Hardly anyone in the legal establishment blew the whistle on what was happening. The insensitivity to the rights of their fellow citizens exhibited by policemen, solicitors, barristers, magistrates and judges is one of the shocking features of modern British history. Parliament or the administration showed itself unwilling to address such abuses. They were too busy congratulating themselves on the fairness of British justice to reform a system that would not have been out of place in a tinpot South American military dictatorship. As Mark suggests:

> [such] practices ... were perfectly well-known to solicitors, to counsel, to judges and to the Press but that nobody did anything about them because there seemed no obvious way to achieve a fair balance between public interest and the rights of wrongdoers. To pretend that knowledge of such malpractices was confined to police alone, as people occasionally do, is sheer hypocrisy.

The journalist Colin MacInnes, surveying the criminal justice system five years later, suggested that the 'police very rarely bring a charge without grounds, simply through malice. But when they *do* bring a charge they are not over-scrupulous on how they make it stick – nor can they afford to be, with the public and official pressures on them to get convictions'.

As a consequence of their activities many provincial policemen grew expert in their knowledge of the homosexual subculture. As confessions became franker and more explicit they began to tap a largely oral tradition of homosexual experience. Homosexual subcultures have always placed a premium on the storyteller and the archives uncovered by the police suggest that many men were keen to preserve the evidence of their histories. It is a source now almost completely lost, the only traces of it surviving in the court proceedings of the period.

By the 1950s the prosecution of homosexuality by the legal establishment was well entrenched. Nothing seemed able to disturb those practices. Anyone listening to or reading the evidence given to the Wolfenden Committee could not fail to appreciate the extraordinary degree of hostility felt by judges, magistrates, barristers, solicitors and policemen against homosexual activity. It had become part of their rationale as guardians of public morality and explained the ferocity with which they reacted to the modest proposals for reform that appeared in 1953. This was a situation that the Wolfenden Committee evaded and one that no British government faced, however liberal its Home Secretary. They seemed powerless to prevent this hostility and unwilling to challenge such a well-established vested interest.

9

The Crusaders

In 1936 Mrs Wallis Simpson was looking for a solicitor to act for her in the divorce action that she was taking against her husband Ernest. She approached the London City solicitor, Theobald Mathew, who refused to act for her. It was one of his proudest boasts.

Mathew belonged to a legal dynasty; his grandfather had been a Lord of Appeal and his father a barrister. Called to the bar in 1921 Mathew practised for only four years before qualifying as a solicitor and establishing a lucrative legal practice in the City of London. In 1940 he joined the Home Office as a temporary civil servant. He had the good fortune to acquire a patron, Labour Home Secretary Herbert Morrison. Mathew became Morrison's troubleshooter and acquired considerable experience of the Home Office, and of the administration of the criminal justice system. The war seemed to excite Mathew's ambitions and he began to intrigue for the post of Director of Public Prosecutions. Morrison pressed the claims of Mathew; with this appointment the Labour politician broke precedent. It was customary for the DPP to be appointed from amongst the chief crown prosecutors, either lawyers who worked within the office of Public Prosecutions or who had served as crown lawyers at the Old Bailey, what were called the Treasury counsel. Mathew belonged to neither of these groups. He had little experience as a practising barrister and the bulk of his legal work had been as a solicitor. Unusually for a Director, he had accumulated through his service in the Home Office connections with the senior members of that office and the Chief Constables of Britain's police forces. Such connections might have been thought to disqualify him from acting as Director: they certainly influenced his direction of the office.

The appointment of Mathew by Morrison was one of the most important decisions the Labour politician ever made. Mathew remained Director of Public Prosecutions for almost twenty years, until his death in 1964. He did incredible damage to the criminal justice system in Britain and seems to have exploited his position to build up a major personal fief as he expanded the size and the scope of his office. The Second World War greatly expanded the British state and men like Mathew acquired a taste for bureaucratic power. They became skilled empire-builders and in the new post-war state massive amounts of money were spent expanding the bureaucracy even further. The Prosecutions of Offences Regulation of 1946 extended and refined the role of the Director of Public Prosecutions, making him more independent of interference from the Attorney-General, the member of the government responsible to Parliament for the operation of the DPP's office (it is one of the curiosities of the British system that, up until 1986, the Director was appointed by the Home Secretary but it was the Attorney-General who was ultimately responsible for the business of the office to Parliament).

Mathew was one of the 'new men' created by the war. The most pernicious feature of Mathew's two decades as Director was the close and rather cosy relationships he maintained with the Chief Constables and the senior mandarins at the Home Office. An immensely clubbable character, he was a regular visitor to the network of conferences held by chief police officers throughout England and Wales, where he was almost invariably the last man in the bar. Whisky was his favourite tipple and by the end of his reign his judgement was seriously impaired by excessive consumption of alcohol. Close connections with the police had been avoided by his predecessors who had been formed in an altogether different tradition, one in which they preferred to see themselves as watchdogs of possible abuse of the prosecution system by the police. Previous occupants of the office had acted as a genuine safeguard for the citizen against the way the police abused their power. As a consequence of his policy Mathew turned a blind eye to the massive abuses of power and corruption which were such a feature of the British police during the post-war period.

It is characteristic of the way in which British historians and political scientists have chronicled the post-war decades that Mathew's existence has barely been registered. While many more visible and vocal characters, many of them a lot less powerful or important, occupy the centre stage, one of the real movers and shakers of his time completely escapes their attention. This is exactly what Mathew desired; he resisted all publicity, preferring to operate behind the scenes in the corridors of power. Few of the records of his office have yet been released by the state – most are embargoed well into the next century. His evidence to the Wolfenden Committee and the file that his office constructed to support his testimony and report are one of the few documents relating to his reign as Director that have been released. They cast an important light on this powerful and secretive man, and expose a strong and determined moralist who was trying to save his nation from a great menace.

Mathew has been described as a 'devout Catholic', as if this offers an explanation for his actions. In fact he was a lapsed Catholic, like one of those other great post-war moralists Sir William Haley, Director-General of the BBC and editor of *The Times*. Perhaps lapsed Christians were more dangerous than the devout variety. Possibly one of the reasons for the growing moralism of early and mid-twentieth-century Britain was the growing number of individuals who retained all the ethical teachings of Christianity (most of them derived from the Old Testament) without many of the mitigating doctrines of the New Testament.

After he had given his testimony to the Wolfenden Committee Mathew was sent a transcript of what he had said by the committee's secretary, which he would then edit before the final document was circulated to the committee as the record of the proceedings. Fortunately Mathew's reply, listing the amendments he wanted to make, survives. In this way the poor historian struggling against the cunning of the secretive mandarins occasionally gets a break. Mathew's principal amendment was the removal of the word 'campaign' from his evidence: 'In 571 I would like to have "because I did a campaign with the Ministry of Education" taken out, because "campaign" is an exaggeration, and I do not want to convey the impression that the Ministry of Education were hostile to the idea.' In fact, as we shall see, 'campaign' was a very accurate word to describe Mathew's prosecuting policies towards certain groups of homosexually inclined men after his appointment in 1944. Sir Theobald Mathew conducted a crusade.

Mathew has a place in homosexual demonology as a member of Peter Wildeblood's trinity of witch-hunters. Mathew makes one of his few recorded appearances in print on the pages of Wildeblood's book. Mathew attended the second Montagu trial in 1954, and was present at the moment when the Office of Public Prosecutions got its revenge on Lord Montagu of Beaulieu. He had, according to Wildeblood, taken 'the liveliest interest' in the case.

Mathew believed, in common with many of his contemporaries, that homosexuality had increased since the war. This he believed had happened because of the 'complete change in the life of the male adolescent' that had occurred in that time. It was as a result of extending 'the period of education', presumably a reference to the 1944 Education Act under which the number of children continuing their education after fourteen increased, but partly also as a result of the introduction of National Service. These two developments had created 'an atmosphere in which these habits [i.e. homosexuality] can be easily acquired and become ingrained'.

Mathew did not believe that any form of treatment or reformation could save an individual once corrupted. He believed that the number of 'genuine' homosexuals who came before the courts was extremely small.

Most offenders did not, 'whatever they say, have this excuse'. They had been corrupted: 'in many cases against their better instincts, through curiosity, hero worship or cupidity, [they have] allowed themselves to be initiated into these practices, and have persisted in them, until their capacity to control or limit their homosexual desires has ceased to exist'. The only way to tackle the problem was

> at a much earlier stage. A decent and healthy community, in this respect, can only be created and maintained by inculcating into the young a clean sex outlook, both physical and mental, through parental influence and by education . . . boys and young men should be taught that these habits are dirty, degrading and harmful, and the negation of decent manhood, and that every practicable precaution be taken that those in charge of boys and young men are themselves free from this taint.

Mathew focused particular attention on schools. 'The history of many accused', he told the Wolfenden Committee, 'has started with being themselves taught minor homosexual practices, when at school, by masters or by older boys. They in their turn have taught younger boys, and have acquired a habit that requires considerable strength of character to eradicate.'

He believed that those in authority had become more lax in their treatment of homosexual offences: 'I have an impression that, at the present time, minor homosexual practices amongst boys at some schools are not being treated, as a matter of discipline, with the same severity as they were a generation ago, and that the supervision of boys at night and out of school hours is not so strict.' Schools seemed to be guilty of moving erring schoolmasters on without bringing them to justice: 'I have had a disturbing number of cases in which masters suspected, on good *prima facie* evidence, of interfering with the boys in one school, have been allowed to resign and have been given excellent references to another school, with disastrous results.'

Using the information collected in the DPP file it is possible to reconstruct Mathew's campaign, a campaign against men in positions of authority and trust having sexual relationships with boys or young men in their care. From the time that he became Director in 1944 the number of cases in which the DPP's office took over the prosecution in homosexual offences from the local police force expanded rapidly. In 1946 his office took 46 such cases; in 1947, 65; in 1948, 75; in 1949, 69; in 1950, 108; in 1951, 154; in 1952, 103; and in 1953, 141. These figures underestimate the number of cases actually taken because they exclude cases in which the accused was solely charged either with indecent assault or gross indecency, but the figures available give us an idea of the general trend. It explains why in many assize calendars in the 1950s three-quarters of the cases concern sex with boys or adolescents under the age of sixteen. The much noticed rise in the number of prosecutions during the period 1945 to 1954, which excited comment at the time and since, was largely a consequence of a prosecuting policy pursued by Mathew. The policy was directed mainly at teachers, youth leaders and other people who had a connection with the young male. This policy was not directed towards sexual assaults on females nor did Mathew tackle the problem of sexual abuse within the family.

Mathew attacked the institutional protection offered to men guilty of exploiting their position for their own sexual gratification. He found that all organisations which employed men to look after young males instinctively covered up. It was, as he told the Wolfenden Committee, common practice for most employers to give an erring employee a good reference and send him on his way. Most schools and youth organisations avoided scandal in this way. The Church of England generally removed the offender from the parish that he was serving, and sent him off for a period of rehabilitation to a religious order (the Cowley Fathers in Oxford was a particularly favoured spot) before reintroducing the individual to parish work in another diocese. In some instances the Church of England sent erring clerics to the colonies, usually the West Indies. Cases were brought only when someone pressed a complaint. Parents were the usual source, though most parents refused to get themselves or their child involved in a prosecution. Another source of complaint was female members of these organisations; male members rarely blew the whistle on an individual abusing his position, and then only if they were disgruntled employees.

The rise in the number of prosecutions for homosexual offences in the post-war period has led many commentators to suppose the existence of a witch-hunt, though they have not pinned down that campaign more precisely. The Mathew evidence to Wolfenden suggested that this has a somewhat different cause than was previously suspected. It was a campaign directed against one group, a campaign which uncovered some fairly dreadful levels of abuse of children and adolescents by adults, exposing a problem which even today remains largely hidden; though one of the consequences of Mathew's campaign was to strengthen the link within the popular and official mind between child abuse and homosexuality. His campaign provided plenty of copy for the court columns of the *News of the World* and the *Sunday Pictorial*.

Mathew met some resistance to his campaign in Whitehall. He put pressure on the Ministry of Education to keep a blacklist of convicted homosexual offenders, a list which was certainly maintained from 1955.

He brought to the attention of the Ministry particularly bad cases to support his campaign. He wanted them to organise more effective supervision, registration and inspection of private schools. His greatest triumph within Whitehall occurred in the Home Office.

On 3 September 1952 the Children's Department of the Home Office issued a circular to all institutions containing children and young people managed by the Home Office, mainly approved schools and Borstals. This instructed managers to record even the most minor acts of homosexual activity in their log books, and they were instructed to inform the local police of any homosexual offence committed on their premises regardless of the circumstances. Institutions lost the power to conduct their own inquiries and inflict their own punishments. This instruction was strongly criticised by the managers of these institutions. They complained to the Home Office and to the Wolfenden Committee that this circular undermined their authority and that they resented the interference of the local police. A study of the assize calendar suggests that the number of such cases involving approved schools and Borstals did increase. The Wolfenden Committee recommended in its report the withdrawal of the circular.

In Mathew's evidence to the Wolfenden Committee and the DPP file we finally find the smoking gun, the piece of the jigsaw which explains why the number of cases for homosexual offences rose so dramatically after 1945. Here was a highly-placed moralist with a very specific axe to grind whose policies have done much to shape British perceptions of male homosexuality. Mathew is a key figure, who really did set the agenda.

The Voice of Justice

The judiciary occupied a position of considerable power, prestige and prominence in mid-century Britain. Surrounded by an immense amount of ceremonial and pageantry, the senior judges of the English courts lived a peculiarly privileged existence. Their office provided them with plenty of opportunities to ventilate their prejudices. An opinionated group of men, firmly convinced of the wisdom of their observations, they used the act of sentencing the wretched men and women who came before them to comment not simply on the inadequacies of the convicted but also on the society they served. These homilies from the bench enjoyed wide circulation through the press, local newspapers usually printing their offerings in full. They rarely provoked disagreement. The homilies provided the leader writers with the chance to sound off about the same evils identified by the judges, inevitably lacing their remarks with liberal praise for the illiberal justices.

In the 1940s and 1950s these judicial commentaries became increasingly vicious. The judiciary had a high sense of its social mission and, as many of the sermons demonstrate, they were keen to cast themselves in the role of tribunes of the people. Judges in the post-war period did much to promote a populist notion of justice by repeatedly tailoring their comments to popular prejudices. Newspapers encouraged judges to sound off and play to the gallery. A society constantly priding itself on its tolerance encouraged reactionary voices, stirring up hate and fear throughout the country.

The judicial style was best exemplified by the Lord Chief Justice, Rayner Goddard, who was never out of the headlines. Regarded as the most reactionary member of the British judiciary in the twentieth century, Goddard has become something of a caricature. He was immensely popular. Never particularly friendly to the state, he took great pleasure in deriding bureaucratic excess at a time when many Conservatives in the country found themselves totally out of sympathy with the expansion of the state. Britons seemed to love his irascibility, for like most judges Goddard seemed to live in a constant state of alarm at the deterioration of British civilisation. Goddard invariably jumped on every moral bandwagon.

Ironically it was the reforming Labour government of Clement Attlee that appointed Goddard to the post of Lord Chief Justice in 1946, an appointment celebrated at the time by Labour because it was 'non-political'. Keen to emphasise their differences from the Tories, Labour decided to end the practice which had made the chief judicial office a piece of political patronage. Previous Lord Chief Justices had been lawyers active in party politics. In retrospect it is clear that this had a moderating role on the judiciary. Goddard was too much part of the culture of the judiciary and achieved extraordinary ascendancy over his colleagues doing much to encourage and promote the populist style of justice which released so much reactionary poison in British society. Certainly not one of the Labour government's greatest achievements.

Introducing Goddard to the Magistrates' Association, Labour's Lord Chancellor Earl Jowitt recalled for his audience his earliest memory of the new Lord Chief Justice. Inevitably enough Jowitt and Goddard had both attended the same public school, Marlborough:

> When my dear old friend, Lord Caldecote, thought it necessary to lay down the cares of his office, I frankly tell you that I suggested to the Prime Minister that Lord Goddard was the man to succeed him. I did not do that because he and I had attended the same school. He

preceded me slightly, but his reputation lived after him. When you went to Marlborough as a small boy you were always expected in the dormitory after lights were out to show what you could do in the way of singing or telling a story. They made Rayner Goddard start by singing but after a few opening bars they came to the conclusion that he had better stop singing, and therefore he stood up and recited to the assembled company the striking and solemn words of the death sentence. It struck terror into the hearts of those listening, and accounts for the comparatively good behaviour of old Marlburians since ... If I had done nothing else for the administration of the law, the fact that I was instrumental in getting [Rayner Goddard] appointed, is in itself a good testimonial to my character and conduct in my great office.

The judiciary are unintelligible without understanding the power of the public schools in the formation of the British élite. Like Goddard they had all been formed by the public school system in its golden age before the First World War. It was at their public schools that their opinions seem to have been fixed. Patriots who had all served King and Country in the Great War, they remembered the British Empire at its finest hour. They had grown to manhood at a time when Britannia seemed to rule the world, a situation that contributed much to their arrogance and faith in their vision of the world. These men were intolerant and narrow-minded. They believed they were right and everything about the office and the legal culture in which they functioned supported this notion. They were victims of an ideological system which refused to accept a pluralistic concept of truth. It was a serious weakness in men called upon to administer the criminal justice system.

Almost all the judges were Protestant, most of them closely associated with the established church. Many judges presided in the church courts and acted as legal advisers to the church administration. Schooled by Anglican clergymen, they celebrated the virtues of British Protestantism.

By virtue of their position, their education and in most cases their birth, most judges were members of the upper classes. An extremely clubbable caste, they entertained on the grand scale. Each evening on circuit, judges were either entertained by local dignitaries or themselves acted as host to the local élite. Every one of them belonged to at least one London club, most to several.

They were not particularly intellectual. While almost all had gone from public school to one of the two ancient universities, few had distinguished themselves academically. Few read much for pleasure and none could really boast any wide cultural interest. Indeed they seemed generally contemptuous of the arts and culture, their philistinism providing another point of contact with the common man.

As Lord Chancellor, David Maxwell Fyfe, Viscount Kilmuir, played a part in curbing the populism of the judiciary. In 1955 Kilmuir sent a letter to all judges encouraging them to stop speaking directly to the press, and this does seem to have had an impact on restraining judicial behaviour. Through his appointments to the bench he helped form a judiciary more friendly to the executive. Lord Chief Justice Parker appointed to succeed Goddard in 1958 was a much less flamboyant character than his predecessor, and he kept away from the limelight. Judges found themselves increasingly drawn into the management of the state, resolving conflicts for the executive, becoming friendlier and friendlier to the problems and difficulties of government, and less tempted to sound off about the moral state of the nation.

10

A Casebook

In this chapter I examine a number of trials for homosexual offences during 1953–4, and one case from 1955–6. These cases give us the opportunity to see how the law worked in practice, and they balance the somewhat distorted picture provided by a concentration on high profile trials.

Homosexual offences were dealt with in three different types of courts. The prosecuting authority, invariably the local police, effectively determined the court in which a case would be heard. All cases went in the first instance to the local magistrates' court and some offences (such as importuning) were tried by the magistrates. The magistrates were usually local big-wigs without any legal background and they were guided in points of law by a full-time clerk of the court, often a fully-qualified solicitor. Three magistrates usually sat together, the chairman of the bench presiding. In large cities such as London the magistrates were full-time and paid; these stipendiary magistrates were always men recruited from a legal background.

In more serious offences (as determined by the police) the magistrates heard the evidence and decided if there was a case to answer. Hardly ever did they reject the prosecution's argument to send the case to a higher court. They might sometimes modify the charge sheet but the committal hearing normally provided an opportunity for the prosecution to outline its case. The court could decide to send the person charged either to the Quarter Sessions or the Assizes. In London where there was no assize cases would be sent to the central criminal courts at the Old Bailey. The Quarter Sessions were also presided over by magistrates but the chairman was almost always a lawyer. Many judges served as chairman of the Quarter Sessions in their home county. In the towns and cities the Quarter Sessions were presided over by a Recorder, a senior barrister often on his way to the judiciary but who still practised law.

The highest courts which could hear homosexual offences were presided over by high court judges. Three times each year the judges of the high court in London descended on the English provinces, hearing the most serious criminal and civil cases that had been committed in the counties of England and Wales. The country was divided into eight circuits to which the Lord Chief Justice assigned two or three judges. This tradition, like so much else in British life, had its roots in the middle ages. London-based judges had first taken justice to the provinces in the thirteenth century. Known as the Assizes, from the Latin word meaning 'to sit', they lasted until 1971 when they were finally abolished as a result of a report by the former ICI executive and physicist Dr Richard Beeching, the vandal who had axed much of the British railway network in the early 1960s.

By the 1950s much of the business of the criminal calendar was sexual – what one journalist described as 'a comprehensive pageant of the seamy side of life'. As this domination of the assize calendar had grown, so British newspapers became more selective in their coverage of the Assizes. Newspapers quite happily carried long accounts of murder, manslaughter, burglary, arson and acts of violence which also fell within the competence of the assize courts, but often lapsed into silence when it came to sexual matters. Local newspapers were more idiosyncratic than national titles and some did report the entire range of the Assizes' business. The most reticent were those operating in the big provincial cities of the Midlands and the north – Birmingham, Manchester, Liverpool, Leeds and Newcastle-upon-Tyne. The local Leeds newspapers managed almost entirely to ignore the efforts of their local Chief Constable who conducted one of the most vigorous anti-vice campaigns in post-war Britain during the late 1940s and 1950s. Many editors and proprietors believed that it was prudent to remain silent about sex. They were, after all, proud to describe themselves as *family* newspapers.

The arrival of the assize judges was a great local event attended by much pomp and circumstance. Cities and towns were proud to play host to the large number of lawyers who descended on them for the duration of the Assize. These events always attracted a great deal of newspaper coverage. The Assize was a privilege jealously guarded. Sixty-three communities across England and Wales welcomed the judges and their company three times each year, in winter (January–March), summer (May–August) and autumn (October–November). Only Leeds held a fourth assize each year in the spring to deal with the huge volume of criminal business generated in West Yorkshire.

The treatment accorded to the judges was magnificent. They were entertained as representatives of the crown doing the king's business in the localities. Special lodgings maintained to the highest standard of luxury, comfort and elegance were provided by the county authorities. The judge was met by local dignitaries on his arrival in the town and his evenings were filled with lavish entertainments at the expense of the county. By the 1950s the old horse-drawn coaches had been replaced by a fleet of Rolls-Royces, again provided by the court. There were many processions and the Assizes offered a variety of dignitaries the opportunity to wear ceremonial costume. The judge of course was resplendent in a long wig and scarlet gown. He was attended by footmen and protected by pikemen. His entry to his lodgings and the court was greeted by a bugle. On the first day of each Assize the judge attended a service in the principal church of the locality. Many of the assize cities and towns were also the sites of a cathedral and these were used to their maximum ceremonial advantage. A senior ecclesiastical dignitary, almost invariably the bishop or a dean, conducted the service and a sermon was read, the entire effort providing divine sanction to royal justice. It was a visible demonstration of the alliance of church and state, a fundamental element in the ideology of the British state. The judges would also inspect a guard of honour from the local county regiment. In the 1950s, well before a rationalisation had transformed the structure of the Army, each county town or city was home to a particular regiment.

On the second day of the Assize the court actually sat. The judges transacted their business in magnificently decorated chambers housed in important local buildings – the castles at Winchester and Exeter, but more usually in the guildhall or shirehall. In some places the business of the Assizes might take no more than a day, though in the large centres of population the court sat for several weeks.

The purpose of this circus was to impress the populace with the majesty of royal justice and the seriousness with which the state took law and order. Most men who got to the Assizes for homosexual offences appeared only briefly before the courts. Most trials for homosexual offences lasted less than an hour because so many of those accused had already confessed. The committal proceedings might take much longer and in some cases could last a day. The magistrates' court often intimidated men intending to plead not guilty and the number of pleas changed before the accused was sent to a higher court is a register of the impact of the proceedings on the man as he saw the tale that the police had spun about him and his character.

Babes in the Wood, January 1953

George Williams, forty-two, was a comedy actor, on the threshold of stardom, according to his *Times* obituarist, when he came before the courts in the early months of 1953 accused of homosexual offences. Williams was playing the part of 'Simple Simon' in a pantomïme at the Kemble Theatre in Hereford, when he struck up an acquaintance with a boy soldier, three months short of sixteen. Williams booked a room at the

Mitre Hotel where he and the young soldier stayed for two nights together. The soldier was a consenting party and refused to blame Williams in court. He had wanted to stay with Williams, telling him a hard luck story. The soldier had spent Christmas at the camp, walking around Hereford in his free time. On one of his excursions to Hereford he met Brian Lloyd, twenty-nine, another member of the pantomime company. It was Lloyd who introduced him to Williams. The soldier brought another boy soldier, sixteen, from the camp (the son of a major in the regular army) who also slept with Williams after he saw the pantomime. He was also a willing partner. Williams gave him money, about £1 in all. Lloyd also took the other young soldier to his lodgings.

It is not clear how the case came to the attention of the police. It is possible that someone at the hotel or lodgings informed them. On 12 January 1953 Williams was arrested and he made a full confession. The case came before Justice Sellers at the end of February 1953. Sellers cleared the court of women 'in the interests of justice'. The court had also been completely cleared for the evidence of the boy soldiers. Lloyd got a sentence of eighteen months.

Williams had a criminal record. He had been convicted of larceny in 1935 and at Nottingham Assizes in 1945 had been convicted of gross indecency and had been sentenced to three years' penal servitude. He had been released from prison in February 1947.

Williams suggested in his defence that he had a quarrel with his fiancée and left his lodgings in a highly emotional state before Lloyd introduced him to the young soldier. Both of the young soldiers were sent to approved schools.

The Hearn Case, January 1953

The chairman of the Northampton magistrates criticised the parents of a fourteen-year-old boy. The parents had allowed their son to spend a fortnight's holiday at Margate with thirty-three-year-old John Hearn. Hearn pleaded guilty to two sexual offences with the boy. The parents had also allowed Hearn to give him 'lavish' presents, totalling in all £160, including a gramophone. When Hearn called at the home of the boy, the parents had left them alone together downstairs while retiring to their bedroom. Police accepted that the boy had been the dominant partner. The case had been referred to the DPP's office which had decided to prosecute Hearn rather than the boy.

Hearn was 'highly valued' as a buyer by a Northampton shoe firm. He told the court in his defence that 'This lad has systematically blackmailed me for thirteen months. When we met outside the cinema he said: "You have had it. If I shouted for help what a position you would be in." They always take the boy's side. So I was introduced to his parents and afterwards my life was hell. The boy said I was tied to him for life unless he got married.' The prosecution seems to have accepted the substance of his story. The boy also warned him that he would expose him if he was ever unfaithful with a woman. He had made no objection, indeed he seems to have encouraged the sexual side of their relationship. Hearn was sentenced to twelve months in prison with a recommendation that he receive treatment.

The Wiles Case

John Wiles, forty, was married and owned his own private school for homeless children in Surrey. Many similar institutions flourished in the 1940s and 1950s (and possibly beyond), as local authorities farmed out unwanted boys and girls to private entrepreneurs who were prepared to look after them, often in conditions reminiscent of Dickensian England. Wiles had a very public affair with a young teenage gardener who worked for his school. The relationship caused such gossip that the staff of the school called a special staff meeting and confronted Wiles about his affair. He quoted the Bible at them: 'Let him who is without sin cast the first stone.' One of them did cast the first stone and Wiles was interviewed by the police.

Wiles adopted a slightly novel defence. He suggested that he had made love to the boy as a form of psychological treatment for himself, advice that he claimed he had obtained after answering a magazine advertisement. Clifford Allen, the Harley Street expert on homosexuality, appeared for him in March 1953 and told the judge at Surrey Assizes, Mr Justice Jones, that there was hope in this case of a cure. He promised to find a suitable institution where Wiles could be treated and the judge agreed that he ought not to be sent to prison. He was bound over for three years on the promise that he receive treatment.

The Ossett Circle

Mr Justice Havers told Mr and Mrs Wilkinson of the small Yorkshire village of Ossett that they had 'both sunk to the very lowest depth of human degradation'. Ethel Wilkinson, thirty-three, acted as a procuress for her husband, setting him up for sex with the youth Roy Hemingway, twenty-two at the time of the trial at the spring Assizes at Leeds in March 1953. The offences had begun six years before during a game of 'Truth and Dare'. One of the dares was for Hemingway to have sex with George Wilkinson, then twenty-nine, a millhand. The relationship had continued from that time. The couple even 'lent' Hemingway to three other men aged between twenty-nine and forty-five, two millworkers and a fettler.

They were in the dock with the Wilkinsons. All pleaded guilty to having had sex with Hemingway, described by the prosecution as a 'positive menace'. The circle had come to light after Wilkinson had disciplined Hemingway, and the young man went to the police. According to the report all the principals 'made graphic statements describing in detail what had been going on'. 'I do not think', said Havers, 'I ever heard a more hideous or revolting case than this.'

The Kensington Blackmail Case

Mr X was a writer who went to Piccadilly Circus and met a youth who took him back to a house in Queensborough Terrace close to Kensington Gardens in west London. They went to bed together. Twenty minutes later Laurence Clarke, twenty-three, appeared at the end of the bed. He claimed to be the landlord of the property and at this stage in the proceedings he introduced a detective, Ronald Headford, twenty-one, who emerged from behind the curtains. The youth, they said, was fifteen-and-a-half years old. Arrangements were made for keeping the matter quiet and Mr X agreed to pay over more money (£20) later at Speakers' Corner in Hyde Park. After leaving the house he immediately went to the police station and Clarke and Headford were arrested by the police when he met them at the agreed spot. R. E. Seaton, the prosecutor, told the court in March 1953 that Mr X had 'certain tendencies' although he was also married. Clarke had a previous conviction for importuning. He had worked as a personal servant of the late J. V. Rank, father of the film magnate. He had also worked on the stage before finding his present employment as a mechanic. Headford was a valet to a peer (unnamed) in Hampshire. The judge Sir Hugh Beazley called it 'about as bad a case of its type as it is possible to imagine'. Both men were sentenced to imprisonment. The youth was not caught.

The Swindon Case, May 1953

Alfred Williams, fifty-eight, an accounts clerk, fainted when the judge sentenced him to ten years' imprisonment in May 1953. He was in the dock with four other men, all single: Richard Edwards, thirty-four, a barman; Cyril Frankum, twenty-eight, an inspector viewer (?); Leslie Hobbs, twenty-three, a gardener; and Patrick Lethaby, seventeen, a junior salesman. The case began when Wiltshire police called at Williams's home in Commercial Road, Swindon, and started to search the premises without a search warrant. They discovered 'letters . . . three of an improper nature' and a film in his camera which they had developed. In this way they were led to Williams's three co-defendants. When police inquired about a green box in the wardrobe Williams claimed that it contained private papers.

He fainted and his companion tried to expose the film that was in the box, but unfortunately he failed. The companion did not appear in court. He was sixteen and had lived with Williams for two years. His parents, who knew Williams, had encouraged the boy to move in with him because Williams seemed 'a charming, middle-aged man living an extremely lonely life'. He was now to be placed in care and protection.

It is not easy to piece this case together as the newspaper accounts are extremely reticent about going into details. It seems that all the men in the case used Williams's house for sex. It was this which presumably so excited and appalled the police and the judge. Everyone made confessions and these presumably went into vivid details about this 'den of iniquity'. Corruption was not suggested in this particular case. Lethaby was described by the police as 'self-satisfied, a prig and above himself'. They were in no doubt that he had been steeped in these practices. The judge placed him on probation and wondered if he was taking a risk. Frankum denounced his former associates and was now, according to the probation officer, 'keeping company with a respectable girl'. The judge presumably thought she could redeem him and placed him on probation. Hobbs got four years and Edwards got three years. These were really savage sentences for a case involving a group of consenting males. The judge said they had behaved 'like animals'. Sobbing, Williams made a long speech from the dock. He had never asked the men to visit him, they had come of their own free will: 'I have been so terribly alone since my mother died. Everyone seems to have someone except me.'

The Rampisham Postmaster

Walter Samson was a leading member of the community in the small Dorset hamlet of Rampisham. As well as his duties as postmaster, he served as church organist and churchwarden. His age was never given by the papers but some friends had known him for fifty years. The villagers rallied around when he was charged with homosexual offences in May 1953, and even though he pleaded guilty they petitioned on his behalf. The Rector provided a character witness. For over twenty years it had been his practice to have a permanent companion, a lad between the ages of twelve and sixteen. The arrangements had always been made with the consent of the parents, whose behaviour appalled both the judge and the prosecutor. The boys had been his lovers. The judge, Mr Justice Byrne, sentenced the corrupter of youth to three years. After the sentence, Samson, clutching a stick, was helped from the court by a prison officer.

The case following Samson's involved a friend of his from the same village, a farmer named Philip Arthur Record. Boys from the village lived at the farm and Record encouraged boys to visit:

Judge: Do the parents know?
Prosecutor: Oh yes.
Judge: An extraordinary state of affairs.

When Record's brother had been questioned about the attraction of the farm for the lads he told the police that they were 'crazy about milking', to which Byrne replied, 'Why [then] did they sleep there?' Record was sentenced to four years.

The Bath Case
Nine youths loitered around some public lavatories in Bath city centre and established a racket extracting money from men who went cottaging there. They did this at least twenty-nine times during February and March 1953. John Walker, sixteen, explained in May 1953 that 'the idea was to get talking to a man, and after reaching a nice quiet spot, the man would commit an improper act. Then the rest of the gang would come up and give two alternatives – the police or money. Violence would come into it if the man got rough.'

On occasion three of them made love to a man in a caravan. Patrick Harding, seventeen, was often used as a decoy – 'apparently when he dressed up in a particular way, he looked a proper softie'. Most of the boys carried coshes. The ringleader was Raymond Stevens, seventeen, who had done time for theft in an approved school. Three of the lads, including Stevens, were sent to prison for a year each, two were sent to Borstal, and the others were put on probation. The offences came to light when one of the victims who had refused to pay and been beaten up went to the police. The case was taken by the DPP's office.

The financial demands made by the gang were exceptionally low. It was calculated by the prosecution that they had collected a total of £15 16s. 7½d., an average of 10s. 6d. a time. This money had been divided between the participants, usually three to five gang members, leaving them with as little as half a crown each.

The court accepted that Ronald Head, seventeen, had not been involved in the extortion. He claimed he had taken part in the offences to get his revenge. His brother had been involved with an older man who had been sentenced to several years' prison for offences against boys during 1952.

The Vicar of Whitley, Lancashire
Terence Davenport received relatively lenient treatment from Justice Oliver at the Cheshire Assizes in June 1953. He was placed on probation: 'I do not propose to say anything which might add to the bitterness of your position' – an unusual degree of judicial restraint. Davenport was

found guilty of sexual offences with two eighteen-year-olds. One he had brought to the vicarage to view his model railway; the other, an apprentice plumber, had come to the vicarage to discuss a dark patch on the ceiling. The plumber shopped him.

A bachelor and a 'conscientious parish priest', Davenport belonged to a well-known Macclesfield family. The condition of his probation was that he enter a mental hospital, which he did, having already resigned his living.

The Cartwright Case, June 1953

Mr Justice Havers, exchanging the northern for the eastern circuit, was appalled once again. This time at a thirty-eight-year-old schoolmaster who came before him at Norfolk Assizes in June 1953 charged with offences with nine of his pupils aged between eleven and fifteen. Cartwright was a housemaster at a private boarding school and according to the prosecutor had lost the respect of the school. He allowed boys 'a most remarkable degree of familiarity'. He was in the habit of telling 'improper stories, using improper language and letting the boys openly call him by his nickname'. The other teachers in the school had issued an ultimatum to the headmaster and he was dismissed. Shortly afterwards he was arrested.

Cartwright was sentenced to five years. He had a chequered career, starting as a medical student before transferring to music. He was a Bachelor of Music and had been a music master at Chelsea Grammar School before coming to Norfolk in 1946. An Anglo-Catholic, he had acted as organist to a number of fashionable London churches.

The Case of Woodham and Jones, July 1953

It was unusual for the newspapers to report a case which ended in an acquittal but the two principals in this case were both clergymen, Haydyn Jones, thirty-two, a chaplain at the Royal Navy Barracks at Portsmouth, and his friend Harold Woodham, forty-one, a curate in Devon. Woodham was staying with Jones and the two of them visited a 'notorious' pub where they got into conversation with three naval airmen, all stationed at HMS *Daedalus*, who accepted the offer of a drive with the clergymen. The sailors stole the car and some money and were arrested by the police. Woodham and Jones had been left at some waste ground. The sailors alleged that some incidents had taken place at that spot and that in revenge they had taken the car and the money. The defence asked them why they went to that particular pub:

'The beer's not too bad.'

Anything else?'

'A game of darts and they have a juke box. I like modern records.'

'Do you approve of the kind of customers they have there?'

'It doesn't hurt me. I am there to have a drink.'

Norman Skelhorn worked very hard for a conviction, quoting Woodham's initial refusal to press charges: 'If the dear boys want the money let them have it. I don't wish to prosecute.' The clergymen were acquitted by a jury at Portsmouth Quarter Sessions in July 1953.

The Walker Case

Lewis Walker lived at the Verger's Cottage in Ongar, Essex, the last stop on the Central Line. Sixty-one years old he was a scoutmaster. In July 1953 he denied a large number of charges of sexual offences with ten boy scouts aged between ten and fourteen. Walker had converted his cottage into a sort of den where he entertained members of his troop. Each quarter he measured the scouts in his troop and took upon himself the task of instructing them on sex, providing practical examples. The boys would undress when they entered the cottage in parties of four or five and Walker was himself naked while he lectured to the boys about sex.

The case came to the attention of the police because Walker himself complained to the police of the 'disgusting way' in which two of his scouts had behaved with a fifteen-year-old girl. During the investigation parents suggested that they thought something peculiar was going on with their sons. Walker defended his right to instruct the boys: 'A Scoutmaster's position is unique. They must be taught about sex.' He circulated books, including *Being Born* and the *Wonderful Story of Me*, as well as nudist magazines.

Walker, a widower, had a previous conviction for similar offences with boys in Hertfordshire in 1946 when he had been imprisoned for eighteen months. The hearing of the case lasted eight hours at Essex Quarter Sessions. Walker eventually changed his plea to guilty after the committal proceedings. He received ten years for what Derek Curtis-Bennett, the chairman of the Quarter Sessions, described as 'one of the most terrible offences in the world'. He had 'never heard a worse case'.

Making Contact

Picture Show was a weekly magazine that cost threepence. The style of the pictures of movie stars suggest that it was catering for a homosexual constituency, something which can be supported from the pen-friends column. Here are some examples:

18 year-old male in Tipton, Staffs, wants pen-friends (males only) anywhere in London. Interests: films, travelling, music, Doris Day, Audie Murphy. (9 February 1952)

21 year-old male from Cheshire wants male pen-friends, anywhere, especially abroad. Interests: swimming, dancing, Latin-American music. Photograph appreciated. (15 March 1952)

26 year-old male nurse from Reading wants pen-friends (22–26) male only, anywhere. Interest: general bodybuilding. Own photo appreciated. (7 June 1952)

24 year-old male from Gravesend: wants pen-friends (males only). Interests: amateur acting, dancing, Alan Ladd. Photo appreciated. (21 June 1953)

Graham Houston from Dalton-in-Furness placed his ad in August 1952. He was nineteen and he was interested in reading, theatre, stage and tap dancing. He received 141 replies. Replying to one of the letters he made an error in the address, turning 151 into 51. This mistake landed him in court. The person who received the letter read it and was appalled. A huge investigation was undertaken by the police and the Post Office. The prosecutor in Houston's case suggested that it was 'through the use of a kind of code [that] perverts got in touch with each other' through the pen-friend section of the film magazine. The prosecution presented the column as a source of corruption. One of Houston's correspondents was seventy. Houston had already committed an act of gross indecency with another of his new pen-friends.

Two other men shared the dock with Houston: Stanley Bernard, twenty-three, a salesman from Caterham and Alfred Baker, thirty-two, a short-hand typist from Plaistow in London. The prosecution explained to the court that the way the correspondent tested the water was by wondering if his new pen-friend 'was broadminded': 'I am . . . are you?' This was the cue for the recipient to open up.

The prosecutor thought that Houston had an inferiority complex; he had tried to make himself more wicked and depraved than he actually was. He was described by the prosecutor as having 'not very high intellectual standards'. His peers looked on him as a bit of a kid and it was suggested that he wrote the letters to feel older and more important. He organised a dancing troupe of small children and gave shows for charity. Baker denied doing the things he claimed in the letter, saying that it was 'just nonsense for excitement'. All three men were fined by the Lancashire magistrates. (There had been a spate of pen-pal scandals in the early 1950s; the *Sunday Pictorial* described the clubs as 'a cover and a breeding ground for blackmailers, street girls, perverts and rogues of every sort', 16 November 1952.)

The Father Forbes Case, July 1953

Police arrested Charles Forbes, thirty-two, a Roman Catholic priest from Gilling Castle in Yorkshire, at the public lavatories at Victoria Station. He pleaded guilty to the charge of importuning. It had been Forbes's second visit to the lavatory that day. He had left earlier with a man and together they tried to find a hotel room in the area without success. On his arrest Forbes said, 'Why pick on me?' He was fined. The magistrate at Bow Street in July 1953 told him that he clearly needed 'advice, medical or otherwise'.

The Bull Case, July 1953

Albert Bull, forty-one, was a clergyman with a distinguished war record. He had been paralysed from the waist down as a result of wounds received during the Allied landings in Sicily during the war. In July 1953 he faced charges for three offences concerning a fifteen-year-old boy, a former pupil. By 1953 Bull was a chaplain at a private school in Hertfordshire. All incidents occurred in a car on Saturday afternoons at Runnymede. What Bull did not know was that he was watched each week by the police. The Bishop of St Albans told the court that he could be rehabilitated. The court fined him £10.

The Worcester Case, July/August 1953

Joseph Cronin, nineteen, was a handyman, who admitted to police that he had committed 'improper behaviour' with between two to three hundred men; he had lost count – he sometimes committed eight or nine incidents an evening. His defiant attitude won him few friends in court. Sentencing him, the Recorder of Worcester R. G. Micklethwaite told him that the court was 'always reluctant' to send a person under twenty-one to prison for a first offence but that he was an 'exceptional case'. He had come

> to the conclusion that you were responsible for all these matters. It is quite clear from the evidence that you systematically and pro-fessionally acted as a sort of male prostitute . . . I am quite satisfied that for the protection of the public you should be away for a long time . . . I am not going to send you to Borstal . . . where you would endeavour to contaminate other young people.

He was sent to prison for eighteen months.

Cronin was arrested one evening in late July at 11.35 p.m. on Worcester racecourse with John Ricketts, thirty, a baker. The men were caught in the act and taken by the police back to the station. There Cronin began to boast about his activities and police began to make a list of names. In the course of the confession he implicated at least five other men whom the police succeeded in persuading to confess. Hubert Barnsley, forty-seven, was a former city councillor who owned a sports outfitter's shop in Worcester and held a commission in the Territorial Army. He confessed to two offences with Cronin, once at the racecourse and on another occasion in his car. William Clarke, thirty-eight, was a storekeeper, who met Cronin outside a cinema. Michael Tomkins, twenty, was a student home from college for the summer. He had been with Cronin, once on the golfcourse and on three other occasions at the racecourse. Thomas Murphy, thirty-three, was a compositor who was found guilty of two offences with Cronin. Thomas Preece, sixty-seven, a pensioner, had sex with Cronin in a shed on the racecourse. None of these men was sent to prison. Barnsley was fined £40, Ricketts fined £15 and Tomkins put on probation. He had already seen a doctor and his college promised to take him back if he underwent treatment. All the other men were conditionally discharged.

The Recorder placed most of the blame on Cronin. He told the other men: [you] 'ought to be thoroughly ashamed of yourselves for having yielded to the temptations of a man younger than yourselves. I expect it happened when some of you had too much to drink. I hope you will take it as a warning and let nothing of this happen again. If you do it will be very serious for you.'

The Vicar of Barnes Bridge, September/October 1953

Francis Wynne was fifty-eight, a long-serving clergyman who had served a succession of parishes across the diocese of London, working for most of the 1930s in the East End of London. By 1953 he was in the suburban parish of Barnes Bridge in west London. In an extremely long-running trial, during which he changed his plea, he was found guilty of ten charges with seven boys. Many other charges were also taken into consideration, the charges upon which Wynne was tried being merely specimens from a much larger number. The boys, aged ten to fifteen, were all choirboys. Wynne recruited his choir sometimes from boys on the street. He gave the boys small presents and small amounts of money for services rendered. The boys were given gin, port, beer and bottled beers at these sessions as well as being shown 'rude books with pictures of ladies with no clothes on'.

Wynne was discovered when a mother searching her son's trousers before washing them found a paper on which her son, a choirboy, had recorded the fees paid by Wynne for a variety of acts; the methodical choirboy had also recorded the acts performed. She went to the police. Wynne was on holiday in Bristol and was arrested at Temple Meads station as he was about to return home. Police found on his person 'a powder box with women's powder and a mirror'.

R. E. Seaton was the prosecutor. He revealed that Wynne already had a criminal record. In 1944 he had been convicted of offences with boys at Lincolnshire Assizes. He had been bound over for three years on the understanding that he would withdraw to a monastic establishment. Seaton told Mr Justice Hilbery: 'This so-called man of God under his guise as such has used it as a cloak for debauching young boys in a way which in your Lordship's long experience is probably the worst you have had to listen to.' The judge was suitably appalled that he had ever been reinstated by the Church of England.

Dr Matheson from Brixton Prison said that there was no question of Wynne being insane, though he was not normal. Judge: 'No man addicted to this perversion can be regarded as normal?' Matheson: 'No.' Dr Arthur Spencer Patterson, a specialist from London, thought that Wynne showed early signs of deterioration of the brain: 'He also told me that he was very much distressed at an early age by his impulses and that he overcame them only by an extremely apathetic and lonely mode of life in which he would spend a whole night in prayer and also by carrying out ritual acts like writing in his own blood promises to resist temptation.'

Wynne felt deeply ashamed and argued that he had not been in control of his own desires. The judge, an Anglican, told him: 'Not the least tragic part of this case is that you being a priest of the Church of England have betrayed the sacred office not only by doing irreparable mental injury to these boys, but lending to the enemies of the church just the sort of weapon that they look for in order to attack all you should stand for. Nobody can measure the harm you have done.' He was sentenced to ten years.

The Fylde Farm School Case, September 1953
Ten boys from this approved school situated near Blackpool were accused of a large number of offences with each other and with other inmates at the school in September 1953. John Williams, nineteen, from Birkenhead, who faced nineteen charges, was identified as the ringleader. In many cases violence had been used against younger inmates. One boy of sixteen told the court that he had been seized by two of the accused on his way to a game of cricket and been raped a hundred yards from where other boys played cricket. Most offences took place in the dormitories at night. Mr Justice Byrne described it as 'appalling conduct'.

The school authorities tried to blame the Home Office circular received in 1952 for undermining their disciplinary regime, but from the evidence this was ludicrous. The institution seems to have been run by a gang of inmates whose activities went unchallenged. There were 110 boys in the school, divided into four dormitories. Williams was described as a 'very clever painter, a genius in a way, coats of arms he [had] painted had been shown at the Royal Agricultural Show at Blackpool'. The judge did not believe 'for a moment that the youths were sexualists' and sentenced them all to Borstal.

The McKeown and Bayliss Case, September 1953

PC Reddin discovered Gerard McKeown, thirty-six, a costs and bonus surveyor, lying in the grass at King George Field, Worcester, with Stacey Bayliss, twenty-two, a shop assistant. The men ran away. PC Reddin chased them and caught Bayliss. As he was arrested Bayliss begged the policeman: 'No please don't. Think of the disgrace to my mother and father.' McKeown was arrested later. They both pleaded guilty to committing an act of gross indecency with other acts taken into consideration by the court in September 1953.

Bayliss had served in the Royal Navy from 1946 to 1952. McKeown had been married but was separated from his wife at the time of the offence. He had a previous conviction for dishonesty. The Recorder of Worcester, R. G. Micklethwaite, was encouraged by the fact that Bayliss 'did not, like most criminals, think of yourself, but of the disgrace of your parents'. McKeown was fined £25 and Bayliss was put on probation.

The Newbury Case, September 1953

In September 1953 a big crowd gathered in the Market Place, Newbury, outside the magistrates' court half an hour before the court opened. As soon as the case began, the prosecution asked the chairman of the bench to clear the court so that the evidence could be held *in camera*. The court was cleared. The prosecution did not want the public to hear evidence 'of a particularly depraved and filthy character'. The court would hear of 'men who defiled young boys' – the youngest individual involved in the case was seventeen – and of men who 'had behaved like animals'. The cases revolved around a former mayor of Newbury, Douglas Cameron, sixty-three, a prosperous local businessman who owned a building company. He had been mayor during Coronation year. It was his case that the crowds had come to hear.

Cameron made a full confession. The connection had been made at a public lavatory in the centre of Newbury where the mayor had picked up other men. From the confession obtained, four other men were charged with offences and put on trial with him. One of them, Arthur King, forty-three, had a long and distinguished record of domestic service. He had worked for many years in the household of the British Ambassador to Russia and had 'testimonials praising [him] from some of the best households in the land'. Only one of the men was sent to prison; all the others were fined, bound over or put on probation.

After his arrest, Cameron collapsed. He went as a voluntary patient to a mental hospital, his family threatening him that they would have him certified if he did not go into the hospital. He attended the proceedings accompanied by a male nurse and arrived and departed in an ambulance. He was placed on probation on condition that he seek medical treatment for at least a year.

The Bedford Case, October 1953

Kenneth Brown, nineteen, was a garage hand described by the judge in October 1953 as 'a menace to society'. He had 'been really little better than a male prostitute' who got money from a small group of men with whom he had sex. Brown hung around a billiards hall in Bedford where he picked up men. Here he met Alfred Clark, sixty-two, an engineer trimmer, Ernest Gray, forty-eight, a kitchen porter and Herbert Edwards, twenty-seven, a bricklayer's labourer. Incidents occurred in the billiards hall, at Brown's home and at Clark's lodgings. Clark had been convicted of a similar case in 1940 and was divorced from his wife. His employers were willing to continue his employment. Gray was completely deaf, blind in one eye and had an impediment in his speech. His employers also spoke in his favour, describing him as a good worker. All three men were put on probation and Brown was sent to Borstal. The judge blamed Brown's behaviour on the fact that his father had died in 1940 and so he had grown up with a lack of control.

The Cornish Cases, October 1953

Of the nineteen men found guilty of homosexual offences at the Devonshire Autumn Assizes in October 1953, Mr Justice Lynskey sent eight to prison. Twin brothers Francis and William Webster, twenty-six, from Redruth in Cornwall, were given sentences of five and four years respectively. All the offences had taken place in Cornwall, allowing the judge to observe of these 'really terrible' cases that there 'is so much filth apparently – in Cornwall particularly'.

A number of the offences took place in a flat in Falmouth. Indeed it was a nosy neighbour who noticed the numbers of servicemen, especially sailors, leaving the apartment early in the morning, presumably to return to their units, that led the police to organise a stake-out. Seven men in all were charged with offences at the flat; others escaped. The men were mostly between eighteen and thirty. The flat was the home of a waiter, John Jago, thirty, who was sent to prison for three years. Jago was a veteran of the North Africa campaign. John Levett, thirty-four, who was depicted as the leader of this 'gang of homosexuals', was regarded as having played an active role in the organisation of this 'nest of corruption'. The court heard of his service record. He was a naval airman stationed at Culrose. He had served as a member of Bomber Command, having been awarded a Distinguished Flying Medal, 'a brilliant record'. He was sent to prison for two years.

According to the prosecution, 'men in public houses were invited freely [back to the flat] in the hope that they would participate in activities at the flat'. The judge told the court that the group 'met and drank in licensed houses, bought more beer and took it back to the flat and there started dancing and cuddling', as a preliminary to the orgies which then developed.

Local newspapers did not carry anything except a list of the men convicted in the other cases, which were apparently the result of following up the confessions of the Falmouth group. It is therefore impossible to discover what the twins really did to lead to such heavy sentences from the court. The ages of these men ranged from twenty-six to sixty-eight, but most were in their late twenties or thirties. They covered a wide range of occupational groups. Two bakers, two male nurses, a baker's roundsman, a machinist, a monumental mason, a cook, a furnace-man, the owner of a hotel, a barman and an engineer.

The Applewhaite Case, November/December 1953

Charles Applewhaite was a magistrate, chairman of his local bench and the holder of a cluster of posts in Hampshire where he had been chairman of the County Council. A senior alderman of the council, he had for many years been chairman of the County Council's Approved School Committee. He was extremely well connected and had competed as a player at Wimbledon in the past. His case came up in November/December 1953 at the same Assize in Winchester as the first trial of Lord Montagu.

Applewhaite was accused of a succession of offences with teenagers, three youths aged between sixteen and eighteen. All three youths had been inmates of the approved school. They had been frequent visitors to his house. He had been a constant presence at the school all through his chairmanship, making friends with the boys and encouraging them to take their problems to him. He took a lot of trouble placing them in employment after their release. He denied the charges but was found guilty principally on the basis of affectionate letters he had written to the boys.

Several prominent individuals spoke in his favour. Frances Temple, the widow of William Temple, Archbishop of Canterbury from 1942 to 1944, was full of praise for his work with young people, describing his manner as a jovial uncle. Lady Portal, another member of Hampshire County Council, chairman of the Children's Committee, also spoke in his defence describing his 'indefatigable' efforts to help youths who had left the approved school.

The Rector of Harlington Hayes, November/December 1953
Alfred Morgan, sixty-three, had been ordained in 1913 and served as a chaplain with the British Army in the First World War. He had been awarded the Military Cross for his gallantry at the battle of the Somme. In November 1953 he was arrested in Soho after police followed him after they watched him 'pick-up' Frederick Cronin, an eighteen-year-old cinema operator from Belsize Park. They followed them to an alleyway off Leicester Square where their meeting had taken place. The police alleged that they witnessed improper behaviour in a doorway. Cronin, it later emerged, had absconded from an approved school. Morgan denied the charges and at two trials juries failed to agree a verdict. His defence was organised with great vigour by G. D. Roberts who accused the policemen of lying and subjected the constables to a ferocious cross-examination. The Crown decided to take the case to a third trial but withdrew the charges on the day the case came to court. Morgan was also helped by Cronin's complete denial of the charges.

He did not get off scot-free. The prosecution refused to apologise for taking the case and instead made a statement which suggested that they still believed the clergyman guilty. The case had, they said, been dropped with some reluctance: 'In view of the fact that the defence in each of the two previous trials consisted of an attack on two young police officers it is felt that the Commissioner of Police, through me, should express his complete confidence in each of these officers and his complete satisfaction in the manner in which they carried out their duty.'

The Moore Case, December 1953
Christopher Moore, forty-five, was a fraud who had awarded himself a doctorate. His real name was Montague Black and he had a long string of convictions going back twenty years. By 1953 he was the owner and headmaster of two private schools at Salisbury and Bournemouth. In December he was charged with eight offences with his pupils. He denied the charge on the grounds that an operation performed in 1949 had

rendered him impotent. The operation had been designed to kill his sexual desire completely.

He had served four prison sentences for offences with boys. His *modus operandi* was always the same. He would buy a private school, commit offences with some of the pupils, get caught and be sent to prison. In the course of his career he bought a succession of schools across England. He belonged to a high camp church called the Evangelical Catholic Communion in which he was an ordained priest and as a result was known as the Revd Dr Moore, Ph.D.

Justice Lynskey sentenced him to five years after a jury took three hours to find him guilty, rejecting his plea of impotence.

The Inquisitive Officer, December 1953

Lieutenant Commander John Welham, thirty-four, was married with children, lived in Norbury in south-west London and worked as an executive officer at the Admiralty. Welham was arrested by police at the public lavatories in Victoria Station. He denied that he was importuning, claiming that he had spent so long in the lavatories because he was curious to study 'this question of homosexuality' that was attracting such attention at the time. The magistrate did not buy his story despite the character reference of his boss at the Admiralty, Commander Paterson, who claimed that Welham had a great thirst for knowledge and that his particular flair for investigation had often led him into trouble. He was fined £20 in December 1953.

The Martin Case, December 1953

Cyril Martin, thirty-nine, was a schoolmaster in Sussex who rolled up to a children's home where he introduced himself as the 'Revd Martin of Willesden'. The managers of the home gave him permission to take a thirteen-year-old boy with him on holiday. Martin assaulted the boy at a hotel in Uxbridge. The boy complained to the police and they arrested Martin. He belonged to another Anglo-Catholic fringe organisation, the Old Roman Catholic Church of England. He had been ordained by Bishop Barrington-Evans of Iver in Buckinghamshire. He was sent to prison for four months in December 1953.

The Eden Case, December 1953

Major Robert Eden, DSO, forty-one, had served bravely in the North Africa campaign; his gallantry was mentioned by Churchill in his memoirs. A regular soldier serving with the British Army in Germany, he was court martialled in Westphalia for offences with German boys in December 1953. He attracted the attention of the local boys by playing his mouth organ and took some of the boys for long rides on his horse, after which the offences occurred. He gave away lots of small bribes: sweets, chocolates, a wristwatch, a football, a mouth organ and in one instance, beer and sausage. His doctor constructed the defence that the twenty-two charges had occurred because he was experiencing a breakdown after years of military service. A German doctor claimed that he could cure Eden within a year. The court accepted his defence and Eden was sentenced to a year's treatment at a German clinic.

The Thrasher, December 1953

The Recorder of Bedford, C. L. Henderson, was itching to launch a witch-hunt. He shouted loudly from the bench about the dangers of keeping silent about the homosexual menace. Fortunately Bedford produced relatively few cases for him to exercise his prejudices.

In December 1953 he made headlines when he praised a fifteen-year-old youth who had given a 'good thrashing' to a man who approached him for sex. Thomas Wagstaff, thirty-six, approached the youth in a cinema. According to the prosecution Kenneth Mitchell gave Wagstaff such 'a good hiding that cosmetically he was in no position to go to the police station'.

Passing sentence, the Recorder said that he had taken into account 'the punishment so ably administered' by Mitchell: 'It may be that a good sound thrashing administered to people like you by a young boy would do a lot of good because usually the victims of the thrashing don't have the courage to stand up for themselves.' He congratulated Mitchell, a modern paragon: 'It is refreshing to come across a boy who will stand up for himself like that . . . It was a public benefit.'

Wagstaff had confessed to several other offences and was imprisoned for eighteen months by the court.

The Davis Case, January 1954

On the morning of 9 November 1953, Kenneth Brooks, fourteen, went missing. Three days later the boy was found in a copse. He had committed suicide by hanging himself from a tree. A post-mortem examination suggested that the 'boy had been interfered with for about twelve months'. Suspicion fell on Raymond Davis, forty-seven, a process worker, who lodged with Kenneth's family at their home in Bridgwater. He had lived there for two years, moving in after the death of his father. He had been a friend of the Brookses for twenty years. Davis shared a double bed with Kenneth, who was a month away from his fifteenth birthday when he died. At first Davis denied the charge, then he confessed at the police station that he and the boy had frequently had sex together. He later retracted this statement: 'At the time I was in panic. I just lost my head completely.'

A jury found him guilty on the evidence of the expert witness, the pathologist. The family stood by Davis and accepted his innocence. Mrs Brooks told the court that they had been 'good pals'. The judge said he did not blame Davis for the suicide, but sentenced him to three years in prison.

The Avery Case, January 1954

William Avery, a sixteen year-old labourer, was described by the magistrate as an absolute menace. He had lived away from home since the age of eight, spending most of his years in an approved school. At the time of his conviction in January 1954 he was living in a hostel run by a local authority in Clapham. Avery was found guilty of an act of gross indecency with a thirty-six-year-old labourer. Avery was described by the hostel warden as a solitary type of boy but he had since discovered that he was going out most evenings soliciting on Clapham Common. He claimed that his pocket money was too small. He claimed that over one weekend he had earned £3. The warden said his attitude was entirely mercenary and he received no satisfaction from the acts. He was sent to Borstal.

The Gordon Case, February 1954

Cliff Gordon, thirty-four, was a writer and actor who lived in Cardiff. In November 1953 he stayed for a few days at the Pheasant Hotel in Newton, Montgomeryshire, in central Wales. He met an old schoolfriend in the town and asked the licensee of the hotel if they could talk in Gordon's room. The licensee reluctantly agreed on condition that they stayed in the sitting room and did not use the bedroom. Twice he checked on the room and saw no light in the sitting room but he did notice the bedroom light on. Sufficiently alarmed, he dashed upstairs and flung open the door of the bedroom. He alleged that he saw Gordon and his friend making love. He threw the men out of his hotel and two months later the police, acting on his information, arrested Gordon for his alleged acts.

The assize jury in February 1954 did not believe him. Gordon conducted his own defence. He told the jury that throughout the whole of his adult life he had fought against his homosexual tendencies to the detriment of his own career. He had sought medical advice and tried many cures. At the time of his arrest he had been a voluntary patient in a mental hospital. Born in Llanelly, he had first appeared on stage when he was fourteen and could list a long and distinguished association with the West End stage and the BBC. He had written *Choir Practice*, a musical that had starred Ivor Novello and had been adapted into the film *Valley of Song*.

He denied the charges. The defence amounted to the fact that it was his friend, who was a witness for the prosecution, who had made the improper suggestion. He had rejected him. Given his struggles with this curse, he claimed he could never have any intention of propagating homosexuality. He even admitted that he had been bound over for a similar offence in 1941. The jury believed him and acquitted him.

The Wellington Case, March/April 1954

John Connolly, thirty-four, owned the Kipps Café in the small Shropshire town of Wellington. The café acquired considerable notoriety, especially amongst soldiers. Connolly had sex with many of them. Many National Servicemen came to the café and either brought partners or met them amongst the café clientele using the bedrooms upstairs. The eleven men eventually charged during March and April 1954 ranged in age between eighteen and forty-four and all were working men: a couple of labourers, a coalman, a salesman, a lorry driver, a decorator, a salesman, a butcher's assistant and two soldiers. The crown withdrew its case against one man whose counsel argued at the hearing that his statement had been extracted under duress. The prosecution decided at the last moment not to test his allegations in front of a jury. All the other men pleaded guilty. Connolly was sentenced to four years, another man to three years, one other to a year and the rest were either placed on probation or bound over.

Mr Justice Lynskey told the men: 'In this country we do not allow men to behave in the quite shocking way you men have behaved with one another. The difficulty, of course, is always to know what to do with men who are convicted of this kind of offence.' He hoped that the time was not far away when some steps would be taken where they could be dealt with – other than being sent to prison – where they would not be a danger to other people but learn to be 'respectable people'. 'This café', he continued 'has for some time been a centre of corruption to which come young men for various reasons or under various pretexts. Almost at once they have been led into this kind of life, not perhaps always needing much persuasion.'

The McGann Case, April/June 1954

On 8 December 1953 *The Citizen*, a newspaper in Gloucester, published a report of a case in which Basil Jordan was convicted on a charge of gross indecency. He was fined £20. On 12 December he received an anonymous letter: 'Dear Basil, On Monday next you will receive an[other] anonymous letter the contents of which are strictly private. You are advised in your own interests to read that letter only when you are alone and then to destroy it immediately.' Jordan was alarmed. He felt someone was trying to set him up so he took the letter to the police. The next letter suggested that Jordan meet the writer for immoral purposes. On 16 December, acting under police instruction, he left a reply at Gloucester Folk Museum. The following day, watched by the police, Robert McGann, thirty-two, a curate connected to Gloucester Cathedral, picked up the letter.

McGann sent a reply to Jordan: 'Dear Basil, Thanks a million for the dates . . . as soon as I can manage it I will send you a theatre ticket for a show at a Cheltenham theatre on a Saturday evening. It will probably start at 8 p.m. Be in your seat in good time. Leave the rest to me. Burn this.' On 23 January 1954 Jordan received another letter asking him to leave another message, this time in a hiding place at Gloucester Central Station. He left it the following day and McGann collected it three days later. The police waited for further contact, hoping to draw McGann further. He drew back. On 7 April, realising that he had withdrawn, the police went to see him. Ten days later he attempted suicide. He explained to the police: 'I have never seen Jordan. I was toying with an idea which I subsequently abandoned and never put into practice. What I did was the result of a sudden impulse which I was foolish enough not to abandon immediately. I could not bring himself to meet the man.'

In June 1954 McGann was charged with two charges of procuring the commission of an act of gross indecency, two charges of sending indecent communications and a charge of attempted suicide. He was placed on probation and was to spend the first year of his probation with the Cowley Fathers in Oxford.

The court report exposes an extremely sad case of a young man, desperately lonely, who wanted to find some way of meeting other men who shared his interest. The newspaper report offered that possibility. The court learned that he had a particularly difficult childhood. His father had committed suicide three days after his birth and his widowed mother kept him out of school until he was twelve, never allowing him to mix in male company. It was the story of a very timid man who had taken a very bold step, only to find himself in trouble with the police.

The Recorder of Gloucester, Raglan Somerset, used the case to draw attention to the problems of reporting trials for homosexual offences. He suggested that a large-scale case at a Borstal in Monmouth involving twelve youths had also occurred as a result of the publicity given to such cases. He believed that silence was the best policy on the part of the press.

The Stevens Case, May 1954
Mr Justice Sellers at Bedfordshire Assizes in May 1954 sent a fifty-year-old railway crossing keeper to gaol for fifteen years. Frederick Stevens pleaded guilty to nine charges of sexual offences with boys, and asked for at least

sixty other offences to be taken into consideration. The charges ran back as far as 1938. Stevens was almost illiterate with a very low IQ. Doctors thought he was too mentally backward for any sort of psychiatric report. Back in the 1930s he had been an assistant scoutmaster but it was his hut at the level crossing that drew hordes of boys, exploiting their passion for railways. He gave boys presents, and vast quantities of sweets and cigarettes were found at his home. He also took boys away on holiday with him each year, with their parents' permission. The case did not come about as the result of a complaint from any boy or parent but rather through the vigilance and curiosity of a local policeman who grew suspicious about the constant stream of boys visiting the hut. Sellers described it as 'the worst case of this type of depravity to come to my knowledge'. None of the local newspapers in Bedfordshire or the surrounding counties reported the case.

The Stakeford Case

One of the most tantalising case reports of the period concerns the mining communities of East and West Stakeford. The only report of this case I have discovered appears in the *News of the World*; no local newspaper carried the story. The six men in the dock were all miners aged between twenty-one and forty-eight. Three youths were also involved aged between twelve and seventeen. The judge, Mr Justice Donovan, disgusted by these youngsters and their brazenness, insisted that their names and addresses be published. None of them was sufficiently remorseful to satisfy Donovan. He told the court on the basis of their evidence that they 'were not innocent. A public service would be done if their names and addresses were published.' The circle, according to the prosecution, had been functioning since 1942, and it is clear from the charge sheets (copies of which are in the Public Record Office) that other men were involved. They presumably did not confess and the police decided, as so often, to prosecute only those members of the network foolish enough to sign a confession.

Most of the offences were committed in the pit. Only one of the men was married. Three of the men were sent to prison for a total of eleven years (the report does not make clear how this was distributed), and the rest were either fined, placed on probation or conditionally discharged. Two of the men in their twenties lived at the same house – partners? The case greatly exercised the judge:

> Great cities and great countries have been brought to ruin because they tolerated these offences . . . Nearly a century ago our ancestors in their wisdom called these abominable offences and prescribed a maximum punishment of imprisonment for life. They took the view

that the men must be punished not because they were weak but because their fellow men had to mark their detestation of the practices to ensure that others did not commit such offences.

The Uren Case, May 1954

Major Ernest Uren, forty-three, was a prominent local businessman in Plymouth, a flour merchant. He had served in the Army during the war in the North Africa campaign and in France. In May 1954 he was found guilty at Devonshire Quarter Sessions of committing a sexual offence with an eighteen-year-old sailor. The major took the sailor for a drive in the country. According to the prosecution, there the offence took place 'without the young man's consent, or at least without his full consent'. Later the sailor complained to the police and Uren was arrested. He was sentenced to six months by Sir Leonard Costello, chairman of the Quarter Sessions. Costello rejected as ridiculous Uren's defence that he committed the offence because he 'had done a hard day's work, [and that] your wife was away and that you had a few drinks'. He believed that Uren had corrupted the sailor. 'It was astonishing', added Sir Leonard, 'with all the publicity there has been lately about this class of offence and offences of a similar nature, [that] anyone with your upbringing, education and record should not have taken heed of the fate which befalls people in these days who indulge in this kind of behaviour.'

The Taunton Case, May 1954

Travelling back to Taunton from Exeter in the early evening of 20 February 1954, Geoffrey Williamson found himself alone in a closed carriage with another passenger. Williamson asked his companion if he would like to do something and indicated that they might have sex. He insisted that his fellow passenger should remove his mackintosh. The man bided his time, contributing to what he later described as an 'improper conversation'. On their arrival at Taunton railway station he arrested the young man. He was an off-duty railway policeman. Williamson was seventeen, a public schoolboy boarding in Taunton. At the police station Williamson told the desk sergeant that: 'It is obvious you know I am a homosexual. That is why you brought me here. You may consider these things morally wrong but I don't.' The sergeant told him that it was rather unusual for a lad to be talking about such matters. Williamson felt challenged: 'Of course I know what I'm talking about. I have been doing it since I was nine. Tony Evans is one.'

The boasting began as the police scribbled down the names he mentioned. He implicated many men including his lover Private John Nixon, an eighteen-year-old National Serviceman stationed at Nunsfield Camp outside Taunton. Nixon it turned out had an even more active sex life than Williamson. Several of their partners blamed the young men for enticing them into sex and Williamson's conduct would certainly suggest that he was capable of making the first move. Police questioned all the men that the pair named and eventually arrested and charged seventeen men who stood trial in Taunton at the Summer Assizes in May.

The court heard stories familiar across the country. Vere Caspar, thirty-seven, a Somerset farmer, thought that it had all been due to his father's death, leaving him with 'a lot of financial worry and heavy responsibilities'. Charles Schofield, a twenty-year-old airman from Rhyl, said 'misconduct' happened because 'he was lonely'. It was only because he 'had read about it in the papers. It only happened because I was away from home. It won't happen again', he promised. Another airman, also twenty, assured the court that he was seeking a course of treatment 'to get over this sort of thing' and that he would like to be 'cured of this kink'. Anthony Evans, twenty-six, a factory hand from Bridgwater, explained that it had all begun with his seduction as a boy, which created 'a stronger attraction for men' than for women. He was the man first named by Williamson in his initial statement.

Others were more defiant. Geoffrey Hilborne, thirty-one, a clerk from Taunton, said that he had

> first become aware of my homosexuality during my service in the Army ... I don't consider it morally wrong for such love-making between males as long as they are above age 20–21, and they are already queer ... I have always held the view that young people should not be corrupted, but if older people agree I see nothing wrong.

Hilborne seems particularly well-adjusted and had maintained a relationship with John Demmett, twenty-three, a cook. The judge was appalled. 'I regard you both', he told them, 'as perfectly hopeless cases.' Hilborne was sentenced to three years and Demmett to two, with an instruction that they be sent to different prisons.

Private Nixon had many admirers across the country, some of whom foolishly wrote to him. He preserved their letters. Walter Sexton, forty-five, a civil servant, was terribly smitten, telling policemen that they had met in Chester when Nixon had been sixteen. He thought he had met a soul-mate. 'My interest in [John] Nixon', he insisted, 'is not limited to one aspect. He has a lively, deep and precocious interest in other things. He was interested in amateur dramatics.' Sexton had advised him not to 'become over-zealous in sexual matters', advice that was probably the product of bitter experience.

It was Nixon's association with a Liverpool industrialist that was destined to hit the headlines. His namesake Gilbert Nixon, thirty-seven, was the vice-chairman of a pharmaceutical company and a lieutenant-colonel in the Territorial Army. A member of the regiment for eighteen years, he had won the Military Cross in the war for gallantry, during the Allied invasion of Sicily. They made love in the officers' mess. The elder Nixon had already successfully hidden a conviction for 'improper conduct', presumably cottaging, from his family and colleagues. A married man with one child, he had much to lose. The judge was disgusted: 'It is terrible to see a man like you, with a gallant military record, in the dock.'

The defence counsel representing Gilbert Nixon included many distinguished barristers, including Norman Skelhorn, QC, a member of the prosecuting team at the Montagu trial during March. The defence counsel relied a great deal on psychiatry in their pleas for mitigation, encouraged possibly by the presence of Dr R. Sessions-Hodge who ran a hospital near Taunton which offered cures for homosexuality through hormone treatment. The judge cross-examined the expert witness, producing a positively medieval exchange:

> Mr Justice Oliver: Does it mean this is a pest or disease which spreads where it strikes?
> Dr Sessions-Hodge: It can become more prevalent.
> Mr Justice Oliver: It seems to me as something rather like an infection or outbreak of some disease in a particular place. I cannot believe that the society of Taunton is naturally so degraded that it would produce a state of affairs like this. I have been on the bench for sixteen years and seen a good deal of this sort of thing, but never have I seen anything like this . . . How could an ancient, historic not very large town like Taunton . . . exhibit as many cases of homosexual crime as in the ordinary way I meet in a whole year?

The answer, he thought, was that the population of Taunton was not necessarily more debased than other groups but that once vice got established it spread 'like a pestilence and unless held in check, threatened to spread indefinitely'.

The judge gabbled on and on. The case clearly exercised him a great deal. Before sentencing, he explained his opinion on the plea for psychiatric treatment: 'That to me is dangerous ground. What the judges have to consider, first and foremost, is the welfare of the community. The sanction behind all law in the end is the fear of the consequences of transgression. The vast majority of people keep the law because they know it to be right but many keep it because they are afraid of the consequences of breaking it.'

Addressing the men in the dock, he told them that they had broken not only the laws of the country but the laws of common decency as well. To safeguard the community he sent nine of the men to prison. Evans the factory hand, described by the judge as 'an incorrigible pervert', received four years. Raymond Davies the ward orderly, whose wife had to be taken from the court screaming, got three years; he was told that he was 'one of the people who spreads this about by picking up people in public urinals'. The Somerset farmer Vere Caspar got two years and Sexton a year. The younger men were either bound over or put on probation. Private Nixon was put on probation for two years. The young soldier announced his cure to the court: 'I have been fighting homosexuality for some months with some degree of success, inasmuch as I am now attracted to women instead of men.' Williamson, whose confession had led to the investigations, was bound over. His upper-middle-class family from Buckinghamshire persuaded the court that they could save their son; the court did not call upon him to recant.

The other public schoolboy on trial, Gilbert Nixon, was less fortunate. He heard his sentence with head bowed and was then taken to the cells below the courtroom. As soon as the door was closed he took a tablet and collapsed, dying instantly. It was his dramatic suicide that brought this story to the attention of the national press. It provoked, however, no outcry.

The Dorset Case, May 1954

The Taunton case led to the arrest in Sherborne of Howard Kent-Jones, thirty-eight, and of two other men in Dorset. Kent-Jones had been named by Private John Nixon to Somerset police, who passed the information on to the Dorset constabulary. Kent-Jones was arrested and made a confession. Kent-Jones was described as an electrician though he also had a private income and had bought his cottage after being demobilised from the army at the end of the war. Single since his divorce in 1949, he entertained a number of young men, all over eighteen and most in their twenties, at his home. He was a member of the Rover Scouts, the senior branch of the scouting movement. Police made much of his large double bedroom where most of the incidents had taken place. Police also found photographs of young men at the cottage. It was claimed that his address book contained the 'addresses and telephone numbers of many well-known men'.

As with Croft-Cooke in Sussex, Kent-Jones was a newcomer in the village of Nether Carne and his activities generated much gossip. Many of his partners were locals with whom he had extremely close friendships. None of them had betrayed him. He had also brought soldiers like Nixon down for weekends at his cottage.

Kent-Jones offered the defence in May 1954 that his homosexual tendencies had brought him punishment throughout his life, 'isolating him from his fellow creatures'. He promised to seek medical treatment. The judge, Mr Justice Oliver, was not in a lenient mood. He sentenced Kent-Jones to seven years, and the other two men were bound over:

> It is perfectly obvious you are a complete and absolute pervert whose one idea is to get hold of youths and young men and bring them to your filthy practices.
>
> You are one of those men whom society regards as a pest and whose interest is to spread filthy doctrines about society. There is one thing in your favour: you have not interfered with children. If you had the sentence would have been fourteen years . . .
>
> The appalling nature of a case like this is the way this viciousness is spread among people who would otherwise be quite uncontaminated. It is my experience over and over again that youths and men who have turned aside to these filthy practices behave like animals.

The Ingram Case, July 1954

Thomas Ingram escaped to his native Ireland after Kent police issued a warrant for his arrest. Accompanied by the young man he described as his secretary, Godfrey Vosper, who also was wanted by the police, the pair planned to settle in the Irish countryside by buying a farm in Donegal. British police caught up with the fugitives in Limerick city and took them back to Dartford where they were remanded in custody before facing a trial at the Summer Assizes in July 1954.

Ingram, always known as Father Ingram, was in minor orders, having been ordained a deacon as a young man in West Africa during the early 1930s. At the time of his trial he was 48 years old. A charming and persuasive Irishman, Ingram had roamed around the world during the 1930s, picking up a couple of sentences for theft and serving two terms of imprisonment, one six-month stretch in Britain and another in Australia. In 1942 he went into partnership and became proprietor and manager of the London Choir School which was moved to Bexley in Kent during 1944 (to the site of a school closed because of the prosecution of the headmaster for homosexual offences with his pupils). The school, which had about a hundred teenage pupils (thirty of whom boarded), supplied choristers to London churches with a taste for ritual but lacking trained singers in their locality.

Father Ingram encouraged homosexuality among the boys and made trips himself to the dormitories at night, slipping between the covers with some of his young charges. When one boy complained to his parents, Ingram complained that it had been a case of mistaken identity and sacked another Irishman on the staff who carried the can for his superior's misdemeanours. Vosper, a pupil at the school, stayed on to become a general factotum, sharing Ingram's bedroom above the dormitory. An Ulster clergyman who discovered this fact denounced his boss and was sacked. Eventually it was he who took his story to the *Sunday Pictorial* in 1951, an action that led eventually to Ingram's exposure.

It was his activities with the school tart, a boy called Roger, that were to earn Ingram his massive sentence. Roger acknowledged the fact that he had slept with other boys but offered a defence rarely heard in an English court: 'I only did what is done by boys in boarding schools all over the country.'

Ingram not only enjoyed having sex with his willing pupil but importing men into the school and watching them perform. He picked men up in the West End, usually accompanied by Roger and Godfrey Vosper. There was a certain Charlie, a couple of soldiers (one of them a Grenadier Guardsman who gave evidence at the trial with immunity from prosecution) and a sailor. In all of these encounters young Roger was the principal attraction. The pliant Roger turned rebel, however, when Father Ingram brought a young negro back to the school. Roger fought, kicked and created a noisy scene. Roger was disgusted by the idea and refused, resisting all Ingram's seducing after that point.

In a bizarre twist Ingram married a divorcée in December 1951 though they lived together only a few months before she returned to her mother. The separation appears to have been amicable and she gave evidence in his favour at the trial. Marriage did not curb his activities, for according to one witness the homosexual activities continued.

It is a measure of Ingram's confidence that he rode out the revelations of his activities that appeared in the *Sunday Pictorial*. He claimed he had been libelled by a clique of homosexual masters that he had been forced to dismiss who were now getting their revenge. He posed as a vigorous opponent of vice and claimed that he was pursuing a case for libel in the courts that would completely vindicate him. The parents believed him and the school continued to function. The police were satisfied by his denials and closed their investigations.

It was love that proved to be Ingram's downfall. For over a decade the mother of one his favourites, a widow, had carried a torch for the Irishman, only to have her suit repeatedly rejected. His marriage turned her into his most dangerous enemy and it was on the basis of her suspicions that police eventually issued a warrant for his arrest on 14 April 1954 and took him into custody. When the policeman came into his study he provided what the prosecution took to be virtually an admission of guilt by asking them if they 'had called about the fire or is it something dirty?'

His admirer's account of a holiday that she had paid for in the summer of 1945 in North Wales was to be one of the most entertaining moments of a particularly colourful trial. Together they rented a three-bedroomed house, a room each. Frequently she found the schoolmaster sleeping in her son's room. She apparently suggested that he should stay in his own room but Ingram laughed off the suggestion. When she visited the school the following term and stayed as Ingram's guest she discovered that the holiday arrangement continued. Her son slept in Ingram's room at the school. 'I had my suspicions about it', she told the court, 'but I understood Father Ingram to be a celibate priest.'

The trial lasted seven days during July 1954. Ingram denied all the charges though he foolishly wrote to witnesses before the trial, providing the prosecution with useful corroborative evidence. To one former pupil he had written: 'I never thought that however much you disliked me you would mention the matters which took place between us as you did.'

The defence even put Ingram into the witness box, an unusual move in a trial for homosexual offences, which provided the prosecutor R. Seaton, QC, with an opportunity for a particularly brutal cross-examination. Dudley Collard, Ingram's counsel, tried to depict him as the victim of circumstances, 'a rather pathetic man trying to free himself of these cruel calumnies' and not as the 'charming and plausible rogue' presented by the prosecution. The all-male jury took only fifty minutes to find him guilty on six of the eight charges. Vosper, accused of a single count of buggery, was found not guilty. He had remained loyal to his former employer: 'I am not saying anything against Father Ingram. He has been very good to me and I will stand by him', he had told the police on his arrest.

Seaton had opened the case with a long speech to the jury, apologising to them for the disgusting things they would have to listen to, some of which would be 'almost unbelievable'. His case was that Ingram's activity had been a planned and systematic corruption of his young charges. The judge agreed. Justice Hallett, an active Anglican, introduced God into his summing-up: 'You took advantage of your position as principal of the London Choir School, which provides boys for the service of God by music to engage in a prolonged and outrageous course of depravity, which may well have serious consequences on the lives of these boys.' The judge had been very animated by the trial, taking an active part in the cross-examination of Ingram and doing much to help the prosecution case. The defence protested but their objection was overruled (it might have provided the basis for an appeal). The judge sentenced Ingram to ten years' imprisonment.

The Hatch Case, June 1954

Major William Hatch was an officer in the Duke of Wellington's Regiment serving with the British forces in Germany. At his court martial held in Germany in June 1954 he pleaded guilty to eight charges of committing sexual offences with four National Servicemen. Some of the offences concerned soldiers who had come to Hatch's quarters to listen to his records of classical music. It emerged that the major, who had a distinguished military record, had at one point thought of being ordained. The Franciscan friars were still willing to accept him.

The Ferris Case, June 1954

Albert Ferris, thirty-four, was an Anglican curate serving a parish in Plymouth. In June 1954 Mr Justice Streatfield sentenced him to ten years' imprisonment. He had pleaded guilty to ten charges of sexual offences with boys, and also asked the court to take into account forty-two other cases. Twenty-eight boys had been involved. The judge rejected his plea of guilty but insane. Streatfield told him that it was his duty 'for the sake of mankind to see that you are kept out of harm's way for a very long time'.

Ferris had one previous conviction. In 1946 he had been found guilty of thirteen charges with thirteen boys. On that occasion he asked the court to take into account eleven other offences. He had been sentenced to five years and had been released in 1949. After a year with the Cowley Fathers in Oxford the church had given him a second chance. He repeated the same pattern of behaviour in Plymouth that he had followed in his previous parishes. He ran a rabbit club as a way of getting to know young boys.

The court heard much about a very strange life. As a boy he had slept in the garden because he believed that his room was haunted. A graduate of Leeds, he had trained for the priesthood at Mirfield. The doctor who examined him found him remarkably free from any sense of guilt or shame.

The Usk Borstal Case, June 1954

So complex had been the couplings between fifty inmates of the Borstal at Usk in Monmouthshire that the prosecution presented special diagrams showing who had had whom. Twelve youths were charged with offences, eighteen were disciplined by the authorities at the Borstal, and a further twenty were given warnings. It was one of the most dramatic consequences of Sir Theobald Mathew's campaign to root out homosexuality from Borstals and approved schools.

The twelve youths charged, ranging in age from eighteen to twenty-one, were put on trial at Monmouthshire Assizes in June 1954 before Mr Justice Finnemore. Three had become soldiers since they left the Borstal and they wore battledress uniform in the dock. When they first appeared in court the accused each had a large label attached to his chest with a number. This was fairly common practice in network trials of this kind. The judge told them to take their labels off as he had prepared his own panel to tell 'who's who'. The forty charges took twelve minutes to read, so the court could discover who had whom. Three of the accused pleaded not guilty and were discharged to be tried separately. As the prosecution made their case they changed their pleas again and rejoined the others in the dock.

It was said that the Borstal was situated in a wooded area, which apparently provided plenty of cover for many nefarious activities. The prosecution blamed the publicity surrounding the Montagu case and the press coverage of homosexuality since the autumn as the principal cause: 'It appears that because of the extreme publicity that has taken place about this type of offence in recent months, involving well-known people, the whole moral outlook at the Borstal has been lowered.' The connection is intriguing. The governor and his staff also seemed to bear some of the responsibility because they relied 'on the moral sense of the vast majority of the inmates to bring to light anything of this sort'.

The incidents, within an elaborately organised system, came to light when an inmate asked to be moved. A youth had been raped one evening and serviced by seven others. Sexual favours became part of the currency of the institution used to repay debts or acquire credit.

The accused were well-schooled, showing a tremendous amount of remorse and shame in court. Keith Stratford, twenty-one, who had become a seaman since he had left the Borstal, said that his 'shame was acute. He insists that he has never done this before [coming to Usk] and would never dream of doing it outside.' Ten of the twelve were sentenced to imprisonment, sentences varying between six to fifteen months. Finnemore remarked:

I do not know what you men in the dock are thinking. If I did it might help me. I do not take the view that you are what are called perverts – those people who are addicted to indecency. I suspect that this began as some sort of joke, and developed into the serious crimes to which you have pleaded guilty. Everyone of you knows that this sort of thing is rotten.

If you do not stop this sort of thing you will ruin your lives altogether. I don't know how this matter began – what is obvious is that . . . the institution became a sink of iniquity and corruption.

You have got to be man enough to stand up and refuse to take part in these beastly practices. Those of you who will go to prison will go to a special one where there will be strict discipline and hard work. It will be the kindest and best thing for you if you work this beastliness out of your system.

Everyone of you can make good if you like . . . But you have got to keep the good on top and the bad underneath.

Let these disgusting and disgraceful practices stop now. They bring only unhappiness and misery.

One inmate tried separately for buggery with an animal was sentenced to four years.

The Oteley Park Camp Case, June 1953

Within a few days of the Monmouth trial Mr Justice Finnemore found himself trying another case involving men under discipline. Eight National Servicemen based at Oteley Park, a camp near Ellesmere in Shropshire, were found guilty of a succession of sexual offences with one another. No civilians were involved. This case could be turned into another example of military prostitution. All the soldiers, aged between eighteen and twenty-five, were consenting partners. Finnemore sent five of them to prison for a year each and placed the others on probation. 'I have', he said, 'come across it again and again. Young men during their National Service in the Army become grossly unoccupied and having long hours with nothing to do and suffering from boredom' become drawn into other activities. 'Boredom', he reminded the court, was 'one of the greatest enemies of character.' He told the soldiers that, 'If you let this sort of thing go on you will destroy your lives utterly and completely.'

The Wignell Case, June 1954

Mothers of three boy scouts gave evidence in June 1954 on behalf of the scoutmaster Stanley Wignell, twenty-eight, who was found guilty of sexual offences with their sons, members of their troops. Wignall, a tool setter from Enfield, was sent for medical reports by magistrates at Middlesex Quarter Sessions. The prosecutor said that the offences took place when the boys went to Wignell's house to try on new uniforms. One mother said that he had always treated her sons with respect on all occasions.

The Fiveash Case, June 1954

'In the old days', said Sir Norman Kendal nostalgically, 'people in temptation were in the habit of repeating the Lord's Prayer.' Kendal, chairman of Buckinghamshire Quarter Sessions was addressing Arthur Fiveash, thirty-eight, kitchen porter from Amersham found guilty in June 1954 of attempting buggery. Kendal asked Fiveash if he knew the prayer. Fiveash nodded. Sir Norman continued: 'When you get to the words "deliver us from temptation" – no that is wrong "lead us not into temptation" – get up, go out and do something else.' Sage advice from the old magistrate.

Fiveash was fined £25. He had approached a sixteen-year-old youth outside a cinema. The boy gave him a 'thorough thrashing': 'You did not know that this boy was old-fashioned enough to defend himself with his fists from this kind of thing. It might well have been some nervous type of boy you were attacking. The law allows a maximum penalty of ten years for this kind of offence. Think about that when you say the Lord's Prayer.'

The Treforest Case, July 1954

Mr Justice Glyn-Jones explained why he had sent Arthur Wallis, a forty-one-year-old unemployed miner from the small town of Treforest in Glamorgan, to fourteen years in prison. Glyn-Jones described the evil which spread like cancer. The case, said the judge, provided a 'striking example of the appalling mischief which would follow if vice were left unchecked'. It was a not particularly subtle signal to the newly appointed Home Office committee.

In the dock with Wallis at Glamorgan Assizes in Swansea in July 1954 were six men. Wallis was charged with eleven counts of buggery, one of which involved a three-year-old boy. Wallis asked the court to take into consideration fifty other counts. These involved seventeen different men and boys aged twelve to fifteen. The prosecution believed that the trouble had begun when Wallis acquired a television set, one of the few sets in the district. Men and youths were invited to view the set and in the process succumbed to sexual temptation: 'in that way', according to the judge, he 'organised a school of instruction in homosexual vice'. Wallis enjoyed 'their bodies when [he] pleased'. In this way he drew into his 'web' a group of men and boys who did 'not display [any obvious] abnormality but are normal people unable to resist temptation'. He was described as a 'ringleader' and an 'instigator'.

The other men, aged seventeen to thirty-one, most of them miners, were placed on probation. Their defence lawyers successfully blamed Wallis as the corrupting agent and they all managed to avoid prison. Wallis had to sit through a long judicial homily in which the judge was clearly addressing

Wolfenden about the dangers of changing the law, or the floodgates really would open:

> Such offences appear to have become very common and the question of what shall be done by the court for those who are convicted of such offences has become a matter of some public interest.
>
> Those who practise this vice must find others to share their work. The cases which have come to my notice seem to me to show that those addicted to the vice usually seek to widen the group of those who share it with them, usually younger men.

He defended the heavy sentence on the grounds that he wanted to 'mark the horror and revulsion with which any decent member of the community' regards such behaviour, to 'deter others following your example' and to make sure 'that for a long time to come you have no opportunity to corrupt others'. The Welsh judge was helping to clean up his homeland.

The Reading Case

The year 1954 was remarkable: in no year before or afterwards were so many trials for homosexual offences reported in the press. This coverage reached its peak during the summer of 1954. It is important to remember that the numbers of trials had fallen since 1951, but this was not the impression conveyed to contemporaries reading newspapers. Judges and magistrates realised that they were addressing a wider audience, and were keen to justify their actions in these trials. R. C. Hutton, sending four men to prison for sentences between three months to eighteen months, said that these cases were becoming too prevalent. As a consequence he had to act more harshly. This was of course untrue; judges and magistrates throughout the 1930s and 1940s had been just as savage: 'At first I and some other courts were unwilling if it could be helped to send down men like you, hitherto of good character, if it was thought that not much damage had been done. But from the way in which practices of this kind are spreading it is obvious that it will have to cease.' These self-important and arrogant professionals really did believe that their actions could change human behaviour. Despite more and more cases the rhetoric never changed, though the voices became angrier and more strident.

Three of the four men came from the Reading area, all of them in their twenties and thirties: a wine merchant, a sales manager, a garagehand and a man whose occupation was not given. Only one was married. The offences involved two boys aged eleven and twelve. These two lads, according to the police, were corrupt long before the men came on the scene. The pair were described as a public danger. According to the prosecution they sold themselves for a florin or a half-crown a time, an activity which had begun in the summer of 1952.

The Rotherham Case, July/November 1954
'This', said Judge Pearson, 'is a perfectly terrible story', as he addressed the seventeen men from the south Yorkshire town of Rotherham on forty-one charges of homosexual sex. All pleaded guilty. At the heart of this network was a twenty-one-year-old saw driver, Brian Hobson. At every stage in the proceedings no opportunity was lost to vilify him. A previous conviction two years before, also at the Leeds Assize, had won him probation and a chance to 'mend his ways'. The charge sheets reveal that Hobson had sexual relations with eight of his fellow accused, eleven of the charges involving him. He asked the court to take into consideration twenty-one other offences not on the indictments. Almost all of the men involved in the case were, like Hobson, natives of the town and working in a variety of unskilled and semi-skilled jobs. Hobson, a puzzling character who wore several masks, appears to have been something of a religious fanatic, a regular feature of Rotherham town centre on Saturday afternoons where he distributed evangelical literature.

It was through a public convenience in Market Street, rather than the chapel, that he met most of his partners, though he picked up Raymond Anderson, a salesman, at the local cinema. From some of them he took money; indeed after his arrest he complained to the police that one man still owed him money for acts performed on credit. The police suggested that he was well-steeped in 'homosexual matters'. The prosecuting authorities successfully prevented his release on bail at the committal hearing at the end of July 1954. He was portrayed as the leader (the word 'ringleader' was actually used) of the Rotherham 'underworld'. According to the trial judge he had 'spread corruption far and wide.'

Hobson's most audacious act was to commit what appears to have been several successive acts of fellatio on a gang of his workmates, six in total, on a works outing. The action took place on back seats of the coach. The coaches had left Rotherham at midnight on 21 September 1951 carrying 700 workers from the factory to spend a day in London during the Festival of Britain. Drink had been consumed and some of his partners on that occasion used their inebriation to excuse their action, probably the oldest and most popular excuse in the book. Hobson seemed to have had a succession of consenting partners who appeared to need little persuasion to have sex with him. Geoffrey Smith, a forty-six-year-old radio engineer, had what the prosecution described as 'a trysting spot' near the Brecks where he took Hobson. Smith was one of five married men in the dock; the rest were bachelors. John Redmond, thirty-two, a miner, is recorded as saying before he began dictating his statement that his 'wife is going to think this is "rough".'

Many of those on trial found it difficult to articulate their experiences. They had simply never put into words before what they had done, and certainly not for what would become a written statement read to a court of law. William Maw, a thirty-nine-year-old labourer, said 'yes' he would make a statement but he warned the police that its contents were 'rude'. He had met Redmond in the cottage in Market Street.

The prosecution pretended to suffer from a similar problem. While they may have had a wider vocabulary with which to describe the action, and certainly an endless supply of outrage, they found the whole exercise terribly distasteful and feared polluting the minds of others with accounts of these outrageous acts. The prosecutor prefaced his reading of Hobson's statement with a strong warning:

> he was sorry to say [that it] was apparent Hobson had behaved like a depraved animal. Throughout [his confession] you cannot help but be shocked and disgusted by his conduct. There are no words which sufficiently describe the way he conducted himself. The acts he performed with these men are too disgusting for words and I do not propose describing them. Frankly they are horrible. Unfortunately you will have to hear of them once.

He then proceeded to read the statement, having distanced himself from its contents and excited his audience about its revelations. Unfortunately the reporter from the *Rotherham Advertiser* pulled down the veil at this point and we are left guessing at the terrible catalogue of crimes to which the young worker confessed.

The police did not like Hobson and they managed to convey their reaction to the courts. By the time he came for trial in November 1954 he was penitent. He had, he claimed, 'mended his way' (a phrase he had used two years before at the Assizes) as well as revived his courtship with Mavis (possibly a real girl, but also another of Hobson's jokes: the name was homosexual slang for the police). Hobson enjoyed shocking the policemen and they disliked his defiance and his insolence. 'A self-confessed pervert', Hobson admitted his offences 'without any sense of shame at all for his infamy. He is thoroughly depraved and nothing is too disgusting for him.' He was a regular demon in fact.

Few of the offences took place in private residences. Most were committed in 'places of public resort'. Frank Small, thirty-five, who fixed radios and televisions and was putting in many hours of overtime in one of the great booming businesses of the decade, was the man who owed Hobson money for services rendered. Hobson kept him company on a few of hese evenings and Small confessed to sex acts at his workplace. The prosecutor reported that he had done so 'without his employer's knowledge'. The police reported the employer's reaction to this improper use of his workshop: he 'was deeply grieved and shocked' to learn about what had happened on *his* premises. The prosecution successfully conveyed the pollution they believed had occurred through the two men's actions.

One of the most curious features of the case was the absence of any reference to effeminacy. At no point was the masculinity of the men in the dock challenged. Horace Moffatt, thirty-two, who drove buses for the corporation, revealed that his initiation to homosexuality had taken place during the war when he was twenty. A flight engineer, his plane was shot down over the Reich in 1942 and he was taken prisoner: 'This business started when I was a PoW in Germany. I have been with one or two men [since], but the only one in particular is a man who works at a wireless shop [Frank Small] . . . that kind of practice had been rife throughout the camp.'

Small was single and lived with his parents. He received one of the longest sentences, three years, but one of his partners had been sixteen. Five men received prison sentences and others were either fined or conditionally discharged. Hobson got five years, which was relatively lenient considering the virulence of the prosecution and the amount of evidence against him. His previous conviction certainly did not help. His probation officer informed the court that while he had been satisfactory he 'had the feeling that he was still interested in homosexual practices', which given the record of the case was something of an understatement.

The judge drew a distinction between men who were able to demonstrate that this had been an isolated act and those for whom it constituted a pattern. The latter were sentenced to imprisonment. The police collected evidence about the working habits of the accused, their industry and punctuality being particularly important. Redmond the miner, who had a previous conviction for an act of gross indecency at Sheffield, was reported to be an 'idler' and a 'waster' by the Coal Board.

It is not entirely clear how the men were exposed. One account suggested that Small was caught cottaging in Market Street and spilled the beans; another account suggests that police received a tip-off about Hobson.

What surprised the prosecuting authorities was the absence of organisation. Though searches were made, no diaries, address books, letters or other incriminating documents were discovered. The prosecution professed to find this more shocking and possibly more sinister: 'The most disturbing feature of these very sordid cases, for those who care about morals to-day, is that they started in such a casual and off-handed manner.

217

You may think that in some cases the extreme casualness in which the offences were committed was a matter for grave disquiet.' You couldn' win; in some cases it was the organisation that was the most disturbing feature, while in this case it was the lack of organisation. The case gener ated many rumours in Rotherham and suggestions were made that men who had been better placed and who could pull strings had escaped arrest.

The Birmingham Case, July 1954

The prosecution prepared a special glossary of terms for a case in July 1954 involving twenty-one men aged from twenty-one to sixty so that the jury would be able to follow a trial that amounted to a caricature of almost every homosexual stereotype. In the most prominent place was Kenneth Walton, a twenty-seven-year-old hairdresser whose personal archive supplied the police with a good deal of their evidence. Walton's address book appropriately enough a small black book, was filled with 'the names addresses and telephone numbers of scores of men living in the Midlands' members of what the prosecution described as 'a vicious clique who have infested the city [of Birmingham] for many years'. Walton kept a score book recording all his conquests, the declining numbers some index poss- ibly of the demands of the archives. Police counted an overall figure of 213 partners, 105 of whom he had met in 1951. Eighty partners in 1952 and a decline to fifty in Coronation year suggest he might have been losing his touch.

While Walton worked and lived in West Bromwich, he spent many leisure hours in a milk bar in the centre of Birmingham, regarded by police as a notorious centre of vice. Walton was Nina to his friends at the bar. Other men in the dock adopted a variety of more exotic camp names Tiger Lil, the Duchess, Garbo, Rita, Jezebel, all revealing the influence of the big screen. The *Birmingham Evening Mail*, the only local paper offering any sort of report of the trial, mentioned the men's practice of using feminine pet-names and supplied a slightly more restrained list than the *News of the World*: Blanche, Georgina and Freda. 'Nina' had once worked in a glass factory and included a personal ad amongst an export consignment to the US: 'Blonde, 22 years of age, who would like to write to someone in your country', signed Nina, with Walton's address. Reports do not record how successful this manoeuvre was. Walton had served his country in the Merchant Navy and was taken into custody carrying sun- tan powder, eyebrow pencil, and the ubiquitous badge of the fraternity a powder puff.

The judge, Pearce, allowed himself to be deeply shocked at Charles English, executive of a brewing company, and at the time of the trial ifty-two. He had been a famous local rugby player who had narrowly missed international honours and the judge thought he should have known better. A public schoolboy, he held a commission in the war and possessed a distinguished war record. The court heard about his caravan holiday with Frederick Element, a twenty-six-year-old mechanic from Warley, described by the prosecution as 'a constant frequenter of the company of effeminate men'. English's name had been first recorded in Walton's books five years ago.

When George Hawkesford, 'Jezebel', was arrested he told the police that he was 'well-known'. A twenty-three-year-old machinist, he got a sentence of two years on two charges of buggery. The men faced eighty-nine charges in total, while a further seventy-three offences were taken into consideration. The men were drawn from across the city's trades, industries and services: a storeman, a spring maker, a rubber worker, a butcher, a chocolate worker, a laundry worker, a packer, a shopkeeper, a farm labourer, a tonguesman, a foreman, a tailor, a cellarman, a milk roundsman, a porter, a record clerk, Walton the hairdresser, English the brewer, Element the mechanic, Hawkesford the machinist, two cooks, three male nurses and three warehousemen. All played their part in the life of the second city, the workshop of the world.

The case had begun with a complaint about Hobson. He was arrested, his home was searched and the police worked through his papers. He made a full confession and was awarded a lighter sentence because of his co-operation. He was sentenced to three years. Twenty-three men received prison sentences. One other man, the rubber worker, got three years for two acts of buggery with a man who did not appear in the dock (the prosecution announced that the court was seeing only a sample of the 'clique'; it is possible the other men sensibly refused to co-operate). Justice Pearce sentenced seven men to two years, including 'Jezebel'. English and Element were among a group of five men sentenced to eighteen months.

The Carlisle Case, July/October 1953

At the Carlisle Assizes in October 1953 twelve men were found guilty of a series of homosexual offences. The case was one of the most viciously prosecuted in the period. Carlisle police left no stone unturned. Their searches of the homes of the accused were so thorough that they even examined annotations on theatre programmes to try to collect incriminating material. Even a scrap of paper with a name on it found in the wallet of one of the arrested men led to the discovery of another of his partners, a local fishmonger whose business was destroyed by the case. It is clear that much pressure was employed to extract a number of the confessions that secured convictions and that all sorts of inducements and threat were employed by the two policemen who organised the case.

The case really began in the summer of 1954 when relatives of Council lor John Gardner, twenty-nine, a postman, approached the police because they feared that he was being blackmailed. In the previous months he had borrowed increasing amounts of money from his relatives, who started to become suspicious as they compared notes. Why they did not confront him is unclear because their action destroyed his political career. Elected as a Labour member of the city council in 1953, Gardner was politically ambitious. On the advice of his family police interviewed Gardner at the police station on a Saturday evening. According to the police report he immediately confessed: 'My mind has been muddled since 1947. I want to get the whole thing off my chest.' Gardner claimed that he was being blackmailed by a colleague who threatened to expose his homosexuality to the Postmaster. In this way Gardner led police to John Woodmass. Gardner and Woodmass, it seems, had been lovers in the late 1940s. Woodmass claimed that he had lent money to Gardner who was refusing to return it.

Gardner had been a Marine. He claimed he had been seduced by a colour sergeant in 1942 when he was seventeen-and-a-half and had a further experience with a corporal while he was in the forces. His counsel suggested that these two incidents had a permanent effect on Gardner. Demobilised, he returned to Carlisle and married. At this stage he claims someone else (from his unit in the Marines) started to blackmail him about his wartime liaisons. It was then that he started borrowing money and then that he got to know Woodmass, to whom he confided his past.

Woodmass was arrested on the following Tuesday. At first he denied that he had ever had 'abnormal relations' with Gardner but he soon confessed. He mentioned another man who he claimed was Gardner's lover. This man was arrested but denied everything and refused all induce ments to confess. He was not prosecuted as a consequence. A search of Woodmass's house uncovered four letters from other men that the police thought suspicious. This led to more arrests. They established a connec tion with Richard Gosling, fifty-one, a maintenance fitter whose activities at a lavatory in the market had provided him with a large number of sexual partners, several of whom were arrested after his confession.

Gosling is a rather shadowy character. None of the newspaper reports discussed his past history. They were mainly interested in one of his part ners, Albert Reynolds, thirty-four, the local Conservative Party agent. Rey nolds was a self-made man as much on the rise as Councillor Gardner. A native of Derbyshire, he had left school for a labouring job, and moved on to a post as a footman to a Harley Street doctor. He studied for a while at a theological college; like many other individuals in this case, he was active in the Church of England. The war made him. After service in the Army he was able to find a job as a press clerk before moving into Conservative Party organisation. The local association rallied around him and it was the intervention of the prospective Conservative parliamentary candidate for the constituency that saved him from prison: 'I am willing to stand by him and assist. He has made a slip, but I do not think he is beyond redemption.' Mr Justice Gorman said that he would act on that advice. As a result Reynolds was bound over. Reynolds sensibly enough refused to make a statement to the police: 'I have heard of statements being read out in court. I don't see that it will serve any purpose having all these details read out.'

Two other men, one of whom had sex with Gosling, were not so lucky. They lived together. Kenneth Palmer, twenty-five, a waiter from London who had formerly been a nursing orderly, described their relationship as 'a deep and sincere friendship'. His partner George Bryden, twenty-three, was a hall porter at a hotel in Keswick. He had met Gosling in the market two years before. They were both sentenced to six months in prison largely because they lived together.

Gosling and Woodmass got four years each. Sam Kidd, twenty-nine, the fishmonger, got a year. William Anderson, a travelling salesman who had met Woodmass at a pageant in Edinburgh, got eighteen months. Police had discovered amongst his effects a theatre programme on which was written 'an expression in French which might be provocative'. The newspaper report does not provide us with more details of these powerful words. Allan Cameron, twenty-seven, a railway guard whom police arrested as he was returning to Carlisle with a train, ensuring maximum humiliation for him, was given a sentence of six months. The other men involved either were bound over or put on probation.

Certainly the most telling comment on the case came from George Bryden who said on his arrest by the police that he 'supposed' someone 'gave you my name. Somebody will have. There is always somebody to split on you.'

An Officer and a Gentleman, September/October/November 1954
Moustached Military Cross holder Lieutenant Colonel Julius Caesar, fifty-seven, was devoted to his regiment, the King's Shropshire Light Infantry. On retirement after nearly forty years as an officer in the regiment he was appointed as regimental administrator responsible, amongst other things, for maintaining the regimental records and maintaining contacts with former members. He continued to live as an officer at the regimental headquarters at Copthorne.

In September 1954 he was arrested on eleven charges, to six of which he pleaded guilty. Soon after his arrest he denied all the charges. By the time of the trial he had changed his mind again.

The case revolved around two soldiers in the regiment, Hryden Woodhouse, twenty, and John Everton, twenty-two. It was claimed that Caesar had seduced Woodhouse on Christmas Day, 1953. Woodhouse served as a waiter in the officers' mess. Caesar gave him four whiskies in the mess and then brought him to his room. They sat on the edge of the bed and then Caesar caught hold of the young man's arm, pulling him towards him. Woodhouse was pulled on to the bed and they started kissing, after which the newspapers report tantalisingly that 'the offence was committed'. On another occasion they had sex at a disused army camp in the neighbourhood. Caesar tried to persuade Woodhouse to come with him for a weekend in the capital.

Private John Everton was accused during the summer of 1954 of an act of gross indecency and sent for trial at the Shropshire Assizes where he would have encountered Mr Justice Finnemore. Everton's commander assigned Caesar to organise the young private's defence. Caesar fell passionately in love with him. They made love together on at least one occasion. The main evidence against Caesar was the love letter he had written to Everton:

Dear John,

. . . since you once again treated me as a normal human being who is trying to help you, things for me are brighter, so much brighter that silly as it may sound and seem to you I have reached the stage when it is hell not to have you around the place.

I am dreadfully afraid that I am desperately in love with you.

Our short meeting yesterday was grand. You were so much your old self, and I just cannot tell you how much it did for me. Since, I have been thinking of you all the time all day, and now that you are dancing.

Please play your part for as long as we can be together, and promise first that nothing will stop us being together from 2.30 on Wednesday until the cows come home.

Promise that you will come out again; promise that you will, should you get inside for a spell write me, and promise that if all goes well stick to me.

It sounds idiotic, but I assure you I have never met anyone of whom I have been so fond.

I promise not to worry you by writing, but I just cannot do so tonight. Please, please, try to make chances to meet me privately somewhere. I want you so much . . . Burn this without fail.

Everton claimed that Caesar had lured him to a meeting in his quarters and made him drunk with sherry. Everton handed the letter over to the regimental sergeant major who passed it on to the commanding officer, who passed it on to the police. They postponed Everton's trial and arrested Caesar.

Amongst the former members of Caesar's regiment who gave evidence in his favour was R. E. Vaughan, Recorder of Birmingham, who had acted as a prosecutor in many trials for homosexual offences. He had served with Caesar as a subaltern in the First World War and tried to suggest in mitigation that he had known no other life than the regiment and that by his actions he had made himself an 'outcast from the society to which he has been accustomed all his life'.

He was without close relatives or a real home. He was sentenced to a year's imprisonment. The defence could offer no explanation for what had occurred.

The Barnsley Case, December 1954

Peter Goodliffe, twenty-four, a glass worker, was beaten up and robbed. Police inquiries soon moved away from these crimes to Goodliffe's sexual history. After an interview with the police he made a full confession linking him to a large number of men in Barnsley. Thirteen of them were charged with sexual offences involving Goodliffe. One man refused to plead guilty and was discharged at the beginning of the West Yorkshire Assizes in December 1954. All the other men confessed.

The chairman of the magistrates' bench at the committal proceedings invited the prosecution to read all the confessions to the court 'word for disgusting word'. He thought that Goodliffe's statement was 'the most shocking document I have read'. He was particularly shocked by the fact that Goodliffe could not remember the names of some of his partners. According to the magistrate the statements had been 'couched in effectively filthy terms'. One of those charged, Leslie Jones, eighteen, a haulage hand, told police: 'It sounds dirty when you're speaking about it afterwards.'

Goodliffe had been 'a pervert for several years'. All the other accused men tried to use this fact to their advantage. They were also helped by the fact that on several occasions he had accepted money for sexual favours.

His most highly placed partner was the Revd Ernest Clark, forty-seven, an Anglican clergyman, who had committed the offence while he was Vicar of Barnsley. The judge discharged him on condition that he seek treatment. His superiors spoke powerfully in his defence. The court was told by one of them that his former parish was one of the most 'depressing' parishes in the diocese, liable to get 'on a man's nerve', and push him over the edge.

The testimony made Goodliffe sound irresistible. George Wood, twenty-seven, a labourer, claimed that he had joined the Army to escape from Goodliffe: 'I knew it was wrong . . . I don't do these things now.' Daniel Pickles, forty-three, an ice-cream salesman, had been picked up by Goodliffe in the road while driving his car. Thomas Ryder, fifty-one, a painter, met Goodliffe in Barnsley bus station and invited him to his home after noticing that he was 'effeminate': 'I know what we did was an offence. I shall never do anything like it again.' Harold Walker, fifty-two, a glassworks packer, said that Goodliffe had constantly pestered him. They had sex at their factory together. He even met Goodliffe one night waiting for him after the theatre.

John Cade, thirty-six, a railway policeman, had been drawn into 'perversions' when he had served with the Royal Engineers in Syria: 'Since I left the Army I've tried my hardest to conquer this habit, but on some occasions it has happened between myself and other men in Barnsley.' Arthur Beverley, thirty-five, a batch mixer, also talked about his military experiences: 'It used to be a common thing in Burma. I don't think it was ever serious.' Beverley had sex with Goodliffe at their place of work when they were alone together. James Whitehouse, twenty-nine, a hospital porter, had gone on holiday with Goodliffe to Great Yarmouth. Bernard Haxby, forty-eight, a master builder, was married with children. He suggested that his reason for 'lapsing' 'might have been that my wife's attitude to sex was rather cold'. He had met Goodliffe and an unnamed friend one evening and taken the other two out to Langsett Moors in his van: 'I have a good wife and two children. I don't want any shame on them. When I've done these things I've wanted to kill myself – I was so disgusted.'

The others involved were also working men: Wilfred Egley, twenty-nine, railway shunter, and Harold Wormersley, forty-nine, cable repairer. Apart from the vicar all of Goodliffe's partners had been drawn from the working men of the Yorkshire town.

Goodliffe said little. It was revealed that he had been active since he was sixteen. The magistrate thought he showed no remorse. Mr Justice Pearson sentenced him to five years: 'It is clear beyond doubt that to a considerable extent you have been the focus of this truly disgusting business which has been going on. It is a great danger to others who may be tempted to go astray. For the protection of others it is necessary that a severe sentence should be imposed.' Three other men were imprisoned, Walker and Egley for a year and Whitehouse for nine months. All the rest were either fined or placed on probation.

The Battle for the Fitzroy

The Fitzroy Tavern is situated on the corner of Windmill Street and Charlotte Street, a short walk from Tottenham Court Road and Oxford Street, at the heart of London's West End. This pub gave its name to the surrounding district, Fitzrovia, a place of particular interest in artistic and cultural history. Tom Driberg, a regular visitor to the Fitzroy, coined the name in an article celebrating the pub in the William Hickey column of the *Daily Express* (27 March 1940). The article explained how the Tavern had adopted a ship of the Royal Navy, the HMS *Fitzroy*. Driberg praised the activities of the landlady Annie Allchip for organising a circle of regulars to knit 'balaclavas, socks, scarves and mittens for the crew' – Bohemia's contribution to the war effort.

Annie was the daughter of the man who had created this British institution, Judah Kleinfeld (always known as 'Pop'), a refugee from Polish Russia who had come to London in 1885 to escape the 'pogroms and oppression' in his native land. A tailor, Kleinfeld had become a master tailor in Savile Row by the outbreak of the First World War. A man clearly of considerable enterprise, intelligence and charm, he had become by that time 'a leading figure in the burgeoning Jewish West End community'. He was responsible for promoting many philanthropic projects amongst his own community. During the First World War he established a business making greatcoats for the Army. The profits from this business provided him with the capital to take over the tenancy of the pub on the corner of Windmill Street and Charlotte Street.

Proud of his adopted country, a patriotic Briton with a powerful sense of history, Kleinfeld renamed the pub after the aristocratic family that had once owned this part of the capital. (King Charles II had granted the manor of Tottenham Court to his minister the Earl of Arlington in 1667. Arlington's daughter and heiress married the King's bastard son Henry Fitzroy, first Earl of Euston and later first Duke of Grafton. His mother was Barbara Villiers, Duchess of Cleveland. All these titles and names are commemorated in this district of London. One member of the family, Henry James Fitzroy, Earl of Euston, was involved in the Cleveland Street Scandal in 1889 when he was exposed by a radical journalist as having patronised the male brothel run by Charles Hammond, employing postal delivery boys as prostitutes.) Kleinfeld decorated the walls of the bar with recruiting posters from the Great War, giving the place a strongly period flavour. His successors added posters from the war of 1939–45, maintaining the patriotic tradition. These became the nucleus of a collection of military and naval memorabilia that decorated the tavern.

Fitzrovia attracted a number of artists because of the cheap rents available in some of the local properties. Augustus John was probably the most famous local resident and he became one of Kleinfeld's first patrons though it is the artist Nina Hamett, a colourful and larger than life figure, who established the Fitzroy Tavern as the headquarters of London's Bohemia. Pining for Paris, she found in the Fitzroy Tavern the place that 'best embodied the atmosphere of the Parisian café'. According to Kleinfeld's daughter, 'Nina would sit in the corner of the bar and sketch'; she had 'an enormous following whom she introduced to the Fitzroy. Sitting erect on her bar stool, she ruled supreme as "Queen of Bohemia".' By the early 1920s the reputation of the pub was established: 'a heady Bohemian mix in contrast to the more sophisticated Bloomsbury set, the other side of Tottenham Court Road, and also distinct from the Sohoites south of Oxford Street, the great divide.' The presence of David Bertorelli's restaurant across the road from the Fitzroy also attracted customers, and in time Charlotte Street became famous for a cluster of restaurants, some of which still survive. The arrival of the BBC at the edge of the district in the interwar period brought another ingredient to this cosmopolitan meeting place.

In the mid-1930s Kleinfeld handed the licence on to his daughter Annie and her husband Charles Allchip, an East End Jew who always spoke in cockney rhyming slang, and came, like his wife, from a family involved in tailoring. During their tenancy the pub began to attract a homosexual crowd, overlapping and complementary to the bohemian types who had provided the main clientele. The strongly gay tone of the pub was firmly established in the 1940s when the Fitzroy attracted large numbers of servicemen, particularly sailors. The pub was also popular with American servicemen. Kenneth Williams, who lived about ten minutes' walk away in Marchmont Street, visited the Fitzroy on a Friday evening in June 1952: 'Went out with Henry W. & L. Drinks at a gay club called "Fitzroy" which really is the gayest pub I know. Charming. Full of sailors and queens with prying eyes and inquisitive nostrils – all searching for some new sensation – all empty vacuous faces devoid of anything, save sexual appetites.' It was cruising at its crudest.

Appropriately enough, Williams talked to his friends about socialism that night. For the Fitzroy counted a number of Labour politicians amongst its clientele, many of them brought along by Tom Driberg. Kingsley Martin, Michael Foot and the Castles, Barbara and Ted, were amongst those he introduced. Hugh Gaitskell, leader of the Labour Party from 1955 until his sudden death in 1963, used to bring his students from the LSE in the late 1920s and 1930s and it was in the Fitzroy that he met his wife Dora Frost, indeed he proposed to her in the bar. He had first noticed her when she threw a pint of beer over a man's head when he had directed an anti-Semitic remark at Annie Allchip.

Charles and Annie Allchip were very popular and well-connected figures in the West End. Commander Robert Fabian of the Yard, Britain's best known and most glamorous policeman during the late 1940s and 1950s, drank in the pub, as did another Allchip friend the public executioner Albert Pierrepoint. Pierrepoint had dispatched Timothy Evans, Bentley, Christie and Ruth Ellis to their maker. By this time a publican from Lancashire, Pierrepoint 'struck up a great friendship with the Allchips . . . He would pop into the Fitzroy when he was in London . . . He never talked about his work except once when he explained to Charlie that his black case contained "the tools of the trade".'

The Allchips maintained and extended the charitable activities of Pop Kleinfeld, organising enormous parties and outings for deprived city children. Ralph Reader, of *Gang Show* fame, organised the entertainment and each year a different celebrity took the role of Santa Claus. Both Richard Dimbleby and Gilbert Harding performed this office during the 1950s. Harding, another regular, interviewed Charlie Allchip one Saturday evening on his TV programme *The Spice of Life*. 'By 1951', according to Sally Fiber, Charlie's daughter, 'the parties had become such a London institution that BBC's Childrens' TV televised it live.' Beverley Nichols was another regular, as was Kenneth Horne who helped get the Allchips' daughter 'into his old boarding school'.

The pub was also well protected by its strong connections with the hierarchy of the Met. The Allchips employed a former CID man to act as their head of security, John Rutherford, 'potman-cum-overseer and minder for the Fitzroy after his retirement from the force'. Rutherford had been one of the original members of the first Flying Squad at Scotland Yard during the 1930s. Other famous detectives of the period, Jack Capstick and Fred Narborough, were also customers.

On the evening of 15 January 1955 the Fitzroy was raided at about ten minutes to ten. It was a Saturday night and the pub was packed. Superintendent Paull from Tottenham Court Road police station told Allchip that the premises had been under observation since 7 January. He was charged with eleven offences, running a disorderly house and serving drink to drunken customers. The case was heard at three sessions during 1955 at Marlborough Street magistrates' court and was not completed until 30 November when the magistrate Paul Bennett found Allchip guilty on nine charges and fined him £1 on each. Allchild immediately launched an appeal.

R. R. Seaton, acting for the Metropolitan Police, depicted the Fitzroy Tavern as a 'den of iniquity', a phrase that supplied headlines in the *Daily Mirror* and *Daily Express* in extremely brief accounts of the case. According to Seaton:

the occupants [of the pub] were quite obvious male homosexuals who dyed their hair and rouged their cheeks and behaved in an effeminate manner with effeminate voices. The other occupants were to a large extent made up of servicemen – sailors, soldiers and marines. There can be little doubt that this house was conducted in a most disorderly and disgusting fashion. These perverts were simply overrunning the place, behaving in a scandalous manner and attempting to seduce the members of the forces.

This description was supported by the testimony of the police officers who had been observing the premises in early January, making head counts of from fifty to eighty 'perverts' on different nights:

The 'perverted behaviour' had apparently involved fingering sailors' buttocks, linking arms with sailors, rubbing their thighs and generally patting each other on the cheek ... they had even put hands up a Seaforth Highlander's kilt! ... According to Mr Seaton [and the police officers], these 'perverted homosexuals' accompanied the brave servicemen down to the gents. The conscientious policemen followed them downstairs to the lavatory, where they saw two 'perverts' and two sailors standing close together and one of the sailors was buttoning up his flies ... The language used was indeed colourful. They addressed each other as Diane, Sylvia, Monica, June and Georgina respectively. One typical comment was, 'I have a very nice flat not far from here. If you come with me, we could have a nice time.' When the sailor replied, 'I can't stay all night,' the 'lady' is meant to have said, 'Don't worry my dear. I shall look after you.' Again Georgina supposedly told her friends, 'It was awful ... He turned out to be a bloody old steamer. Two pounds for all night.' 'I bet you told him what he could do with it,' Sylvia answered to gales of laughter. Another rich interchange reported by the police ran as follows:

'Excuse us, we are going down the hole,' said the sailor.

'If you are going to wash your hairbrush, can we come and dry it for you?' the 'pervert' responded.

'I don't get it but I'm willing to learn,' the bewildered sailor said.

This brought titters from the packed courtroom.

A further sample was, 'I think you are two lovelyboys. You must both come home with me when we leave here.'

Even more extreme, according to the police, was when one 'lady' stood on one leg on the bench seat, exclaiming, 'Here I am Cupid, God of Love,' and was complimented on a 'nice round bottom'. The police would testify that during their periods of observation sailors trooped off with 'homosexuals' for assignations together outside the pub.

The magistrate accepted that Seaton had made a compelling case: 'I feel that I am bound to accept that the place was full of men with very few women, which proves right away in a public house in the West End or anywhere else, that there is something extraordinary about it . . . My view is that there was plenty going on.'

Allchip offered a vigorous defence. G. D. 'Khaki' Roberts defended him in court. Roberts had of course been Rupert Croft-Cooke's defence counsel in 1953 and had been prosecutor in the second Montagu trial. Roberts's cross-examination of the police was extremely tough and he exposed so many inconsistencies in their stories that Allchip successfully appealed against his conviction in January 1956. Roberts also presented a large number of character witnesses for Allchip. Wynford Vaughan Thomas, the broadcaster, spoke eloquently in favour of the charitable publican. Many former senior Scotland Yard policemen, including Fabian, were also willing to testify to Allchip's good character. Roberts also made much of the fact that Allchip had received no word of warning from the police, indeed Superintendent Paull's predecessor at Tottenham Court Road police station had officially commended Allchild for his co-operation with the police.

Almost certainly the appeal benefited from a line of questioning by Roberts to the Superintendent that probably came from other policemen in the Met. Roberts exposed Paull as a zealot:

The Superintendent admitted that the covert spying operations had taken place on his instructions . . . [and] that he had acted for self-aggrandisement in the force . . . Under cross-examination he was forced to agree how difficult it was for a licensee or a member of the bar staff to decide if the man he was about to serve was a 'pervert'. A high-pitched voice and a gentle, even effeminate manner didn't necessarily mark out a person as such.

The brewery who owned the pub, Charringtons, suspended Allchip's tenancy after his conviction on 30 November. They were bombarded with letters in his support and he was reinstated after his appeal. On that day Allchip hoisted the Union Jack on the roof of the tavern and all drinks were on the house – he had won the 'Battle of the Fitzroy'.

The Allchips retired from the pub soon after the case. The trials had taken a heavy toll and it had soured their relations with the brewery. Bernard Levin wrote a eulogy to them and the tavern in the *Manchester*

Guardian, the day after their enormous farewell party. He celebrated the pub where 'The Arts and Politics' mixed, but he did think that 'some of the men in the bars might have raised the eyebrows of their predecessors', the only allusion to the gayness of this important West End space.

11

The Montagu Trials

Two homosexual trials during 1953 and 1954, both involving a peer, Lord Montagu of Beaulieu, made front page news in contrast to the hundreds of other cases that went unreported. Because of the social prominence of the accused and the nature of the accusations, the Montagu trials received more press coverage than any trial for homosexual offences since Oscar Wilde's in 1895. The Montagu trials occupy an important position in social histories of the period and are much cited. Most citations can be traced back to an important book written by one of Montagu's co-accused in the second trial, Peter Wildeblood, whom we have already encountered as a witness giving evidence before the Wolfenden Committee. Wildeblood's *Against the Law* is a powerful polemic recounting his experiences on trial and, after his conviction, in prison. It was an influential book much read by gay men in the 1950s and 1960s, originally published by Weidenfeld and Nicolson in 1955 and soon reissued as a Penguin paperback.

Wildeblood's account of the Montagu cases was extremely partisan, a piece of propaganda that has limited value as a historical record of the trial. That historians have elevated it into a primary historical source says much about their credulity and negligence and their desperate wish to believe Wildeblood that the trials of Lord Montagu and his friends were the show-trials of a homosexual witch-hunt launched by a reactionary administration.

Contemporary records of the evidence that actually emerged in court show the trials in a different light and challenge the rather one-dimensional version to be found in *Against the Law*.

The Accusations

The story of the Montagu trials begins in the summer of 1953. It started with two accusations made by two boy scouts against Lord Montagu and his friend, an assistant film director, Kenneth Hume, on 3 August 1953, Bank Holiday Monday. The scouts made their allegations to their scoutmaster who then presented them to the police. The police were told about the allegations three days later on 6 August and began their investigation under the head of Hampshire CID, Detective Superintendent Jones. There is no evidence that this was a set-up. The genesis of the trials lies in these accusations by the two scouts.

The scouts had spent that Bank Holiday Monday working as guides at Palace House, Beaulieu, Montagu's home, which had been opened to the public for the holiday. The two scouts stayed behind for tea. Montagu invited them and one of his house-guests, Kenneth Hume, to go for a swim in the sea at Warren Beach on the Beaulieu estate. The scouts claimed that each had sex with the peer and the director in a beach-hut where all four changed after the swim. Montagu and Hume denied this. They did not deny that they changed in the beach-hut or that they paired off, going into separate rooms so that each man was alone with a scout. Neither did Montagu deny lending the scout changing with him his towel. The scouts claimed the door between the rooms was shut but Montagu claimed it was ajar.

These were serious charges, and after police interviews the scouts stuck to their stories. On 8 August Montagu was interviewed by the police. According to his own account delivered under oath in the witness box he was shocked when the police told him of the allegations. He denied them vigorously: 'It is fantastic. I deny it. I was there with my friend and was not alone. I suppose they have not got me mixed up with my friend – I cannot answer for anything he has done.'

Montagu believed that the police had come to discuss some property that had gone missing from the beach-hut on that busy Monday. The disappearance of a camera and silver cutlery has produced a wonderful red herring in sympathetic accounts of this case. The implication is made that Montagu accused the scouts of the theft and they in revenge con- cocted their story of impropriety in the beach-hut. Peter Wildeblood's book is once again the source of this tale.

In August 1953 ... Edward Montagu told me of a strange incident which had occurred at Beaulieu during the Bank Holiday period. Palace House, as usual, had been open to the public, and a troop of local Boy Scouts had acted as guides for the visitors. Edward and one of his guests, a film director named Kenneth Hume, had gone down to the beach hut with two of the Scouts to bathe; later Edward discovered that an expensive camera was missing, and informed the police. The latter, however, when they came to interview him about the loss, appeared to be less interested in the camera than in Lord Montagu and Mr. Hume. The boys apparently, had complained that an indecent attack had been made upon them in the beach hut.

I thought at the time – and still think – that this was an extremely unlikely story. If Edward had had anything to hide, the last thing he would have done would be to telephone the local police station and ask for an inquiry.

The effect of the story is clear. It provides the scouts with a motive for making the allegations and effectively exonerates Montagu. Wildeblood's account does not tally with Montagu's own account. He told the court that he and a group of friends had a picnic lunch at the beach-hut. On their return the butler realised that some property was missing. It was to retrieve that property that led Montagu to suggest the swim, so that they could refresh themselves and search for the lost items.

Montagu was about to announce publicly his engagement to Anne Gage, an event that had taken place on 28 July. The notice appeared in *The Times* on 6 August. In the following weeks the police inquiries continued and the case was handed over to the Director of Public Prosecutions. This was normal procedure in what was obviously a high-profile case. Montagu wrote a letter to the Chief Constable denying the charges and informing him that he would be defending himself vigorously against them. This was going to be a tough struggle.

On 22 August Montagu went to France on the day that a summons was issued for his arrest. On 25 September his solicitor, according to some press reports, told the police that he was going into voluntary exile. On 26 September he arrived in America by air from Paris. By the start of November he had returned to France and on 7 November he bravely returned to face the music at home. The justification he offered for his absence was the marriage of his sister which had taken place on the previous Saturday. He did not want that event overshadowed by criminal proceedings. In the event the wedding was covered by all the newspapers and made many front pages the following Sunday morning. Several items had appeared in the press speculating about Montagu's whereabouts. One report in the *Telegraph* had him recovering from his ordeal in a Texas nursing home.

On 14 and 21 November Hampshire magistrates heard the case against Montagu and Hume. They decided that there were cases to answer and both men were sent for trial at Hampshire Assizes. They were to be tried separately.

Montagu's trial opened on 14 December. The prosecution case was constructed on three elements: the suspicious behaviour of Montagu in inviting the scouts to the beach and the division of the quartet in the hut into two pairs using separate rooms; the testimony of the scouts and their allegations; and the ten weeks that Montagu spent out of Britain knowing that warrants had been issued for his arrest.

The first witness in the box was one of the scouts, described by the *Telegraph* as 'fair-haired with a fresh complexion'. The defence sought to show that the scout was a liar. This they did chiefly through a very tough cross-examination of the boy. They believed that his cocky manner and his obvious enjoyment of his moment of fame worked against his credibility as a witness. Fearnley-Whittingstall, Montagu's counsel, exposed the implausibility of the more serious charge that Montagu had sodomised the scout. There was much discussion about what the boy meant and a lot of time was spent finding a common vocabulary to describe various homosexual acts – part of the trial unfortunately not reported in the press. The boy was five foot eight inches tall, and weighed eight-and-a-half stones. He maintained that the act had occurred without his consent. A better-coached witness might have said that he consented because it made no difference in law whether he had consented or not, the older man would still face the same penalty. By refusing to say that he consented, the scout allowed the defence to score an important victory. The judge intervened at what was a critical point in the trial:

Judge: Why did you not shout out?
Scout: It would have been no good.
Judge: The other scout was in the other room?
Scout: Yes, but so was Hume.

A medical examination of the scout which had taken place a few days after the alleged assault proved inconclusive. The senior Home Office pathologist giving evidence on Montagu's behalf thought that unless there was co-operation during a serious act it would have been extremely difficult to commit the offence. He thought the medical evidence unconvincing. Montagu was acquitted on that charge.

The prosecution tried to muddy the waters in many different ways. A sweepstake taken at tea to guess the numbers of visitors to the house that day and handed over to the scouts was made to seem like a payment for services rendered. The sum was very small, a few shillings. A generous act was given a twisted interpretation by the police and prosecutor. They sought to portray Montagu as a liar by suggesting that during September 1953 he had slipped back to England before going to America. As evidence of this the prosecution provided Montagu's passport.

They claimed that his passport contained a stamp showing that he had left France for England on 23 September 1953. The passport was shown to the judge, Mr Justice Lynskey. He asked for a magnifying glass and announced that the date stamp had been altered. The passport had been in police possession since 7 November. It had obviously been tampered with by the police. Perhaps not surprisingly this fact was underplayed by both the press and by the judge in his summing up, an indication, if one were needed, of the protection commonly offered by the legal establishment and the press to the police. It was a humiliating moment for the Hampshire police and the office of Public Prosecutions. We now realise that it has been common practice over many decades for English prosecuting authorities to manufacture evidence in high-profile cases. The disclosure ought to have provoked a chorus of outrage, though it only generated some criticism in the *New Statesman* and *Spectator*.

A number of character witnesses appeared for Lord Montagu.

After having retired for forty-five minutes the jury returned to ask the judge if they could hear another witness. They claimed that without the testimony of Kenneth Hume they found it difficult to come to a verdict. The scout had claimed that he had been propositioned by Hume during the afternoon of his Bank Holiday at Beaulieu. He alleged that after they had smoked a cigarette together Hume had tried to assault him. The scout had drawn a knife on him warning him to 'Cut that out'. He told the other scout that Hume was 'rather queer'. Montagu had seen them leave Hume's apartment together but said nothing. Hume's testimony would help to establish the scout's veracity and possibly set the events of that day in a broader context. It was certainly odd that defence had not called him because he might at certain points have supported Montagu's defence. The judge said that they must judge the case on the evidence they had heard and sent them back to reach a verdict.

On the second charge the jury divided seven/five, so Montagu faced a retrial on that charge which the judge set for the following Assizes. He also postponed Hume's trial to that time as well. Their awful ordeal would continue.

In the meantime, a kit search of some British airmen serving in Korea led the RAF special investigators to a homosexual network within the service. The searches accumulated more and more evidence and produced letters mentioning Lord Montagu, linking him with two airmen involved in the network. The RAF passed this material to the Director of Public Prosecutions, and it must have come into his possession in the middle of December 1953 at around the time of Montagu's trial. For an office that had lost a key case in the public eye, the arrival of fresh evidence of further possible misdemeanours by the young peer was a godsend. It is surely not too difficult to account for the decision to collect evidence for a new case. In the last days of 1953 and the first ones of 1954, the office of Public Prosecutions and the Hampshire police gathered material that would vindicate their decision to prosecute Lord Montagu.

Meetings

It was Peter Wildeblood who had established Montagu's connections with the airmen. In the spring of 1952 Peter Wildeblood, twenty-eight, a gossip columnist on the *Daily Mail*, picked up a young airman, Edward McNally, twenty-three, at Piccadilly Circus underground station, one of London's busiest homosexual pick-up points. Wildeblood took McNally back to his flat in Kensington.

Wildeblood and McNally became lovers, establishing a relationship that lasted for fifteen months. McNally visited Wildeblood whenever he had weekend leave. Wildeblood records cosy domestic evenings in Kensington spent listening to records, and excursions to Kew Gardens and the Tower of London. They exchanged intimate letters. Wildeblood destroyed those he received; McNally kept his. We know little else about their relationship. Wildeblood claimed later that it had often been painful: 'there grew up between us that extraordinary, passionate tension which resulted in quarrels when we were together and misery when we were apart.' By the autumn of 1953 Wildeblood believed they were drifting apart. By then he had moved into a new home in Islington. He was planning a more stylish existence and planned to employ a manservant, a valet/butler, and McNally offered his services. Wildeblood rejected his offer. McNally was hurt and according to Wildeblood he began to become slightly menacing.

The nature of the relationship can be glimpsed from some of the correspondence that passed from Wildeblood to McNally, correspondence which was eventually read out in court; the letters opened, 'My dearest darling Eddie'. In April 1953 Wildeblood was on the brink of an extremely successful promotion. He was about to become Diplomatic Editor of the paper, a post that brought much foreign travel and a salary well in excess of any cabinet minister.

> At the moment there is only one thing in my life and that is work ... I honestly feel [that] if I am to get on at all I must seize the chance of proving it now ... The editor says he is planning to give me the biggest job on the paper and make me diplomatic correspondent which means more money.
>
> The last man who got the job got £4,500 a year and that in due course I shall live as I want to ... at the moment I am in such a state of crisis I just do not know where I am. (letter dated 28/4/53)

Wildeblood was frightened but he was also excited. Ambitious and talented, he was about to land a glittering prize while only thirty-one. It is difficult to assess the impact of this promotion on his lover, working as a nursing orderly in a RAF hospital at Ely – a not particularly glamorous

Lord Montagu of Beaulieu (left), the peer accused by a boy scout of impropriety.
Montagu would later win fame through his collection of vintage cars.
Journalist Peter Wildeblood (right) was arrested in January 1954 for a series of
homosexual offences.

part of England nor was McNally doing a particularly glamorous job. Wildeblood was boasting and it may have excited envy in the young serviceman. He wrote to McNally on 16 June 1953:

> The last few weeks have been an absolute hell of overwork and anxiety about the future but now it is all settled.
>
> When I was at Ascot to-day I heard finally that the editor had approved my appointment as diplomatic correspondent, the best job on the paper . . .
>
> I have bought a little house so that I can live with whomsoever I choose. It is in rather a poor quarter at Islington [St Paul's Road, Canonbury] but it is very pretty, Georgian design, a little garden, wrought iron balconies and with eight rooms.
>
> The firm is making me take three weeks holiday after Ascot. I am going down to Beaulieu for a few days . . . is there any chance of your being able to get away?

'I can live with whomsoever I choose' – a carrot or a stick? Wildeblood had secured his prize and bought a new home, he was on his way up. They had spent the previous summer on holiday as the guests of Lord Montagu at Beaulieu, but did not go again during the summer of 1953. The police later claimed that the relationship between the two men had come to an end soon after this letter. They met again in November 1953 for about half-an-hour and McNally spent a weekend with Wildeblood during December 1953, and McNally claimed that they had again made love.

Wildeblood had boasted about his friendship with Lord Montagu in an earlier letter telling him that the peer had just returned from New York and 'bought a lot of new records including a very sexy one by Miss Dietrich: "Miss Otis Regrets" in German'.

McNally acted as a go-between and introduced the peer to his friend John Reynolds who also worked as an orderly at RAF Ely. Reynolds was eighteen when he was introduced to Montagu. He had been in the RAF since June 1951. McNally claimed that he had described his blond friend as 'a young, nice-looking bloke'. Montagu, he claimed, had asked him if Reynolds was queer and McNally had assured him that he was. He provided Montagu with a photograph. McNally had given Montagu's telephone number to his friend. Reynolds made a reverse charge call to the peer: 'I said I was Johnny and Lord Montagu replied he was Eddie. I told him I could see him in London and he replied "that would be lovely".'

Montagu challenged McNally's account. Montagu denied asking him if his friend was queer. He could not challenge the fact that he and Reynolds made a foursome with Wildeblood and McNally for an evening,

12 August 1952, seeing Agatha Christie's *Dial M for Murder*. There were drinks back at Wildeblood's flat in Kensington. Reynolds and McNally claimed that Montagu slipped off to a bedroom with Reynolds where Reynolds claimed they made love. Montagu and Wildeblood disputed this version of events. The airman believed they were drinking champagne, Wildeblood reports that it was champagne cider. Whatever happened that night, it was at the time regarded as a success. It was agreed that Reynolds should join McNally and Wildeblood on their summer visit to Beaulieu. Montagu was off to Austria on the following morning.

The prosecution would try to portray Montagu and Reynolds as lovers. A letter that Montagu wrote to Reynolds after his return from Austria suggests intimacy:

Dear Johnny,

A rather annoying thing has happened. I have to have my brother and also my sister in the flat all the following week, which means it will be impossible for me to put you up in London that week, and rather complicates life.

I am sorry, but I cannot get out of it. Loking forward to seeing you, Regards to Eddie [McNally].

Certainly it seemed odd that a peer of the realm should be accommodating a young airman on his weekend leaves to the capital.

Summer Holidays

Reynolds was met at Brocklehurst railway station on 24 August 1952 by Lord Montagu and a friend, identified in court only by his occupation, an assistant film director (Kenneth Hume?). Wildeblood and McNally had arrived two days earlier. On the night of Reynolds's arrival there was a party in one of the beach-huts on the estate. What happened there was much disputed. Reynolds and McNally claimed that there was much drinking and dancing at the all-male gathering. Montagu and Wildeblood did not dispute the fact that only men were present at the party but said that it was a good deal more sober than the airmen suggested. They claimed that the airmen were exaggerating and misinterpreting an exhibition of a skating act by one man which a few others copied while the others sat around drinking. They denied that Reynolds had slipped away with Montagu and made love together in another part of the hut.

The following morning there were photographs, photographs that would later surface as evidence, photographs kept by all the principals, taken with Montagu's camera, presumably the one lost on the August

Bank Holiday of 1953, a present from his tenants on his coming of age in 1951. Lord Montagu was going to America on business and left that day for the United States. Wildeblood with the two airmen took up the invitation of Montagu's first cousin Michael Pitt-Rivers, a Dorset land-owner, to spend the remainder of their holiday on his estate, Larmer Lodge. Pitt-Rivers had been staying at Beaulieu and had been among the guests at the beach-hut party.

Reynolds said that he never saw Montagu again. He claimed that he received four or five letters from the peer, all but one of which he destroyed. According to Reynolds these letters contained requests by Montagu to spend time with him in London. Reynolds said that he did not reply because by then he 'was seeing Pitt-Rivers'. The airman claimed that he made love with Pitt-Rivers a number of times and that a relation-ship developed between them. Pitt-Rivers had attempted to bugger him, he claimed, but he had not let him.

In Dorset the four men paired off, Wildeblood and McNally sleeping together in a hut in the grounds and Pitt-Rivers and Reynolds in the house. After the holiday the association between Reynolds and Pitt-Rivers continued. Reynolds saw him about half-a-dozen times at Pitt-Rivers's London flat in Clarendon Street near Victoria railway station. Pitt-Rivers gave him a cigarette case for his birthday. A search of Pitt-Rivers's flat uncovered a photograph of Reynolds among his possessions: one of the photographs taken by Montagu at Beaulieu and described by the prosecution at their trial as 'a sexy photograph of Reynolds'. Rey-nolds's letter to Pitt-Rivers written after his return to his duties at Ely on 1 September 1952 was read in court:

Dear Michael,
    Here is the letter I promised you and as early as possible. It is only 8.15 a.m. so that I could not do much better could I?
    You are probably fast asleep by now, or are you living up to your criterion and being early to rise and shine? It seems awful to be back after the lovely time I have had, but I suppose I will get used to it in a few days. I want to thank you for the wonderful holiday you made possible.
    I should have made a better job of it at Bournemouth railway station, but Mac and Peter would hang on until the last minute and I hate saying goodbye to anyone . . . Take care of yourself and keep out of trouble. Bye bye for now, love, Johnny, X.

The Trials

On 23 December 1953, six days after the end of Lord Montagu's trial, McNally and Reynolds were interrogated by the RAF at Acton in west London. Reynolds spent eleven-and-a-half hours being questioned, one session lasting for as long as five-and-a-half hours. McNally spent eighteen hours being interrogated. Both men faced the prospect of a court martial, dismissal from the service and prison sentences. The letters implicating Lord Montagu were found in a search of Reynolds's kit on the second day of Montagu's trial, 16 December. By 28 December, after a horrible Christmas, both men agreed to make a deal with the authorities. In return for giving evidence against Montagu, Wildeblood and Pitt-Rivers they were offered immunity from prosecution for their own crimes.

We know nothing about the way in which this deal was brokered. The Director of Public Prosecutions almost certainly played a leading role in a manoeuvre designed to salvage the reputation of his office and vindicate its prosecution of Montagu. Whatever happened, he would throw enough dirt at the peer to sully his reputation. Other interpretations of his action have been offered. It is possible that he was motivated by a powerful sense of the immorality of these acts or that he sought to teach well-placed men who indulged in homosexual activities a lesson. He may also have disliked the cross-class nature of the associations, which certainly shocked some contemporaries. Whatever his motive, he found the instrument of revenge in the two young airmen. Throughout the trial of Montagu, Wildeblood and Pitt-Rivers he sat with the prosecution in the crown court at Winchester.

At 8 a.m. on 9 January 1954, police in London, Hampshire and Dorset made simultaneous arrests of Peter Wildeblood, Lord Montagu and Michael Pitt-Rivers. It was a well co-ordinated operation. To the arresting police officers Pitt-Rivers announced that, 'It is all part of this ridiculous witch-hunt going on all over the country.' Montagu and Pitt-Rivers were driven to Lymington police station a few miles from Beaulieu and invited to make statements. They refused. Wildeblood, possibly identified as the weakest link in the trio, was brought to Scotland Yard where he did make a long incriminating statement. He confessed to his involvement with a sailor from HMS *Vanguard*. Police had successfully kept him away from a solicitor for several hours; a similar tactic was used against the other two men. That day, without obtaining search warrants, the police searched the properties of the three arrested men. This was a common practice, though completely illegal. Courts in the 1950s rarely challenged material obtained in this way.

That afternoon all three men were brought to Lymington magistrates' court, and charged at 5.30 p.m. with a succession of sexual offences. The extra twist in the indictment was a charge of conspiracy: that the three accused worked in concert to procure sexual partners. This was the first time this charge had been used since the Wilde trials in 1895. The lawyer who drew up the charges possibly had been studying the Victorian case from the many accounts which appeared in the early 1950s. It allowed for a trial that embraced the three accused so that the full extent of the association could be presented to a jury rather than a series of individual trials narrowly focused on specific actions. It made the presentation of a prosecution case easier. In total there were nineteen charges against the men. They were accused of buggery, attempted buggery, and gross indecency; Montagu and Pitt-Rivers were charged with counselling and procuring homosexual acts, and Wildeblood was charged with aiding and abetting the commission of such acts.

All three men were bailed, with Kenneth Tynan, the drama critic of the *Observer*, acting as surety for Wildeblood. Wildeblood, it was noted, left the court in a chauffeur-driven car.

It was no accident that the arrests took place on a Saturday. Journalists were well-briefed that morning and the story dominated the front pages of the Sunday newspapers. Whoever planned the arrests appreciated that the Sunday papers would provide much more space for the case than the dailies. As the accounts of the case that appeared in Saturday evening newspapers suggest, fairly detailed briefings of the press had taken place soon after the arrests. These provided material for sensational copy, and the story would stay on the front pages until the three men were convicted on 24 March 1954. The crown rehearsed its case at the committal proceedings in late January. The trial at Winchester during the Hampshire Spring Assizes opened on 15 March and lasted for eight days.

Modern accounts of the trial are all based on Wildeblood's version of events. His account is extremely misleading. He, and those who have followed him, make the two airmen the principal agents responsible for the conviction of the three men. The crown would almost certainly have lost the case had it relied entirely on the evidence of the two airmen. The existence of the letters and the nature of the association between men of such diverse backgrounds were what ultimately secured the conviction: letters of a kind which were 'extremely sentimental, emotional and contained endearments of an unusual kind for men to exchange'.

McNally and Reynolds were vilified by everyone. At the end of the trial they were booed and spat upon as they left the court under police protection. They were presented as a pair of odious fairies. Peter Rawlinson described them as 'rotten, worthless miserable creatures . . . evil little men'. McNally he described as an 'ugly hideous witness'. Outlining the case for the prosecution at the start of the trial, G. D. Roberts warned the jury that the two men should be treated with caution. They were 'put forward as perverts, men of the lowest moral character'.

They faced extremely savage cross-examinations at all stages of the proceedings. The defence suggested that they had been coached by the prosecution but the transcripts of the trial suggest that they were more credible because they made many small errors, errors ludicrously magnified by the defence attorney. It was often the nature of trials for homosexual offences that one party tried to save his skin at the expense of others and the defence certainly exploited this fact. Rawlinson, who spoke in his closing statement of the crucifixion of his client Peter Wildeblood, was characteristically brutal with Edward McNally. He suggested that McNally was shielding his lover, a young man called Jerry. McNally had spent a night the previous November with a man named Jerry at the Regent Palace Hotel. In a letter that McNally had written to a friend he described Jerry as 'my husband dear'. Rawlinson, intent on exposing McNally as depraved, asked him what the expression meant. McNally claimed that Jerry was 'just a gentleman friend' – the word 'husband' had been a foolish expression. Rawlinson also insinuated that McNally had kept the letters for sinister purposes, probably for blackmail. Rawlinson asked him why he had not thrown the letters away:

McNally: I never gave it a thought to throw them away.
Rawlinson: Did you ever think they would be useful?
McNally: I do not know what you mean by useful.

It turned out that McNally had kept all his letters from other partners as well.

Both young men were actively homosexual and had been so for several years. Neither seemed to have a problem about his homosexuality. Reynolds, explaining the subculture to the court, told them a special language or code existed between queers and that he had picked up other men in pubs in the West End. He and McNally belonged to a group of four at the hospital who shared their interests. The barristers seemed puzzled about how this group had been formed. Reynolds insisted that he knew 'by instinct' that others shared his tastes. They were not lovers, just friends.

Hospitals were one of the many places in society where homosexual coteries flourished, and the RAF hospital at Ely does not seem to have been an exception to this fairly widespread phenomenon. Mary Renault's 1953 novel *The Charioteers* sets a wartime homosexual romance in a hospital, and it is clear from other cases that came before the courts that the world of male nurse and orderly was one that homosexually inclined men found attractive.

One of the most perverse features of the case was that the two airmen ended up being identified as the homosexual monsters, the perverts. We should remember the dilemma they faced, their youth and the fact that they could not afford lawyers of the quality representing Montagu, Wilde-blood and Pitt-Rivers.

However much they vilified the airmen, the defence could not really explain the association between individuals from such entirely different worlds. Asked why he had taken McNally and Reynolds with him on holiday, Wildeblood explained that it was to have someone to do 'the washing-up'. Wildeblood claimed to be impotent, a condition he had experienced for three years, and claimed that his relationship with McNally had never been sexual. He said that his job writing for a news-paper made him live a very social life covering royal engagements and garden parties. He liked to relax with somebody who was quite simple and fond of him. He found that person in McNally.

Montagu and Pitt-Rivers denied any homosexual interests, which made their association with the others even more puzzling. Wildeblood said that he was an 'invert', a description used by both the prosecution and his own counsel. He was not like the airmen who were 'perverts'. The question put by G. D. Roberts, prosecuting counsel, eliciting his confession, was very cleverly constructed:

Roberts: Your character has been put at the highest, and I agree nothing has ever been brought against your character. You can hold your head high, but you are an invert?
Wildeblood: Yes.
Roberts: Through no fault of your own you are subject to temptations and desires to which a normal man is not subjected?
Wildeblood: That is true.

Both Montagu and Pitt-Rivers claimed that they had not known about the sexual proclivities of their friends. Neither of them apparently knew that Wildeblood was an invert.

Class difference helped to convict the three men, as they could offer no plausible explanation for their association. Wildeblood tried in his book, as he had done in the witness box, to suggest that the three men espoused an egalitarian philosophy that led to their downfall. Wildeblood took on the mantle of a warrior against the British class system. Montagu was

one of the most completely unsnobbish people I have ever met, and I thought this remarkable in an Old Etonian who had been a peer from the age of three . . . I do not suppose it ever occurred to Edward Montagu that there were certain dangers in rejecting the class-system which so many of his friends and neighbours held sacred. He did it quite unconsciously. His guests, both at Beaulieu and in his London flat, formed an extraordinary assortment of conflicting types: business men and writers, duchesses and model-girls, restaurateurs and politicians and musical comedy actresses and Guards officers and Americans wearing hand-painted ties. He was always busy and often merely used to introduce his guests to each other and then disappear; a most disconcerting habit. I remember him doing this once in the middle of luncheon, leaving two big businessmen and a Canadian ice-hockey player staring at each other and wondering what on earth to talk about. Trivial though it may seem, this kind of behaviour enraged some people who took themselves extremely seriously and expected Lord Montagu to do the same. He made enemies, as well as friends.

Montagu becomes, in this version, a martyr sacrificed to perpetuate the class system.

Wildeblood tried hard to minimise and de-glamourise his existence. Even a cursory examination of the life he led suggests otherwise. The three men mixed in fashionable London. Wildeblood's friendship with Tynan went back to Oxford and he had hopes of writing a play for the West End stage. Pitt-Rivers had been married to the daughter of Hermione Baddeley. While Wildeblood was not wealthy, he was well-connected. Montagu was an aristocratic entrepreneur, one of the first peers to realise the commercial possibilities of stately homes. Already building up the collection of classic cars that still draws crowds to Beaulieu, Montagu had become a director of a public relations company in the autumn of 1953, a company he had been working for since 1949. Neither the prosecution nor the press established these connections at the time, but the social prominence and position of these three men would have been quite obvious to any jury.

This was an extremely difficult case to defend. All three men could afford distinguished and able counsel. They tried everything they could to secure the acquittal of their clients, chiefly by attacking the credibility of the airmen. The greatest success of the defence was that Peter Rawlinson managed to have the incriminating statement by Peter Wildeblood ruled as inadmissible by the court. Rawlinson persuaded the court that it had been extracted by the police under duress. The jury did not hear his arguments, nor were they reported in the press. As a consequence some of the worst excesses of the police were not exposed.

The police had behaved appallingly throughout the case. It was an issue that the defence decided to soft-pedal, and both the prosecution and judge went out of their way to defend the integrity of the force – who were only doing their duty. Such practices as confessions produced under duress, inducements offered to secure more information and searches of property without authority were standard practice in cases involving homosexual offences, and probably other categories of crime as well. Roberts, the prosecutor, tried to get Lord Montagu to criticise the police during his cross-examination of the peer:

Roberts: Are you complaining against the police?
Montagu: I think I have reason to.
Roberts: Do you realise the police have their duty to perform whether they are arresting Lord Montagu or Bill Sykes?
Montagu: I do.

The judge defended their behaviour in his summing up to the jury: 'You may think it not unreasonable that the police should, and I think did, arrest the accused men at 8 o'clock in the morning and search their premises and when satisfied that the premises had been searched, allowed them to get in touch with their solicitors and have all the proper facilities for their defence.'

All three accused men produced character witnesses. Montagu's cousin, a colonel, was asked if he had ever seen any signs of homosexual interest in his cousin. 'Never', he replied. Pitt-Rivers called another colonel: his former commanding officer from the Welsh Guards told the court that Pitt-Rivers had been 'extremely brave' against the enemy. Wildeblood's former boss, the editor of the *Daily Mail*, was a good deal less friendly in his very grudging endorsement:

Rawlinson: Did you see anything which in any way could cause you to suspect that Wildeblood is as he describes himself, an invert?
Edward Schofield: No, I always considered him to be in appearance and manner rather effeminate, but I never had the slightest reason to suspect anything.

The jury found them guilty. After the verdict and before sentence, defence counsel offered speeches in mitigation. A doctor appeared for Wildeblood suggesting that the journalist was suicidal and under terrible pressure. He felt that there was a strong likelihood of a cure in his case. The judge seemed to agree: '[Wildeblood's] problems must be surely, a medical problem first and foremost. It must be a problem which can only be solved – if a man, worthwhile as he, is not to be thrown away on the rubbish heap of humanity – by some form of medical treatment.' This opinion did not stop the judge giving him a custodial sentence. It was quite impossible, the judge claimed, for him to pass over these offences, though he reminded them that he was dealing with them in 'the most lenient way I possibly can'. Wildeblood and Pitt-Rivers were sentenced to eighteen months each and Montagu was jailed for a year.

The Myth of the Witch-hunt

I am horrified to read headlines in the evening papers that Donald Maclean and Guy Burgess have absconded . . . I fear this will mean a witch-hunt.

– Sir Harold Nicolson's diary entry, 7 June 1951

Peter Wildeblood had his revenge. He suffered a terrible prison sentence and lost his job and this understandably made him angry. He directed that anger at the legal establishment, the police, the judiciary, the prison authorities and, above all, the Home Office. He quickly produced his book soon after his release; he was writing it at the time that he gave evidence to the Wolfenden Committee.

In his evidence to the Wolfenden Committee, as we have already seen, Wildeblood poses as the spokesman for the 'good homosexual'. In his book he continued to promote this image: the good homosexual was a thoroughly decent fellow and keen to be a respectable member of society. This led Wildeblood to distance himself from men whom he called pederasts and pansies. It is not clear where Wildeblood drew the line between a lover of boys and a lover of men but he did argue in the book for an age of consent at twenty-one, so possibly that is where he would have drawn the line. He felt that: 'they form a quite separate group from men like myself. Although I regard them with just as much distaste as anyone else, I have tried hard to understand their point of view, but we have no common ground for discussion.'

He was venomous in his condemnation of effeminate men:

Everyone has seen the pathetically flamboyant pansy with the flapping wrists, the common butt of music-hall jokes and public-house stories. Most of us are not like that. We [the respectable homosexuals] do our best to look like everyone else, and we usually succeed. That is why nobody realises how many of us there are. I know many hundreds of homosexuals and not more than half a dozen would be recognised by a stranger for what they are. If anything, they dress more soberly and behave more conventionally in public than the 'normal' men I know; they have to, if they are to avoid suspicion.

When I ask for tolerance, it is for men like these. Not the corrupters of youth, not even the effeminate creatures who love to make an exhibition of themselves, although by doing so they probably do no harm; I am only concerned with the men who, in spite of the tragic disability which is theirs, try to lead their lives according to the principles I have described. They cannot speak for themselves, but I shall try to speak for them.

Wildeblood also condemned homosexual society, the underworld:

The homosexual world is, of necessity, compact and isolated. It is also extraordinarily out of touch with reality. I have already mentioned that a number of homosexuals, respected and discreet, were courageous enough to offer evidence to the Home Office Committee when it was set up. These, however, were exceptional. The great majority of the homosexual community shrugged its shoulders, expressed the opinion that the law would never be changed, and carried on with its dangerous and tragic way of life. Our case caused a momentary flutter, and a number of the better-known homosexuals left the country for a time, until they decided that it was safe to return. I am obliged to admit that most homosexuals are furtive and irresponsible, and that if a more tolerant and just attitude towards their condition is ever adopted by this country it will not be through their efforts.

Wildeblood emerges from his *apologia* as a not particularly attractive individual and it is in these uncharitable and narrowly conceived passages that he is at his most unpleasant. Of course it was these passages that made him such a liberal hero. The model of the respectable homosexual as promoted by Wildeblood dominated liberal reform rhetoric up until 1967. When things turned out differently after 1967 and gay liberation emerged, the most critical voices were raised by the liberal reformers who found the new model of homosexuality with its aggression, flamboyance and visibility a very bitter pill to swallow. Wildeblood's conformist who was willing to accept second-class status was a much more attractive image, the embodiment of the consenting male adult in *private*. According to Wildeblood the homosexual 'will always be lonely: he must accept that. He will never know the companionship that comes with marriage, or the joy of watching his children grow up, but he will at least have the austere consolations of self-knowledge and integrity.' The outcast in Eden, observing the heterosexual dictatorship in all its magnificence and glory.

★   ★   ★

Wildeblood places his conviction in a wider context, and in establishing this connection propagated the myth of the homosexual witch-hunt. He and his co-accused were the victims of a witch-hunt organised by the British legal establishment: 'a political manoeuvre, designed to allay American fears that people susceptible to blackmail were occupying high positions in Britain.' In this interpretation the Montagu trials were deliberately planned by three key members of the legal establishment: the Home Secretary Sir David Maxwell Fyfe, the man responsible for securing the approval of the cabinet for the establishment of the Wolfenden Committee; the Director of Public Prosecutions Sir Theobald Mathew; and the Commissioner of the Metropolitan Police, Sir John Nott-Bower. Wildeblood believed that these three men were motivated by a desire to convince the Americans that the British were getting tough on homosexuality because of the defection of Guy Burgess and Donald Maclean to the Soviet Union in May 1951. They were imitating a witch-hunt of homosexuals taking place at that time in America as part of the McCarthyite crusade against deviance.

A number of historians and biographers have taken up this interpretation. Probably the most important disseminator of this explanation was Harford Montgomery Hyde in his history of homosexuality in Britain, *The Other Love*. This book has been used widely in conjunction with Wildeblood's original memoir and they have persuaded a considerable number of writers that a homosexual witch-hunt was attempted in Britain during 1953–4. The most skilful use of this idea has been made by biographers, Humphrey Carpenter in his biography of Benjamin Britten, Margaret Drabble in her biography of Angus Wilson, but most influentially by Alan Hodges in his life of Alan Turing. It has won general acceptance and as an interpretation has gained considerably by Alan Hollinghurst's use of the witch-hunt of 1953–4 as the basis of his popular and highly acclaimed novel *The Swimming-Pool Library* (1988). The interpretation has now taken on the status of an established truth.

All are agreed that the witch-hunt came unstuck as a result of the Montagu trials. Questions were asked in Parliament and articles written in the press supporting some measure of homosexual law reform. Wildeblood found six articles written after the second Montagu trial that criticised the prosecution, across the whole media. According to Wildeblood and those who follow him this led the reactionaries to cave in. They did not simply put up the white flag but agreed to establish an inquiry into the operation of the laws relating to homosexuality. Robert Boothby, one of the MPs who asked questions in the Commons, claimed credit for bringing that pressure about, and many have been willing to cast him in that role. Wildeblood too has been seen as an important agent in bringing about the Wolfenden Committee. The witch-hunt had been a complete failure: indeed, it produced consequences entirely the opposite to those which its orchestrators had hoped for. In this way Wildeblood and the others become the pivotal figures in stopping the witch-hunts and setting up a committee that would lead to a reform of the law.

There are many problems with this interpretation, notably the implausibility of the government's surrender. The cabinet papers show that the proposal came through the Home Office, which must have decided late in 1953 or in the first few weeks of January 1954 to push for a royal commission to discuss prostitution and homosexuality. Nothing about the genesis of the measure suggests that it developed out of a bungled prosecution. If there had been a conspiracy then it would have had to include the boy scout who first accused Montagu in August 1953 and the Hampshire police who decided to prosecute the case. Had they not prosecuted then they would have been liable to accusations of favouring a local dignitary. Another odd feature of the interpretation is the speed with which the administration decided to stop appeasing America. In the autumn of 1953 they supposedly were willing to bring a case to do so but by the spring of 1954 this had ceased to be a motive. It is also odd that they should have waited over two years after the defections before showing the Americans that they were getting tough. In all the records exposed in America under the Freedom of Information Acts nothing has appeared to support the idea of a witch-hunt, nor has anything surfaced elsewhere. The interpretation does not fit in with other information that we know about how the British authorities dealt with the Burgess and Maclean case.

What is attempted in this chapter is an examination of how Wildeblood came to believe in a witch-hunt and the information upon which it rested. It will be seen that something important did happen in the early 1950s but that it was nothing planned or orchestrated by the state, but came about as a result of developments in Fleet Street, where newspapers reported homosexuality more widely and more frankly than at any point this century. This change in reporting had extraordinary consequences for the ways in which most Britons perceived homosexuality. It also incidentally fostered the myth of the homosexual witch-hunt.

The American Witch-hunt

That an officially orchestrated witch-hunt did take place in the United States seems to be without doubt. It was triggered by the publication in 1948 of Alfred Kinsey's report on the sexual behaviour of the human male which caused a sensation when it appeared. Kinsey was a scientist interested, unlike Wolfenden and his committee, in what was really happening sexually in his society. During the 1940s he had assembled a team of researchers at the University of Indiana, funded for much of the time by the Rockefeller Foundation, to undertake thousands of interviews about people's sex lives: in all, 17,000 men were interviewed for the 1948 report. Kinsey found that over a third of American men had had at least one homosexual experience and that at least 10 per cent of American males were predominantly or exclusively homosexual. Kinsey developed the model of a sexual spectrum which suggested that while some people were exclusively heterosexual or homosexual, most sat somewhere in between.

Kinsey's report received massive publicity inside the United States. His work sanctioned a public discussion of sexuality that newspapers and magazines were eager to embrace. Because of his status as a scientist, Kinsey licensed such discussion. His work also coincided with the emergence of art and writing with a strongly homosexual element: the plays of Tennessee Williams, the novels of Gore Vidal, the stories of Truman Capote, the photographs of Bob Mizer, the drawings of George Quaintance and Neel Bates and the films of Kenneth Anger. These cultural developments laid the foundations for the emergence of the modern homosexual identity that was to flower during the 1970s.

It would not have been possible for a British academic to establish a project similar to that instituted by Kinsey. He would almost certainly have lost his job. No British academic institutions would have tolerated such research. He could never have hoped for funding from such a prestigious body as the Rockefeller Foundation. If his researchers had gone round the English provinces they soon would have found themselves in front of the local magistrate. American society at mid-century gave rather more liberty to the scholar than his counterpart received in Britain.

It is possible also that the Kinsey survey reflects the existence of an academic culture which had a much greater respect for sociology. All discussions of homosexuality in Britain during the 1950s completely lacked a sociological dimension. The subject was not studied in most British universities and was generally held in low esteem amongst intellectuals. This had many damaging consequences for the shaping of public policy, and British understanding of its own society.

The Kinsey Report, by identifying the existence of the homosexual minority, also allowed politicians to create the idea of a homosexual menace, linked with and patterned upon communism. It could be depicted as a force that was, like communism, undermining American values at the beginning of the Cold War. There was a strong element of opportunism in the way that some Republicans exploited these issues after 1948. The Republican Party was desperate for electoral success; its defeat in the presidential election of 1948 was its fifth successive defeat. Since the victory of Franklin D. Roosevelt in 1932 the Democratic Party had dominated the American political system. There was therefore a strong element of desperation in the Republicans' tactics in the late 1940s and early 1950s as they struggled to dislodge the Democrats.

Republican politicians used the presence of homosexuals in the Democratic administration as a sign of that party's decadence. This was a classic political smear. Social Democrats in Germany before the First World War had exploited the Eülenberg scandal involving members of Kaiser Wilhelm II's entourage to depict a similar decadence in the Imperial regime. It was also possible to suggest that homosexuals were more prone to betray their countries' secrets and as a consequence that they were security risks. This particular fear was frequently used in the United States to justify the removal of homosexuals from official employment. According to a congressional report in 1950:

> homosexuals and other sex perverts are not proper persons to be employed in Government for two reasons: first, they are generally unsuitable, and second, they constitute security risks . . . it is generally believed that those who engage in overt acts of perversion lack the emotional stability of normal persons. In addition there is an abundance of evidence to sustain the conclusion that indulgence in acts of sex perversion weakens the moral fiber of an individual to a degree that he is not suitable for a position of responsibility . . . The Federal Bureau of Investigation, the Central Intelligence Agency, and the intelligence services of the Army, Navy and Air Force . . . are in complete agreement that sex perverts in Government constitute security risks.

It was this reasoning which justified a purge of homosexual men from the American bureaucracy.

The McCarthyite witch-hunt was widely reported in Britain. Few reports mentioned the homosexual element or else described it euphemistically as an attack on deviants. There were fears in Britain in the early 1950s that the Conservative government elected in October 1951 would use the Burgess and Maclean defections to support a purge of left-wingers from British institutions. On 16 February 1952 the left-wing tabloid the

Sunday Pictorial congratulated the Foreign Secretary, Sir Anthony Eden, for not launching a witch-hunt.

McCarthyism was condemned by both the left and the right in Britain, and was a way in which many members of the British élite could legitimate their anti-American feelings. It became part of a wider attack on American materialism, immaturity as a world power and the intolerance of American society. It was from America that the word 'witch-hunt' gained currency in British culture during the 1950s and it was David Astor, editor of the *Observer*, who first applied the word to the policing of homosexuality in Britain.

Male Vice

Wildeblood based his account of the British witch-hunt on a single newspaper article by Donald Horne that appeared in the *Sydney Sunday Telegraph*, Australia, on 25 October 1953. Many writers since have lifted passages from this article and used it interchangeably with Wildeblood's text to support the witch-hunt interpretation. The article is usually cited from the extract in Wildeblood's book (where he gets the title of the newspaper wrong). The article is printed here in its entirety, with the passages quoted by Wildeblood in italics.

BIG NAMES INVOLVED IN LONDON CLEAN-UP OF MALE VICE

London, Sat[urday] – The sensational charges this week against Lord Montagu of Beaulieu and actor Sir John Gielgud are the result of a Scotland Yard plan to smash homosexuality in London.

The plan originated after strong United States advice to Britain to weed out homosexuals – as hopeless security risks – from important Government jobs.

One of the Yard's top-rankers Commander E. A. Cole, recently spent three months in America consulting with F.B.I. officials in putting finishing touches to the plan. But the plan was extended as a war on all vice when Sir John Nott-Bower took over as the new Commissioner at Scotland Yard in August [1953].

Sir John swore he would rip the cover off all London's filth spots. Montagu and Gielgud were the latest accused in his drive against the shocking crime of male vice which is now linked with drives on call-girl rackets, obscene postcards and the widespread vice trade.

Under laxer police methods before the US-inspired plan began and Sir John moved to the top job at the Yard as a man with a mission, Montagu and his film director friend Kenneth Hume might never have been charged with grave offences with Boy Scouts.

This week's conviction of Gielgud for persistently importuning sprang from increased police vigilance.

So did the conviction for importuning of W. J. Fields [*sic*] who has now resigned his seat in the House of Commons, his reputation destroyed and his career ruined.

Other well-known casualties in this new police drive have been author Rupert Croft-Cooke, sentenced to nine months for offences against two sailors, and the Rev. Francis Wynne, vicar of Barnes, in Surrey, jailed last week for ten years after admitting offences against choir boys.

Apart from the security risks, like many other Londoners Scotland Yard's new chief was appalled that London had the . . . ne [illegible in original] of being beneath its ultra-respectable surface, one of the most vicious cities in the world.

He knew that a vast underground pervert ring was flourishing in central London, to which perverts from other countries including Australia – were freely admitted.

Almost his first act when he moved into the top job at the Yard was to close down a notorious male establishment in Notting Hill the sleazy district where killer Christie hunted for his victims, and for long one of the favorite haunts of perverts.

Police have also been . . . unofficial means to wipe out infamous advertisements found in shop windows in the side streets of cosmopolitan, prostitute-ridden Soho.

Then Sir John swung into action on a nationwide scale.

He enlisted the support of local police throughout England to step up the number of arrests for homosexual offences.

For many years past the police had turned a blind eye to male vice.

They made arrests only when definite complaints were made from innocent people or where homosexuality had encouraged other crimes.

They knew the names of thousands of perverts – many of high social position and some world famous – but they took no action.

Now meeting Sir John's demands they are making it a priority job to increase the number of arrests.

In West London Court alone 600 men have been convicted of homosexual offences this year.

These are not pleasant facts to write about, but this shocking perversion has become so widespread that Scotland Yard's Special

Branch had already begun a behind the scenes probe of political and diplomatic circles before requests from the US began.

Says Lieutenant-Colonel Marcus Lipton, M.P.: 'The problem of homosexuality among government officials – particularly diplomats – is of growing magnitude.

'These people, some of whom occupy important positions, are an obvious target for blackmailers.

'The authorities have become increasingly alarmed.'

The Special Branch began compiling a 'Black Book' of known perverts in influential government jobs after the disappearance of the diplomats Donald Maclean and Guy Burgess, who are known to have pervert associates.

Now comes the difficult task of side-tracking these men into less-important jobs – or putting them behind bars.

Meanwhile Sir John continues at full-tilt the all-out war on female prostitution he began as Deputy Commissioner, when he decided to make West End streets respectable for the Coronation.

Visitors from the dominions and the US have been appalled by the over-painted women who flagrantly parade some of London's most crowded streets.

Here Sir John has a tough job for an army of extra police would be needed for this mammoth task.

However this week police finished a clean-up of a vice ring which operated a £100,000 'call-girl' racket when the last of a series of vice queens behind the racket was jailed.

Central figure in this big clean-up was tall, brunette Heather White, prettiest policewoman in London, who posed as a prostitute in London's unsavoury underworld to get the evidence needed.

She walked the West End streets in a skin tight black dress, red swagger coat and a little black hat, heavily made up and throwing suggestive looks around her.

She was a successful decoy, and the vice queens who hire well-dressed spivs to hunt for new 'talent' soon got into touch with her – and gave her the evidence that put them in jail.

The latest series of arrests have caused panic in the call-girl racket, and many of the crooks who run them are temporarily out of business.

Similarly successful has been the drive on obscene publications and postcards.

Acting on police complaints, the courts have ordered the destruction of more than 50,000 obscene postcards in the last two months.

But the fight against the drug trade has had less spectacular results.

The drugs rings have long since learned how to fool the police by going completely underground.

The tragedy of drug addiction in which even boys of 16 and 17 become victims still grows unchecked.

Indeed London's thousands of vice crooks must now be waiting for the storm to blow over.

They are cynical customers with a tough survival value, and they believe London is such a vast complicated warren that no police force in the world can smoke them out.

from *Sydney Sunday Telegraph* 25 October 1953.

Donald Horne produced an extremely sensational account of the capital city of the British Empire and Commonwealth, exposing metropolitan vice to a virtuous readership in the Antipodes. It was not unique. Many articles on London as a den of inquity appeared in newspapers in the United States and the Commonwealth during 1953. The Coronation of Queen Elizabeth II that summer had brought many journalists to London and focused a good deal of media attention on the city. Horne, as the full version of his article shows, draws connections between a number of disparate events to expose the depravity to which the great city had sunk.

The article is littered with errors and full of silly inconsistencies. Horne misunderstands the extent of the police commissioner's jurisdiction: there is no national police force in Britain; each force is autonomous – there is no central directing executive. Sir John Nott-Bower directed the police only in the capital, and even there his jurisdiction did not include the City of London which has its own police force.

One of the most surprising features of the article, and almost certainly its most misleading feature, one which was not challenged by Wildeblood or others, is the statement that prior to 1953 the British police forces 'had turned a blind eye to male vice'. This is absurd: the files of Britain's courts for the previous three decades give no support for this notion. What the Horne/Wildeblood account does is to direct attention away from the much more sinister developments in Britain since the 1920s, the series of locally directed police campaigns against homosexuality that were an unchallenged part of English legal culture by the 1950s. There was no single nationally organised campaign in 1953–4. Even the Home Office figures, which are extremely problematic, suggest that there were fewer convictions in 1952 and 1953 than there were in 1951. By directing our attention to a specific campaign, which turns out to be without foundation, we miss the real witch-hunts in the English provinces which were mainly directed at working-class men.

Horne makes all sorts of connections which are difficult to sustain when examined closely. He mentions four other cases apart from Montagu's. Two of those cases involved the arrest and conviction of prominent men for importuning. In early January 1953 the thirty-seven-year-old Labour MP for Paddington, North, William Field, was arrested for importuning in the West End. He fought the case vigorously, taking it eventually to the Court of Criminal Appeal. At every stage he was found guilty and when he eventually lost in front of the appeal court he resigned his seat in the Commons and retired from public life. Sir John Gielgud was arrested at a public lavatory in Chelsea on the evening of 21 October 1953. Gielgud pleaded guilty the next morning and was fined, like Field. Unlike Field, Gielgud did not retire into the shadows; he continued to appear on the stage, and his friends in the theatrical world rallied round and gave him tremendous support. Neither of these arrests was a set-up, neither man denied that he had been in a public lavatory, and both men were unmarried. Gielgud's case did not spring from 'increased police vigilance'. We know from the documentation provided by the Metropolitan Police to the Wolfenden Committee that the police had been operating a system of surveillance for several years, indeed more policemen had been deployed in the late 1940s than in the early 1950s but that was related to nothing more sinister than problems of manpower.

The Croft-Cooke case was also introduced by Horne to support his argument. Once again the genesis of this case makes it difficult to imagine that it was a set-up. The sailors who supplied the incriminating evidence had been guests at Croft-Cooke's house, and their first point of contact with the Croft-Cooke household was through a meeting in London's leading gay bar. The fourth was that of Revd Francis Wynne, discussed in Chapter 10.

Horne cited these cases as if prominent men had never been convicted of homosexual offences before. There had been arrests, even convictions in the past, but they had not triggered massive publicity of the kind associated with Lord Montagu and his friends. Bobbie Shaw, the eldest son of the Tory MP Nancy Astor, had been found guilty of gross indecency by a court in 1931 and sent to prison. Lady Astor was able to mobilise her family to prevent publication of the case: the Astors owned *The Times* and the *Observer* and the family was able to appeal to other newspaper proprietors not to report the case. Lord Beaverbrook secured the same treatment when his gossip columnist Tom Driberg was brought to court for homosexual offences in 1935. He was acquitted and went on to become an MP, and eventually chairman of the Labour Party. Sir Paul Latham, Conservative MP for Scarborough and Whitby, was found guilty of ten homosexual offences and sentenced to two years' imprisonment in 1941.

Some newspapers reported the case but the only one to do so in any detail was the *News of the World*. Angus McBean, the leading theatrical photographer of the period, was sent to prison for two years for homosexual offences in 1942, a case treated by the press in a way similar to Latham's. In 1943 the Earl of Lauderdale successfully fought an accusation of having sex with a young man in a Soho alleyway. None of these cases produced major coverage by Fleet Street. But by the early 1950s things were beginning to change and after 1953 and the first Montagu trial all newspapers were prepared to report trials for homosexual offences.

There are a number of other factual errors in Horne's piece. He reported an inaccurate statement by the magistrate in the Gielgud case that his court dealt with six hundred importuning cases a year. This was greater than the total number of such cases for the whole of London for either 1952 or 1953. The mission of one of the 'Yard's top-rankers' to the United States suggests that the British authorities were co-ordinating action with the Americans, and this has been seen repeatedly by historians and commentators as the crucial point of contact between the American witchhunters and their British counterparts. In fact, as we have seen, this mission was led by a Home Office official, Philip Allen, and it was reported in the newspapers that he studied two subjects – prostitution and parking meters. Allen did not find the Scotland Yard officer very helpful; he thought he was 'a bit dim'. Allen's report led to the decision to establish an inquiry to investigate the laws relating to prostitution, the terms of which were eventually broadened to include homosexual offences. It was not quite as sinister as some have imagined.

There are problems of chronology as well. The new campaign is supposed to coincide with the appointment of Sir John Nott-Bower as Metropolitan Police Commissioner in August, yet three of the cases cited as evidence of the get-tough policy were begun several months before he came to office.

Horne may be accused of embellishing the truth and of drawing connections from a series of unrelated stories, but he cannot be accused of fabrication. The speculations that he printed came from official sources and from other journalists. Wildeblood and others have tried to suggest that other newspapers, particularly those in Britain, did not carry the story because they were part of some sort of official British cover-up. This is not true. Amongst British newspapers the *People* and the *Sunday Pictorial* carried similar speculations about a clamp-down on vice. Indeed a survey of the previous two decades shows such stories to be a regular and recurring item in the British press. The *News of the World* reported at least eight such campaigns between 1932 and 1952. The source is not difficult to find: in every case it was Scotland Yard's press offices boasting that its police officers were leading the campaign to crack down on vice.

What the Horne article opens up is a more interesting picture of the way in which homosexuality suddenly surfaced as an issue in the autumn of 1953 and the way in which different elements in the metropolis tried to extract some advantage from the issue. Three sources can be identified for Horne's article: the British press in the weeks before his report appeared (journalists constantly refashion one another's articles), the press office of Scotland Yard and the Labour Member of Parliament for Lambeth, Colonel Marcus Lipton. It was the Yard and Lipton who supplied Horne with the homosexual spin that has made his article of interest to posterity, and it is these two sources that we shall examine in more detail.

Scotland Yard

The news machine at Scotland Yard had been feeding Fleet Street with stories for decades. There existed a close relationship between the upper echelons of the Metropolitan Police and the fourth estate. Newspapers provided much protection to the police force and built up myths about the police which deflected criticism from them.

Few British institutions in the early 1950s took the press as seriously as the Metropolitan Police. Under Sir Harold Scott, Commissioner from 1945 until 1953, the Met's press office was greatly expanded. Scotland Yard deliberately courted and cultivated the media. The crime reporters of the national newspapers enjoyed privileged access to the Yard. Policemen of all ranks supplemented their earnings by establishing connections with interested journalists. In the case of senior policemen such relationships could pay long-term dividends. Popular newspapers regularly published the heroic memoirs of the senior members of the Met and some like Commander Fabian (immortalised in a television series) graduated to well-paid consultancies with national newspaper groups. After his retirement Fabian worked for many years as an employee of the Kelmsley Press, a group which owned a large number of newspaper dailies including two national Sundays, the *Sunday Times* and the more popular *Empire News*.

It was a stunning public relations success. The press office did much to nurture a positive image of Scotland Yard and the Metropolitan Police as crime fighters: this image appeared in newspapers and books and increasingly on cinema and television screens as well. The greatest triumph of the Scott regime was the creation of Sergeant George Dixon, a London policeman who inhabited the fictional world of Dock Green. Dixon as played by veteran British actor Jack Warner epitomised the public image of the British police for post-war Britain. According to Geoffrey Gorer in *The English Character* (1955), the policeman had become 'for many Englishmen the ideal model of masculine strength and responsibility'.

Dixon made his debut on the big screen in the movie *The Blue Lamp* (1950). The police collaborated closely with the film-makers. Warner described the relationship in his autobiography:

> Although the story was fictional the film was almost documentary. It was made with the full co-operation of Scotland Yard and with the invaluable help of many members of the Metropolitan Police. The Commissioner in office, Sir Harold Scott, visited Ealing Studios to see rushes of some of the early scenes and on his advice any technical inaccuracies were corrected. Filming took place at several police stations but the focal point for the cameras was at Paddington Green – hence Dock Green – where Chief Inspector Wilkinson and his staff coached us in the manning of the station . . . To ensure the accuracy of every detail of police procedure we had Inspector Leonard Pearoy, an instructor at the Peel House Training School, attached to the film unit as technical adviser. A car used in some of the early scenes was 'doctored' by Yard officers so that it looked like a real police car. In the final exciting cops-and-robbers chase, we were also allowed to use police radio cars. They were loaned on a carefully worked out availability rota.
>
> Scenes of the activity at Scotland Yard's Information Room where all 999 calls are received and communications maintained with and between radio cars, were filmed in short takes on two successive Sundays. The cameras panned in on genuine police officers – Inspector Law, PC King and PC Fleet, who were seen and heard sending radio messages to police cars in the final scenes.

Warner joked that there were 'probably more real policemen than actors in *The Blue Lamp*'.

The film enjoyed a great deal of popular acclaim. Warner was voted top male star by *Motion Picture Herald* and the film was shown across the world. In 1952 it was converted into a play, with runs in Blackpool and Oxford before coming into the West End. In 1955 the BBC took up the characters and setting and launched the television series *Dixon of Dock Green* that ran for twenty-one years, achieving audiences of fifteen million in its heyday. It was voted the most suitable programme for family viewing by Mary Whitehouse's National Viewers' and Listeners' Association, 'a clean show from which sex and violence were absent'.

The film told the story of the worst crime that Britons could imagine in the 1940s and 1950s, the murder of a policeman. Forty-five minutes into the picture Sergeant Dixon is shot by a young delinquent called Riley. Dixon dies later in hospital. The remaining thirty-five minutes were spent tracking down the murderer. Riley is rejected by the criminal fraternity, who play a major role in bringing him to justice: they too share the sense of outrage caused by the murder of a British bobby. Eventually Riley is run to ground at a dog track and arrested. Dixon was such a popular character, avuncular and genial, that his creators resurrected him for his transfer to the small screen.

The attractions of the role for Warner are fairly obvious: 'I realised that the murder of a policeman, far from eliminating him, really gave him a martyr's crown as a man never to be forgotten and that any audience would readily understand the spirit of the film and the message it conveyed.' Nobody disguised the fact that this was pure propaganda, the sort of publicity money could rarely buy. It did much to reinforce the sorts of myths previously propagated on the printed page and began an association between the police and film and television that has brought many benefits to the boys in blue and that was, as we shall see, almost total fantasy, a fantasy which too many Britons wanted to believe.

This publicity machine fed Horne and other journalists their stories. In the case of Horne's article the spotlight is on Scott's successor at the Yard, Sir John Nott-Bower who took over as Commissioner during the summer of 1953 after the Coronation; there are eight positive references to him, and many implied criticisms of the Scott regime. It is clear that Horne was being briefed by press officers eulogising Nott-Bower. Few would have recognised the police Commissioner from this flattering portrait. He was in fact prone to indecision and generally regarded as ineffective. He postponed any re-examination of the force and ludicrously supported his officers whenever they were accused of corruption, excessive violence or interference in the course of justice, regardless of the evidence. He courted the force and saw himself as the defender of the London policeman, repeatedly making speeches about the superiority of the Met as the greatest police force in the world. According to D. Ascoli, 'Nott-Bower was the "safe" Tory reaction . . . he had spent twenty years in the Indian Police Service before coming to Scotland Yard . . . in 1933 . . . He had a good brain and all the social graces, and was an expert horseman . . . and a devoted bridge player . . . Above all, he was excessively idle . . . Of the nineteen holders of the office of Commissioner Nott-Bower is the least memorable'.

Horne also features WPC Heather White who appeared in all the British popular newspapers that third week of October for her undercover work in exposing a prostitution ring. It was the sort of human interest tale that Scotland Yard knew the papers lapped up, especially when it concerned a beautiful young woman playing a prostitute in the line of duty: good girl masquerades as bad girl and emerges eventually as a very good girl.

The comments that the police made on male homosexuality almost certainly were spoken by officers briefing Horne and others as part of a wider crusade to 'clean-up' the city, a recurring element in police rhetoric from at least the 1920s though never before explicitly mentioning homosexuality. The reason for introducing this new vice is to be found in the arrest and conviction at a London magistrates' court of the actor Sir John Gielgud, three days before Horne's article appeared, an event which triggered an extraordinary number of articles in the British press about the 'homosexual menace'. Scotland Yard were reacting to that concern by showing that they were taking action in dealing with this 'problem'.

Horne was being sold a line, a line he bought because it could be fitted into his exposure of metropolitan vice that would presumably comfort, console, shock and alarm his readers back in Australia. The Met were happy because they secured another few inches of newsprint that cast them in a favourable light.

Colonel Lipton and the Cambridge Spies

Another of Horne's sources was the south London MP, Colonel Marcus Lipton, a Labour backbencher who specialised in hatching conspiracy theories and who devoted much of his energies in the 1950s to the Burgess and Maclean case. He promoted a witch-hunt of the diplomatic and security services. Lipton believed that there had been a cover-up in 1951 when the two spies had disappeared and that there were further spies to be exposed. He named Kim Philby as the third man in the spy ring in Parliament during 1955, causing a major embarrassment for the government which had publicly exonerated Philby as an innocent party. Lipton can be cast as a fearless exponent of open government but we should also recognise that he was proposing the sort of purge associated with Joe McCarthy in the United States. Lipton wanted to expose the guilty men and remove all 'unreliable' elements from British intelligence – that of course would include homosexuals. Horne reported Lipton's view that 'The problem of homosexuality among government officials – particularly diplomats – is of growing magnitude.'

The government resisted Lipton's demands. A loner, he was regarded by members on both sides of the House of Commons as having behaved extremely badly for actually naming Philby as the third man in the spy circle. By naming him in the Commons Lipton denied Philby the opportunity to sue him. Lipton reacted to his ostracism by briefing journalists on the implications of the case. He found a particularly receptive audience amongst journalists from the United States and the Commonwealth who always played up the homosexual elements in the story of the spies.

The Burgess and Maclean defections did not trigger a witch-hunt. The government invested in a cover-up and did little to please the Americans. The two men left England on Friday 25 May, but it was not until the 29th that the Foreign Office learnt of their departure. Robert Cecil, a friend of Maclean's and his deputy in the American Department, remembered that:

> The defection plunged Whitehall into a state of shock, in which nobody, Ministers included, grasped the need to recognise what had happened and limit the damage. Instead, all hopes were pinned on recapturing the defectors and repressing all information. It was an understandable reaction, but it resembled that of a driver who, after a fatal accident, walks away from the scene, trying to convince himself that it was a nightmare that will eventually go away. The Diplomatic Service with its links to the throne had always gone on the assumption that its loyalty was irrefragable; that its status and tradition set it apart from, and above, the rest of the Civil Service. In pursuance of this belief, it had long been administered much as a kindly Victorian paterfamilias would run a large family ... At one blow this whole framework of mutual confidence and trust had been shattered ... Two intelligent men from the right class had been practising disloyalty for sixteen years.

The Foreign Office had little time to recover before the *Daily Express* broke the story on 7 June after an indiscreet leak from the Paris police. The *Daily Express* had a circulation of almost four million and was run by the Canadian tycoon Lord Beaverbrook as a vehicle for his private vendettas and what amounted to a long-running conflict with established institutions. He despised the British establishment and the story of the two defectors allowed him to embarrass one of the chief pillars of that establishment, the Foreign Office. All other newspapers took up the story, which quickly crossed the Atlantic. The Korean War was in progress and many American politicians and commentators doubted Britain's commitment to the struggle. They seized on the story to support their opinion and brought to the fore the homosexuality of the two men, something which British newspapers had initially marginalised. The Americans were keen to highlight the corruption and decadence of the British. The British élite were generally perceived by Americans as effete, an image that had been promoted by Hollywood.

The Foreign Office responded foolishly. A statement was issued on 7 June saying that it was known that the two men had gone to France and that 'Mr. Maclean had a breakdown a year ago owing to overstrain but was believed to have fully recovered.' This led the press and its readers to believe that they had simply taken a holiday on the spur of the moment without telling anyone else, suggesting that the two men were merely missing, giving the episode its name: 'The Missing Diplomats'. It was a terrible piece of news management. The US State Department put pressure on the Foreign Office to release a franker statement as the amount of press space devoted to the story multiplied. The Foreign Office resisted this pressure. The Foreign Secretary, Herbert Morrison, made a statement to the Commons on 11 June but made no suggestion that the two men had defected to Russia. He protected his department by invoking national security and the need for secretiveness on such a sensitive issue. The CIA refused to work any longer with Kim Philby, who was serving in Washington as the liaison officer between British and American intelligence. The Americans now regarded him as a spy. He resigned from the secret service.

Newspapers searched for stories about the two defectors. W. H. Auden, the poet, on holiday in Italy, provided headlines with his comment that Maclean had known 'quite a lot about the Atom Bomb'. Still the Foreign Office sat tight, oblivious to the impact of its poor handling of the case on opinion on both sides of the Atlantic.

The cabinet established a committee of three wise men to investigate the affair, a committee which sat and reported in private. Sir Alexander Cadogan, a former head of the Foreign Office, served as chairman and was assisted by a retired Ambassador, Sir Neville Bland, and the Cabinet Secretary, Sir Norman Brook. It was, wrote Cecil, 'evident that no outsider was to peep behind the curtain whilst the Foreign Office washed its dirty linen'. The committee met five times in the summer of 1951 and interviewed seven witnesses. According to Cecil:

> [the] seventh witness was a psychologist. His evidence did not give the committee much encouragement to believe that homosexuals could necessarily be detected at the stage of recruitment into the Service. His view was that homosexuality, as practised in private in a relatively uninhibited way, would be unlikely to lead to open scandal. This danger would be more likely to occur at a stage later than that of recruitment in the case of a repressed homosexual, whose urge had been bottled up by moral or other restraints.

Neither the expert witness nor the report of the committee pinpointed homosexuality as a problem. The committee's chief recommendation was to introduce positive vetting. In practice this turned out to be an extremely limited exercise. New recruits were required to provide the names of two referees and it 'was not, in the early days, a very testing examination' of background. As a result of the Cadogan report 'four officers left the Service on account of undefined "political activities and associations"'. It is significant that they did not identify homosexuality as a particular problem for the foreign service.

The Foreign Office hoped that it might bury the affair but it would not go away. Mischievous popular newspapers (most notably the *Daily Express* on the right and the *Sunday Pictorial* on the left) kept the pot boiling and the defection became a useful way to berate the élite. Indeed it was largely through the coverage of this affair that the concept of the establishment was properly defined. The defections fascinated readers of newspapers and books more than the earlier cases of Alan Nunn May and Klaus Fuchs, chiefly one suspects because the two defectors were so well-connected and had so obviously belonged to the English upper class. Both men were public-school-educated Cambridge graduates. Burgess was an Old Etonian and Maclean was the son of a cabinet minister. So Fleet Street began its association with the Cambridge spies, a story that has never died and which brought together the popular press's 'long tradition of self-righteousness and the specious identification of profitable sales with public interest'.

Despite a careful combing of the archives in Washington there is little evidence to suggest at any point after the defection that the British government took any action that might have appeased American fears of the Soviet infiltration of British intelligence. The affair certainly damaged Anglo-American relations and it provided a splendid pretext for the Americans not to share more of their secrets with the British. But it is probable that had not Burgess and Maclean been exposed the Americans would have found other excuses. America and Britain were uneasy allies and the degree of co-operation between the two states was not always high.

It is important to recognise that British governments after 1945, Labour as well as Conservative, were keen to avoid any systematic purges of government personnel. A recent study of the different strategies adopted by the British and American governments to deal with dissidence and deviance during the Cold War suggests that the British authorities were much more restrained than their American counterparts: 'The Communist Party in Great Britain was at least as strong and effective – indeed probably more so – than the Party in the United States, but there was no parallel attempt to discover, expose and root out Communism in every aspect of British life.' David Caute suggests that there was 'obviously some controlling mechanism [that] operated in British politics, a tacit code of restraint.' It was a policy that enjoyed support at the highest level. Sir Percy Sillitoe, head of MI5 from 1946 to 1953, outlined in his memoirs his personal preference for avoiding witch-hunts: 'I myself, would rather see two or three traitors slip through the net of the Security service than be a party to the taking of measures which would be calculated to result in such a regime [a police state].'

This policy brought many benefits to British political culture and avoided the horrific nightmare of McCarthyism. Indeed, neither political party made capital out of the affair in the early 1950s, a situation helped by the fact that it had been a Labour government that was in power during the defections and which established the Cadogan Committee. Lipton was a monomaniac with a bee in his bonnet whose time would come during the early 1960s, when the Labour Party would use security and scandal to electoral advantage and he was able to cast himself as a man vindicated by events, a prophet spurned. In the early 1950s he was a voice crying in the wilderness and his chief audience was foreign newspapermen like Donald Horne.

An appointment made in the spring of 1954 seems to confirm this reading of the policy of restraint being pursued by the government. The Admiralty advertised a vacancy for a post in the British Embassy in Washington for a clerk to assist the Naval Attaché working in the embassy. After interviews, twenty-nine-year-old John Vassall was selected. Within a year Vassall had been compromised by the Russian authorities and began his seven-year career as a Russian agent.

13

The Press

An unmarried person in this country is a social misfit, and is suspect.
— Sunday Pictorial, 16 August 1953

There are only about twenty murders a year in London and not all
of them are serious — some are just husbands killing their wives.
— Commander G. H. Hatherill of Scotland Yard, Observer,
2 January 1954

It's unfortunate but true: the West End of London spells VICE in
searing capital letters. There's plenty of it to be found in other parts
of the capital of course, and in other British cities, towns and even
villages. But for the black, rotten heart of the thing look to London's
golden centre.
— from the memoirs of Chief Superintendent Arthur Thorp of Scotland
Yard, News of the World, 11 April 1954

Suddenly in late October 1953 newspaper articles about male homosexuality began to proliferate. A few called for a reform of the existing laws. Journalists, principally in the *New Statesman* and the *Observer*, suggested that it was time Britain adopt laws on homosexuality similar to those operating in France and several other continental countries: the decriminalisation of homosexual acts in private between consenting adults. This modest proposal, the first major public attack on these laws, produced a ferocious reaction from the legal establishment. They found a useful ally in the press, most of which rallied to the defence of the existing laws; indeed, many articles called for tougher legislation. The reaction revealed the degree of commitment that existed amongst judges, lawyers and policemen to these laws. It brought into play one of the most ruthless antagonists to male homosexuality, the popular press. The controversy raged for most of the autumn and winter of 1953/4. The Montagu trials added fuel to the coverage. It was to defuse this controversy that the

Home Office added homosexuality to the terms of reference of the inquiry it was proposing to investigate female prostitution.

The spark that ignited this controversy was the arrest of Sir John Gielgud on the evening of 21 October 1953, at a public lavatory in Chelsea, and his conviction the following morning 'for persistently importuning'. Newspapers were rapidly extending their coverage of society in the early 1950s. The publication of the Kinsey Report on female sexuality during the summer of 1953 provoked some of the most explicit articles on sex to have been published in the mainstream British press, articles that were condemned from the pulpit as pornography. Editors were allowing journalists greater freedom to explore taboo subjects. The most notable subject to emerge during 1953 was the speculation surrounding Princess Margaret's romance with a divorcé, Group Captain Peter Townsend. Stories such as this led groups such as the Church of England successfully to promote the establishment of the Press Council in 1953 to regulate Fleet Street.

The Gielgud case licensed newspapers to write about a subject that had previously been veiled in secrecy, male homosexuality. Gielgud was possibly the leading actor of his generation and a dominant figure in British cultural life. He pleaded guilty to the charge of importuning. He lied on the charge sheet about his occupation and described himself as a clerk, almost certainly in the hope of avoiding publicity. This was a common practice, a way in which the arresting police rewarded a man who pleaded guilty, exploiting his hope that his case would not be picked up by the press. It apparently worked sometimes. But it did not work for Sir John: someone at the police station tipped off the press and Gielgud faced a packed press gallery when he came up before the magistrate the following morning.

The arresting police officer reported that the famous actor said 'I am sorry' when he was arrested. In the only statement that he made to the court Gielgud explained: 'I cannot imagine I was so stupid. I was tired and had had a few drinks. I was not responsible for my action.' The magistrate, with journalists scribbling down his comments, clearly enjoyed his few minutes of fame. He advised Gielgud to see his doctor: 'See your doctor the moment you leave here and tell him. If he has any advice to offer take it because this conduct is dangerous to other men, particularly young men and is a scourge in this neighbourhood.' He fined the actor £10. With a full press gallery he decided to make some more general comments about the problem of importuning: 'I hear something like 600 of these cases every year and I begin to think they ought to be sent to prison as there were many more of them. I suppose on this occasion I

Sir John Gielgud survived his conviction for persistently importuning other males in a public convenience. He continued to be a prominent figure in the British theatre.

can treat you as a bad case of drunk and disorderly and fine you but nobody could do that again.' He was exaggerating, of course. It was impossible for him to have heard 600 cases of this type; as previously noted, there had been fewer than four hundred cases for the whole of London during 1952, and the total for 1953 was similar.

Every single national newspaper and many local ones carried accounts of the case. Gielgud was due to open in a play the following week at the Royal Court, in N. C. Hunter's *A Day by the Sea*. Directed by Gielgud and with a stellar cast, the play was destined for the West End. Gielgud would also be appearing on cinema screens later that month when the Hollywood version of Shakespeare's *Julius Caesar* would be released.

Chiefly a vehicle for Marlon Brando who played Mark Antony, its cast included a number of British actors clearly included to add class to the production. Gielgud played Cassius.

There was speculation that Gielgud would withdraw from the play, but he decided to tough it out. Almost all of his fellow professionals rallied round and the audiences during the run of the play were extremely warm. The reviews of the play and of his part in the Hollywood epic were particularly fulsome. Gielgud was a popular figure in the British theatre and he benefited from the enormous fund of goodwill that existed towards him.

First Reactions

The Gielgud case provoked two different reactions. Amongst one group of commentators it provided an opportunity to focus on the absurdity of the criminalisation of all homosexual sex in Britain. The Gielgud case was not really applicable to their argument, for he had pleaded guilty to soliciting for sex, and defending importuners never formed part of the case for decriminalisation. The reformers simply sought the decriminalisation of homosexual acts between consenting adult males in private. The Gielgud case merely allowed a few newspapers to carry features and comment on this issue in a way that had never happened before. Those calling for reform were extraordinarily tame. They all hedged their proposals for reform with plenty of safeguards to ensure that the young would continue to receive the protection of the law and that everything would happen in private – never in public. It was clear that a number of liberal individuals did feel that the existing law was unjust and were willing to say so.

The Gielgud case also provoked a moral backlash against homosexuality, and a reaction against the articles calling for changes in the law. This backlash was fuelled by the seeming leniency of Gielgud's sentence and the fact that it had not damaged his career. Moralists wanted him to be punished for his crime, humiliated, not celebrated. What's more, they smelled a liberal conspiracy in the campaign for decriminalisation that now emerged. What seemed to make it worse was that Gielgud had recently been dubbed a knight, and there were suggestions that he ought to be deprived of the honour. The previous summer Gielgud had received an honorary degree from the University of Oxford along with the Home Secretary, Sir David Maxwell Fyfe, the deputy leader of the Labour Party, Herbert Morrison, and Jacob Epstein.

Leading the hunt against Gielgud was one of Lord Beaverbrook's chief lieutenants, John Gordon, the editor of the *Sunday Express*:

Sir John Gielgud should consider himself a very lucky man to have met a gentle magistrate. I am loath to make his punishment heavier by provoking wider discussion of his delinquency but this moral rot implicit in the charge against him – 'persistently importuning male persons' – menaces the nation much more than most people realise.

Because the offence to which Gielgud pleaded guilty with the excuse that he had been drinking is repulsive to all normal people, a hush-hush tends to be built up round it.

Sensitive people shrink from discussing it. Newspapers are disinclined to switch on the searchlight of public exposure regarding it as a peculiarly unsavoury subject.

What have been the consequences of that delicacy? The rot has flourished behind the protective veil until it is now a widespread disease.

It has penetrated every phase of life. It infects politics, literature, the stage, the Church . . . and the youth movements as the criminal courts regularly reveal to us. In the exotic world of international politics it seems at times to be an occupational disease . . . It is not purely a West End plague . . . It is often pleaded on behalf of these human dregs that they are artistic or intellectual creatures who because of their special qualities should have special freedoms. This is not so. The vice is as prominent among the lowbrows as it is among the highbrows. The Assize calendars show that.

The suggestion that peculiar people should be allowed peculiar privileges is arrant nonsense. The equally familiar plea that these pests are purely pathological cases and should be pampered instead of punished is almost as rubbishy.

It is time the community decided to sanitise itself. For if we do not root out this moral rot it will bring us down as inevitably as it has brought down every nation in history that became affected by it.

There must be sharp and severe punishment. But more than that we must get the social conscience of the nation so raised that such people are made into social lepers.

It is utterly wrong that men who corrupt and befoul other men should strut in the public eye, enjoying adulation and applause however great their genius. Decent people should neither encourage them nor support them.

And I would suggest that in future the nation might suitably mark its abhorrence of this type of depravity by stripping from men involved in such cases any honours that have been bestowed upon them.

Gordon specialised in invective, and in homosexuality he found a subject on which he could exercise all his talents. Like most of the attacks penned by Gordon, it reflected his own narrow-minded and misanthropic prejudices which so delighted the proprietor of the newspaper he edited, Lord Beaverbrook. Violently anti-American, he was no friend to the rise of the state, which he pilloried endlessly. He invariably flattered the readers of the *Sunday Express*, reassuring them that they were normal, decent and full of common sense. He posed as the spokesman of the little man against the big battalions and the corruption of the world. John Junor, a Gordon protégé who maintained the Gordon tradition, characterised his mentor in his memoirs: 'John Gordon was one of the greatest journalists of his time. He had an enormous capacity for sensing what ordinary people were thinking. He himself came from a humble background in Dundee. He remained throughout his life a Scots Presbyterian but he was an extraordinarily difficult man to like. He had a huge conceit of himself and an absolute unwillingness ever to admit having been wrong.'

Gordon was of course a Scot. Almost all of the most virulent homophobes operating in Britain during the 1950s were Scottish. It seemed to go with the territory, almost certainly a legacy of the powerful social and cultural position enjoyed north of the border by the Presbyterian church. In an earlier generation Gordon would have delivered his hell-fire moral condemnations from the pulpit of the kirk; instead he found a pulpit that brought him into the homes of millions of Britons.

According to Gordon, the following week, the 'problem of these peculiar men' had produced 'an exceptional response' from readers. Most of course 'expressed strong approval' of his comments 'but a number plead, some most movingly, the case for the afflicted'. Later he returned to the issue. With the usual modesty of the journalist he announced that since he had 'taken the opportunity provided by the case of Sir John Gielgud to draw attention to this male perversion menace ... the subject has become a national talking point'. Gordon claimed that the 'sinners' were glorying in the 'limelight'. He attacked those individuals calling for reform as if they were homosexual. He predicted that 'punishments in this country are more likely to become heavier than lighter'. Ever eager to act as a national barometer, he was certain that the 'temper of the country' was such 'that the spectacle of these depraved men flaunting themselves in the public eye and flourishing on their notoriety will not be tolerated'. Gielgud's survival still rankled: 'They have earned social criticism and they should get it. And they should certainly be stripped of any honours the nation may have conferred upon them. For while they remain public idols demonstrations that fame not shame has been the fruits of depravity, they draw other men to the depths with them.'

After another fortnight Gordon entered the fray again, this time to berate the *New Statesman,* the *Observer* and the *Spectator* for publishing articles advocating decriminalisation of homosexuality for adult males in private. It was David Astor, editor of the *Observer,* who first associated the notion of a witch-hunt and homosexuality in an article that he wrote on 1 November 1953. He described Gordon and others as speaking 'in the rabble-rousing tone of the witch-hunt'.

Correspondence columns provided one outlet for expressing opinions on this question. Under the title 'A Human Problem' the *Daily Telegraph* opened a controversy that raged for several days in mid-November, with the number of letters equally divided between reformers and moralists. The controversy was triggered by a man writing from Wells on 2 November suggesting a reform in line with the Code Napoléon, which operated in many European countries, which ignored homosexual acts committed in private between consenting adults. The correspondence provided an opportunity for the caricatured *Telegraph* reactionaries to let off steam. A Harley Street doctor suggested: 'that the laws relating to homosexuality should be printed in bold letters and exhibited. It may have no more deterrent effect than the poster for "Keeping death from the roads". But the Black Plague was finally controlled when rats and their attendant fleas were exterminated.'

The few articles which appeared in newspapers and magazines calling for reform of the law often passed critical comments on judges and policemen for the severe ways in which they enforced the laws on homosexuality. This annoyed both the judiciary and the police. It was in reaction to this type of comment that someone at Scotland Yard, probably the new Commissioner or someone close to him, decided to brief some journalists about the 'drive against male vice'. It is a measure of the extremely protected position that the judiciary and the police occupied in British life, and the important position occupied by the laws on homosexuality in the legal establishment's image of itself as the nation's moral guardians, that quite mild criticism could produce a ferocious reaction. The journal *The Practitioner* devoted a special number to homosexuality published in April 1954. Captain Athelstan Popkiss, the Chief Constable of Nottingham, was selected by his fellow Chief Constables to present their views:

Homosexuality is beginning to eat into the very vitals like a cancer. The public would be horrified if they knew its extent, and it is on the increase . . . And no wonder when we read in the public press that a body styling itself 'The Progressive League' has expressed the view that, while recognising the need to protect the minors, it nevertheless calls for an amendment to the law so that homosexual practices should not constitute a legal offence . . . In which direction do they suggest we should 'progress' if we legalised practices from which they agree minors should be protected? The police know only too well the evils that flow from such progress . . .

The high court judges were on circuit when the first articles appeared, trying cases in the provinces at the Assize courts. In November three members of the bench used the opportunity provided by sentencing men convicted of homosexual offences to answer their critics. They did so chiefly by drawing attention to the 'menace' (a word invariably used by moralists when discussing homosexuality) posed by a rising tide of homosexuality that they were valiantly trying to keep in check.

Mr Justice Lynskey, trying four men in what he described as a 'gang of homosexuals' at Exeter Assizes, pointed out that the 'law is quite clear although some people take the view that this offence ought to be treated leniently'. He, however, 'had only to look at this calendar' to appreciate the folly of such notions. 'These cases', he reminded his audience, 'are really terrible. This calendar, including the case I am taking now shocks me. People must be taught that this sort of conduct cannot be tolerated. It is bad not only for the individual but for the nation.' His brother judge, Streatfield, sitting at Norwich, was equally appalled and outraged:

It is a most distressing thought that this particular type of offence is so rife in this county [of Norfolk] at this time. It is an indication of moral decadence that is wholly regrettable. It is perfectly appalling that when judges go out north, south, east and west in the country on circuit they find the criminal calendars packed full of cases of indecent assault and gross indecency between males. It is a most distressing thought . . . An indication of moral decadence, that is wholly regrettable.

Two weeks later Mr Justice Cassels, sentencing a twenty-year-old man to three years' imprisonment at Hereford Assizes for five sexual offences with men over twenty-one, explained: 'This type of offence seems like a disease sweeping through the country, no assize court seems to take place without a case of this kind coming before it. So far as the law is concerned it must be stamped out.' Mr Justice Stable spoke at Leeds Assize of 'a great black spot on the national life. It's getting bigger and bigger. It is very alarming . . . One is beginning to wonder whether there is any possible method of dealing with this problem, except by making it clear that if these men are caught, to prison they will go. It will be an exception if they are not sent to prison so far as I am concerned.'

All these comments were picked up by national newspapers and provided 'evidence' for the sort of moral decadence exposed by the Gielgud case. They helped to generate a sense of outrage, and fed the reaction against homosexuality. The *News of the World*, unique amongst British national newspapers for covering trials concerning homosexual offences each week for decades, offered its support for the judiciary in an editorial titled 'AN EVIL IN OUR MIDST'. It set the tone for much press coverage of the subject that autumn:

> It is safe to say that it takes a lot to shock Her Majesty's Judges. Day after day in London or on circuit to the assize towns, they preside over courts that probe the failings of their fellow men and women. Their humanity and understanding, their deep insight, their wisdom – all these are by-words.
>
> During the past week it has fallen to two Judges [Lynskey and Streatfield] to call attention to the great and growing problem of moral offences ... [the judges' warnings and reflections are repeated] ...
>
> These are grave words, relating to grave happenings. For all who read the newspapers – or who simply walk about with their eyes open – know that things are going on in some of our towns (and our villages) that constitute a direct challenge to this Christian nation.
>
> Pious resolutions alleging 'Press sensationalism' in reporting certain cases just ignore the real question. Some recent criticism appears to have come from people who fondly believe that the less you say about an ugly subject the sooner it will die – if indeed any menace exists at all!
>
> Why should any of us dwell in a fool's paradise? The grip of this particular form of vice is ever tightening. Only the searchlight of public opinion will reveal the extent of the evil in our midst.
>
> 'People must be taught that this sort of conduct cannot be tolerated' said Mr. Justice Lynskey. We think that the most salutary way of teaching them is by publishing the punishments. Nobody must be able to say: 'I didn't know I was committing an offence.'

The leader writer was too modest. For decades the *News of the World* had served as a national pillory advertising to the nation the vices of their fellow citizens. In 1953 alone the paper covered more than one hundred trials for homosexual offences. In the two previous decades the words 'homosexual' or 'homosexuality' had appeared only three times. The paper, as this editorial shows, traded in euphemism that helped to make the danger even more sinister.

The political affiliations of the *News of the World* were staunchly conservative. (The *Sunday Pictorial*, by contrast, was extremely hostile to the Conservative Party: the newspaper used the issue of homosexuality to embarrass the élite and the Conservative government.) After another stonewalling performance by the Home Secretary in the Commons to further calls for an inquiry from two MPs, the *News of the World* presented Maxwell Fyfe's steadfastness as a great virtue:

> All praise to Sir David Maxwell Fyfe, Home Secretary, for bringing down to earth the arguments about moral offences.
>
> Her Majesty's Judges, of course, have never had their heads in the clouds when it comes to dealing with evil – and particularly the form of vice which one of them recently called 'a great black blot on our national life' and into which the Church of England called yesterday for an official inquiry.
>
> Almost daily in the assize courts the judges see not only those who have been called to account for their conduct; they see the victims as well. And we don't hear so much about the victims from the theorists who talk so glibly about 'treatment' for moral offenders.
>
> Maybe the law should be brought up to date in light of modern knowledge. Maybe more can be done in the way of prevention and treatment. But Sir David puts first things first.
>
> Certain people are a danger to others, he told the Commons, and so long as he is Home Secretary he will give no support to the view that they should be prevented from being such a danger . . . 'I have a duty to protect people, especially the youth of this country.'
>
> That, we think, is about the most sensible pronouncement we have heard on this dark subject for a very long time.

Moralists took up the issue of the homosexual menace and used it to explain a host of national and moral problems. One of the most spectacular outbursts was delivered by Lord Samuel on 5 November 1953 in process of making a speech in the House of Lords in the debate to mark the opening of the parliamentary session. Samuel was a few days away from his eighty-third birthday, to be celebrated with a special dinner by his fellow parliamentarians, and his selection to speak first was an honour accorded him by his colleagues. He decided to give the nation the fruits of a wisdom that had accumulated over many decades. His warning that Britain might be about to succumb to the 'Vices of Sodom and Gomorrah' made headlines in every newspaper. These vices 'appeared to be rife among us. If they become common, then retribution would be found not in any earthquake or conflagration but in something much more deadly, the insidious poisoning of the moral sense.' He was deeply anxious about the moral character of the people at the beginning of the second Elizabethan Age: juvenile delinquency; violent crime; sexual laxity; divorce and separation: 'One found in literature and drama and in life that adultery was regarded as a jest and divorce a mere unimportant incident.' The speech won him enormous praise. Many newspapers devoted their editorials to agreeing with the peer. For weeks afterwards, in letters to editors, in sermons and in articles his speech was taken as a reference point to articulate the moral decline of post-war Britain.

The press excitement over homosexuality brought a different reaction from other quarters. Even though much of the commentary condemned homosexuality, many moralists preferred complete silence on the issue. This was the response of the Prime Minister, Sir Winston Churchill, and it was a sentiment that struck a chord in Whitehall and amongst churchmen. In mid-November the Bishop of London, Dr Wand, addressing a diocesan conference, announced that the Church of England had established a committee examining the question of homosexuality that would report soon. He hoped that their recommendations could provide the basis for a national policy. He tried to discourage the sensational treatment of the subject:

> Let us not panic about the 'vice wave' which is supposed to be surging over the country at the present time. We have lately had a great deal of discussion in the Press and elsewhere about vice ... People are saying 'What is the Church doing about this?' implying that it is doing nothing at all. Nothing could be further from the truth.
>
> The Church itself does not stand idle. We have the Moral Welfare Council, which has at the present time, a committee inquiring into the particular sort of vice about which we have read so much. The committee is composed of real experts – not only clergy but lawyers and doctors. They are trying to thresh the whole matter out as thoroughly as they can ... We must not allow ourselves to be driven into any sort of encouragement of panic legislation.

Wand was trying to demonstrate that he and his colleagues in the episcopate had the matter in hand, that the Church of England was *doing* something. Wand, however, like other moralists, questioned the wisdom of giving so much space to the issue. The Bishop's fear that there was too much discussion of the subject was taken up by the Archbishop of Canterbury, Dr Geoffrey Fisher, in a pastoral letter that he delivered to his archdiocese in late November.

Fisher blamed the popular press for giving too much space to homosexuality. His criticisms were part of the campaign waged by moralists during 1953 against what they described as the pornography of the popular press. Fisher's attacks had begun with his opposition to televising the Coronation. He found much that offended him in the press during 1953: the graphic reports of the necrophiliac murderer Christie in the summer; the publicity given to Kinsey's report on female sexuality during August; and overshadowing everything else, the reports of Princess Margaret's romance with Townsend. The Press Council, used by Fisher, in its first report in September condemned the way in which the popular press were treating the monarchy, sex and crime in their pages.

Fisher and Wand preferred to work behind the scenes. They supported the activities of the Public Morality Council, a body which since 1899 had worked quietly to police public morals. They rarely advertised their concern to the public, preferring instead to mobilise authority in their support. This strategy was of course completely at odds with the policy of the popular press, who clearly enjoyed the opportunities that the breaking of the silence about homosexuality gave them. By the end of 1953 the genie was out of the bottle.

The National Pillory

Strafford Somerfield, *News of the World* journalist from 1945 and editor from 1959 to 1969, described his paper as 'The most widely read of any paper, a household name, a gold mine and a force to be reckoned with'. During the 1930s and 1940s it was the only British national newspaper that regularly reported the many trials that took place for homosexual offences across Britain. A broadsheet, the paper had some affinity with its tabloid namesake today. Like its modern heir, the *News of the World* devoted a good deal of its space to sex and violence, activities which it condemned while ruthlessly exploiting the prurience of its readers, who were clearly intended to be titillated as well as shocked by what they read.

The *News of the World* is one of the great success stories of newspaper history. By the 1950s it was a national institution that was as much a part of the British Sunday as the roast. Copies of the newspaper found their way into three-quarters of all British homes. With a circulation of eight million and an estimated readership of twenty-four million, it was not afraid to boast that it had the largest circulation of any newspaper in the world.

Founded in 1841 the paper's first half-century was remarkably uneventful. Having achieved a circulation of 40,000 in the 1850s its readership slowly declined until reaching 10,000 in the late 1880s. The paper was close to collapse but was saved by a remarkably talented consortium led by a London solicitor, George Riddell. Riddell was a Victorian entrepreneur who had started his working life as a humble office boy in a city solicitor's firm. Born in a modest home in the suburbs he died a multimillionaire, in his sixty-ninth year, in 1934. Like many newspaper proprietors before and since, Riddell used his position to acquire political and social influence. As his voluminous diaries reveal, Riddell was an *éminence grise*, the confidant of many influential politicians, most notably David Lloyd George (Prime Minister, 1916–22). Riddell managed the British press for the government during the First World War. He was rewarded with a knighthood in 1916 and a peerage two years later. It was an extraordinary success story. A considerable philanthropist, he left his entire fortune to charitable causes, a remarkably generous act.

He was obsessed with detail. It was, he believed, his mastery of facts that brought him success. Lloyd George's secretary and mistress Frances Stevenson recorded in her diary:

> No incident is too small for him to notice, no trivial fact escapes his alert mind. Everyone and everything concerns him and contributes to his interest in life and human nature. He probes and prises to find out the why and wherefore of this and that and he will take immense trouble to satisfy himself as to . . . the smallest details of the lives of the people with whom he comes into contact.

His newspaper was stuffed full of information, dozens of items competing for attention, satisfying some of the readers' curiosity about the world in which they lived. Well into the 1940s the paper was heavy with words (in sharp contrast to the same title today). Pictures occupied only a tiny proportion of the space.

Riddell's newspaper found most of its stories in the courts and in the provincial press. The journalists on the paper lifted huge chunks of their material from local newspapers, shaping the copy to the house style and providing their own angle and headline. It was a skilful operation. The paper's greatest extravagance was the money spent to acquire the rights to the best murder stories of the age. Accounts of executions were a recurring feature of the paper, with plenty of details: 'The weight of the victim, the length of the drop and the last words on the scaffold.'

The formula Riddell imposed gave the paper a unique character. The format of some columns ran unchanged for decades. Each week a column providing details of unclaimed money from recent wills excited hopes of a legacy amongst its readership. Another column which seems to have run for seven decades gave details of missing persons, supplying names, aliases and a physical description, chiefly trying to put families in touch with lost relatives. Whether or not the missing person wanted to be found was debatable.

The coverage of sport was excellent, long and detailed reports of matches and competitions and covering sports such as pigeon racing that were popular with the working man. Each week the paper published the music and lyrics of a popular song. Riddell had acted as solicitor for Sir Oswald Stoll and had a financial interest in the chain of music halls with which he was associated. As a consequence there was always considerable space provided for the music hall. Neither did Riddell's paper ignore news; politics was his governing passion and readers were treated to a front page completely devoted to news. Riddell and his successors employed many distinguished names to write features. Winston Churchill was a regular contributor in the 1930s. Leslie Hore-Belisha, the popular War Secretary sacked by Churchill in 1940, provided a weekly commentary on the progress of the war. Somerset Maugham reported on France in the early months of 1940, assuring readers that Britain's ally was ready, willing and able to resist the Germans. After 1945, maverick Tory MP Bob Boothby wrote a weekly column interpreting domestic and international politics for the readers.

It is easy to see why so many Britons turned to this newspaper to fill their time on what often seemed to be the longest day of the week. It provided entertainment on a dull day when most other forms of entertainment were closed.

Until the 1940s there was a remarkable degree of continuity amongst the paper's personnel. Young journalists recruited in the 1890s and 1900s, largely from South Wales, remained on the paper for the rest of their careers. Sir Elmsley Carr, nephew of one of the consortium of 1891, became a Fleet Street legend: editor for fifty years from 1891 until his death in 1941. His half-century in the editorial chair was celebrated by a dinner at the Dorchester attended by Winston Churchill taking time off from prosecuting the war. Senior figures from the worlds of politics and the press paid their respect to Carr. Churchill praised Carr as 'one of the strong proofs of the continuity of life in this country . . . Long may he continue to educate and amuse the British race.' Major J. J. Astor, the owner of *The Times*, presided over the gathering and King George VI sent a congratulatory telegram.

A Conservative newspaper, the *News of the World* was a pillar of what would be christened in the 1950s 'the Establishment'. It supported all established institutions. The judiciary occupied a particularly elevated place; columns appeared each term on the energy and industry of the judges in going through the growing calendar of civil and criminal cases. Judges nicknamed it their 'trade paper' and some judges were known to delay their summing up until the *News of the World* man was in the press box. Judicial casebooks were also published by the paper after the judge had retired from the bench, the closest one gets in Britain to a judicial memoir.

The police clearly provided valuable inside information on many cases. The adulation accorded by the paper to the police and in particular to Scotland Yard was second only to that lavished on the judiciary. Retired policemen wrote their memoirs for the paper. The *News of the World* was an insider, it conformed, it did not rock the boat, it had found a tried and trusted formula that worked, attracting more and more readers each year, and it provided Britons with a news service that they could find nowhere else in the British press.

In all items from the court a particular formula was invariably followed by the reporter. The offence was mentioned in the first sentence which also contained the name, age, occupation and address (usually down to the number of the house) of the person accused or convicted. The following paragraphs were based on the speeches of the prosecutor, defending attorney and judge, usually ending with the verdict of the jury.

'We may', said the editor George Riddell, 'publish the crime but we also publish the punishment.' A mention in the *News of the World* was an added humiliation for the person accused or convicted of a crime. It was its emphasis on punishment that licensed the *News of the World* to report subjects which were generally regarded as taboo. With this justification it could produce the most sensationalising reports in Britain. It was Riddell's greatest legacy to the newspaper because it protected it from attack by moralists or the élite.

The juiciest cases were those from the divorce courts, with prosecutions for bigamy and breach of promise also filling much space. Homosexual offences were never particularly prominent. In the early 1930s they supplied about thirty items a year, in a total number of cases well in excess of one thousand.

The words 'homosexual' or 'homosexuality' were rarely used. Indeed, in the quarter-century from 1932 until 1959, I can locate only half a dozen uses of these words by journalists on the paper. The *News of the World* instead resorted to euphemisms that conveyed to readers familiar with the paper a long-practised code to tell them exactly what was going on. Most offences were 'serious' which seems to equate with the charge of gross indecency but could also be used to cover an indecent assault by a male on a female. 'Grave' was more serious than 'serious' and might be employed to suggest buggery or attempted buggery, or rape in hetero-sexual offences. 'Grave' was a word much used by the editorial staff and was often employed in the late 1930s to discuss the deteriorating international situation, as in 'Grave Situation in Danzig'.

Poisoned Papers

The Sunday newspaper market was extremely lucrative and the *News of the World* had many rivals. None, curiously, applied the same formula but all instead offered something different; in particular they provided less text and more pictures. As the circulation figures of the *News of the World* fell during the 1950s its editors started to imitate its rivals, reducing the amount of text and increasing the amount of space devoted to pictures. There were three main rivals for the popular market: Lord Beaverbrook's *Sunday Express*, the *Daily Mirror*'s Sunday sister paper the *Sunday Pictorial* and the Odham group's *People*. All achieved circulation levels in excess of four million during the 1950s.

Papers were so cheap that many households bought several. As a result, British newspapers relied to a considerable extent on advertising revenues, more so than their continental counterparts. The cover price contributed only a small proportion of the total income earned by the paper. In the 1950s the competition for advertising grew stronger and as a consequence the competition for readers became even more fierce. The hysterical tone adopted by many popular newspapers at the time was a direct consequence of this struggle. It was a competition which did much damage to British society and was often based upon the demonisation of a number of people who could be presented as different: sexually different (as in the case of prostitutes and homosexuals), socially different or marginal (criminals, single mothers and those people who lived entirely off the state – a much smaller number in the 1950s than today), or racially different. In this way an incredible amount of poison was released into British society, with some terrible cultural consequences. This process of demonisation was constructed around the notion of normality which newspapers suggested were the characteristics shared by the broad mass of their readers: ordinary, decent, honest, hard-working, and above all else respectable. Every reader, it was assumed, was completely heterosexual; if single, they aspired to marriage, and when married they aspired to become parents, remained faithful to their partner and dedicated themselves to providing a good home for their family. Of course many of the journalists shared these prejudices. Fleet Street in the 1950s was overwhelmingly male and dominantly heterosexual, as reflected in the material that they wrote.

The Wizard

God, it was fun!
Hugh Cudlipp on his career as a journalist, editor and publisher

Whenever I feel really depressed about the stinkingness of politics, I
take a dive into Fleet Street and see what stinkingness really is.
from The Backbench Diaries of Richard Crossman,
entry for September 1952

The man who more than any other orchestrated many of these developments was a Welsh journalist called Hugh Cudlipp. Cudlipp lives today
in retirement in Chichester. Ennobled by his friend Harold Wilson in
1976, he seems to spend much of his time ensuring that historians will
not forget him. Cudlipp has always been his own best publicist, celebrating
his leading role in what he likes to call 'the tabloid revolution'. Obituarists
will celebrate him as one of the greatest journalists of the century and
much praise will be lavished upon him. Newspapermen, hardened cynics
much of the time, become sentimental when they remember their own
past; famous editors become heroic figures, and journalism becomes a
vocation. All this will come to Cudlipp. He has outlived most of his
enemies so there is nobody left to assassinate his character or reputation.

Cudlipp played a major part in the development of a press tradition
which vilified homosexuality and did much to celebrate normality. What
is more, he has boasted of the fact.

Cudlipp's 'log cabin to White House' biography begins in a modest
home in South Wales, a major recruiting ground for British popular journalists. The son of a commercial traveller, Cudlipp grew up in Cardiff,
the youngest of three brothers who all became journalists. Each one of
them became editors of national newspapers. Percy Cudlipp was editor
of the *Evening Standard* and the *Daily Herald* while Reg was editor of the
News of the World (1953–9). Percy had become an editor at the age of
twenty-eight, the year before his kid brother arrived on Fleet Street to
join the staff of the *Daily Mirror* in 1935. Hugh was twenty-one and had
already served a seven-year apprenticeship on the provincial press. Within
four years of arriving in Fleet Street he was appointed editor of the *Sunday
Pictorial*. For ten days during 1953 the three brothers were all editors of
national newspapers at the same time. All three sons owed much to their
ambitious mother and to the moral education provided by their parents
and the local chapel and Sunday school run by the Wesleyan Methodists.

Cudlipp joined the *Daily Mirror* at an important moment in its history.

His contemporaries on the paper included some of the most talented popular journalists of the century, notably William Connor, Donald Zec and Sydney Jacobson. They would remain together as a group for nearly four decades and they were a very powerful Fleet Street network.

Owned by the Rothermere family, the paper had been steadily losing circulation for years. According to Cudlipp it was 'Fleet Street's most identifiable lame duck' when he joined it in 1935. The Rothermere family had many more profitable titles including the *Daily Mail*, the paper upon which their fortune had been built. In 1934 the family handed the paper over to a new company in which Cecil King, a nephew of Esmond Rothermere, Lord Northcliffe, was given a watching brief. A shy and ambitious character, King was determined to make himself an even greater press baron than his famous uncles. With a remarkably talented group of journalists and advertisers he set out to establish one of the most popular British newspapers in history.

The new-look *Mirror* was re-launched as a Labour Party paper and directed itself towards the masses. A key element in this process was the recruitment of Basil Nicholson from the American advertising giant, J. Walter Thompson. It is a paradox that one of the pillars of the British Labour movement should have owed so much to one of the great agents of American capitalism and advocates of free enterprise. The Mirror Group would become a savage critic of liberal economics and a major supporter of Labour's plan to nationalise the British economy. In only one market did they support competition and a free market – the media. The former employees of J. Walter Thompson set the paper apart from its rivals:

> It was ... apparent that the leading American advertising agencies, with their sales appeal to the masses in strip-cartoon form had evolved a technique which the editorial pages of a pop newspaper would be wise to emulate. J. Walter Thompson were the masters of the new 'art' form, so it seemed prudent to acquire some of their know-how and talent: they were skilful exponents of marketing [and] consumer research.

There were plenty of pictures and lots of cartoons.

Cudlipp mainly worked to 'humanise the feature pages', in which task he was brilliantly successful. Moved to the paper's Sunday sister as editor in 1938, he acquired the reputation of a man with the Midas touch, adding 400,000 readers in the two years before he quit Fleet Street to serve his country in 1940. By the time he returned from the war, having edited the newspaper of the British forces and worked in government propaganda,

Cudlipp took over a newspaper that had faithfully followed his formula and been rewarded with a circulation of five million.

The company that ran the papers had no major shareholder and was run by a small board of directors who were for ever intriguing against each other. In 1949 Cudlipp fell foul of a faction that was temporarily in the ascendant and was sacked. Lord Beaverbrook immediately employed him on the *Sunday Express* and groomed him to be editor of that newspaper. Fortunately for Cudlipp the faction led by his patron Cecil King regained control of the Mirror company and Cudlipp was brought back in the summer of 1952 to edit again his creation, the *Sunday Pictorial*. Within a short while he was placed in editorial control of the whole group but the 'Pic', as he liked to call it, always absorbed most of his time. Eventually the court intrigues at the company would lead to Cudlipp engineering the dismissal of Cecil King in another boardroom coup, but that was far in the future. 'It was', reported Cudlipp, 'ironical that a newspaper that was successful because of its sense of human values, its compassion and its sincerity and warmth should be produced in a climate of rumbling malevolence and rivalry.'

Cudlipp's attitude to British life was coloured by the 1930s. Like many members of his generation, he believed that the mass unemployment of the 1930s should never be repeated. He constantly advocated full employment, which became one of the great sacred cows of the men who made British opinion in the post-war era. Even more significant was the feeling that the agreement between Neville Chamberlain and Adolf Hitler at Munich in September 1938 had been a betrayal of the British people. It is difficult to uncover exactly what Cudlipp thought of Munich at the time, but with the passage of time his opposition to this diplomatic manoeuvre coloured his entire political outlook: 'those who were right were utterly right and those who were wrong were incredibly wrong. History offers no other period of the recent past in which it is so hard to understand and sympathize with those whose judgement erred.'

For Cudlipp (and for others also) Munich had been a plot hatched by the established authorities to hoodwink the British people. It sanctioned his attacks on what he called 'the Establishment', a moving target which covered a multitude of individuals, institutions and policies which Cudlipp and his friends despised. In truth, Cudlipp's own political philosophy was extremely naïve, completely without any historical understanding and with absolutely no comparative dimension. It revolved around the special role of the press in the political and social life of the nation and on a sentimental regard for the people. He cast himself as their tribune. There was clearly a sexual dimension to this struggle against the establishment, which was often depicted as effete, smooth and unmanly in contrast to Cudlipp and his allies, who were presented as masculine, virile and *totally* heterosexual.

The idea of a single monolithic 'British Establishment' is of course ludicrous, a journalistic invention. Britain like every other state has a series of sometimes competing and sometimes complementary establishments. Cudlipp himself belonged to one of the most powerful twentieth-century establishments, a network of left-wing journalists and politicians associated with the Labour Party which championed a number of 'progressive causes' from the 1940s through the 1970s – by which time it was beginning to feel its age and its members were retiring to the House of Lords and to their country retreats to ponder on what had gone wrong with their particular version of the New Jerusalem. The defining moment for these men and women had been Labour's triumph at the polls in 1945, which seemed to herald the dawning of a new age. As yet no biography has appeared of Cudlipp but Dick Crossman's diary presents a particularly compelling image of Cudlipp as machinator, plotting, scheming and making mischief amongst the Labour élite, a power broker and fixer. Like Beaverbrook, another man who promoted the myth of the 'British Establishment', Cudlipp desperately desired to pose for his public and for posterity as an outsider – the fearless crusader against established authorities.

The Mirror company cultivated men who felt marginalised or ignored by what they liked to call 'the Establishment': Bishop Barnes of Birmingham, the modernist Anglican cleric ostracised by the Church of England, was provided with a platform for his heretical ideas; Basil Liddell-Hart, the military thinker whose views on warfare were ignored by the top brass, was given space to explain his criticisms of the commanders; Lord Vansittart, the diplomat whose warnings about Hitler were ignored in the 1930s, occupied a specially favoured position in the counsels of the company: 'The significance of Vansittart was that, like Churchill and our newspapers, he was vindicated by events.'

Munich and appeasement were the sticks with which Cudlipp and company would beat their enemies throughout the 1940s and 1950s. When what Cudlipp called the 'unpopular newspapers' attacked the sensationalism of the *Daily Mirror* and the *Sunday Pictorial* he retaliated by dredging up Munich. William Haley, editor of *The Times*, was reminded about his famous predecessor Geoffrey Dawson who eliminated all anti-appeasement comment from his paper, while David Astor, editor of the liberal *Observer*, was reminded about the antics of his mother and her friends at Cliveden, a circle popularly believed to have promoted the cause of the fascist dictators in Britain during the 1930s. It made Cudlipp even more self-righteous, even more pleased with himself and presumably made him even more cocky and self-confident.

Cudlipp of course owed his position to his talent as an editor and journalist but much of his power in the Mirror Group came from his association with Cecil King. King lived a hermit-like existence and used Cudlipp to act as his mouthpiece. He was able to articulate King's ideas and plans and put them into everyday language. Both men were obsessed by power and desperate to influence and shape events. King once said to Cudlipp: 'Let us get together and make a dent in the history of our times.' Together they promoted the Labour Party and would claim credit for the 1964 victory; they promoted and defended the state of Israel; they called for a 'modernisation' of British institutions beginning with a much-publicised campaign to modernise the monarchy; they called for an end to Empire and made heroes out of the men who led colonial struggles against the British. They were in favour of the players against the gentle-men and played a major role in shaping Labour ideology during the 1950s and early 1960s. Cudlipp was particularly keen to attack the 'old men' and repeatedly called for the promotion of the 'young'. For many years the *Sunday Pictorial* carried the slogan 'For the Young at Heart' on its front page. This campaign was one way of irritating the proprietor of the *Express*, Lord Beaverbrook, who particularly celebrated the wisdom of age. During the early 1950s Britain really did seem to be ruled by a gerontocracy.

Cudlipp and King were much courted by the Labour élite; with Dick Crossman and Barbara Castle operating as a link between the paper and the parliamentary party. Both Crossman and Castle wrote columns for the papers and Castle's husband Ted was a journalist on the *Mirror*, and for many years responsible for the northern edition. George Brown, deputy leader of the Labour Party from 1960, was industrial adviser to the group.

Few newspapers have ever so strongly, so passionately and so aggress-ively presented the male heterosexual viewpoint as the *Daily Mirror* and the *Sunday Pictorial*. There were always plenty of pictures of scantily clad females. One of the most famous features of the *Daily Mirror* was the strip cartoon character Jane, a girl who lost her clothes at the drop of a hat. Andy Capp was another regular cartoon feature; he owed his existence to Cudlipp who wanted something for northerners: 'Realistic, down to earth, essentially northern flavour ... Thus began the most fabulously successful cartoon character since Jane ... Andy Capp was created solely by Reg Smythe, who was born in Newcastle and still *thinks* Newcastle. His lay-about callous bounder became a universal symbol of how all men (occasionally) would like to treat women.'

With the re-creation of the *Daily Mirror* in the mid-1930s, 'The English People', according to A. J. P. Taylor, had 'at last found their voice.'

Evil Men

The *Sunday Pictorial*'s association with the subject of male homosexuality began in June 1951 when a former teacher from the London Choir School came to the paper's office and told a remarkable story of his former boss, Father Thomas Ingram: hence Cudlipp's suggestion that homosexuals flourished 'mainly in private schools'. The Ingram story had several ingredients that were particularly attractive to the journalists who worked on the paper. Ingram had strong 'establishment' credentials, his benefactors included several aristocratic ladies and he was closely connected with upper-class Anglo-Catholic circles in the capital. Even the fact that most of his qualifications were bogus and that he had a criminal record appealed to the journalists. The newspapers tipped off the Prime Minister's wife and she prudently withdrew from her planned visit to the school to hand out the prizes at the end of the summer term. In the event, Ingram's case did not come to court for another two-and-a-half years, so all went quiet after the initial publicity about the school, which focused mainly on Ingram's bogus qualifications and did not mention the sexual accusations that had been levied against him by his former colleague. For over two years the *Sunday Pictorial* sat on this story, which it would eventually present as an attempt to silence the press.

On 25 May 1952 the *Sunday Pictorial* opened its three-part series 'Evil Men', the first major examination of what Cudlipp called 'the homosexual problem'. The decision to produce these articles was Cudlipp's. He had recently returned to the editor's chair at the *Sunday Pictorial* and was keen to register an impressive increase in circulation, to gain even more notoriety, to make a mark. He achieved it as usual through sensationalistic reporting of social issues, in this case breaking the silence and eliminating the 'last taboo'. The sequence of articles left no stone unturned in vilifying and demonising homosexuality and promoting a tradition of newspaper reporting of homosexuality that has lasted for over four decades.

> Apart from jokes about 'cissies' and 'fairies' on the stage, one taboo obstinately survived, for newspapers did not talk about homosexuals. Vicars, teachers and choirmasters passed in sordid parade through the court columns of the *News of the World*, but Parliament, press and public alike evaded any serious discussion of the homosexual problem.
>
> The *Sunday Pictorial* considered the time had come for this taboo, also, to be swept away ... a series of articles on 'Evil Men' ... stripped the subject of the careful euphemistic language in which it

Evil Men

- TODAY the 'Pictorial' begins an investigation into a grave and growing social problem.
- IS IT TRUE that male degenerates infest the West End of London and the social centres of many provincial cities?
- IS IT TRUE that their influence is exerted in important spheres of national life?
- EMINENT JUDGES and social workers have been concerned with this problem for many years. It is time the public knew the facts.
- THIS INVESTIGATION has been conducted by

DOUGLAS WARTH

THE natural British tendency to pass over anything unpleasant in scornful silence is providing cover for an unnatural sex vice which is getting a dangerous grip on this country.

I have watched it growing—as it grew in Germany before the war, producing the horrors of Hitlerite corruption, and as it grew in classical Greece to the point where civilisation was destroyed.

I thought, at first, that this menace could best be fought by silence—a silence which Society has almost always maintained in the face of a problem which has been growing in our midst for years.

But this vice can no longer be ignored. The silence, I find, is a factor which has enabled the evil to spread.

Homosexuality is an unpleasant subject, but it must be faced if ever it is to be controlled.

Parents Must Face This Danger

MOST parents recognise the dangers of prostitution, and warn their teen-age children against the painted, disease-ridden women who parade the streets of our cities.

Few, I find, recognise the corrupting dangers of the evil men who, in increasing numbers, pervert youngsters to their unnatural ways.

Most people know there are such things as "pansies"—mincing, effeminate young men who call themselves "queers." But simple, decent folk regard them as freaks and rarities. They have become, regrettably, a variety hall joke.

There will be no letting about thi...

[...] people realise

...ports assert, ...nown homo... ...th numbers ...teeply since

...effeminate ...remain in ...any, who ...book, are as "sus-...

...theatrical ...makers ...rcentage

...chiatrist ...his field ...on the ...found ...ell.

...ly as ...and ...dmirals. ...xers. ...nany ...fact ...the ...hey ...ld

and a little girl of thirteen, at Winthorpe, Skegness. He asked for twenty-seven other offences to be taken into consideration.

The police found a black book in his possession, containing the names of 850 boys, against the names of 392 of them there were various symbols.

One man, as Mr. Justice Stable said at the time, had been able to corrupt many young people. "Nobody will know how many ruined, broken lives you have caused," he said.

The Unproven Offences

IN a notorious case, sixteen years ago, twenty-nine men were committed to trial from Altrincham, near Manchester on allegations of homosexuality.

Some were discharged. Others received sentences ranging from seven years to eighteen months. Among them were prominent local citizens.

This case, which depended on the statement of one prisoner incriminating another, arose after the facts had been dragged from one boy—a terrified victim of this wide vicious ring.

Most cases which get into the newspapers are couched in such careful language that the true warning cannot be read by large sections of the community.

Perhaps more significant than the relatively rare court action — for most offences, committed behind locked doors, remain unproven—is the naming of Guardsmen of a number of public houses frequented by perverts, near their London barracks.

Guardsmen with their fine physiques and smart uniforms have long been sought after by many rich degenerates. A little over a year ago the officer commanding the Brigade of Guards had his attention drawn to the problem.

An inquiry showed him to what an extent these fine soldiers had become involved in this world of unnatural vice.

The Language of Corruption

THIS evil affects people in all walks of life. Public school masters will admit privately that the vice is rife among those very adolescents who are being trained to take leading places in the community.

Certainly it is rampant at the universities. Some months ago I saw for myself what a hold it has got among certain sections in Oxford.

Homosexuals have their own private language, constantly changing as some of their expressions go into common usage. They recognise each other by the phrases they use.

Make-up, which they sometimes wear, is "slap." Putting on women's clothes is "dragging up."

A man whom they recognise as unsympathetic to them, and likely to mock and scoff at their mincing ways, is a "send up." Anyone strutting and posturing as they do is "very camp."

There is a freemasonry among them which brings the rich, pampered de-

...generate into touch with the "rough" who acquired his unnatural habits from some corrupting youth club leader — although, of course, the vast majority of youth leaders are decent, upright people.

In Diplomatic or Civil Service circles perversion is regarded as a special danger, for there is always the accompanying complication of possible blackmail.

Blackmail

IT is this blackmail danger which makes the perverts such a problem to the police. Homosexuals support each other. Influential ones will often go to extreme limits to compromise anybody who pries into their secret affairs.

That is why a number of doctors believe that the problem could best be solved by making homosexuality legal between consenting adults. They point to the fact that some...

of the most flagrant cases are helpless misfits who are physically unfortunate.

But this solution would be quite intolerable — and ineffective. Because the chief danger of the perverts is the corrupting influence they have on youth.

Widespread

IF this vice were limited to the few freaks who frankly, are victims of a glandular disorder, the problem could be dealt with as a medical one.

But so many normal people have been corrupted and, in turn, corrupt others that the problem no longer belongs to the medical field.

Habit is strong in all of us and, once a callow youth has become enmeshed in the practices of the pervert — through ignorance, curiosity, drink, blackmail or flattery—it is hard to win him back to normal life.

Even psychologists are taught, in their text books, that it is almost impossible

CONTINUED ON PAGE 15

—NEXT SUNDAY

The menace in London, and the big provincial cities

Bernard Dobson, a young Londoner, shows his amusement at the *Sunday Pictorial* feature 'Evil Men'. Dobson's photograph provides evidence of a defiant attitude shown by many young men at a period when their sexuality was publicly vilified.

had always been concealed. Doctors, social workers and the wretched homosexuals themselves recognised this as a sincere attempt to get to the root of a spreading fungus, but the taboo was still strong; so absolute, in fact, that nothing practical was done to solve the worst aspect of the problem – the protection of children from the perverts.

These characters flourished mainly in private schools because of the incredibly slack state of the law, and the apparent indifference of the Ministry of Education.

'Evil Men' was a way of exploring the 'problem' while they waited for Father Ingram to come to court. The series of articles was written by Douglas Warth, a young staff reporter who had celebrated the birth of his baby daughter with readers the previous year. Warth would soon acquire a column on the paper. He devoted his first column to bullfighting, an activity which during the middle decades of the twentieth century was often celebrated by heterosexual writers as a way of affirming their masculinity. According to Warth, 'the whole idea' of bullfighting 'is to show [that] Man, with his skill and artistic sense can rise above the brutishness of animal violence and subdue it . . . [the] Bullfighter is a high-priest [who] teaches the bull to dance. He gives it such nobility as it would never achieve on its painful way to an ordinary slaughter-house.'

The series of articles on homosexuality was part of a sequence of features focusing on particular 'social problems' and presenting them in an extremely exaggerated manner. In October 1951 the newspaper had offered an exposé of 'Black Magic', an activity having much in common with male homosexuality: 'many men and women who delight in wickedness and who, subscribing to the cult of black magic take part in unbelievable debauchery . . . Black magic is not practised by a few crazy individuals. It is the cult of many organised groups . . . they include people who are nationally and internationally famous . . . young people are being ensared.'

The rising drugs menace was associated with the rising tide of immigration of 'coloured' peoples to Britain. A series on the 'shameful cities of Britain' focused particular attention on illegitimacy and the mothers of such children. The articles blamed American servicemen and the girls themselves; even their mothers did not escape blame. A female welfare officer from Oxford explained her pet theory:

I think these girls are mostly to blame, and their mothers encourage them. The mothers can't forget that during the war many English girls got good American husbands. I think the trouble is partly that so many of these American visitors are mothers' darlings. Americans spoil their boys, and when the boys are left on their own in a strange country they naturally take to womanising.

The implication was that the British system of child-rearing did not have these consequences for the British male. Once again it was possible to trace the source of this problem back to the female, in particular the mother who was a principal culprit in the search for the causes of homosexuality.

The three articles that made up the series 'Evil Men' were constructed around the notion that it was time to lift the 'veil of secrecy' that surrounded this subject because it was being used by the 'evil men' to corrupt others. The articles were based on the assumption that male homosexuality in Britain was growing because 'numbers have grown steeply' since 1939:

> The natural British tendency to pass over anything unpleasant in scornful silence is providing cover for an unnatural sex vice which is getting a dangerous grip on this country ... [Douglas Warth] thought, at first, that this menace could best be fought by silence – a silence which Society has almost always maintained in the face of a problem which has been growing in our midst for years.
>
> But this vice can no longer be ignored. The silence, I find, is a factor which has enabled the evil to spread.
>
> Homosexuality is an unpleasant subject, but it must be faced if ever it is to be controlled.

It was particularly important that parents should be warned:

> Most parents recognise the dangers of prostitution and warn their teenage children against the painted, disease-ridden women who parade the streets of our cities.
>
> Few, I find, recognise the corrupting dangers of the evil men who, in increasing numbers, pervert youngsters to their unnatural ways ... It is a problem which every parent must take into serious consideration. For the first time every family must face up to the fact and say: 'This is something that threatens our own children so long as silence is allowed to reign' ... Bringing the horror of the situation out into the open is the first necessary step to getting control.

According to Warth most people underestimated the problem because they believed that homosexuality was confined to effeminate men. This, he claimed, was not so; *they* were everywhere: 'Most people know there are such things as "pansies" – mincing, effeminate young men who call themselves "queers". But simple, decent folk regard them as freaks and rarities. They have become, regrettably, a variety hall joke.' In this way the danger had been minimised: 'There will be no joking about this subject when people realise the true situation.' It turned out that, 'Few of them look obviously effeminate – that is why people so often remain in ignorance of their danger.'

While homosexuality was 'rife in the theatrical profession' it was also to be found amongst 'the most virile professions as well':

They claim success not only as writers and in the arts, theatre and poetry, but also as generals, admirals, fighter pilots, engine drivers and boxers.

The brilliant war records of many homosexuals is explained by the fact that, as the Spartans, they fought in the company of those whose opinion they valued most highly ... Indeed a famous general in World War One was a known pervert [presumably Lord Kitchener].

Male homosexuality had taken root amongst the British élite:

This evil affects people in all walks of life. Public school masters will admit privately that the vice is rife among those very adolescents who are being trained to take leading places in the community.

Certainly it is rampant at the universities. Some months ago [reported the intrepid journalist] I saw for myself what a hold it has got among certain sections in Oxford ...

This decadent vice, which to a large extent has spread downwards from the over-civilised and public school classes ...

Swansea police reported that 'the vice is most rampant among the "socially elevated" classes although they take their unnatural desires down to the dockland.' Paradoxically, however, 'Borstal institutions tend to be veritable nurseries for this sort of vice.'

There was a huge market for male prostitutes, who earned more than their female counterparts and were much busier and could be found in every major British city. If homosexuality were decriminalised or tolerated in any way then Britain 'would rapidly become decadent'. In France the toleration of homosexuality had led to 'an alarming fall in the birthrate'. Clifford Allen, the psychiatrist, warned readers: 'In the past battles may have been won on the playing fields of our public schools, but numerous lives have been broken in the dormitories.' Allen was one of the two main sources who supplied Warth with information and was possibly his principal source.

The other source was a Methodist clergyman based in Manchester whose ministry was to 'save' homosexuals. He told Warth that Manchester was 'the worst city for homosexuality that I have been in ... The old ones are like hags. You see them huddled up pathetically at night on the seats in the sunken garden in Piccadilly.' It was difficult to understand how anyone could be attracted to this vice because behind the superficial glamour there was the 'loneliness and secret misery which always lurks behind the brazen face of vice'.

Dr Allen's main contribution to the series was that he offered a solution; he felt that a cure was the 'prime need of the hour' and he was ready to find one. A Harley Street specialist, he was described in the articles as 'the great psychiatrist Clifford Allen'. He used the *Sunday Pictorial* to peddle his own pet project, the establishment of institutions where homosexuals could be treated and over which presumably he would preside. Prisons were completely unsuitable, offering even more possibilities for recruitment: 'In prisons the homosexuals find vast numbers of potential recruits to their perverted habits among their fellow prisoners.' Allen envisaged 'a new establishment for them, like Broadmoor. It should be a clinic rather than a prison and these men should be sent there and kept there until they are cured.' It would have many scientific benefits: 'Doctors and psychiatrists would welcome the idea. There is a great deal to be learned about the delicately balanced endocrine glands which determine whether or not a man could take to these unpleasant activities.'

Warth managed to suggest that the increase in the amount of male homosexuality could have even more serious consequences for Britain: 'I have watched it growing – as it grew in Germany before the war, producing the horrors of Hitlerite corruption and as it grew in classical Greece to the point where civilisation was destroyed.' On a trip to Hamburg later in 1952 he discerned the sinister revival of Nazism.

Sometimes his material produced some rather wonderful images. Describing the spread of homosexuality to the provinces, he reported that in 'Newcastle-upon-Tyne perverts from a wide area around the town congregate at a small buffet', while back in the capital a key meeting place was 'a snack bar where they leave each other messages'.

This was Cudlipp's great scoop, the breaking of the 'last taboo', a sequence of articles that presented a completely negative and hostile picture of male homosexuality and was intended to titillate and terrify the readers of the newspapers, to promote ignorance, intolerance and hatred. Another demon was presented for inspection to the great British public.

Despite all Cudlipp's talk of a 'green light', no other national newspaper followed his lead; it was only the Gielgud arrest in October 1953 which triggered a breaking of the silence across the rest of Fleet Street.

Calling for a Witch-hunt

During the 1950s the *Sunday Pictorial* campaigned intermittently for a witch-hunt. It sought the removal of homosexuals from schools and from the civil service. It demanded purges. It wanted registers and lists to protect children and state security. In the pages of the *Sunday Pictorial* homosexuals were presented either as potential child molesters or as potential spies. The purpose of these campaigns was to embarrass the Conservative governments of the period, to show that they were 'soft' on homosexuality. It was one element in the fierce polemic that both the *Daily Mirror* and the *Sunday Pictorial* employed in their support of the Labour Party.

The Father Ingram case started the ball rolling. When he was convicted and sentenced to ten years' imprisonment (as discussed in Chapter 10) the *Sunday Pictorial* crowed at its triumph. Ingram would always remain a major trophy, even finding his way into Cudlipp's memoirs as one of his newspaper's greatest achievements. Whenever a schoolmaster was found guilty of sexual offences with boys the *Sunday Pictorial* returned to the attack.

After another scandal in the summer of 1956 the *Sunday Pictorial* devoted its front page to a long article with a huge banner headline: NOW WILL THE MINISTER OF EDUCATION STOP DITHERING AND ACT TO PROTECT OUR CHILDREN (22 July 1956). In March 1957 after yet another case the *Pictorial* reminded its readers: 'Many times the Sunday Pictorial has lambasted the Ministry of Education for failing adequately to protect schoolboys from homosexual schoolmasters. Many times honey-tongued words from the Ministry have met our protests. And each time a new case has arrived to shock the public and to prove the justness and urgency of the Pictorial campaign.' By September 1957 it reported that 'no real positive steps have been taken to root out the perverts and crooks who still infest Britain's private schools'. It also printed a warning after a limited register was introduced that autumn: 'If any school where homosexual teachers corrupt the kids succeeds in getting a place on the national register the Minister can expect no mercy from parents – or from the Pictorial. WE SHALL BE WATCHING!' It helped that this campaign could be run in tandem with an attack on private schools, which were presented as dangerous agents promoting class division in Britain: what the *Sunday Pictorial* called 'nasty little snob schools'.

By the mid-1950s the *Pictorial* was calling for the witch-hunt. In January 1955 the newspaper reported that Burgess and Maclean were playing a key role in shaping Soviet policy towards the West, though the only concrete example that they mentioned was the decision to send the Spartak

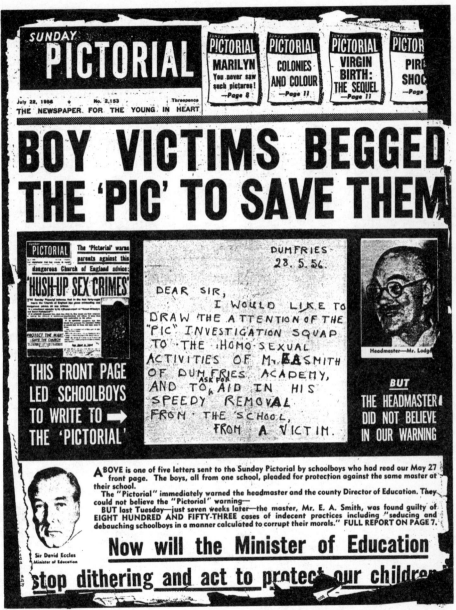

Hugh Cudlipp used stories of child abuse to win support for his witch-hunt during the 1950s. This front page indicates the way that he and his journalists sensationalised the issue during the period.

Moscow football team to play friendlies in Britain. That article had nothing in it about homosexuality. But on 25 September the *Sunday Pictorial* printed 'THE SQUALID TRUTH' about Burgess and Maclean on its front page: 'The wretched squalid truth about Burgess and Maclean is that they were sex perverts.' Something which was hardly news. Significantly upping the ante, the newspaper explained why the spies had remained so long undetected:

They were protected during most of their careers by men who knew or ought to have known about their homosexual tendencies.

There has for years existed inside the Foreign Office service a chain or clique of perverted men.

Whatever the current medical or social view, the danger of such men in public service is obvious. Homosexuals – men who indulge in 'unnatural' love for one another – are known to be bad security risks . . .

This sordid secret of homosexuality – which is one of the keys to the whole scandal of the Missing Diplomats – is ignored by the Government . . . it is urgently necessary that this hoodwinking of the public should cease.

On this occasion a Tory backbencher, Captain Harry Kerby, a diehard at odds with the Tory leadership, wrote about the traitors who were apparently 'notorious perverts' and called for a clear-out. Labour frontbencher George Brown was given an inside page to attack 'F.O. Flops' who drew attention to the feudal, aristocratic and effeminate character of the Foreign Service.

On 13 November Alf Robens, Shadow Foreign Secretary and a leading member of the Labour Party, made similar noises revealing that Soviet agents were blackmailing prominent homosexuals, thus exposing Britain to attack:

Part of the stock in trade of the enemy agent is blackmail. The easiest people to get into an agent's clutches are perverts – men who indulge in unnatural practices; men who drink heavily.

Agents of foreign Powers give such men facilities to drink to excess and give vent to their homosexual tendencies. Cunningly concealed cameras secretly take photographs and their blackmail begins.

That is one reason why the Prime Minister must agree to a thorough inquiry into recruitment, appointments and promotion at the Foreign Office.

The debate on the Burgess–Maclean scandal has left too many questions unanswered.

Both Maclean and Burgess drank heavily and were homosexuals. Both men were in a position to be blackmailed. Both were in a position to have access to secret documents.

I am not seeking to become a judge of their morals or their drunken behaviour. All I want to know is this: How did these two men keep their jobs for so long after their behaviour became common gossip in the circles in which they mixed? . . .

Does the system of recruitment and promotion within the department produce a 'close association' of personal loyalties which creates the keep-it-quiet complex?

Only a thorough inquiry can give the answers . . . The public are entitled to know that there are no more Burgesses and Macleans left and no more coming up.

All this coverage supported Sydney Jacobson's description of the period as 'The Backstairs Age' in November. It was all part of a polemical battle against the Conservatives, who were increasingly depicted as decadent because of their refusal to take a tougher line on homosexuals in the civil service and in the schools.

In December 1958 the paper offered advice to young people about homosexuality, and exposed another demon. An article constructed two 'real life' experiences. The first was that of a nineteen-year-old boy who had read extracts from the Wolfenden Report and feared that he was homosexual. He went to his doctor who 'cured' him and he acquired a girlfriend who led him safely back to heterosexuality: 'if he hadn't sought professional help he'd have been condemned to a lifetime of misery.' The second, the case of Margaret, a Cornish girl, moved the *Pictorial* into new territory. Margaret went to a café in Charing Cross and accepted a cigarette from a woman who became her lesbian lover for three years before she 'escaped'. The anonymous doctor offering advice warned: 'Lesbianism is far more dangerous than male homosexuality for this reason. A woman demands body and soul. For a man the body is sufficient. Margaret alone could never have broken the stranglehold of this woman. But with medical help she was freed. The last time I saw her she had a steady boy.' The wise doctor believed that far more lesbians were seducing/corrupting girls than male homosexuals were seducing/corrupting boys.

The Liberace Trial

Cassandra ... The name of a daughter of Priam sought in love by Apollo, who gave her the gift of prophecy; when she deceived him he ordained that no one should believe her prophecies, though true.

Oxford English Dictionary

Throughout the 1950s much interest was generated in the British media by the arrival of the big names of American showbusiness in Britain, generally to appear at concerts and shows at the Albert Hall or the London Palladium. Usually the stars crossed the Atlantic on a Cunard liner and docked at Southampton where they were greeted by large crowds, fans, well-wishers and journalists. A first-class train took the star into Waterloo Station where even larger crowds waited. The star was usually mobbed before being taken off to one of London's prestigious hotels in the West End. It was like a royal progress and produced an incredible amount of publicity for the star concerned.

In September 1956 Liberace, the flamboyant American entertainer and pianist, arrived at Southampton and received the usual treatment. Liberace had become a household name through his astonishingly extravagant dress. One of the earliest stars created by television, he was already a multi-millionaire with homes dotted across the United States. A bachelor he preferred the sexual company of members of his own sex – something which he quite obviously did not advertise. Of course many men certainly regarded him as a homosexual, but it was his remarkable female following that excited the jealousy of so many heterosexual men. How was it that a fairly obvious queer should send large numbers of females into ecstasy? A woman in a letter to the *Leicester Mercury* during October 1956 explained that it 'was time you [men] learned what we women want and how to keep us happy. In my long career I can only recall two men who made me feel glad that I was a woman and this I think is a great pity. So here and now I am advocating more Liberaces in Great Britain and then perhaps we shall have less mental patients and divorce cases.' She signed her letter, 'Still Hoping'.

One man was completely revolted by the whole exercise: William Connor, the journalist who wrote the Cassandra column in the *Daily Mirror*, was one of the bright young men who had transformed the *Mirror* in the mid-1930s. He was a close friend and colleague of Hugh Cudlipp. They regularly drank together at El Vino's in Fleet Street with their other chums. He drank heavily and read prodigiously. By the late 1950s Connor was feeling his age; he was growing increasingly stubborn, cantankerous and prickly and his columns often took on a very hard edge; his writing, according to his son, 'was as sharp as a scalpel'. When his columns 'were vitriolic which they often were during [the 1950s] ... they were *very* vitriolic. Blisteringly, punishingly so.' A big man, he was 'interested in money, cars and women' and, as he grew older, in cats as well: 'he loved them almost obsessively' and regularly wrote about them in his columns with a lot more sympathy than he usually allowed his human subjects. His cats conducted correspondences through his column with other cats, including the Wilsons'. He hated beards and moustaches and had an instant distrust of men who decorated their faces in this way. He was 'Irascible, excitable, passionate, testy and tetchy ... He used his pen like a club' and had 'a talent for robust invective'.

Connor's own pedigree certainly qualified him to adopt the moralising tone that he usually preferred to employ. His father was a Protestant Ulsterman and his mother a Scot, both strong lifelong Presbyterians. His biographer in the *Dictionary of National Biography*, former colleague John Beaven, suggested that: 'In Connor's denunciation of the wicked and praise of the virtuous, it was often possible to catch echoes of the Presbyterian pulpit beneath which Connor had regularly sat through his youth. About his religion he was publicly ambiguous although he was a deeply spiritual man and regularly read his Bible and Prayer Book.'

He was strongly anti-establishment. Beaven believed that he participated in a fashion among his friends 'for contrived rudeness as an antidote to the smoothness and alleged effeteness of the Establishment'. It is a manner that has become popular with many columnists. Connor was a pioneer, knighted in 1966 on the recommendation of his friend Harold Wilson for his services to 'journalism' and presumably for his services also to the Labour Party, of which he was a long-standing member. According to Beaven the 'knighthood [was] an inspiration of Harold Wilson [which] gave him and his friends great delight; and he enjoyed the irony of its bestowal on a life-long professional critic of the Establishment'.

In September 1956 Connor decided to call Liberace's bluff. It was a stupid mistake, for the effeminate entertainer fought back.

It was Liberace's triumphal reception at Waterloo that triggered Connor's tirade:

YEARN-STRENGTH FIVE

On August 20, 1939, when war was absolutely inevitable between Great Britain and Nazi Germany, I went and had a drink – I needed one more than anything before or since – at Berlin's most violent, most vulgar and most picturesque bar, the Haus Vaterland.

This vast establishment had about twenty bars . . . a round-up of the drinking habits of the world. In the Yachting Bar they had a drink to end all drinks.

It was called 'WINDSTARKE FUNF' – or Windstrength Five.

It was the most deadly concoction of alcohol that the Haus Vaterland could produce in those most desperate days.

On behalf of Mr. Chamberlain and Mr. Hitler I had five.

I have to report that Mr. Liberace, like 'WINDSTARKE FUNF', is about the most that a man can take.

But he is not a drink.

He is YEARNING WINDSTRENGTH FIVE.

He is the summit of sex – the pinnacle of Masculine, Feminine and Neuter. Everything that He, She and It can ever want.

I spoke to sad but kindly men on this newspaper who have met every celebrity arriving from the United States for the past thirty years.

They all say that this deadly, winking, sniggering, chromium-plated, scent-impregnated, luminous, quivering, giggling, fruit-flavoured, mincing, ice-covered, heap of mother love has had the biggest reception and impact on London since Charlie Chaplin arrived at the same station, Waterloo on September 12, 1921.

This appalling man – and I use the word appalling in no other sense than its true sense of 'terrifying' – has hit this country in a way that is as violent as Churchill receiving the cheers on VE Day. He reeks with emetic language that can only make grown men long for a quiet-corner, an aspidistra, a handkerchief and the old heave-ho.

Without doubt he is the biggest sentimental vomit of all time.

Slobbering over his mother, winking at his brother, and counting the cash at every second, this superb piece of calculating candy-floss has an answer for every situation.

On Religion: 'I feel I can bring people closer to God through my appearances. I happen to be a religious man, and I want my marriage to be blessed with my faith.'

On Mother Love: 'I think it is my mother love which so many of them (middle-aged women) do not get from their children.'

On Worldly Love: 'I want to spread the word of Love. Love of Family. Love of God and Love of Peace'.

On Money: 'I think people love lovely things – and they are deductible from income tax. I earn about nine million dollars a year and could earn more if I tried harder; but I only manage to keep nine cents out of every dollar I earn.'

On the occasion in New York at a concert in Madison Square Garden when he had the greatest reception of his life and the critics slayed him mercilessly, Liberace said: 'The take was terrific but the critics killed me. My brother George cried all the way to the bank.'. . .

Nobody since Aimee Semple McPherson has purveyed a bigger, richer and more varied slag-heap of lilac-coloured hokum.

Nobody anywhere ever made so much money out of high-speed-piano-playing with the ghost of Chopin gibbering at every note. . .

There must be something wrong with us that our teenagers longing for sex and our middle-aged matrons fed up with sex, alike should fall for such a sugary mountain of jingling claptrap wrapped up in such a preposterous clown.

Daily Mirror, 26 September 1956

Mr Angry vented his spleen at American popular culture but principally at effeminate homosexuality. It was clear what he was calling Liberace. Connor used words normally reserved for the sort of bar-room banter that he indulged in at the end of each day. The lawyers immediately saw the problems and advised the editor to spike the article. Hugh Cudlipp, editorial director of the *Mirror* and the *Pictorial*, overruled them and sanctioned the printing of the column in its entirety. He would stand by his mate. It was also bound to attract more controversy and that is what Cudlipp knew sold papers; as always he revelled in the notoriety. On 23 October 1956 Liberace issued a writ for libel. It took nearly three years before the case finally came to court.

The case opened on 8 June 1959 and lasted for six days. It has traditionally been read as an example of Liberace's hypocrisy and the lengths to which the entertainer went to deny his homosexuality. Liberace enjoyed teasing his audiences with his sexuality and it is now extraordinary to think that anyone was ever taken in, certainly as Connor's piece suggested some weren't. But it is also possible to read the case as a humiliation for the sort of tabloid journalism practised by Cudlipp and Connor under the banner of a free press, a journalism which has done so much to poison our society. Cudlipp and his friends celebrated an aggressive heterosexuality and were irked by an effeminate man who was breaking all the rules and making a fortune. Certainly the case injured Connor; according to his son who wrote his biography he never recovered from the hours he spent under cross-examination during the trial. He believes that it led to Connor's early death. In the years that followed the trial, his journalism lost its sting.

Liberace, the popular pianist who enjoyed an enormous female following, successfully persuaded a British jury that he was not a homosexual.

Liberace won his case due to the skill of his counsel, the extremely gifted courtroom lawyer Gilbert Beyfus who had practised in the courts for almost four decades. Beyfus scored many triumphs in his cross-examination of Connor. It was according to spectators pure torture watching the normally ebullient Connor being gored by a more skilful operator. Beyfus's hundred-and-fifth question provoked a notable riposte:

'What I suggest you were trying to do was hack out a good living for yourself by making yourself useful to the newspaper?'

'In the same way', replied Connor, 'as distinguished advocates of the Bar do the same thing.'

'I was going', returned Beyfus, 'to refer to your rudeness in a moment but perhaps you have given a good illustration.'

Like a pair of veteran prizefighters the barrister and the journalist traded punches but it was Connor who found himself more often on the canvas. His testimony grew less confident as he began to appreciate that Beyfus was making him look like a buffoon. Beyfus made a detailed scrutiny of all Connor's writings and succeeded in depicting Connor as 'a literary assassin who dips his pen in vitriol instead of ink and is hired by this sensational newspaper to murder reputations and hand out to the public day by day these sensational articles on which its circulation is built'.

He made much of a critical piece Connor had written about the popular broadcaster Richard Dimbleby who commanded much public affection. Connor's performance suggested that his 'command of English was written not spoken: his speaking voice was poor'.

Beyfus had even more fun with Cudlipp. He plundered his book *Publish and Be Damned* to expose his irresponsible approach to news and his support for sensationalism. In his summing up he suggested that these popular newspapers were 'vicious and violent, venomous and vindictive, salacious and sensational, ruthless and remorseless', employing Connor's own language. It was, he said, not 'quite up to Cassandra's standard but it is the best I can do'. The court burst into laughter.

Defending the action for the *Daily Mirror*, the Labour lawyer Gerald Gardiner clearly found this a difficult case to fight. He hoped to ridicule Liberace during his cross-examination, but found him extremely clever at answering his questions, often quite witty and continually raising a laugh in the court. The *Mirror* had tried to dredge up stories about Liberace's private life but found nothing they could use.

Connor invoked Munich and the menace of Hitler when the effete élite had been appeasing the dictators. He even tried to associate Liberace with the Nuremberg rallies: 'I am always suspicious of people gathered together in large numbers. I saw the Nuremberg rallies, people persuaded by propaganda, searchlights, speeches by Goering, driven by herd instinct. That is a bad thing. When I saw these young and impressionable people gathering outside Waterloo station [to welcome Liberace] I did not like it.'

The jury found for Liberace, awarding him costs and £8,000 damages. Amongst the crowds cheering him as he returned to a celebration at the Savoy were a group of drama students shouting that they wanted 'Fatso'.

Liberace died of AIDS in February 1987. He is supposed to have told his lover on his deathbed that he did not want 'to be remembered as an old queen who died of AIDS'. Inevitably his end has cast a long shadow over his career as it has done with Rock Hudson. Yet it would have been career suicide for either of these men to have admitted their real sexuality. They were willing to maintain the illusion that turned them both into 1950s pin-ups. Hudson was often celebrated as a clean-cut hero, in contrast to other more ambiguous males like James Dean. Hudson was at the height of his popularity in the late 1950s. In March 1958 a *Sunday Pictorial* report from their Hollywood correspondent described the star: 'Too many actors have been sensitive and spooky like Jimmy Dean. The public got tired of decay. So here's Rock Hudson. He's wholesome. He doesn't perspire. He has no pimples. He smells of milk. His whole appeal is cleanliness and respectability. The boy is pure ... In person Hudson seems curiously unreachable. His serenity is belied only by his ragged finger nails. He says: "I've picked at my nails since I was a kid. Nerves, I guess." Rock adds "My nails are the only visible sign of any discomfort. Otherwise I am outwardly at peace."

Since Cudlipp broke the 'last taboo' in 1952, the popular press has maintained an interest in male homosexuality that has continued to perpetuate the fantasies developed by men like Cudlipp, Warth and Gordon. Cecil King and Hugh Cudlipp became tycoons during the late 1950s, using the profits generated by the *Daily Mirror* and *Sunday Pictorial* to buy up newspapers and magazines and build the largest media empire in Britain. Amongst the titles they acquired was the *Daily Herald,* the official paper of the Labour movement. The *Daily Herald* had been losing circulation throughout the 1950s and was almost certain to be another casualty of the intensely competitive struggle for readers that killed off many titles during the late 1950s and early 1960s. Cudlipp and King promised that they would keep the *Daily Herald* going for at least seven years. It was hoped that Cudlipp's Midas touch would revive its fortunes before that deadline. The *Herald* did not revive despite a dramatic makeover in 1964, when the paper was relaunched with a new title, the *Sun.*

In 1969 two new players entered the Fleet Street game, Robert Maxwell and Rupert Murdoch. They were desperate to get a foothold in this potentially lucrative market. The controlling interest in the *News of the World* was keen to sell its share-holding, and after a titanic battle Murdoch emerged triumphant. The editor of the *News of the World* campaigned vigorously against Maxwell, whom he insisted on referring to as Jan Hoch. The anti-Semitic nature of the smears was barely concealed.

Cudlipp decided to sell the *Sun* and again Murdoch and Maxwell entered the lists. Once again Murdoch triumphed. He now had his base to launch his tabloid revolution. Cudlipp remembers in his memoirs a conversation with Rupert's father, the Australian newspaper magnate Sir Keith Murdoch, during the early 1950s: 'I'm worried about my son Rupert. He's at Oxford and he's developing the most alarmingly left-wing views.' Sir Keith need not have worried, it was only a passing phase, possibly even a pose. Rupert Murdoch went on to create the most virulently right-wing tabloids operating in Britain, and brought hostility to male homosexuality to completely new levels. He found plenty of journalists willing to produce material continuing the great tradition begun by Douglas Warth.

14

La Dolce Vita

G. Ramsay-Willis: 'Vassall' means a spy who is a homosexual?
Bernard Mulholland: Yes.

> *— from evidence given at the Radcliffe tribunal in 1963*

A small man, described officially as weak and not too bright, fooled all his highly educated superiors and sold his country and (in the future) thousands of young men in ships to those who would destroy what is left of our world. For seven years. Not seven weeks, before somebody noticed him, but seven years. Nobody is to blame. It just happened. Just how far can tolerance go?

> *— Spectator, 3 May 1963*

Attorney-General: ... It has been said that you are a known pervert ... that you are a person who has homosexual tendencies? That is right is it not?
Vassall: Yes.
Attorney-General: ... And that unhappily you also practise it occasionally?
Vassall: Yes.

> *— from evidence given at the Radcliffe tribunal in 1963*

A succession of homosexual scandals kept homosexuality in the headlines. In November 1958 a junior minister at the Foreign Office, Ian Harvey, forty-four, Conservative MP for Harrow, was caught *in flagrante delicto* with a Guardsman in Hyde Park during the early hours of the morning. He resigned his seat in the Commons. In 1962 a former Labour Party chairman and trade unionist, George Brinham, forty-six, was murdered by a sixteen-year-old cellarman he had befriended. The youth was acquitted of the murder on the grounds that Brinham had made homosexual advances to him, and this was accepted as an act of provocation. After the trial the young man sold his story to the *News of the World*. Later that year Ian Horobin, sixty-five, a former Conservative MP and for a time a junior minister, was convicted of homosexual offences with members of a boys' club that he ran in the East End. When he was charged, Horobin told police that he had been having sex with teenagers from the club for the forty years he had run the club. He proudly boasted that he had sex in recent years with the sons, and even grandsons, of boys he had had in previous decades. Peter Rawlinson, the barrister who had represented Wildeblood, acted as his attorney. Horobin was sentenced to four years in prison. Each of these stories occupied the newspapers for a few days and then quickly died.

The Vassall scandal, which surfaced after the exposure of a Russian spy in September 1962, excited the interest of the popular press and the Labour Party and drew on many of the myths that had been propagated about homosexuality during the 1950s. It also played a part in bringing about the downfall of Harold Macmillan, the Conservative Prime Minister.

On the evening of 19 March 1955 John Vassall, a clerk at the British Embassy in Moscow, had been invited to a ball to celebrate St Patrick's Day at the American Club. Vassall was a party animal 'showered' with invitations, 'so that it was not uncommon to have two embassies to visit each evening and meet new friends as they arrived week by week'. He lived in a social whirl, and just as gratifying was his sex life. Good-looking Russians seemed to be lining up to sleep with him and on the 19th he went on a date with a boyfriend he nicknamed 'the skier'. Tantalisingly the skier promised him an introduction to another young friend. Vassall decided not to go to the ball.

'The skier' met him at a railway station and introduced him to his friend, a good-looking blond in a military uniform. Vassall was smitten and they travelled to an apartment block somewhere in the suburbs where one thing led to another and Vassall found himself alone in a bedroom with the soldier. At no point in this encounter did Vassall think about what he was doing, and then he rarely thought, showing levels of naïvety in his dealings with his hosts that bordered on the lunatic. 'The skier', the soldier and the others were plants controlled by a special division of the KGB to trap westerners into compromising positions. Vassall recalled the incident in his autobiography:

> He came into the room, and walked slowly up to me, looking very smart and strong in his uniform. He looked into my eyes and grasped my hands. He was a tall man, very quiet and gentle but firm as he held my hands in his grip. There was no resistance from me. We remained there like this for some time, neither partner really wanting to talk yet having a desire to start something. How was it to happen?

Would his eyes give the signal, or would we be overwhelmed by the desire to kiss one another? I found a kind of sanctuary in his arms, as he held me, saying hardly a word.

There was nothing faked about his love-making. Suddenly the light went out. For a second I could not understand. What was going on? Somehow I knew it was not a power failure. I was suddenly cold and terrified. I started to shiver. In the distance I could hear chains and bolts being moved and voices whispering in the darkness. I wondered what on earth was going on. There was no word from my military friend in bed with me. Then the most dreadful feeling of shame and humiliation came over me. I realized something appalling had happened to me ... the lights came on and there was a polite but firm knock on the door and a voice told me to come into the next room when I was ready. The officer got up, dressed himself and left. He did not say anything to me but seemed intent on disappearing as quickly as he could. It was all *terribly embarrassing*. They must have known what was going on and had arranged to interrupt at the psychological moment.

Vassall was interrogated for seven hours by two officers from the KGB, 'sinister figures dressed in black' who showed him a box of photographs chronicling his extra-curricular activities in Moscow, going back it seems to the autumn of 1954, a few months after his arrival in the city. They threatened him with exposure. He might be imprisoned in the Soviet Union for his crimes or they might even send the photographs to his superiors. Astonishingly, Vassall had received no training in the techniques the Russians might use to trap embassy staff. Indeed, he had been warned only in the briefest and most general way about the situation he faced in the Russian capital. The Russians released him and let him return home to his flat. Vassall lived two miles away from the British Embassy; for reasons of economy the Foreign Office housed embassy staff around the city. The Americans housed everyone in the embassy compound or at the American Club. Vassall's apartment block was guarded by Soviet militia. He met the KGB for another session on 20 March, by which time they were less threatening and began to massage his not inconsiderable ego, flattering him and encouraging him to talk about himself. By the time he returned to his desk in the embassy he had made friends with the secret policemen. Foolishly he did not report his entrapment. As a result he was recruited by the Russians as a spy, and was actively involved in espionage until his exposure in the summer of 1962, by which time he was occupying a clerical position in the Admiralty in Whitehall. Other men were entrapped in the way that Vassall had been and had owned up.

They were sent home, the affairs were hushed up and presumably the men were moved into less sensitive work.

Vassall could not do this. His posting in Moscow mattered too much to him; he was having the time of his life. He decided to live a divided life. He was well paid by the Russians, as a consequence enjoying a lifestyle far above anything he could maintain on a clerk's salary. The Russians were clever and his controllers used the soft approach. Nothing more was heard about the photos. Gregory, his controller in London, seemed shocked by 'the idea that our activities came under the category of espionage'. Soviet officials possessed an even greater talent for euphemism than the British.

For Vassall Moscow was an escape from a dreary existence, living in St John's Wood with his elderly parents. A clerk in the Admiralty, he was lucky to have a job. All appraisals of his work showed that he had little aptitude for administration, he disliked the routine tasks that he was set and was constantly applying for transfers to new departments. Tom Galbraith, in whose office he worked for eighteen months, told him that 'fundamentally I don't think you really like working with paper. I think you like travel and meeting people and doing odd things suddenly.'

In December 1953 Vassall applied for the post of clerk at the British Embassy in Moscow in the office of the Naval Attaché, a position that had to be filled by a member of the Admiralty. Vassall was not a diplomat and was only temporarily a member of the diplomatic service. The two-year post offered Vassall a chance to escape from his dull life, an opportunity to play out his fantasies of a life overseas.

Few other clerks were attracted to the post. It was difficult to persuade civil servants to live and work behind the Iron Curtain where severe restrictions were imposed on all personnel. Cold War Moscow was not a particularly inviting place in which to live. Stalin was barely cold in his tomb and the future still looked glacial. The field of applicants was weak, though forty civil servants applied. Vassall's application was helped by the fact that the Treasury decided that in the interests of economy a single rather than a married person ought to be appointed. It all boiled down to a shortage of accommodation. Vassall had recently been received into the Roman Catholic church and made a good impression on the panel as a strongly religious individual and consequently reliable. On 7 March 1954, in the middle of the second Montagu trial, he left for Moscow.

Vassall may have been an incompetent clerk but he possessed a range of social skills and interests that made him a great success in the tightly-knit diplomatic colony in Moscow. He was a particular favourite of wives, who reacted positively to his attentions and his confidences. His love of classical music, the opera and the ballet won him many friends, and his

Catholicism brought him into contact with many well-placed foreigners who found him a very congenial companion. He also mixed with Russians and had soon constructed a social diary 'almost like that of an Ambassador'.

He was less of a hit amongst his fellow nationals. The British Embassy was strongly hierarchical and many of his seniors did not respond well to his chumminess or the social life that he had constructed for himself outside the embassy. Captain Bennett, the Naval Attaché in whose office he worked, was at first appalled by his effeminacy: in an official report he described Vassall as having 'the handicap of an irritating effeminate personality'. Bennett discussed Vassall's homosexuality with the Ambassador Sir William Hayter, who dismissed it as an irrelevance in a light-hearted manner. Bennett's successor as Naval Attaché described Vassall as a 'pansy' and few of Vassall's colleagues were in doubt about his sexual proclivities. His peers called him 'Vera Vassall' and he took a prominent part in the embassy amateur dramatics, winning a favourable notice from the Ambassador for his role in Rattigan's *Harlequinade*. Captain Bennett warned Vassall that 'someone, he would not divulge who, had brought to his attention that I was moving in circles too high for my position or station at the embassy'. That must have stung.

One of the more extraordinary explanations that Vassall made for his treachery was his social ostracism by his fellow countrymen. Repeatedly in his memoirs, written two decades after his entrapment, he contrasted the warmth and friendship that he found amongst foreigners with the cold shoulder he received from his compatriots: 'The secret is that foreigners are informal; and if they like you as you are, you are always acceptable', unlike the stuffy British. Vassall loved the exotic worlds in which he increasingly found himself, a far cry from Whitehall and St John's Wood. 'Sometimes', he wrote with some feeling, 'I wished that I had lived on the Continent, for their way of life is more expressive of mind and acceptance of others. I feel saddened that this kind of love and tenderness is such a rare find in my own country.'

Vassall built up a particularly strong resentment against Sir William and Lady Hayter. He hoped that they would take him seriously, but they ignored him: 'I was someone of no consequence in the Ambassador's world. It did not worry me.' Of course it did. He spread the story amongst his friends that the Hayters were close personal friends. He imagined himself as being the social equal of the Hayters and he indulged in a belief that his own family were a good deal grander than they really were. Vassall tried to cultivate the impression amongst others that he was in fact socially well-connected. In particular, he led others to believe that he possessed a private income. While it was his homosexuality that allowed the Russians

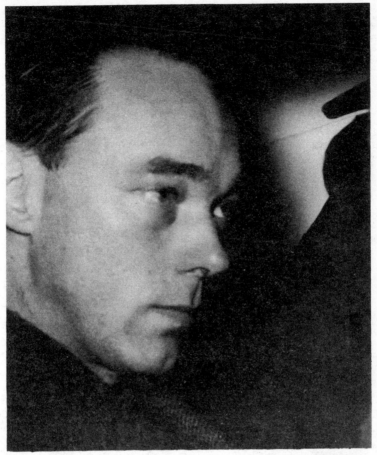

John Vassall, an Admiralty clerk, whose treachery provided further support for the alleged connection between homosexuality and espionage. The greedy and vain Vassall was well paid by his Soviet masters.

to collect an album of incriminating photographs, it was his social ambition, his dreams of a grander life and the resentments that he felt towards his superiors that led to him becoming a spy. Vassall was a blackmail victim who grew richer, not poorer. Burgess, Maclean, Philby and Blunt spied because they believed in communism; Vassall spied because it allowed him to indulge his social fantasies.

He returned to London in 1956 and served in a succession of low-level clerical posts over the next six years, passing more and more secrets to his controllers. The Soviet Union paid for regular trips abroad to visit the vast network of friends he had met in diplomatic Moscow and enabled him to rent a flat a stone's throw from the Houses of Parliament in Dolphin

Square. He applied often for promotion to the executive grade but failed to pass two promotion boards. Vassall was not destined to advance above the clerical level: 'his Annual Reports were never very encouraging and the problem seems to have been rather to find work that he could do.'

A sympathetic boss found him a more congenial move in the spring of 1957 by placing him in the personal office of the junior minister in the Admiralty. Surely a kind gesture, a realisation that 'a substantial part of his duties would consist of looking after the personal arrangements of [the minister] . . . on his official side, the kind of duty for which it was thought that Vassall might have special aptitude'. For two years Vassall helped to manage the minister's diary. His ingratiating manner was perfectly suited to the work and the young minister, Tom Galbraith, a Scottish nobleman, found himself served by a most devoted retainer. Vassall even brought black boxes to the minister's home in Scotland, travelling north on the night train. Vassall admired the minister. He kept his photograph on a chest of drawers in his bedroom and allowed those he knew to believe that they were tied together by more than red tape.

The Russians dignified Vassall's activity by sanctioning his interpretation of the homosexual witch-hunts of the early 1950s which seemed to show the appalling way that Britain behaved towards its deviants:

> I told them what I felt. If you were like this you never mentioned it to anyone, and it was a dangerous fact to be known in official circles. One had to conceal this part of one's life from that world. There was a constant fear that you might be exposed and threatened by police action, which could lead to a prison sentence. I instanced the case of Lord Montagu of Beaulieu, which was still very much in my mind at this time because of the treatment he had received. They were aware that homosexuality was widespread in high circles but they said that many gifted men were like that. They had the openness to admit this to me, and this frankness made our relations much easier, since I felt I had nothing to fear under their protection.

Vassall wrote later of the Montagu affair that it 'was yet another witch-hunt on the part of the British establishment, cruel and vindictive in the extreme'. Thus Vassall justified the protection of the KGB, the most notorious secret police force on the planet, and the Soviet Union, the most brutal and dehumanising regime on earth. It does not seem ever to have crossed his mind to inquire into the Soviet policies on homosexuality. In fact most of Vassall's colleagues knew about his homosexuality and were placed in the dock by the British popular press for tolerating his presence in the Admiralty and at the embassy. The British bureaucracy was attacked after his exposure because they had not behaved like the Soviets and gone poking into his private affairs, the penalty of tolerance.

In September 1962 Vassall was arrested by the police and put on trial for espionage and went to prison for eighteen years, eventually serving only ten. He confirmed the connection that existed in the minds of many that homosexually inclined men were peculiarly susceptible to treason. His case was added to those of Redl, Casement, Burgess and Maclean to support this prejudice. Vassall's exposure as a spy caused a press furore and did a great deal of damage to the Macmillan government. This spy case came on top of two other recent intelligence scandals, the Portland spy ring and the George Blake case. Neither case had involved homosexuality and as a consequence they were not linked into the Burgess and Maclean affair of the 1950s. The Macmillan government bought time by promising a major review of security.

The Attorney-General was away from London when the Director of Public Prosecutions called to tell the crown's law officers of the arrest of Vassall. Sir Peter Rawlinson had been appointed Solicitor-General in July 1962 and was deputising for the Attorney-General that September:

> I was minding the shop. I was certainly not in a mood to anticipate trouble when the Director of Public Prosecutions, Toby Mathew, was announced. I knew him well, but, in my new glory I received him, standing rather grandly in front of the fireplace.
>
> 'Sit down, Solicitor,' Toby said genially as soon as he came through the door. He was looking decidedly pleased with himself. 'Sit down. You will need to. We have arrested a spy who is a bugger, and a minister is involved.' I duly sat.

So it was that Vassall reunited two of the principal players in the Montagu case.

The popular press and the Labour opposition smelled blood; heads had to roll. A sort of frenzy broke out in Westminster and Fleet Street that autumn as the wildest stories gained currency and the Labour Party tried to use yet another homosexual scandal to reveal the decadence of the party in power. How could the Admiralty have sent a 'known homosexual' to a sensitive security posting in the Soviet Union? All sorts of popular stereotypes were exploited to destabilise the Macmillan administration.

The Mirror group of newspapers (Messrs King and Cudlipp), trading in their usual hypocrisy, made an even more damaging connection. The *Sunday Pictorial* bought Vassall's story. Morality did not seem to come into this transaction. They won the auction for his story by offering him £6,500, beating their rival the *News of the World*. This gave them access to Vassall's flat in Dolphin Square. A journalist paid a call, and reported that it was like a 'woman's flat':

> The perfumes, the bath essences and the soap – I washed my hands and they smelt nasty for two days – that was all there for anyone to see, anybody at all. The bedroom was strictly a female's bedroom. I think there were roughly about nine or ten bottles of various perfumes and cologne, talc powders of various types – I think Elizabeth Arden was one of the manufacturers . . . the display of perfumes, one felt that only a fairy queen would have.

He noticed Vassall's cuddly toys and his cuttings from French newspapers of 'stocky, hirsute rugby players'. He opened a couple of mail order catalogues selling women's underwear and using journalistic licence created the story that Vassall had worked in the Admiralty wearing women's underwear. Vassall never denied buying such garments but he insisted he had worn them only in his flat in the company of close friends and never in Whitehall.

The reporter, N. F. Lucas, read through all Vassall's letters that had been returned by Scotland Yard to the flat. He noted a reference to Gilbert Harding but focused most of his attention on a file of letters written by Tom Galbraith, Conservative MP for Glasgow, Hillhead, and the minister in whose office Vassall had worked as a clerk. These letters excited Lucas. He came to believe that they suggested an intimate connection between the minister and the clerk.

Journalists found it difficult to accept that Vassall was working alone and these letters allowed the press to extend the case and build up a much greater scandal. The press was searching for a 'Mr Big' who had acted as Vassall's protector and patron, presumably a homosexual, another member of the freemasonry of deviants. John Freeman, editor of the *New Statesman*, a former Labour MP and one of the individuals most involved in exploiting this case for the opposition, suggested that: 'Somewhere among the senior officials lurks a "Mr Big" who is able to protect homosexuals from the stringent inquiry to which others are subjected when they take over secret jobs.'

The press believed the security service hype that positive vetting was a tough investigation and therefore speculated that Vassall could have come through the procedure only with the assistance of some senior figure. From the moment that Vassall's homosexuality had been identified, the search had begun for a homosexual mafia inside the Admiralty.

The *Sunday Pictorial* on the basis of twenty-four letters and notes from Galbraith fed his name into the rumour mill. The newspaper showed the file to the deputy leader of the Labour Party, George Brown. In a debate on 5 November 1962 Brown suggested that Vassall had had a protector within the government. Brown was a virulent homophobe. His speech insinuating a connection was one of the most tasteless from a politician who often descended into the gutter. The Labour leader, Hugh Gaitskell, was alarmed at the moralising approach Brown was adopting. Brown sought to embarrass the government on the issue and make political capital out of the scandal.

Some elements in the security services briefed the press to watch Galbraith. They claimed to have information that he was about to abscond to the Soviet Union. It is clear that all concerned felt that they were re-enacting the case of Burgess and Maclean. It was further suggested that Vassall had been about to escape before his arrest but had been prevented from doing so by the vigilance of Scotland Yard (it is not particularly difficult to discover the provenance of this tale). A sinister connection was drawn between the fact that Vassall had planned a September holiday in Italy and the Galbraiths had also holidayed there during the same month. Newspapermen were interested in Vassall's trips to deliver papers to Galbraith in Scotland, which became the basis of assignations in the country. The rumours grew so strong that Galbraith resigned on 8 November in order to clear his name and to take legal action against the press.

Harold Macmillan was furious. Galbraith, an extremely honourable Scottish patrician, denied any sexual association with Vassall. Macmillan saw the letters and notes and regarded them as completely innocuous. They revealed 'nothing more damaging than Galbraith's interest in his office carpets, crockery and paper clips'. They were the sort of letters and notes a man on the move might write to his office in Whitehall. In one of the longest letters he gave his consent to Vassall's plan to do some spring cleaning while the minister was in Pakistan. Along with his wife, he had visited Vassall's new flat for twenty minutes in October 1959. All that he could be accused of was over-zealous paternalism, taking an interest in his subordinates and thanking them for helping him perform his work. The publication of all the correspondence sent by Galbraith to Vassall did nothing to stop the speculation, which took on a life of its own.

On the evening of Galbraith's resignation the political editor of the *Daily Sketch*, Boyd-Maunsell, had dinner with a young Conservative MP, Peter Tapsell. They talked about Galbraith and Boyd-Maunsell said that someone either at Scotland Yard or in Admiralty Security had told the paper's crime editor that Galbraith, not Vassall, was the man to watch. Tapsell went to the Chief Whip who in turn went to the Prime Minister. Macmillan, exhausted by his activity in the Cuban missile crisis, one of the tensest moments in the Cold War, decided to act. On 14 November he announced the establishment of a judicial tribunal under the senior judge Lord Radcliffe to investigate the Vassall affair: 'the purveyors of lies should be punished. It was important that an incipient McCarthyism should be stemmed without delay.' The tribunal bought time, which in politics is always a valuable commodity. The tribunal heard evidence in January and February 1963 and reported in March 1963. Macmillan thought that in 'a curious way, I may have gained by this incident, as it has helped to re-establish my ascendancy over the House of Commons'.

The press was put on trial. Journalists were subjected to brutal cross-examinations and made to look ridiculous in public. Three journalists were sent to prison for refusing to disclose their sources, martyrdoms that rankled in Fleet Street but not in the country. One journalist recanted but the two others actually served their sentences. The tribunal wanted to know who had leaked information to the press but got no names. The press protected their valuable sources in Scotland Yard, the Foreign Office, the Admiralty and the security services. Journalists pretended that they had simply invented or imagined particular stories and connections. The government was teaching not just the press a lesson but their contacts in the bureaucracy who fed them so much of their news.

A great deal of time was spent by the tribunal and its highly-paid lawyers discussing the question of how one knew a homosexual. Was 'pansy' a synonym and were all effeminate men homosexual? What was the significance of Vassall's after-shave and the attention he paid to his clothes? How had the press known he was a homosexual? Journalists appeared, telling of their trips to London's gay clubs and pubs where they had collected information. Such evidence was always prefaced by the comment that they were happily married with several children. The proprietors of several clubs gave evidence to the tribunal. The state and the clubs colluded together to show that Vassall had never visited their premises. Membership books were examined and no mention was found of the Admiralty clerk. It was the first official acknowledgement that a network of homosexual clubs and pubs existed in the West End.

The state wanted to show that nobody could know that Vassall was a homosexual. It had to negotiate some difficult evidence, most notably the reports of his superiors who had referred to the fact, never of course explicitly, but euphemistically. It seemed that everyone who met Vassall knew. One old lady, a retired civil servant with whom he shared an interest in cats, had acted as his referee when he was positively vetted in 1956, during which process she had told the Admiralty of his lack of interest in women. Because nobody had seen Vassall making love and nobody could be found to whom he had confessed his proclivities, the state felt itself

exonerated. The greatest problem was that the Russians had shown themselves to be a lot more perceptive than the British. Indeed it was a Russian
employed by the British Embassy who had set Vassall up. They had
briefly been lovers, and a female typist in the embassy had warned her
superiors of this connection and the fact that the Russian had confessed
to her that he was a spy. Her evidence was ignored. The Radcliffe Report
gave everyone in authority the benefit of the doubt, except the official
responsible for Vassall's appointment, and he was conveniently dead.
The distinguished judge applied a liberal coat of whitewash to hide the
discomfiture of the state. In a surprising paragraph the tribunal explained
the particular problem that the state faced in discovering homosexuals
and what had in fact been state policy in the past:

> Government departments, whether or not their work involves dealing
> with much classified material, are not constructed on the basis that
> it is the duty of colleagues to report to some superior or to a central
> Security Department every instance of a 'character defect', drunk-
> enness, pecuniary irresponsibility, sexual intemperance or perversion,
> etc., that they may chance to detect or suspect in each other. However
> 'security conscious' each individual officer ought to be, such a system
> of delation would be intolerable, and, in our view, its encouragement
> would be inimical to the spirit of the Civil Service, or, indeed, of any
> decently conducted organisation of human beings. The question of
> 'character defects', which has a real, though indirect, bearing upon
> security, must be distinguished from observation of direct breaches
> of security, suspicious in themselves, as for instance, if Vassall had
> been seen by someone while abstracting documents or had been
> detected searching in a registry to which he had no right of access.
> In such cases, we think, there is a general and positive duty to report.

The tribunal even in 1963 could court public disfavour by its defence of
traditional élite behaviour based on the honour system of the British public
school which so powerfully stigmatised the informer.

Paul Johnson shrewdly assessed the impact of the tribunal in an item
in the *New Statesman*:

> The case of the two imprisoned journalists has failed to stir the public,
> but it has left Fleet Streeters seething with anger. They blame the
> judges but, above all, they blame Harold Macmillan, who made it
> quite plain, in outlining the Vassall's tribunal terms of reference to
> the Commons, that he was out to get the press. I wonder if Macmillan
> quite understands what he has let himself in for. He is about to fight
> an election in which he will need every friend he has got. At the

moment he has none whatsoever in Fleet Street ... Between now and polling day, political news reporting (and of course, the slanting of news) will be heavily pro-Labour. I think that has already been reflected in the coverage of [Harold] Wilson since he has become leader, which has been far more favourable than ever his most optimistic supporters have expected. At the same time a Tory minister or MP (or, for that matter, judge or barrister) who gets involved in a scandal during the next year or so, must expect – I regret to say – the full treatment.

Macmillan felt triumphant in the spring and early summer of 1963. His ministers had been vindicated. Tom Galbraith was brought back into the government and won substantial damages from the press. The Vassall case, however, lit the fuse that would bring down Macmillan's government in the autumn of 1963.

Labour sought to depict the Tories as feudal and decadent while presenting themselves as the party of virtue and modernity. Homosexuality was a useful stick with which to beat the administration and the Labour front bench were able to associate the practice of homosexuality once more with the upper classes. In Harold Wilson's speech in the debate on the tribunal, Vassall became a member of the establishment, a deliberate misreading of the report: 'I wonder if the positive vetting of Vassall would have been so casual had he been a boilermaker's son who had gone to an elementary school?' In our Soviet enemies, he told the Commons, 'we face a ruthless, highly professional service – and when one fights professionalism in the gentlemanly posture of the Establishment, one is broken before one starts'.

Fred Bellenger, a Labour backbencher, felt there was too much tolerance of 'peculiarities and abnormalities' in high places. He told the House: 'It is quite evident that a new pattern is now emerging among spies. In earlier days, the spy was the glamorous Mata Hari sort of woman who used to get her man. Now it seems that persons with weak tendencies towards homosexuality, are easy prey to the Russians, who seem to specialise in this sort of trap.' George Wigg, who according to Harold Macmillan had set upon himself 'the role of unofficial keeper of morals and protector of security', warned the country that 'we are dealing with a long-term grim battle which involves not only the security of this country, but the whole concept of the Western way of life'.

Expressing sentiments reminiscent of the much-maligned Joe McCarthy, Labour was trying hard in that debate and in the accompanying propaganda to suggest that homosexuals offered easy prey to Russian subversion and that the decadent and aristocratic Tories were soft on homosexuality and sexual perversion. Such a tactic had a long pedigree; before McCarthy the German social democrats had used a similar smear against the Wilhelmine regime before the First World War. The re-launched *Sunday Pictorial*, now more accurately titled the *Sunday Mirror*, obligingly produced an article on 'How to Spot a Homo' to further help the Labour cause.

One Labour MP, Neil MacDermott, did not accept the party line and promoted instead the cause of homosexual law reform. He suggested that there was a connection between the prominence of homosexuals in espionage and the criminalisation of homosexual activity:

> It is not that homosexuals are more likely to be traitors. The point is that homosexuals in this country are peculiarly vulnerable to blackmail. It is because of our attitude of extremely prudish embarrassment towards the whole subject of homosexuality that a person who has been compromised in a homosexual situation is fair game for a foreign intelligence ... It seems to me that we are paying the price as a country for our attitude to homosexuality, and that, from a security point of view, the sooner we give effect to the recommendations ... of the Wolfenden Report the better.

Unfortunately this did not fit the fact in the espionage activities of Burgess, Maclean, Blunt or Vassall. Only one of that quartet had been compromised by the Russians; the other three had ideological reasons for spying for the Soviet Union. In Vassall's case sheer greed seems to have been the predominant motive; attempts to turn him into a victim are rather absurd. Vassall wrote in his memoirs of the pleasure that the passage of the 1967 Act gave him: 'I was on tenterhooks when at last the Wolfenden proposals were finally passed and I gave an enormous sigh of relief that never again could anyone be blackmailed or fear being prosecuted, as had been the case in the past.'

MacDermott's speech provided an opportunity for the MP for Cheadle, William Shepherd, to deliver a rant about homosexuality. Homosexuals, he claimed, 'were dangerous from two points of views, their promiscuity, and second, from the fact that they have a grievance against society, and are prepared therefore, if necessary, to go against society. Whatever might be done in the reform of the law will not alter the attitudes of society.'

The debate made Macmillan reflect on Wolfenden. Relaxing afterwards with his private office he asked them:

> how did you recognise a homosexual? It was said that women could do so more easily than men. Would acceptance of the Wolfenden recommendations make blackmail more difficult? Probably not. It

was not the avowed and complete homosexual who was vulnerable, but the man who did not go quite so far, who in part had a normal sexual life and felt ashamed of his aberrations.

In an interesting twist, the true homosexual was less of a risk than the bisexual. Perhaps Macmillan was thinking of his wife's lover Bob Boothby, whose bisexuality would cause problems for the government of Macmillan's successor, Sir Alec Douglas-Home.

In early June 1963 the Prime Minister went away to Scotland to shoot some grouse. On the 4th he received an alarming message from London. John Profumo, Secretary of State for War, a senior minister outside the cabinet, announced that he had lied about his liaison with a prostitute, Christine Keeler. He had lied to Macmillan and he had lied to the House of Commons. George Wigg, Labour's ever vigilant expert on security and sex, had been building up evidence on Profumo since the beginning of 1963. He had established a connection between Christine Keeler and the Soviet Naval Attaché, Captain Ivanov. Profumo, the minister in charge of the Army, was sharing a prostitute with a member of the Russian Embassy. Newspapers after the Vassall tribunal had been cautious about pursuing the story, but once Profumo admitted his guilt they used this opportunity to revenge themselves on the Macmillan government. All sorts of wild rumours circulated:

> a kind of Titus Oates atmosphere prevailed with the wildest rumour and innuendo against the most respectable Ministers. Altogether, partly by the blackmailing statements of the 'call girls'; partly by the stories started to or given to the Press; and partly (I have no doubt) by Soviet agents exploiting the position, more than half the Cabinet were being accused of perversion, homosexuality and the like.

Macmillan said in a press interview that he was not going to 'have the British Government pulled down by the antics of a whore'.

The *News of the World* gave the whore a platform, publishing her confession on 11 June 1963. They paid £23,000 for Christine Keeler's story, denying their rivals what was generally regarded as the scoop of the century. Macmillan appointed Lord Denning, Master of the Rolls, another judge, to examine the case, buying a bit more time. He reported on 12 September 1963 and within six weeks Macmillan had resigned as Prime Minister. Added to the problems of that summer was the exposure of Kim Philby as the 'third man', the diplomat who had tipped off Maclean. Philby had escaped in March 1963 from the Lebanon to Russia. It seemed as if the business of the 'missing diplomats' would never go away. The press began searching for the fourth man but he did a deal with the security services that preserved his immunity from exposure for sixteen more years. What sort of scandal would have developed had Sir Anthony Blunt, yet another homosexual, been exposed during 1963–4? It would have been more extraordinary than anything that had followed the exposure of Vassall. R. A. Butler, Macmillan's deputy who expected to succeed him as Prime Minister, could not conceal his delight: 'Oh Harold, how are you standing up to things?' he crowed. Macmillan was indeed feeling the strain. 'I do not remember', he confided to his diary on 7 July 1963, 'ever having been under such a sense of personal strain. Even Suez was "clean" – about war and politics.' This 'was all "dirt"'.

It was no accident that it was a homosexual and a prostitute who brought down the Macmillan administration and played a major part in ending thirteen years of Conservative rule. Both had been demonised throughout the 1950s and early 1960s by an increasingly hysterical popular press driven towards unbelievable excesses by their desperation to win readers. It was all too tempting for the Labour opposition, which was the principal beneficiary of all the scandal, finally coming to power in October 1964 after thirteen years in opposition. There are certainly parallels with the Republican Party in the United States during the late 1940s and early 1950s because exclusion from power can make political parties willing to resort to any means to regain power. The Macmillan administration of 1957–63 was no worse and no better than most British governments before or since, most of whom have more successfully hidden their vices. All the government was guilty of were too great a tolerance in the employment of homosexuals and the fact that a minister slept with a prostitute.

Appendix: Membership of the Wolfenden Committee

John Wolfenden, chairman.

James Adair, Scottish solicitor and former Procurator Fiscal of Glasgow.

Mrs Mary Cohen, Vice-President, Scottish Association of Mixed Clubs and Girls Clubs; Vice-President, City of Glasgow Girl Guides.

Dr Desmond Curran, Consultant Psychiatrist at St George's Hospital, Tooting.

Revd Victor Demant, Regius Professor of Moral and Pastoral Theology at the University of Oxford and Canon of Christ Church, Oxford.

Kenneth Diplock, barrister, Recorder of Oxford; appointed a judge in Queen's Bench in 1956.

Sir Hugh Linstead, Conservative MP for Putney, 1942–66; pharmaceutical chemist and barrister.

The Marquess of Lothian, junior minister at the Foreign Office.

Mrs Kathleen Lovibond, chairman, Uxbridge juvenile courts.

Victor Mischcon, solicitor and Labour leader of the Greater London Council.

Goronwy Rees, Principal of the University of Wales at Aberystwyth.

Revd R. T. Scott, Scottish Presbyterian minister.

Lady Stopford, doctor and magistrate; wife of the Vice-Chancellor of the University of Manchester.

W. T. Wells, Labour MP for Walsall, 1945–74, barrister.

Dr Joseph Whitby, GP in north London with psychiatric experience.

Source References

References in the text have been identified by citing the first four words of each quotation followed by its source. The abbreviation PRO has been used throughout for all documentary material found in the Public Record Office, London. In many cases, particularly where evidence from the transcripts of the Wolfenden Committee have been cited, only the first quotation from a particular testimony has been cited.

Introduction

p.1 'The telephone call from' J. Wolfenden, *Turning Points* (1976) p.129; p.2 'Frankly it's an unpleasant' R. Crossman, *Diaries of a Cabinet Minister* (1976) p.196; p5. 'A considerable body of' PRO CAB 129/66/C. (54) 60; p.6 'designed to prohibit the' PRO CAB 27/20 (4); p.6 'he pointed out that such legislation' ibid.; p.6 'If such legislation were' PRO CAB 129/67/C. (54) 121; p.7 'The task which the' HO 345/6: 15/9/54; p.7 'I am rather grimly' Cambridge University Library, Templewood Papers, Vol. XVI: I, Wolfenden to Templewood, 23 May 1954; p.7 'a brilliant product of' S. Faulks, *The Fatal Englishman* (1996) p.212; p.8 'it is true to' *Dictionary of National Biography 1981–5* (1990), p.431; p.9 'Here is a book' *The Observer*, 11 April 1976; p.9 'Their devotion was complete' Wolfenden ibid., p.134; p.17 'meat' HO 345/2: Roberts to Wolfenden, 22 September 1954.

PART ONE: Ventilating Prejudice
Chapter 1: The Wolfenden Committee, 1954–7

p.15 'It is always safer' HO 345/2: Wolfenden to Roberts, 18 November 1954; p.15 'The ordinary plain citizen' ibid., 22 November 1954; p.15 'It is an extremely' HO 345/4; p.17 'distasteful' HO 345/2: Roberts to Wolfenden, 31 December 1954; p.17 'more distasteful part of' HO 345/12/7; p.18 'Dunne: Everything said here' HO 345/14/37; p.18 'The record is entirely' HO 345/14/41; p.18 'We can talk perfectly' HO 345/16/56; p.19 'I think the only' HO 345/14/39; p.19 'the widespread modern belief' *New Statesman*, 4/7/53, p.21; p.19 'our great difficulty is' HO 345/14/39; p.22 'simply dirty-minded heterosexuals' HO 345/15/45; p.22 'a person unable to' HO 345/14/38; p.22 'Some of them far' HO345/9/94; p.22 'compulsive characters' HO 345/16/62; p.23 'I should have thought' HO 345/14/31; p.23 'the normal homosexual, in' HO 345/14/39; p.24 'the sodomist is closer' HO 345/16/54; p.24 'buggery is an offence' HO 345/14/41; p.24 'generally speaking, one could' HO 345/16/59; p.24 'My own private view' HO 345/16/53; p.24 'It lives I believe' HO 345/15/47; p.24 'if you go far' HO 345/16/53; p.24 'Where do young people' HO 345/12/7; p.24 'was laid down in' HO 345/14/34; p.25 'the British public's admiration' ibid.; p.25 'experienced homosexuals . . . possessed certain' HO 345/14/36; p.25 'homosexuals have a curious' HO 345/14/37; p.25 'the greater the disparity' HO 345/14/36; p.25 'Appetites are progressive, and' HO 345/14/37; p.25 'if two men do' HO 345/15/47; p. 25 'they have this funny' HO 345/15/41; p.26 'Homosexual practices tend to' HO 345/9/95; p.26 'Rees: Would it not' HO 345/14/30; p.27 'the removal of homosexuals' HO345/13/25; p.27 'move on to heterosexuality' HO 345/15/48; p.27 'a boy of 16' ibid.; p.28 'persons who have thrown' HO 345/14/39; p.28 'damage to the State' HO 345/14/38; p.28 'an enemy of the' HO 345/15/50; p.28 'Wherever . . . the same ugly' HO 345/15/47; p.28 'The common report from' HO 345/14/39; p.28 'The idea of a' R. Gosling, *Personal Copy* (1980) p.14; p.30 'In the turbulence of' *News of the World*, 26/12/54; p.31 'We never really find' ibid.; p.31 'the national interest requires' HO 345/15/47; p.31 'I believe the practice' HO 345/16/60; p.32 'the State has an' HO 345/15/41;

p.32 'The homosexual should be' HO 345/14/36; p.33 'revolt against domesticity . . . associated' HO 345/13/28; p.33 'An appeal from you' HO 345/13/26; p.33 'For heaven's sake start' HO 345/13/27; p.33 'the whole trouble really' HO 345/14/31; p.33 'there is such a' HO 345/12/11; p.34 'Everything which helps to' HO 345/15/50; p.35 'a most refreshing testimony' HO 345/16/53; p.35 'to describe homosexual acts' ibid.; p.36 'the vital experience of' HO 345/13/19; p.36 'recommends that homosexuality' HO 345/4; p.36 'I find myself personally' ibid.; p.37 'We propose to the' HO 349/9/93; p.39 'fortunate . . . solve American problems' HO 345/12/1; p.39 'What about our Huntley's' HO 345/4; p.39 'exhibitionists', ibid.; p.39 'to reprent the beliefs' ibid.; p.39 'The more I think' ibid., Wolfenden to Roberts, January 1955; p.40 'Some members felt, however' HO 345/5; p.40 'I confess I am' HO 345/2: Wolfenden to Roberts, 23 May 1955; p.40 'The imprisonment of men' HO 345/ 8/51; p.40 'They just happen to' HO 343/13/24; p.42 'gay night life of' M. Drabble, *Angus Wilson* (1995), pp.348–9; p.43 'Winter . . . my point of' HO 345/14/32; p.46 'to accuse a man' HO 345/ 12/8; p.48 'It is terribly difficult' HO 345/13/19; p.48 'tremendous increase' HO 345/12/13; p.50 'After some conversation about' HO 345/9/92; p.50 'known to the police' HO 345/2: Roberts to Wolfenden, 8 August 1955; p.51 'It is a case' HO 345/15/47; p.51 'My aim, first of' HO 345/14/ 39; p.52 'essential in the environmental' HO 345/16/54; p.52 'I regard homosexuality as' HO 345/ 14/39; p.52 'The best insurance policy' *New Statesman*, 6 June 1960, p.88; p.52 'are we to think' ibid., 30 July 1960, p.159; p.52 'satisfactory response' HO 345/14/39; p.53 'some kind of medical' HO 345/16/55; p.53 'The prison officer would' HO 345/9/95; p.53 'an inherently medical question' HO 345/14/31; p.54 'it is for the' HO 345/14/40; p.54 'In general I am against' HO 345/15/41; p.55 'is sometimes a euphemism' HO 345/14/40; p.55 'having been referred to' HO 345/9/94; p.55 'One of the most' HO 345/15/41; p.57 'Obligate, Facultative, Pederasts, Adult-seekers' HO 345/9/86; p.57 'They live for notice' HO 345/15/41.

PART TWO: Shadow Boxing
Chapter 2: Men in Uniform
p.61 'one of the most' HO 345/12/6; p.61 'my view about it' HO 345/12/13; p.61 'It is quite easy' HO 345/15/47; p.63 'a visit to Portsmouth' Q. Crisp, *The Naked Civil Servant* (1968, Fontana paperback edition) p.97; p.66 'for the most part' R. Croft-Cooke, *The Verdict of You All* (1955) p.12; p.66 'a book which caused' ibid., p.11; p.67 'If you are found out' HO 345/16/52; p.67 'From what we have' *News of the World*, 11/11/53; p.68 'We in the Home' HO345/12/1; pp.70–72 This account of the Curzon Street case is based on the report in the *News of the World*, 15/4/51, 29/4/54; p.71 'I do know about' HO 345/12/7; p.72 'they had the guardsmen' HO 345/12/8; p.72 'Hilbery asked me to' HO 345/2: Wolfenden to Roberts, 14 January 1955; p.72 'Hilbery let me read' ibid., 19 January 1955; p.73 'we have a good' HO 345/13/19; p.73 'The age of consent' HO 345/7/12; p.74 'Most of our cases' HO 345/13/25; p.75 'A man might be' HO 345/14/38; p.75 'Those who confess to' HO 345/13/25; p.76 'when trains arrived from' H. M. Hyde, *The Other Love* (1970), p.207; p.77 'I and most of' Q. Crisp, *The Naked Civil Servant* (1968), p.96; p.77 'It would be the' P. Parker, *Ackerley: A Life* (1989), p.114; p.77 'the scarlet jackets and' ibid., pp.113–14; p.78 'beloved friend and chief' P. Quennell (ed.), *A Lonely Business: A Self-Portrait of James Pope-Hennessy* (1981), p.xvi; p.78 'They were received by' ibid., p.xvii; p.79 'My son was expelled' *The News of the World*, 12/7/36; p.79 'I enquired, did not' S. Raven, 'Body Will be Boys', *Encounter* (1960); p.80 'Sir Hugh thought that' HO 345/6: 21/2/56.

Chapter 3: Thin Ice
My account of Rees is largely drawn from the excellent memoir and biography by his daughter Jenny Rees, *Looking for Mr Nobody: The Secret Life of Gorony Rees* (1994), cited hereafter as Rees. The account of Jeremy Wolfenden relies almost entirely upon Sebastian Faulks account of his life in *Fatal Englishmen* (1996), hereafter cited as Faulks.
p.82 'Holidaying for the weekend' HO 345/2: Wolfenden to Sir Frank Newsam, 21[?] March 1956; p.83 'awkward and embarassing little' ibid., 19 April 1956; p.83 'if they come through' ibid., Roberts to Wolfenden, 6 May 1956; p.84 'He was a human' *The People*, 11 March 1955; p.84 'any opinion about the' ibid.; p.84 'The most painful part' ibid., 18 March 1955; p.85 'the public must be' ibid., 8 April 1955; p.86 'Rees lost his head' *Times Literary Supplement*, 11 February 1973, p.142; p.86 'all my cards on' Faulks p.225; p.86 'Afloat! Afloat! I know' ibid., p.224; p.86 'preferred to seduce womaniser' ibid.; p.86 'Where do we go' ibid., p.222; p.87 [1] 'That to stay' ibid., p.241; p.87 'the shallow emotions and' ibid., p.244; p.87 'The two would put' ibid., p.253; p.87 'two pivots of his' ibid., p.280.

Chapter 4: Dark Corners

p.89 'the homosexual community, and' HO 345/14/37; p.89 'I can envisage men' *Parliamentary Debates (Hansard)*, Fifth Series, Volume 596, House of Commons, col.443; p.90 'Although few generalisations can' R. Hauser, *The Homosexual Society* (1962), p.28; p.91 'has the appearance of' D. Reynolds, *Rich Relations: The American Occupation of Britain, 1942–1945* (1995), p.253; p.91 'Outside of two very' ibid.; p.92 'used to meet a' *Walking After Midnight: Gay Men's Life Stories* produced by the Hall Carpenter Archives Gay Men's Oral History Group (1989), p.47; p.93 'an unhappy group' HO 345/14/35; p.93 'There are certain predisposing' HO 345/14/35; p.94 'were people who were' L. Hobson, *Consenting Adult* (1975), p.35; p.96 'a gay Mexican western' R. Tanitch, *Dirk Bogarde: The Complete Career Illustrated* (1988), p.96; p.96 'like a latterday Queen' ibid.; p.96 'was the wisest decision' D. Bogarde, *Snakes and Ladders* (1979), p.241; p.96 'I said "There's no" ibid.; p.98 'what seems at first' Tanitch ibid., p.105; p.98 'It is commonly believed' HO 345/12/1; p.102 'Blackmailing was mentioned and' HO 345/6: 12/3/56; p.102 'These figures represent an' *Report of the Committee on Homosexual Offences and Prostitution*, Cmnd.247, p.40; p.103 'long-haired and glassy' *News of the World*, 15/12/37; p.103 'I am going to' *Manchester Guardian*, 29 March 1955 and the *News of the World*, 24 April 1955; p.104 This account of the Walker suicide is based on a report of the inquest that appeared in the *Cambridge Daily News* 8 June 1955, pp.8–9, 13, and an interview with John Russell Taylor. I am grateful to Mr. Taylor for his help, and for giving up so much of his time to discuss this event. Walker's suicide had a considerable impact on is contemporaries, two of the leading figures who started the campaign for homosexual law reform were college contemporaries: Andrew Hallidie Smith and Tony Dyson. The pivotal importance of Pembroke College, Cambridge in the campaign for gay rights has previously passed without notice – the site possibly of a future pink plaque?

Chapter 5: Report and Response

p.110 'We believe that there' *Report of the Committee on Homosexual Offences and Prostitution*, Cmnd.247, p.33; p.110 'The report would have' HO 345/6: 4/10/55; p.110 'the Committee's wording must' ibid., 12 March 1956; p.110 'the claim that homosexuality' *Report of the Committee on Homosexual Offences and Prostitution*, Cmnd.247, p.16; p.111 'the more we take him' HO 345/6; p.112 'I do not know' *Evening Standard*, 4 September 1957; p.112 'The presence in a' *Report of the Committee on Homosexual Offences and Prostitution*, Cmnd.247, p.118; p.112 'apprehended that the proposed' HO 345/6: 4/10/55; p.113 'consumed ... textual criticism ... profitable' HO 345/10: Curran to Wolfenden, 21 June 1956; p.113 'We feel bound to' HO 345/9/107; p.116 'the living image of' *Daily Mail*, 24/11/58; p.116 'The Pansies Charter' *Sunday Express*, 8/9/57; p.116 'Why did the Government' *Daily Express*, 5/9/57; p.116 'The Wages of Sin' *News of the World*, 8/9/57; p.117 'I speak for the' *Empire News*, 8/9/57; p.118 'The report finds no' *The Times*, 5/9/57; p.120 'Looking back to when' *Parliamentary Debates (Hansard)*, Fifth Series, Volume 260, House of Lords, col.136; p.121 'Observers said only a' *Daily Mirror*, 5/9/57; p.122 'Among the 60 people' *News Chronicle*, 5/9/57; p.122 'You see I've tried' *Daily Mail*, 24/11/58; p.122 'that the Chief Constables' HO 385/5.

Chapter 6: Implementing the Wolfenden Report, 1957–1967

p.123 'a malignant canker in' *Parliamentary Debates (Hansard)*, Fifth Series, Volume 596, House of Commons, col.417, hereafter cited as *Hansard*, Commons; p.123 'It is better,' ibid., col.440; p.124 'From point of view' ibid., col.414; p.124 'never known a Report' ibid., col.454; p.125 'provincial pogrom' *Spectator*, 3/1/58. Reid had campaigned for homosexual law reform for many years. A former Headmaster of King's Taunton, he had been convicted of a homosexual offence in 1937 (see *News of the World*, 17/3/37). He wrote to Gordon Lang, Archbishop of Canterbury, and William Temple, Archbishop of York soliciting their support for the cause as early as 1938: Lambeth Palace Library, Lang Papers Vol.164 ff.266–72. It was a letter from Reid on 2 November 1953 advocating homosexual law reform that provoked a long correspondence on the subject in the *Daily Telegraph*: see page 273; p.128 'There are unfortunately people' *Hansard*, Commons Vol.625, col.1496; p.128 'In my opinion, all' ibid., col.1474; p.128 'revolting creatures of odious' ibid., 1482; p.128 'A life without children' ibid., 1484; p.129 'obviously effeminate, flauntingly exhibitionist' ibid., 1479; p.129 'a very small minority' ibid., col.1453; p.130 'these unfortunate people deserve' ibid., col.1455; p.131 'distasteful and even repulsive' ibid., col.1453; p.133 'an uninspiring advocate;' P. Devlin, *Easing the Passing: The Trial of Dr John Bodkin Adams* (1985), p.40; p.133 'What was almost unique' ibid., pp.39–40; p.134 'To condone unnatural offences' *Parliamentary Debates (Hansard)*, Fifth Series, Volume 266, House of Lords, col.645, hereafter cited as *Hansard*, Lords; p.134 'after the age of' ibid., Vol.267, col.342; p.135 'They are the odd' ibid., Vol.266, col.73; p.135 'What we are now' ibid., col.112; p.135 'Sir John Wolfenden has' ibid.; p.136 'What astonishes me is' ibid., Vol.267, col.396; p.136 'I really must protest' ibid., for this exchange col.396–99; p.137 'I object to this' *Hansard*, Commons, Vol.724, col.840; p.138 'I am sure we' ibid., col.843; p.138 'we had retired to' B. Castle, *The Castle Diaries 1964–70* (1984), p.103; p.139 'a vicious attack . . . the' *Hansard*, Lords, Vol.267, col.295; p.140 'it is becoming more' ibid., Vol.274, col.615; p.140 'Roy was able to' R. Crossman, *The Diaries of a Cabinet Minister: Volume Two, 1966–8* (1976), p.97; p.141 'among fatherless boys there' *Hansard*, Commons, Vol.731, col.262; p.141 'This is no occasion for' *Hansard*, Lords, Vol.285, col.523; p.142 'that a better piece' A. Grey, *Quest for Justice: Towards Homosexual Emancipation* (1992), p.128; p.142 'placating the implacable' ibid., p.128; p.142 'Paris was worth' ibid., p.266; 1.143 'the pressures for social' A. Horsfall in R. Cant & S. Hemmings (ed), *Radical Records: Thirty Years of Lesbian and Gay History* (1988), p.15; p.143 'tended to congregate in' ibid., p.15; p.143 'They saw the condition' ibid., p.21; p.144 'that sympathetic MPs would' ibid., p.30; p.144 'within a few weeks' Grey, ibid., p.154; p.145 'the alteration of the' *Hansard*, Lords, Vol.266, col.82; p.145 'I have been connected' *Hansard*, Commons, Vol.749, col.1503.

PART THREE: Homosexuality on Trial
Chapter 7: Introduction
p.151 'Saw Peggy. She's quite' J. Lahr (ed), *The Orton Diaries* (1986), p.233; p.151 'Went up to see' R. Davies (ed), *The Kenneth Williams Diaries* (1993), p.308; p.151 'I walked him to' J. Lahr, ibid., p.251; p.152 'an ugly Scotsman who' ibid., p.38; p.152 'a dwarfish creature' ibid., p.264; p.152 'we walked in the' ibid., p.259; p.153 'Kenneth who read the' ibid., p.125; p.153 'went down to . . . Holloway' ibid., pp.121–22.

Chapter 8: The Operation of the Law
p.157 'Until then sodomy has' *Hansard*, Lords, Vol,266, col.86; p.167 'a very successful, fairly' R. Mark, *In The Office of Constable* (1978), p.52–3; p.168 'such practices . . . were perfectly' ibid., p.53.

Chapter 9: The Crusaders
p.172 'In 571 I would': PRO, DPP 6/66. Mathew's evidence to the Wolfenden Committee and the supporting material can be found at PRO, DPP 6/66. I suspect that this file was not properly weeded or classified, some of the material that it contains is concerned with 'recent' (i.e. less than a century) police operations which normally ensures either that the offending material will be removed or that the whole file will be closed for at least a hundred years after the date of the most recent file. This one seems to have slipped through the net; p.172 'the liveliest interest' P. Wildeblood, *Against the Law* (1955), p.70; p.172 'a complete change in' PRO, DPP 6/66; p.176 'When my dear old' *The Magistrate*, vol. VIII. No.2 (1947), p.65.

Chapter 10: A Casebook
p.181 'Babes in the Wood' *News of the World* [hereafter cited as *NW*], 25/1/53, 22/2/53; *Hereford Times*, 23/1/53, 30/1/53; p.182 'Hearn Case' *NW*, 25/1/53; p.183 'The Wiles Case' *NW*, 1/3/53, 8/3/53; p.183 'The Ossett Circle' *NW*, 8/3/53; p.184 'The Kensington Blackmail Case' *NW*, 15/3/53, 5/4/53, 12/4/53; p.184 'The Swindon Case' *NW*, 17/5/53; *Swindon Evening Advertiser*, 15/5/53; p.185 'The Rampisham Postmaster' *NW*, 24/5/53; p.186 'The Bath Case' *Bath and Wilts. Chronicle and Herald*, 23/3/53, 30/3/53, 22/4/53, 27/4/53, 28/4/53, 28/5/53; p.186 'The Vicar of Whitley, Lancashire' *NW*, 7/6/53; p.187 'The Cartwright Case' *NW*, 7/6/53; p.187 'The Case of Woodham and Jones' *NW*, 5/7/53, 12/7/53. 9/8/53; p.188 'The Walker Case' *NW*, 15/7/53, 26/7/53; p.188 'Making Contact' *NW*, 26/7/53. *Ulverston News*, 24/7/53; p.190 'Father Forbes' *NW*, 2/8/53; p.190 'The Bull Case' *NW*, 2/8/53; p.190 'The Worcester Case' *NW*, 13/9/53; *Worcester Evening News and Times*, 10/9/53; p.191 'The Vicar of Barnes Bridge' *NW*, 20/9/53, 4/10/53, 18/10/53; p.192 'The Fylde Farm Case' *NW*, 27/9/53, 18/10/53; p.193 'The McKeown and Bayliss Case' *Worcester Evening News and Times*, 9/9/53; p.193 'The Newbury Case' *NW* 20/9/53, *Newbury Weekly News*, 17/9/53; p.194 'The Bedford Case' *Bedfordshire Times*, 9 October 1953; p.194 'The Cornish Cases' *NW*, 1/11/53; p.195 'The Appelwhaite Case' *NW*, 1/11/53, 8/11/53, 20/12/53, *Eastleigh Weekly News*, 19/11/53; p.196 'The Moore Case' *NW*, 6/12/53; p.197 'The Inquisitive Officer' *NW*, 6/12/53; p.197 'The Martin Case' *NW*, 6/12/53; p.197 'The Eden Case' *NW*, 20/12/53; p.198 'The Thrasher' *NW*, 3/1/54; p.198 'The Davis Case' *Somerset County Herald*, 30/1/54; p.199 'The Avery Case' *Clapham Observer*, 8/1/54; p.199 'The Gordon Case' *NW*, 31/1/54, 21/2/54, *Montgomeryshire Express and Radnor Times*, 30/1/54, 20/2/54; p.200 'The Wellington Case' *Shrewsbury Chronicle*, 19/3/54, 9/4/54,

SOURCE REFERENCES

9/7/54; p.200 'McGann Case' *NW*, 2/5/54, *The [Gloucester] Citizen*, 27/4/54, 15/6/54. 16/6/54; p.201 'Stevens Case' *NW*, 16/5/54; p.202 'The Stakeford Case' *NW*, 23/5/54; p.203 'The Uren Case' *Western Evening Herald*, 18/5/54, 23/5/54; p.203 'The Taunton Case' *NW*, 30/5/54, *Somerset County Gazette*, 6/3/54, 29/5/54, *Wells Journal*, 28/5/54, *Somerset County Herald and Taunton Courier*, 6/3/54, 10/4/54; p.206 'The Dorset Case' *NW*, 30/5/54, *Dorset County Chronicle*, 3/6/54, 22/7/54; p.207 'The Ingram Case' *NW*, 6/6/54, 18/7/54; *Dartford, Crayford and Swanley Chronicle*, 16/7/54, 23/7/54; p.210 'The Hatch Case' *NW*, 6/6/54; p.210 'The Ferris Case' *NW*, 13/6/54; p.210 'The Usk Borstal Case' *NW*, 13/6/54, *South Wales Argus*, 12/6/54; p.212 'Oteley Park Camp' *NW*, 13/6/54; p.212 'The Wignell Case' *NW*, 4/7/54; p.213 'The Fiveash Case' *NW*, 4/7/54; p.213 'The Treforest Case' *NW* 11/7/54; *Weekly Mail and Cardiff Times*, 27/3/54, 10/7/54; *Glamorgan Times*, 20/3/54; p.214 'The Reading Case' *NW*, 25/7/54; *Berkshire Chronicle*, 23/7/54; p.215 'The Rotherham Case' *NW* 25/7/54, 21/11/54; *South Yorkshire and Rotherham Advertiser*, 24/7/54, 20/11/54; p.218 'The Birmingham Case' *NW* 1/8/54; *Birmingham Mail*, 28/7/54; *Evening Despatch*, 28/7/54; *Birmingham Post*, 29/7/54; p.219 'The Carlisle Case' *Cumberland News*, 23/7/54, 8/10/54; *Carlisle Journal*, 8/10/54; *Cumberland Evening News*, 6/10/54, 7/10/54; p.221 'An Officer and a Gentleman' *NW*, 21/11/54, *Shrewsbury Chronicle*, 17/9/54, 28/11/54; p.223 'The Barnsley Case' *NW*, 12/12/54, *Barnsley Chronicle and South Yorkshire News*, 14/8/54, 18/12/54; p.225 The Battle for the Fitzroy is mainly drawn from the excellent history of the pub written by the daughter of Charles and Annie Allchip, Sally Fiber, *The Fitzroy: The autobiography of a London Tavern* (Temple House Books, Sussex, 1995). I am grateful to the bar staff at the Fitzroy for bringing this book to my attention. Bernard Levin's account of the pub can be found in the *Manchester Guardian*, 27 March 1956.

Chapter 11: The Montagu Trials
The account of the Montagu cases presented in this chapter has been constructed by weaving together contemporary newspaper accounts. The most detailed record is to be found in the *Daily Telegraph*, from which much of the testimony cited in this chapter has been taken.
p.232 'In August 1953 ... Edward' P. Wildeblood, ibid., p.44; p.236 'there grew up between' ibid., p.38; p.244 'the washing up' ibid., p.39.

Chapter 12: The Myth of the Witch-hunt
p.247 'they form a quite' Wildeblood, ibid., p.6; p.247 'Everyone has seen the' ibid., p.7; p.248 'The homosexual world is' ibid., p.185; p.248 'will always be lonely' ibid., p.3; p.249 'a political manoeuvre, designed' ibid., p.69; p.252 'homosexuals and other sex' P. Higgins (ed), *A Queer Reader* (1993), pp.160–1; p.253 I am grateful to the Australian National Library at Canberra for sending me a copy of this article; p.258 'a bit dim' remark made to me by Lord Allen; p.260 'for many Englishmen the' G. Gorer, *English Character* (1955), p.296; p.260 'Although the story was' J. Warner, *Jack of All Trades* (1975); pp.134–5; p.260 'probably more real policemen' ibid., p.135; p.261 'a clean show from' ibid., p.202; p.261 'I realised that the' ibid., p.133; p.261 'Nott-Bower was the "safe"' D. Ascoli, *The Queen's Peace: The Origins and Development of the Metropolitan Police, 1829–1979* (1979), pp.269–70; p.263 'The defection plunged Whitehall' R. Cecil, *A Divided Life: A Biography of Donald Maclean* (1988, Coronet edition 1990), pp.211–12; p.264 'Mr. Maclean had a breakdown' ibid., p.214; p.264 'evident that no outside' ibid., p.224; p.264 'seventh witness was a' ibid., p.225; p.265 'was not in the' ibid., p.226; p.265 'four officers left the' ibid.; p.265 'long tradition of self-righteousness' ibid., p.216; p.266 'The Communist Party in' J. Mahoney, '*Civil Liberties in Britain during the Cold War*' (unpublished Cambridge Ph.D thesis, 1989), p.318; p.266 'obviously some controlling mechanism' D. Caute, *The fellow-travellers, a postscript to the Enlightenment* (1973), p.342; p.266 'I myself would rather' P. Sillitoe, *Cloak Without Dagger* (1955), p.181.

Chapter 13: The Press
p.268 'I am sorry I' *Westminster & Pimlico News*, 23/10/53; p.271 'Sir John Gielgud should' *Sunday Express*, 25/10/53; p.272. John Gordon was one' J. Junor, *Listening for a Midnight Train* (1990), pp.96–7; p.272 'problem of these peculiar' *Sunday Express*, 1/11/53; p.272 'taken the opportunity provided' ibid., 8/11/53; p.273 'in the rabble-rousing' *Observer*, 1/11/53; p.273 'that the laws relating' *Daily Telegraph*, 14/11/53; p.273 'Homosexuality is beginning to' *The Practioner*, April 1954; p.274 'gang of homosexuals ... law' *NW*, 1/11/53; p.274 'a great black spot' ibid., 15/11/53; p.275 'AN EVIL IN OUR' ibid., 1/11/53; p.276 'All praise to Sir' ibid., 8/11/53; p.276 'appeared to be rife' *Hansard*, Lords, Vol.184, col.56; p.277 'Let us not panic' *Church Times*, 20/11/53; p.278 'The most widely read' S. Somerfield, *Banner Headlines* (1979), p.9; p.279 'No incident is too' ibid., pp.60–61; p.279 'The weight of the' ibid., p.37; p.280 'one of the strong' *NW*, 4/5/41; p.281 'We may

publish the' Somerfield, ibid., p.44; p.283 'God, it was fun' H. Cudlipp, *Walking on the Water* (1976), p.401; p.284 'Fleet Street's most identifiable' ibid., p.49; p.284 'It was . . . apparent that' ibid., p.52; p.285 'It was ironical that' ibid., p.67; p.285 'those who were right' H. Cudlipp, *At Your Peril* (1962), p.62; p.286 'The significance of Vansittart' H. Cudlipp, *Walking on the Water* (1976), p.99; p.287 'Let us get together' ibid., p.259; p.287 'Realistic, down to earth' H. Cudlipp, *At Your Peril* (1962), p.157; p.288 'Apart from "cissies" and' Cudlipp, ibid., p.317; p.290 'the whole idea . . . is' *Sunday Pictorial*, 14/9/52; p.290 'many men and women' ibid., 28/10/51; p.290 'I think these girls' ibid., 19/10/52; p.291 'The naturl British tendency' ibid., 25/5/52; p.292 'the vice is most rampant' ibid., 1/6/52; p.293 'prime need of the' ibid., 8/6/52; p.293 'Newcastle-upon-Tyne perverts' ibid., 1/6/52; p.294 'Many times the Sunday' ibid., 17/3/57; p.296 'Part of the stock' ibid., 13/11/55; p.297 'if he hadn't sought' ibid., 12/57; p.299 'was as sharp as' R. Connor, *Cassandra: Reflections in a Mirror* (1969), p.31; p.299 'interested in money, love' ibid., p.43; p.299 'a talent for robust' *Dictionary of National Biography* 1961–70; p.301 The account of the Liberace case has been drawn from contemporary newspapers: the fullest is to be found in the *Daily Telegraph*. Liberace's lawyer Gilbert Beyfus was the subject of a biography, *The Old Fox* by Ian Adamson (1963), which contains a very full acount of his role in the case; p.306 'He is wholesome. His' *Sunday Pictorial*, 16/3/58.

Chapter 14: La Dolce Vita

p.306 G. Ramsay-Willis: Vassal, *Vassall Tribunal on the Vassall Case and Related Matters – Minutes of Evidence*, Cmnd.2037 (1963), p.137; p.306 'Attorney-General: . . . It has' ibid., p.354; p.307 'showered . . . so that it' J. Vassall, *Vassall: The autobiography of a spy* (1975), p.104; p.307 'He came into the' ibid., p.63; p.309 'fundamentally I don't think' *Interim Report by the Committee of Inquiry into the Vassall Case. November 1962.* Cmnd.1871, p.12; p.310 'almost like an Ambassador' Vassall, ibid., p.99; p.310 'the handicap of an' R. West, *The Vassall Affair* (1963), p.88; p.310 'pansy' *Report of the Tribunal appointed to Inquire into the Vassal Case and Related Matters*, Cmnd.2009 (1963), p.11; p.310 'Vera' Vassall, ibid., p.34; p.310 'someone he would not' Vassall, ibid., p.39; p.310 'The secret is that' ibid., p.42; p.310 'Sometimes I wished I' ibid., p.75; p.310 'I was someone of' ibid., pp.71–2; p.312 'his Annual Reports were' *Report of the Tribunal appointed to Inquire into the Vassall Case and Related Matters*, Cmnd.2009 (1963), p.16; p.312 'I told them what' Vassall, ibid., p.79; p.312 'was yet another witch-hunt' ibid., p.42; p.313 'I was minding the' P. Rawlinson, *A Price Too High: An Autobiography* (1989), p.87; p.314 'Somewhere among the senior' *New Statesman*, 16/11/62, p.689; p.315 'nothing more damaging than' H. Macmillan, *At the End of the Day, 1961–3* (1973), p.430; p.316 'the purveyors of lies' ibid.; p.316 'a curious way, I' ibid., p.431; p.317 'Government departments, whether or' *Report of the Tribunal appointed to Inquire into the Vassall Case and Related Matters*, Cmnd.2009 (1963), p.63; p.317 'The case of the' *New Statesman*, 22 March 1963, p.417; p.318 'I wonder if the' *Hansard*, Commons, Vol.677, col.266; p.318 'pecularities and abnormalities . . . in' ibid., col.291; p.318 'the role of inofficial' Macmillan, ibid., p.438; p.318 'we are dealing with' *Hansard*, Commons, Vol.677, col.313; p.319 'It is not that' ibid., col.343; p.319 'I was on tenterhooks' Vassall, ibid., p.156; p.319 'were dangerous from two' *Hansard*, Commons, Vol. 677, col.344; p.319 'how did you recognise' H. Evans, *Downing Street Diary: the Macmillan years, 1957–63* (1981), p.229; p.320 'a kind of Titus' Macmillan, ibid., p.443; p.320 'have the British Government' Evans, ibid., p.283; p.321 'Oh Harold, how are' ibid., p.271; p.321 'I do not remember' Macmillan, ibid., p.441.

Index

INDEX

Chavasse, Christopher 37–8
Cheshire 186, 187, 189, 204; Birkenhead, 192, Cheadle, 128; Chester, 204; Macclesfield, 187
Chesser, Dr Eustace 19, 23, 51, 52
Chichester 283
Christie, J. R. 227, 254, 278
Church Army 53
Church of England 22, 75, 109, 125, 126, 130, 134, 144, 181, 185, 187–8, 196, 209–10, 221; Wolfenden's membership of 7–8; represented on the Wolfenden Committee 9; opposition to sensationalising popular newspapers 268, 277–8; Anglo-Catholics and 138, 187, 197, 207–10, 288; support for the Wolfenden Report 133; Cowley Fathers in Oxford 201, 210; Anglican Franciscans 210; Mirfield 210; contribution to Wolfenden Committee 35–8; Moral Welfare Council of, calls for an inquiry into the problem of male homosexuality 276, 277; evidence to the Wolfenden Committee 35–8; erring clerics 186–7, 190, 191–2, 196, 200–201, 207–10, 210, 223–4, 288, 294
Church of Scotland, represented on the Wolfenden Committee 9; mentioned 112, 272, 99
Churchill, Winston 6, 25, 197, 277, 280, 286, 300
Citizen, The 200
Clark, Alfred 194
Clark, Ernest 223–4
Clarke, Laurence 184
Clarke, William 191
Cleveland Street Scandal 225
Cliveden 286
Cluskey, Lewis 49–50
Cohen, Mrs 65, 72
Cole, Ernest 4, 253, 258
Collard, Dudley 209
Collins, Canon John 125
Collister, Thomas 103–4
Communism 252, 266
Conesford, Lord 136
Connolly, John 200
Connor, William, and Liberace 298–304; character, personality and career, 298–9; mentioned 284
Conservative Party 220–1, 296, 297; fall of the Macmillan government, 306–21
Cook, Robin 146
Cornwall 194–5; Callington 166; Falmouth 194
Coronation of Queen Elizabeth II (1953), 255, 256; Archbishop of Canterbury's opposition to the televising of 278
Costello, Sir Leonard 203
cottaging *see* importuning
Crawford, Joan 108
Criminal Appeal, Court of 257
Criminal statistics 20, 158–9, 256–7

Crisp, Quentin 63, 77; author of *The Naked Civil Servant* 77
Croft-Cooke, Rupert 65–70, 78, 206, 229, 254, 257; author of *The Life for Me* 66; and *The Verdict of You All* 67
Cronin, Frederick 196
Cronin, Joseph 190–1
Crosland, Anthony 131
Crossman, Richard; reflections on the 1967 Sexual Offences Act 2–3; comments on Fleet Street 283; divorce 2; support for homosexual law reform 131, 140
Cuban Missile crisis 315
Cudlipp, Hugh 80, 117, 313; reflection on his career as a journalist and editor 283; personality and career 283–7; as an innovating editor 284–5; political and social outlook shaped by the 1930s 285–6; connection with Cecil King 286–7; critical depiction of the British elite by 285; promotes a series of articles on the 'problem' of male homosexuality 288, 290; campaigns for the removal of homosexuals in schools and in state security 294–7; and the Liberace libel 299, 301–4; sells *Sun* to Rupert Murdoch 304–5
Cudlipp, Percy 283
Cudlipp, Reg 283
Cumberland 219–21; Barrow-in-Furness 105; Carlisle 219–21; Keswick 221
Curran, Desmond 17, 38, 54, 65, 80, 99, 112–15
Curtis-Bennett, Derek 188
Cuthbertson, Munro 78–9

Daily Express 116, 225, 263, 264
Daily Herald 283, 304, *see also* the *Sun*
Daily Mail 116, 122, 236, 246
Daily Mirror 80, 117, 121, 282, 286, 298–9, 300–301, 304; re-creation as a popular newspaper 283–7; aggressively articulates a strongly male heterosexual outlook 287; attack on Liberace by William Connor 300–301; successfully sued for libel by Liberace 301–4
Daily Sketch 315
Daily Telegraph 81, 82, 112, 116, 234, 273
Darlington, PC 45–8
Dawson, Geoffrey 286
Davenport, Terence 186
Davenport-Hines, Richard 10
Davidson, Miss 27
Davies, Raymond 206
Davis, Raymond 198
Day, Doris 189
Dean, James 304
Dearden, Basil 96
Delinquency, Institute for the Study and Testament of 52
Demant, Vigo 35–6, 65, 93, 109–11, 114
Demmett, John 204

INDEX

INDEX